MANAGING URBAN AMERICA

Managing Urban America

Fourth Edition

David R. Morgan
University of Oklahoma

Robert E. England
Oklahoma State University

Chatham House Publishers, Inc.
Chatham, New Jersey

MANAGING URBAN AMERICA
Fourth Edition

Chatham House Publishers, Inc.
Post Office Box One
Chatham, New Jersey 07928

Copyright © 1979, 1984, 1989, 1996 by Chatham House Publishers, Inc.

Publisher: Edward Artinian
Production editor: Katharine F. Miller
Cover design: The Antler & Baldwin Design Group, Inc.
Composition: Bang, Motley, Olufsen
Printing and binding: R.R. Donnelley and Sons Company

Library of Congress Cataloging-in-Publication Data

Morgan, David R.
    Managing urban America / David R. Morgan, Robert E. England. — 4th ed.
        p.   cm.
    Includes bibliographical references and index.
    ISBN 1-56643-019-4
    1. Municipal government—United States. I. England, Robert E. II. Title.
JS331.M668   1996
352′.0072′0973—dc20   95-17977
                                        CIP

Manufactured in the United States of America
10 9 8 7 6 5 4 3 2 1

To Professor Carolyn Stout Morgan, my wife,
whose humor, thoughtfulness, and support have
sustained me throughout my academic career.
I can never thank her enough. — D.R.M.

To Eric Reid England, my son, my best friend,
and a true little rascal. May your love
of books never die. — R.E.E.

Contents

PART THREE
Internal Management Processes

PART FOUR
The Urban Future

Preface

About sixteen years have passed since the appearance of the first edition of *Managing Urban America*. This fourth edition finds many of the problems facing cities at the beginning of the 1980s still facing public officials in the 1990s. Fiscal stress, doing more with less, productivity enhancement, privatization, cutback management, retrenchment, and economic development are still very much part of the vernacular of urban management. A few new themes have surfaced since the last edition. In particular W. Edwards Deming's Total Quality Management (TQM) and David Osborne and Ted Gaebler's *Reinventing Government* have achieved considerable popularity among elected officials and deserve our attention.

The purpose of the fourth edition basically is to update earlier versions. We review new literature, introduce and discuss such new themes as "reinventing government," and provide new census and other statistical data. The structure, purpose, and thesis of the book remain the same. No new chapters have been added, nor have any old ones been deleted. The book is intended to provide a reasonably comprehensive overview of urban management, including the environmental context, political structures, service delivery, management processes, and strategic planning and economic development. To our knowledge no other urban politics/administration text grounds students in the management literature as does the present text. In contrast, a number of excellent urban *politics* texts are available to students. The thesis of the book remains unchanged: one can be an excellent administrator and still fail in urban management. Without a thorough understanding of the "politics" of city administration, city leaders are destined to be less than completely successful.

The book has been used most frequently by junior- or senior-level undergraduate students and graduate students. One might suggest, however, that the text could be used as the primary text for an introduction to public administration course, with the emphasis and examples shifted from the federal level to that arena where most government takes place —the local level. In fact, the title of the book easily could be changed to Public Administration at the Local Level.

As in previous versions, we offer an ample number of case studies to illustrate key concepts and themes. We have found that students, particularly undergraduate students, find case studies useful in providing a bridge to the "real world" of city government. In-service students can often provide "me too" experiences after reading various cases.

This fourth edition finds a couple of major changes. Bob England joins me as a coauthor. Bob is my former student and frequent collaborator. In addition, the publisher of the text has shifted from Brooks/Cole to Chatham House. We are most pleased to be working with Edward Artinian and his staff.

A number of people deserve special thanks for their assistance in this and previous versions. For their help with the first edition, I would like to thank two of my former colleagues at the University of Oklahoma, Kenneth J. Meier and Steven C. Ballard. Several other readers of an early draft offered useful suggestions as well: Kent Chabotar of the University of Massachusetts at Boston, Robert Daland at the University of North Carolina at Chapel Hill, Lynn S. Miller of Sangamon State University, Jeremy Plant of the State University of New York at Albany, Ed Stene of the University of Kansas, David Williams of West Virginia University, and Donald Wolfer of San Diego State University. The second edition benefited from the perceptive comments of Richard D. Bingham, now of Cleveland State University, Timothy D. Mead of the University of North Carolina at Charlotte, and Clifford J. Wirth of the University of New Hampshire. For their helpful comments for the third edition, I thank Jerry Gilbert of Jacksonville State University, Hubert Locke of the University of Washington, Leonard Ruchelman of Old Dominion University, Bernard Ross of American University, Keith Snavely of Southern Illinois University, Charles Spindler of the University of South Florida, and Robert Waste of San Diego State University.

Pat Fitzgerald, then at Duxbury Press, served ably as the editor of the first edition; Henry Staat and Marquita Flemming of Brooks/Cole helped in a variety of ways as editors of the second. As editor of the third edition, Cindy Stormer deserves thanks for her cooperation and assistance.

A number of individuals at Oklahoma State University helped prepare the fourth edition. A special thank you goes to Kelly Spurrier, Pam

Amos, and Carrie Kearns. Saundra Mace, also at Oklahoma State University, provided assistance above and beyond the call of duty. Much of the new, and some of the old, artwork is her creation.

Irene Glynn did an outstanding job as copy editor of the book.

Finally, Katharine Miller at Chatham House was a great editor and friend. She guided the book from start to press in an efficient and effective fashion.

Our sincere thanks goes to all.

The Need for Improved Urban Management – Now More Than Ever

Improving Public Management: An Overview

Things are changing in city government and not necessarily for the better. Until recent years, many practitioners and students of urban politics alike assumed that city governments would continue to grow, if not prosper. After all, state and local government payrolls expanded enormously during the 1960s and 1970s, much faster than at the federal level. Cities were doing more than ever, responding to new needs and demands. Keith Mulrooney, a former city manager of Claremont, California, describes his activities in the late 1960s:

> confronting antiwar demonstrators, holding council meetings in Chicano houses, sitting with hippies in a park discussing last week's narcotics bust, bargaining against a labor pro, or contracting with the Black Students Union to conduct reading improvement programs for low achieving black school children.[1]

These were the challenges of city management two decades ago, and they represented a significant departure from earlier issues such as building city infrastructures and developing a science of administration that would allow cities to be managed efficiently. "The shift in ... priorities ... [was] from the physically oriented to the human oriented."[2] Along with these new problems came lots of federal dollars and a sharp increase in municipal employment and programs. Between 1960 and 1980, for example, the number of federal grant-in-aid programs grew from 132 to well over 500 with a corresponding dollar growth of $7 to $91.5 billion.[3] In some communities, local officials developed new programs

I

solely for the purpose of hustling federal dollars. Growth and expansion seemed inevitable. In fact, a report from the International City Management Association (ICMA) suggested that the inevitability of growth was so widely accepted it functioned as fact.[4] This pervasive view of local government called for growth in every imaginable area: urban populations would grow, budgets would expand, federal grants would increase, municipal jobs would multiply, and benefits would rise as cities were forced to undertake an ever-enlarging list of responsibilities.

But things do change. Federal aid to cities began to shrink in the late 1970s. Then came the "Reagan Revolution," which brought major reductions in federal domestic spending, including additional cuts in financial assistance to state and local governments. Between 1980 and 1987, federal aid as a percentage of total municipal revenue dropped 55 percent. In 1978, cities received almost 16 percent of their revenue from federal sources; that figure is now around 5 percent.[5] Holding the line—and, yes, retrenchment—became the order of the day. For a number of reasons, the situation improved some in the latter half of the 1980s. Cities showed more resilience than pessimists thought they would. Cuts were made, budgets were balanced, and taxes were raised in a number of communities; cities did learn to manage with less. Some would argue that a lot of cities cleansed themselves during this period of fiscal crisis, emerging stronger and more independent than ever. To the extent that this is true, a great deal of credit must go to those tough-minded city officials forced to make hard choices that often upset employees and clientele groups alike. Also, state governments deserve recognition as they proved to be thoughtful parents of their legal offspring and provided much needed relief, both programmatically and fiscally.

It is imperative to understand, however, that the era of fiscal austerity is not yet over for American cities. In fact, some would argue "that the phrase 'urban crisis' has returned to the American vocabulary"[6] and that this time neither the federal government nor state governments will be able to provide much assistance. The federal government is broke, with a FY 94 deficit of over $300 billion and a national debt of more than $4 trillion. Similarly, some observers are calling the 1990s the "decade of red ink" for state governments.[7] In other words, this time around it would seem that "cities [are] on their own."[8] Now more than ever, improved municipal performance management is a must. Managing with less demands more dedicated, competent, and politically astute municipal managers. And in the broadest sense that is what this book is all about—improving the management of city governments, from both a technical and a political perspective.

FINANCIAL PRESSURES

Times are tough. A recent Gallup poll, for example, found that "one out of five Americans had their take-home pay cut [and] ... had been forced to pay higher medical insurance premiums in the past twelve months. The poll found that about one out of six said they now work a second job...."[9] Frustrated workers frequently become frustrated citizens, demanding more from government for less. According to Alexander E. Briseño, city manager of San Antonio, "Citizens want more services and there's not enough money. Managing local government today means having your back to the wall. You find yourself peering into hats, desperately hoping to see a rabbit."[10] The mayor of Cleveland, Michael White, agrees: "If cities are looked at as a giant rubber band, we've been stretched just about as far as we will go."[11] In fact, in June 1991 the rubber band snapped, and Bridgeport, Connecticut, made national news by declaring bankruptcy.

Cities cannot relax and return to the good old days of growth and revenue expansion; financial pressures are likely to remain, or perhaps even intensify, for some time. The days of wine and roses have been replaced by the days of beer and daisies. For example, according to the National League of Cities' Eighth Annual Opinion Survey of Municipal Elected Officials, fully 51 percent of the officials surveyed report that in their cities "overall local economic conditions worsened in 1991. That proportion rose from 14 percent in 1989 to 36 percent in 1990."[12] Penelope Lemov notes that similar bad news comes from the National League of Cities fiscal survey report released in July 1991, "one of four city governments faces a budget gap of more than 5 percent this year." Comparable figures were about 11 percent in 1987, 9 percent in 1988, 6 percent in 1989, and 11 percent in 1990.[13] According to Lemov, "the misery is worse this time around: budget cuts seem deeper, harsher, and meaner."[14]

Not all cities are hurting, but nearly all local officials continue to face hard budgetary choices. In Long Beach, California, in the 1990–91 budget year all agencies were cut except police and fire; in the next fiscal year all services were cut.[15] Tom Lewinsohn, personnel director of Kansas City, Missouri, notes that in response to fiscal stress his city imposed a one-year salary freeze in 1989 and eliminated three departments through consolidation.[16] Bob Flanagan, city assessor of New London, Connecticut, is forced to scratch $2 million worth of real estate and equipment from the city's taxable property after the closing of Thames Valley Steel. The city may have to raise its property tax 7 or 8 percent (or more), which provides the seeds for a taxpayers' revolt.[17] People everywhere continue to ask what they are receiving for their tax dollars. And local governments, being closer to home, feel these pressures more than do the state and national governments.

THE POLITICS OF MANAGING WITH LESS

As cities hold the line and try to get by on less, they face new political pressures. As long as the municipal treasury is expanding, everyone has hopes of getting more. But as the pie shrinks, the competition among groups to keep their share grows intense. Over time, it becomes difficult to obscure who is winning and who is losing. As political scientist Charles Levine observes, without growth it is harder to buy off the losers.[18]

So retrenchment produces dissatisfaction among interest groups, service recipients, and, not least, public employees. And this means a disenchantment with elected officials and their appointees that voters do not forget at the polls.[19] Perhaps it is the fear of adverse public reaction (if not the loss of their jobs) that leads many local officials to embrace short-term solutions to their problems. For example, cutting the capital budget has been a favorite strategy, one that is now beginning to hurt. Evidence is mounting that the public infrastructure of our older cities and counties is deteriorating at an alarming rate as a result of inadequate expenditures for capital improvements. Another strategy, holding down personnel costs, has led many of the best-qualified and most highly motivated municipal employees to seek work elsewhere. What we may well see, then, is a long-term decline in management capacity.[20] What is needed is not short-term solutions to long-term issues; local governments must engage in productivity enhancement.

INCREASING MUNICIPAL PRODUCTIVITY

Among the 20 Western democracies, Americans pay the least in taxes, in proportion to the size of the economy, but seem to protest them the most. Beyond the protest, however, long experience has shown that Americans demand a high level of public services and are willing to pay for them if they are being treated fairly. The tax revolt has not changed that.[21]

As this remark by long-time city commentator John Herbers suggests, citizens are not unreasonable. They are, however, demanding more than ever that city officials maximize the use of scarce resources. Faced with financial constraints, urban public leadership can do one of several things: raise revenue by increasing taxes or fees, cut costs and services, and/or improve operating productivity. There is little popular support for tax-based revenue schemes. And although popular pressure is likely to keep costs down, the public does not want services cut. In fact, most people want more and better services. Obviously this does not leave urban administrators much choice: they have to increase productivity, and that's not an easy job. An understanding of the process, the problems, and the politics of managing today's city can help, which is the purpose of this book. Indeed two practitioners recently observed that "in most respects the critical problem facing local governments today is not a lack of resources but the ability to use existing resources efficiently and effectively."[22] As the following case study suggests, productivity enhancement is a must in an era of "managing with your back to the wall."[23]

CASE STUDY

MANAGING WITH YOUR BACK TO THE WALL

ACCORDING to city manager Alexander E. Briseño, gains in productivity often can be made with proper analysis of city services.

- After adding two fully equipped emergency medical service units to San Antonio's fleet of nineteen at a cost of $2 million for equipment and one year's staffing, average response time was cut by only twelve seconds. In-house data-processing staff working with the fire department, and with an investment of less than $100,000, developed a program for the computer-aided dispatch system that anticipates by location, time of day, and day of the week emergency calls. Instead of sending the ambulances back to the fire stations, they are positioned near the anticipated calls. The result has been the reduction of 1.5 minutes in average response time, a big difference in life-and-death situations.
- The city improved productivity in the police department by adding more civilians to handle report writing and responses to nonemergency calls. The proportion of officers' time spent on preventive patrol increased from 22 to 28 percent.
- Faced with a possible elimination of the city's $850,000 summer recreation program, the private sector was called on for help. Churches, community groups, and schools were able to raise $165,000 to go with the $250,000 the city was able to scrape together.
- For the next budget year the city appropriated up to $100,000

for new library books. Using a challenge grant, for every one dollar raised in the private sector, the city will match with one dollar. The expectation is that the full $200,000 will be secured to buy new books.

SOURCE: Adapted from Alexander E. Briseño, "Managing Local Government with Your Back to the Wall," *Governing*, October 1991, 11.

Other observers argue that productivity enhancement is simply not enough. Instead, today's critical problems call for fundamental changes in the way cities are governed and managed. The patient (the city) does not need a Band-Aid (e.g., delayed capital spending) or even a physical examination (e.g., systematic analysis of service delivery). What is needed is reconstructive surgery; city government must be transformed. Or, in the words of journalist David Osborne and former city manager Ted Gaebler, the major proponents of the proposed transformation, we must "reinvent government."[24]

REINVENTING/REDISCOVERING GOVERNMENT: BEYOND PRODUCTIVITY?

Osborne and Gaebler's *Reinventing Government*[25] has made a big splash. Public officials at all levels are debating the merits of this best-selling volume. For example, Osborne served as a consultant to President Clinton, who frequently mentioned the idea of reinventing government on the campaign trail. The governor of Oklahoma requires all department heads to read the book. Similarly, a number of city managers have informed us that they too require department heads to read, study, and where possible implement the reinventing government prescription.

This prescription lists ten principles. Government should be:

1. A catalyst, directing activities more than running programs
2. Community-owned, involving and empowering clients and citizens
3. Competitive, encouraging and promoting competition in service delivery
4. Mission-driven, stressing overall goals while minimizing rules and requirements
5. Results oriented, concerned more with outcomes and less with inputs or resources used
6. Customer-driven, treating service recipients as valued customers
7. Enterprising, interested in earning as well as spending money

8. Anticipatory, preventing problems (e.g., recycling) instead of merely curing them (abating pollution)
9. Decentralized, flattening the organizational hierarchy to encourage more participation and teamwork among employees
10. Market oriented, leveraging change by using government incentives to affect market behavior

The chapters that follow will include examples and case studies of how local officials are using these ten principles to improve if not transform municipal operations. Our frequent reference to Osborne and Gaebler's book should not be construed as an unequivocal endorsement. But *Reinventing Government* has drawn so much attention, stimulated so many ideas, and generated so much response that any discussion of managing local government would be deficient without acknowledging its influence. The book has its detractors, of course. And, in the pages to come, we try to take account of some of these objections. For example, many state and local officials think the book is "long on suggestions and short on steps for actual implementation."[26] For now, however, we might offer two general observations. First, Osborne and Gaebler offer little new in the way of management techniques or wisdom. In all fairness to them, however, in the preface of the book they acknowledge that they "are not inventing new ideas so much as synthesizing the ideas and experiences of others."[27] In fact, Charles Goodsell, one of the most astute students of public administration today, in a critique of the book argues that what Osborne and Gaebler really do is "rediscover" government.[28] Second, most of the changes called for in *Reinventing Government,* or in any of the other "new" management innovations, such as "reengineering" government[29] or Total Quality Management (TQM), are in one form or another tied to the concept of productivity. As productivity expert Marc Holzer reminds us, various management programs and strategies are fundamentally aimed at enhancing productivity—from reinventing government as a broad program to TQM, quality circles, joint labor-management committees, contracting out, performance measurement, public-private partnerships, and performance budgeting as strategies.[30]

BETTER MANAGEMENT IS NOT ENOUGH

Few would quarrel with the basic position outlined above: America's cities must improve their management capacity. But improving managerial skills alone will not solve all the city's problems. We also must recognize the special context in which urban management functions. In particular we must be sensitive to the limits imposed on administration by such factors as the culture and values of the community, organizational inertia, the political environment, and the personal qualities of those in top leadership positions.

COMMUNITY VALUES. — The technical know-how and the managerial tools for urban problem solving are available, both from the private sector and from other levels of government. Why aren't they used routinely in city governments?

In their early work on city politics, political scientists Edward Banfield and James Q. Wilson wrote:

> To the extent that social evils like crime, racial hatred, and poverty are problems susceptible to solution, the obstacles in the way of their solution are mostly political. It is not for lack of information that the problems remain unsolved. Nor is it because organizational arrangements are defective. Rather it is because people have differing opinions and interests, and therefore opposing ideas about what should be done.[31]

Obviously urban managers do not grapple continuously with issues of crime, race, and poverty. Administration, planning, budgets, crisis management—all are time-consuming aspects of urban management life. But even in these less-critical areas urban managers often face obstacles essentially unrelated to their technical knowledge of the problem. In the late 1960s the city of Oakland received a large sum from the Economic Development Administration to create job opportunities for unemployed and underemployed residents.[32] One of the major projects was the construction of a large hangar to be built for and used by World Airways. A number of problems delayed the project's implementation. One was the company's reluctance to comply with federal hiring requirements. The city and the federal government's program to put the hard-core unemployed to work bumped squarely against the company's resistance to hiring people it considered unqualified. Two competing values—work for the jobless and the traditional goal of hiring the best people available—created a prolonged delay in a needed urban project.

Another example is the school busing issue.[33] Technical know-how can tell us when to bus, what busing will cost, and the extent to which we can affect black-white enrollment ratios. But benefit-cost analysis cannot gauge values and emotions, and these values, emotions, and even prejudices play the most powerful role in determining how well a solution works.

INSTITUTIONAL INERTIA. —Bureaucrats are comfortable with routines. In fact, most of us prefer an environment in which we are not constantly forced to adapt to the vagaries of change. Rules, regulations, and established procedures accumulate as organizations mature. Organizational inertia, bureaucratic infighting, agency imperialism, and other forces complicate the task of enlarging the management capacity of city government.

THE POLITICAL ENVIRONMENT. —One of the big differences between public and private management is the degree to which public managers must operate within a political environment. A local administrator offered these comments about private managers who went public:

> their biggest problem was what to do when someone says, "You can't do that, it's not politically feasible." They (private managers) tend to say "what do you mean—it's right, we've got the money, and we must do it." The public sector is different. You may waste a half million (by private standards) but you have to take people's attitudes and feelings into account.[34]

More to the point, no matter how good the management techniques and no matter how much money is available, the solutions to most complex urban problems require political judgment.[35] Priorities must be assigned, the level and type of taxes must be decided, and the allocation of resources must be made. In the final analysis these decisions involve judgments on what is best for the people. Under our form of government these are political decisions, and no amount of improvement in management capacity can change that fact.

CASE STUDY

POLITICS AND URBAN ADMINISTRATION

WHEN the old-line city manager left Middleburg (a suburban community of less than 50,000), his young assistant, Roger Masters, was named to replace him. Masters had been with the city for several years as public works director and for two years as assistant city manager. He was under thirty, progressive, and ambitious. Some people felt, however, that he angered easily and took things too personally.

Soon after Masters took over, the police chief resigned. A new chief, Lon White, was named to fill the vacancy. Chief White had just come to Middleburg. A retired chief of detectives with the central-city police department, he had not planned to take on another full-time position but apparently found his retirement check did not go as far as he had hoped. White was a patient, conservative man, wary of change. He first met the city manager at his initial interview for the chief's job, but knew the mayor and two council members quite well.

After White's appointment, Masters paid him a visit and shared his thoughts about the police department. Masters apparently advised the new chief that in his judgment some reorganization—officer reassignment or even dismissal—was necessary to improve the department's performance. According to Masters, the chief was impressed with his concern and promised to act on it as soon as he became more familiar with personnel and procedures.

Some months later, Masters received a complaint from a parent about a police officer's handling of an incident involving the possession of marijuana by a high school student. According to Masters, when he spoke to the chief about the matter, White got angry. He told the manager that he would handle disciplinary matters in the police department and not to interfere. Several similar incidents came up over the next few months, and again manager and chief disagreed. Clearly there was trouble ahead.

A few months later, White approached Masters with a plan for reorganizing the police department. Whether the plan called for demotions or dismissals is unclear, but apparently Masters pushed the chief to fire one officer and demote another—presumably the officers involved in several of the disciplinary arguments. The chief balked, at which point the manager ordered that the action be taken anyway. When White refused, Masters fired him. Later that day, the city manager announced the dismissal of one officer and the demotion of a ranking member of the department.

The matter did not end here. Middleburg has a personnel board with the authority to reinstate employees that it found to have been improperly disciplined or terminated. The chief appealed to that board and took his case to several council members. Although under the city charter the council has no authority over personnel matters, a majority of that group voted to investigate the manager's conduct in the affair. Also, two council members privately urged the personnel board to reinstate White. Their motives were not clear, but the local chapter of the Fraternal Order of Police was rumored to have been instrumental in their election. One member of the personnel board, angry at this interference, resigned in protest; but the other members voted to put White back on the payroll.

At this point Masters went before the council to announce he would not work with White: one of them had to go. Then he asked for a formal vote of confidence from the council. When he did not get it, he promptly resigned. White was reconfirmed as chief by a 4–3 vote of the council, and an acting city manager was soon named.

SOURCE: This case actually took place in a suburban community in the Oklahoma City metropolitan area. Because some of the facts are not a matter of public record, fictitious names are used for the community and the participants. The account is adapted from a graduate term paper by Ted M. Williams for one of the authors' courses in urban management.

Personnel conflict is anything but unusual in city government. Urban administrators must be prepared to deal with pressures and demands emanating from a variety of sources, some internal to the municipal organization, others external to it. To survive, much less to be effective, urban managers must be politically sensitive and skillful. No matter how good their administrative abilities, successful managers must learn the art of the possible—how to bargain, how to compromise, and how to negotiate what may appear to be irreconcilable conflicts among competing interests.

LEADERSHIP QUALITIES.—Finally we must consider managers' personal characteristics. No amount of managerial knowledge can take the place of the basic leadership resources—intelligence, courage, daring, tenacity, and flexibility.[36] And we might throw in intuition and luck for good measure. If you get the impression that good urban managers must be some sort of superpeople, you are not far wrong. Our cities have enormous problems. Although improving managerial skills may help solve them, we need very special people as well.

The Book's Organization

This book is organized in four parts. The first part, The Environment of Urban Management, includes chapters 1 and 2, which sketch out the social, economic, and political world of urban managers. We begin with the context in which urban managers operate. Politics is a critical area, and prospective managers must know something about the nature of the urban world that creates the pressures and demands bearing so directly on the performance of municipal government. Adding to the external forces with which managers must contend are the various governmental entities that impinge on the city—the federal, state, and other local governments.

In chapter 2 we again consider the managers' external world, the nature of the local governmental structure. To gain a proper perspective on how appointed administrators fit into the local political system, you must understand the basic forms of municipal government.

Part Two, Making and Implementing Urban Policy, includes chapters 3 through 7. These chapters discuss how policies are formulated, how decisions are made, how analysis is used in making decisions, how municipal services are delivered, and how managers can improve productivity. In the third chapter we begin to focus more directly on activities that concern professional administrators on a regular basis. The particular topic is urban policymaking. The process by which municipal governments make policy can be reviewed from several approaches, each of which we treat briefly. Then we examine the nature of the positions held by those who actually function as urban policymakers—chief executives (mayors as well as managers), city councils, and urban bureaucrats.

Policymaking is closely tied to another basic management function, decision making, which is the subject of chapter 4. Managers above all are decision makers. We discuss the decision-making process in general and as it applies to the urban context. We identify the approaches to and the limitations of rational decision making, discussing those tools managers can use to make better decisions.

Chapter 5 is actually an extension of chapter 4. Here we examine ways to make the decision process as systematic as possible, using several case studies to review the use of analysis in urban decision making. And we discuss management information systems as one way to use analytic tools to make more effective decisions.

What does the policy process and all the decision making produce? At the local level the answer is services. Chapter 6 explores several features of urban service delivery—the issues involved and the importance of measurement, implementation, and evaluation.

Chapter 7 addresses a topic of expanding significance to urban administrators—the problems cities face in contending with budget cutbacks. The discussion focuses on efforts to improve productivity and the process of cutback management.

Part Three, Internal Management Processes, incorporates chapters 8 through 10. Here we deal directly with management operations, personnel management, and budgeting and finance. Beginning with chapter 8, we examine some of the management practices and techniques employed at the municipal level. The preceding chapters have covered the broad policy process, how decisions are made, and the result—urban services. But how do urban managers move their organization from here to there? We discuss motivation, leadership, and management approaches such as Management by Objectives, Total Quality Management, and organization development.

Nothing gets done without people, of course. In chapter 9 we address the issue of organizing for personnel administration and consider the common personnel functions. In addition we deal with two major areas of continuing interest—affirmative action and collective bargaining.

Where do the funds come from to operate city programs? What are the prospects for expanding the revenue base? All managers worry about how revenue is raised and spent. And the process by which funds are allocated, the budget, looms large as well. In chapter 10 we consider the vital areas of urban finance and budgeting.

The last part of the book, The Urban Future (chapters 11 and 12), includes a chapter on economic development as well as a discussion of the future of urban management. City governments must have the resources and the people to get the job done, but more and more communities have begun to realize how much their progress depends on the strength and vitality of the local economy. Chapter 11 considers the growing importance of economic development as cities strive to remain or make themselves vital, attractive, and competitive. Around the country, economic development has become recognized as perhaps the number-one issue facing cities of all sizes. The chapter addresses some of the options cities have open to them in their quest for economic development and some of the problems they may face as they pursue various strategies for improvement.

The book concludes with a consideration of what tomorrow's urban managers will face. We look closely at what the job of the urban manager demands today and the ways in which education may help. And once more we consider the pervasiveness of politics in urban management. How can managers enhance their capacity to operate effectively in a thoroughly political environment? Surely management skills are crucial, but learning the political ropes may be just as critical to a manager's ultimate success.

Notes

1. Keith F. Mulrooney, "Prologue: Can City Managers Deal Effectively with Major Social Problems?" *Public Administration Review* 31 (January/February 1971): 6.

2. Thomas W. Fletcher, "What Is the Future for Our Cities and the City Manager?" *Public Administration Review* 31 (January/February 1971): 5.

3. George J. Gordon, *Public Administration in America*, 4th ed. (New York: St. Martin's Press, 1992), 88–89.

4. Elizabeth K. Kellar, "Get By with Less," in *Managing with Less*, ed. Elizabeth K. Kellar (Washington, D.C.: ICMA, 1979), 2.

5. See David R. Morgan and Michael W. Hirlinger, "The Dependent City and Intergovernmental Aid: The Impact of Recent Changes," *Urban Affairs Quarterly* 29 (December 1993): 256–75.

6. Jonathan Walters, "Cities on Their Own," *Governing*, April 1991, 27.

7. Penelope Lemov, "The Decade of Red Ink," *Governing*, August 1992, 22.

8. Walters, "Cities on Their Own," 27.

9. As reported by Richard Morin, "Moonlighting More, but Enjoying It Less," *Washington Post National Weekly Edition*, 7–13 October 1991, 37.

10. Alexander E. Briseño, "Managing Local Government with Your Back to the Wall," *Governing*, October 1991, 11.

11. As quoted in Walters, "Cities on Their Own," 27.

12. William Barner and David Dickinson, *The State of America's Cities: The Eighth Annual Opinion Survey of Municipal Elected Officials* (Washington, D.C.: National League of Cities, 1992), 7.

13. Penelope Lemov, "The Axe and Its Victims," *Governing*, August 1991, 26.

14. Ibid.

15. Ibid., 29.

16. Jeffrey L. Katz, "When Bad Things Happen to Good Bureaucrats," *Governing*, December 1990, 64.

17. Penelope Lemov, "The Road to Tax Revolt Is Lined with Empty Buildings," *Governing*, February 1991, 64.

18. Quoted in "Get By with Less," 3.

19. Charles Levine, Irene Rubin, and George Wolohojian, *The Politics of Retrenchment* (Beverly Hills: Sage, 1981), 211.

20. Ibid., 14.

21. John Herbers, "Read My Lips: The Tax Revolt Hasn't Had All That Much Impact," *Governing*, April 1990, 11.

22. Brian Rapp and Frank Patitucci, "Improving the Performance of City Government: A Third Alternative," *Publius* 6 (Fall 1976): 67.

23. Briseño, "Managing Local Government with Your Back to the Wall," 11.

24. David Osborne and Ted Gaebler, *Reinventing Government* (Reading, Mass.: Addison-Wesley, 1992).

25. Ibid.

26. Jonathan Walters, "Managing the Politics of Change," *Governing*, December 1992, 40.

27. Osborne and Gaebler, *Reinventing Government*, xvii.

28. Charles T. Goodsell, "Reinvent Government or Rediscover It?" *Public Administration Review* 53 (January/February 1993): 85.

29. John Martin, "Reengineering Government," *Governing*, March 1993, 27.

30. Marc Holzer, "The Productivity Movement," in *Public Personnel Administration: Problems and Prospects*, 2d ed., ed. Steven W. Hays and Richard C. Kearney (Englewood Cliffs, N.J.: Prentice Hall, 1990), 168–69.

31. Edward Banfield and James Q. Wilson, *City Politics* (New York: Vintage, 1963), 2.

32. Jeffrey Pressman and Aaron Wildavsky, *Implementation* (Berkeley: University of California Press, 1973), chap. 3.

33. Taken from Matthias E. Lukens, "Emerging Executive and Organizational Responses to Scientific and Technological Developments," in *Governing Urban Society: New Scientific Approaches*, ed. Stephen Sweeney and James Charlesworth (Philadelphia: American Academy of Political and Social Science, 1967), 120.

34. Reprinted from Robert R. Cantine, "How Practicing Urban Administrators View Themselves," in *Education for Urban Administration*, ed. Frederic Cleaveland and Thomas Davy (Philadelphia: American Academy of Political and Social Science, 1973), 3–4. Copyright © 1973 by the American Academy of Political and Social Science. All rights reserved.

35. This argument is taken from Lukens, "Emerging Executive and Organizational Responses," 121.

36. Jeffrey L. Mayer, "Managers, Machiavelli, and Michael Oakeshott: A Caveat," *Publius* 6 (Fall 1976): 104–5.

Suggested for Further Reading

Banfield, Edward, and James Q. Wilson. *City Politics*. New York: Vintage, 1963.

Kellar, Elizabeth K., ed. *Managing with Less*. Washington, D.C.: ICMA, 1979.

Levine, Charles, Irene Rubin, and George Wolohojian. *The Politics of Retrenchment*. Beverly Hills: Sage, 1981.

Newell, Charldean, ed. *The Effective Local Government Manager*. 2d ed. Washington, D.C.: ICMA, 1993.

Osborne, David, and Ted Gaebler. *Reinventing Government*. Reading, Mass.: Addison-Wesley, 1992.

Rapp, Brian, and Frank Patitucci. *Managing Local Government for Improved Performance.* Boulder, Colo.: Westview, 1977.

Ukeles, Jacob. *Doing More with Less: Turning Public Management Around.* New York: AMACOM, 1982.

PART ONE

The Environment

of Urban Management

The External World
of the Urban Manager

City governments today stand amid a host of pressures and conflicts. Even in smaller communities, urban managers must constantly respond to the demands of the groups, institutions, and governmental entities that constitute the external world of the urban polity. These political pressures do not materialize out of thin air: competing and conflicting demands on urban government emerge from the racial, ethnic, social, economic, and governmental diversity so characteristic of urban America. To perform effectively, an urban manager must comprehend and come to terms with the often turbulent environment created by these outside forces. Learning to negotiate, to bargain, to persuade, and to compromise thus may be as crucial to a manager's success as is the exercise of traditional administrative skills.

In this chapter we study the social and economic milieu in which urban managers must operate. We examine the intergovernmental forces that affect city governments. And we look at several ways in which the citizenry makes its voice heard at city hall.

The Changing Urban Place

Unlike the 1960s and 1970s, most people no longer speak of an "urban crisis." Some claim we never had one; others insist that we are in the midst of "Urban Crisis II."[1] Regardless of the debate and rhetoric, a number of municipalities, in particular older central cities, continue to experience serious hardship; they remain the home of those with special needs and problems. As Mayor Sidney J. Barthelemy of New Orleans notes, "Cities are viewed as hopeless places."[2] The mayor of Cleveland,

Michael White, expresses similar sentiments, "Big cities are becoming a code name for a lot of things: for minorities, for crumbling neighborhoods, for crime, for everything that America has moved away from."[3]

What the nation's response should be to the continuing plight of these cities remains unclear. Some stress the need for inner-city revitalization. Indeed, the 1980s were marked by a boom in the construction of office buildings and condominiums in our big cities, many of which sit vacant today because of overbuilding. John Herbers contends that government policy is to blame for some of the fiscal problems facing today's cities: "The failure of Washington and the states to achieve some semblance of equity through targeting aid is a major reason some urban areas continue in distress."[4] Others think the change in the basic function of the old central city is not only inevitable but good; their solution is not to encourage people to remain but to use federal programs (e.g., VA and FHA mortgages, the interstate highway system, open housing laws, antidiscrimination employment laws) to facilitate their movement to other locations, to areas where jobs are more plentiful and housing and services more readily available.

Although this is not the place to air all the competing theories, local leaders, regardless of the state of health of their own communities, would be unwise to ignore the social and economic circumstances of less-fortunate places. No city exists in isolation. Moreover, regardless of the overall level of affluence, human service problems exist in all cities: crime, drug abuse, the homeless, and the special needs of the elderly and minorities are problems that can be found in virtually every community.

What are the social and economic changes that have produced service problems for municipalities? And in what ways are cities coping with these problems?

POPULATION SHIFTS

U.S. cities have been decentralizing for many years. The year 1970 marked the first time more people lived in the suburban rings of metropolitan areas than anywhere else in the country. Suburbia, despite some valid criticism, does offer open space, cleaner air, better schools, and above all a chance for homeownership. Polls show that all groups, regardless of age, class, race, or geographic location, prefer either suburban or small-town living. And it is not only the positive pull of suburbia; in many places the central city exerts a negative push. As Mayor White of Cleveland noted above, people leave to escape crime, congestion, deteriorating housing, poor services, inferior schools, and, in some cases, minority neighborhoods.[5]

Of course not everyone can escape. The outward flow has been dominated essentially by the white and the well-to-do. Left behind are the racial minorities, the poor, the unskilled, the uneducated, and the elderly.

Are conditions in large cities as bad as they were a decade or two ago? We hear about *gentrification*—people, especially young professional families, moving back to the inner city. Doesn't this suggest that outward migration has been reversed or at least substantially slowed? No doubt in some big cities a few areas are being revitalized, but these isolated pockets remain the exception. For example, according to the 1960 census, Detroit's population was 1,670,000; now it is 1,028,000. Between 1970 and 1990 the population of Atlanta decreased 20.7 percent, while the surrounding metropolitan area increased 173 percent.[6] In short, a number of large cities continue to experience considerable social, economic, and fiscal hardship. Those most adversely affected are the old industrial centers that have not been able to adapt successfully to the changing nature of the U.S. economy. In contrast, most places offering a broad range of financial and service activities have rebounded admirably.[7] Such service centers as New York, Boston, and San Francisco are doing reasonably well these days. Still, two pervasive problems continue to plague even large service centers where employment is expanding: (1) poverty, especially among nonwhites; and (2) fiscal problems. Apparently much hard-core urban poverty is unaffected by improvements in a city's service economy.

How are cities dealing with these problems? In particular, how is all this affecting their management?

SOCIAL CHANGE AND CITY MANAGEMENT

Municipalities always have provided extensive local services. Since the turmoil of the 1960s, however, city governments have found it necessary to pay special attention to human problems.

This concern for the disadvantaged undoubtedly has contributed to the fiscal squeeze faced by so many large cities. As cities took on new commitments, spending increased at unprecedented rates. Much of this new money came from the federal government as an outgrowth of the War on Poverty, Model Cities, Head Start, the Comprehensive Employment and Training Act (CETA), and other programs. In many large cities these programs were lifesavers. The changing demographic and social complexion of those cities had created an unprecedented need for various social services to aid the elderly, the poor, and the disadvantaged minorities. But as the federal government cut domestic spending, many of these urban programs were eliminated or reduced substantially. Cities were caught in a real bind—raise taxes or decrease services. Cities often did some of both, except in states where spending limits had been imposed by the electorate. Yet cuts hurt. Reductions in police protection, health services, education, and transportation not only aggravated urban problems but induced further flight by middle-income families. This in turn reduced revenue, forced more cutbacks, and so on. These cities, then, were caught in a vicious circle, one that left them highly vulnerable.

In the face of these difficult challenges, what can city governments do? One response is to search for less traditional methods of handling urban problems. Recent literature is full of discussions about ways to hold down costs by turning to alternative sources of urban services. Many see contracting out to the private sector as an especially promising option. Others urge greater cooperation between the public and private sectors. As a community struggles with serious financial difficulties, the private sector may be able to provide assistance and resources that normally would not be available to local government. This was the case in Niagara Falls, New York.

CASE STUDY

PUBLIC-PRIVATE COOPERATION IN NIAGARA FALLS

IN the mid-1970s Niagara Falls was suffering from a mounting fiscal crisis: the budget deficit for 1975 was $5 million; the last budget surplus had been in 1967; and the city's credit rating was slipping. In response, business and financial leaders met with local officials to explore a joint effort to tackle the growing problem. The chamber of commerce and another private industrial group decided to recruit a high-powered management team from the private sector to work side by side with city department heads as consultants. The goal of the volunteer City Management Advisory Board (CMAB) was to restore financial integrity and management effectiveness to city government. William H. Wendel, president of Carborundum Company, was named chairman of the board, whose participants read like a *Who's Who* for Niagara Falls. A Carborundum vice president, Edward H. Belanger, was chosen to be CMAB's task force leader. In all, twenty-two CMAB consultants were to spend a minimum of four hours weekly on city problems. Many spent much more than that. The Niagara Falls city manager, Donald J. O'Hara, headed the public-sector team.

Tough problems had to be tackled immediately. To head off

bankruptcy, the city council increased property taxes and water and sewer rates. Across-the-board personnel cuts were ordered, resulting in a 20 percent reduction in the workforce. Hundreds of thousands of dollars were saved by persuading reluctant municipal unions to waive pay raises for 1976. During this period CMAB advisers and department heads worked around the clock searching for ways to cut costs and increase productivity. At one point Belanger commented, "I eat more meals with Don O'Hara than I do with my own family."

By the end of the year this public-private effort had produced a number of accomplishments:

- The establishment of a basic financial control system to monitor nonpersonnel expenses
- The creation of monthly appropriation forecasts to permit management to act before a financial crisis hits
- The preparation of stringent purchasing policies
- The evaluation of park and street crew sizes, which reduced worker hours without reducing output
- The reduction and elimination of unnecessary street lighting
- The reorganization of city departments, which reduced their number from seventeen to ten
- The introduction of zero-base budgeting and Management by Objectives to city hall

By 1977 public officials were announcing a budget surplus of $865,000; the city's slide to financial ruin had been stopped.

Mayor Michael O'Laughlin heaped praise on the cooperative effort to save Niagara Falls: "This city could not pay for the skill, expertise, and experience given us by industry." CMAB's chairman Wendel observed that success was made possible because of the cooperative atmosphere in both the public and private sectors. "It took the right ingredients and the right people," he said. The head of the task force, Belanger, praised the caliber of the government employees with whom the group worked. "I learned that government is a lot more complex and difficult to manage than people think. I also learned that being in government is like being in the proverbial goldfish bowl ... everybody is watching you. It's hard to make rapid decisions because of the many groups you must consider."

SOURCE: Adapted from Lee J. Stillwell, "The Niagara Falls Experiment," in *Managing with Less,* ed. Elizabeth K. Kellar (Washington, D.C.: ICMA, 1979), 52–56.

Although federal funding cuts have prompted many cities to search for alternative sources of assistance, external support from federal and state agencies still represents a vital source of city revenue. No review of the external forces that impinge on urban government would be complete without considering some of the federal programs aimed at urban problems. Moreover, intergovernmental relations have a horizontal dimension, so we should examine how cities relate to other local government entities, particularly within metropolitan areas. The role of the state needs to be considered as well, especially in the light of the increasing trend to return more responsibilities to state and local governments.

Intergovernmental Relations

As we noted earlier, beginning in the late 1970s, federal aid to cities began to dwindle. During the 1980s, that decline accelerated, as state and local governments suffered cuts of unprecedented size as part of Ronald Reagan's New Federalism. Sometimes people claim that government programs never die. Not so. During the past decade, cities lost General Revenue Sharing and Urban Development Action Grants, two popular and visible urban aid programs. Job programs were sliced to the bone or eliminated, water and sewer programs were reduced, and welfare programs were fundamentally altered. Some observers, who thought cities had become overly dependent on federal funds, argued that this profound change in the relationship between the national government and the cities was overdue and basically healthy. Yet this newfound independence came at a price. Most cities did cut services, a step that often fell hardest on low- and moderate-income families. And to make up for lost revenue, cities tended to turn to more regressive measures, such as fees and charges, which again adversely affect the economically disadvantaged.

Despite all these changes, important federal urban aid programs remain. And even though few cities engage in the level of "grantsmanship" of past years, we need to review the nature and characteristics of key federal programs designed explicitly to assist municipalities.

FEDERAL GRANT PROGRAMS

Federal grants are a mixed blessing. All cities can use outside funding, but the federal government rarely provides money without providing guidelines for its spending. In fact, local officials frequently object to what they feel are excessive restrictions accompanying federal grants. A member of the Oakland city manager's staff complained:

> The strings attached to most federal programs cause all kinds of trouble. For instance, there was a big build-up last year on a new jobs program, with a lot of publicity which raised a lot of hopes. But there were so many restrictions attached the program couldn't do what we had hoped it would. Sometimes there are so many strings that it's hard even to spend the money.[8]

Not all federal money comes packaged the same way or with the same restrictions. Federal aid can be classified along two basic dimensions: how the money is distributed, and how the money is spent by its recipient. Federal funds are distributed in two ways:

1. *Formula grants* provide funds to local governments automatically on the basis of a formula established by law; examples include Aid to Families with Dependent Children, the Job Training Partnership Act, and the Work Incentive Program. All block grants and about 33 percent of categorical grants (see below) to state and local governments are distributed according to some predetermined formula.[9]
2. *Project grants* are awarded competitively (i.e., at the discretion of the granting agency) and must be applied for by the recipient government. Project grants are the most numerous, accounting for about 68 percent of all categorical grants in 1989. A large number of project grants are in the functional areas of elementary, secondary, and vocational education (e.g., bilingual education and literacy programs); social services (e.g., programs for aging); and health (e.g., mental health centers and community health centers).

When considered from the viewpoint of how local governments can spend the money, federal grants take two forms:

1. *Categorical grants* may be spent only for narrowly defined purposes, and often recipient governments must match a portion of the federal funds; examples include Head Start (80 percent federal share); urban forestry assistance (50 percent federal share); and asbestos school hazards abatement (50 percent federal share).

2. *Block grants* combine several related categorical grants in the same functional area or grants-in-aid in related functional areas into a single grant program; examples are the Community Development Block Grant program and the Alcohol, Drug Abuse, and Mental Health Services Block Grant. Although the federal government can provide some direction in spending, historically recipients of block grants have had considerable leeway in shifting money around within a broadly defined area.

Most of the close to 500 grants (492 in 1989) are categoricals (478); only 14 are block grants. Of categorical grants, 323 are project grants and 155 are formula grants. Categorical grant dollars represent about 87 percent of all federal intergovernmental aid.

PROS AND CONS OF CATEGORICAL GRANTS. — Most of the criticism of federal financial assistance is directed at categorical grants. As the number of these grants multiplied in the 1960s, the list of complaints grew: problems of overlap, duplication, excessive categorization, insufficient information, varying matching and administrative requirements, arbitrary federal middle-management decisions, and grantsmanship were just a few. But the money was welcome, even with strings attached; cities scrambled for the newly available federal dollars.

Beyond the immediate financial relief they provide for hard-pressed cities, categorical grants can be defended from an economic point of view. Many governmental activities provide benefits, called *spillover effects*, for those who do not live within the boundaries of the government providing the service. Education, pollution prevention, parks, and recreation services are just a few examples. Local voters, to the extent that they recognize the situation, may be reluctant to fund activities that offer advantages to people who do not pay for the service. Categorical grants allow the federal government to support local programs that have large external benefits.[10]

CHANGES IN FEDERAL URBAN AID. — Despite the continued existence of a host of categorical federal programs, considerable change has taken place in federal urban aid in recent years. The main thrust of this movement is toward greater decentralization. For example, in 1981, seventy-seven categorical grants were collapsed into nine new block grants. Although many of these changes have federal support, the principal rationale has been to lessen federal influence in determining how such funds are spent. As the following case study suggests, however, even block grants are not immune from the legislative desire to attach "strings" to federal largesse.

Pressures to reduce federal domestic spending and contain the federal debt, however, finally caught up with the grant program that had given local officials the most discretion of all; in late 1986 General Revenue Sharing (GRS) was abolished. When the program was first created in 1972, the Advisory Commission on Intergovernmental Relations (ACIR) described its passage as "perhaps the major development in intergovernmental finances in American history."[11] Revenue sharing was extremely popular among city officials, largely because it provided them with so much flexibility in spending. The loss of these funds hit many cities hard; on average, general revenue sharing accounted for about 3 percent of cities' operating revenues.[12]

CASE STUDY

Congressional Earmarking, Block Grants, and Intergovernmental Relations

Cheryl Arvidson suggests that in the last couple of years Congress has begun a practice that may very well "signal the end of the philosophy of giving greater discretion to state governments that was a hallmark of the Reagan years." The practice is to set aside or earmark a percentage of the funds associated with various block grants. The "practical effect is to put strings back on some federal 'block grants' that were created a decade ago precisely to make those monies string-free." One of the early examples of adding such strings was in 1988 when Representative Henry A. Waxman (D-Calif.) led the congressional move to stipulate that half the drug money states receive under the Alcohol, Drug Abuse, and Mental Health Block Grant must be used for services to IV drug users. Waxman also led the effort to require that 55 percent of the mental health federal dollars associated with the same block grant must be used to support new or expanded mental health services instead of ongoing programs. With the backing of Senator Claiborne Pell (D-R.I.), another proposal would require 65 to 75 percent of vocational education block grant funds be spent on high school vocational education programs. Currently the law permits state leaders to split the money however they wish between high school and postsecondary vocational education programs.

Why the new requirements on grants created to be virtually string free? Members of Congress: (1) want to take credit for delivering funds back home for specific, often highly visible programs, which is harder these days in an era of declining categorical grants and funding; and (2) the "strings" represent congressional value judgments. After all, the essence of politics is deciding who gets what, when, where, and how.

SOURCE: Drawn from Cheryl Arvidson, "As the Reagan Era Fades, It's Discretion vs. Earmarking in the Struggle over Funds," *Governing*, March 1990, 21–27.

With the abolition of general revenue sharing, the principal remaining federal grant program aimed at cities is the Community Development Block Grant. Or in the words of William Althaus, mayor of York, Pennsylvania: "It's [CDBG] our last little baby."[13]

THE HOUSING AND COMMUNITY DEVELOPMENT ACT OF 1974.— The passage of the Housing and Community Development Act in 1974 was a significant development in federal support for cities. Originally a three-year program with an $11.3 billion budget, the act consolidated a number of categorical urban development programs—Model Cities, urban renewal, neighborhood facilities, open-space land, public-facility loans, water and sewer facilities, and code enforcement—into a block grant. The formula for grant distribution is based on the community's population, the number of persons living in poverty, the extent of overcrowded housing, and the amount of housing built before 1940. All cities with populations of 50,000 or more and urban counties with at least 200,000 residents are eligible automatically for funds (about 900 entitlement jurisdictions in FY 1990), but 30 percent of the money is reserved for communities with populations of less than 50,000, which must compete for their share of the remaining funds.

In fiscal year 1991 total CDBG funding was about $3.2 billion. Localities can use the Community Development Block Grant (CDBG) funds for a variety of purposes, including public improvements, housing rehabilitation, and economic development. Each project, however, must meet one of the program's three national objectives: benefiting low- and moderate-income persons, eliminating or preventing blight, or meeting some urgent community need. In 1988 entitlement cities spent about 35 percent of their funds on housing-related activities, 21 percent on public facilities, 13 percent on economic development, 14 percent on planning and administration, and the remaining funds on other projects.[14] Community development grants have spawned an enormous range of improvements, from spruced-up storefronts, freshly painted homes, and new sidewalks in New Haven, Connecticut, to lights for baseball fields in affluent Scottsdale, Arizona.[15] The mayor of Cleveland called CDBG a "catalyst" to garner support from banks, businesses, and foundations. Without it, Cleveland would be a disaster area, he remarked.

Nonetheless, an early evaluation of the CDBG by the General Accounting Office raised questions about the program's targeting capacity. It found that cities often spread funds too widely, thus diluting their effect on revitalization.[16] Other critics, noting the considerable increase in support for economic development projects in recent years, complain that downtowns get too much of the action with no proof that lower-income people will benefit. They maintain that cities should be required to show how downtown projects will provide jobs, business opportunities, or training programs for the less advantaged.[17] Even with the problems of targeting, most observers consider the CDBG program a solid success. Despite its accomplishments, as with most federal aid, the funding level for the program dropped during the 1980s, from an earlier high of over $4 billion to a little over $3 billion.

URBAN ENTERPRISE ZONES. — Should small distressed areas be carved out of large cities and given special tax breaks to stimulate economic redevelopment? This is the essence of the various proposals urging the creation of urban enterprise zones. In March 1982 President Reagan unveiled what he termed the linchpin of his urban policy: a proposal to establish enterprise zones in twenty-five American cities. Under the Reagan plan all three levels of government—federal, state, and local—were to be involved. The cities were to be chosen on the basis of a package of tax and deregulation incentives. Local areas might offer reductions in local taxes and less stringent zoning, building codes, and licensing requirements. The target areas had to have sustained high levels of poverty, unemployment, and general distress.

Although federal legislation establishing enterprise zones was not passed, a number of states adopted variations of this idea. In general, and as the case study of Baltimore that follows suggests, many times these programs do not create the islands of unfettered enterprise envisioned by the early Reagan proposal. Instead they rely heavily on traditional tax incentives coupled with extensive public support in the delineated areas—infrastructure investment, training of disadvantaged workers, business loans, and technical assistance, for example.[18]

The original enterprise zone concept, although attractive to many, had its detractors. Tax incentives may be nice, but venture capital is the

key need of small businesses, according to Walter D'Alessio of the Philadelphia Development Corporation.[19] A recent assessment of enterprise
programs operating in several states revealed that the successful ones bear
little resemblance to the original plan embraced by the Reagan administration. In fact, a reduction in taxes is about the only principal provision
retained by many of the states. Economists Marc Bendick and David Rasmussen concluded that enterprise zones, as they have evolved among the
states, do not represent a real alternative to the more traditional approach
to urban revitalization.[20] Roy Green and Michael Brintnall would probably take exception to the negative press associated with state enterprise
zones. Based on the results of a 1985 survey mailed to the chief administrative officers of state enterprise zones, the authors conclude that "the
states are at it again—experimenting, adapting, sometimes disagreeing,
but in particular innovating with a timely policy issue."[21]

CASE STUDY

BALTIMORE'S FAILED ENTERPRISE ZONE

IN the early 1980s Maryland became one of the first states to establish enterprise zones. Substantial property and income tax breaks
were given by cities and the state to businesses inside the zones.
Park Circle, a 49-acre industrial park touted as one of the most successful zones in the nation, was opened in 1982. In the same year
Ronald Reagan visited, with Jack Kemp following in 1989. "But after a decade the zone has had no tangible effect on the neighborhood."

A new business in Park Circle pays only 20 percent of its property tax for the first five years and then 10 percent more each following year until after a decade it pays full rate. Income tax breaks
vary from $500 for a new or rehired employee to $3,000 over three
years for hiring a new disadvantaged worker. Despite the incentives, business owners say they chose the area because of its low
rents and its location close to downtown Baltimore. The president
of Cindarn Plastics, Steve Wasserman, claims he moved the company to Park Circle before tax incentives because of emotional ties
to the city. Parks Sausage, the largest minority-owned meat proces-
sor in the nation, moved to the area when it lost its downtown site
to a parking lot for the Camden Yards baseball stadium.

Few zone employees live in the area. In fact, a 1989 General
Accounting Office study of Maryland zones found that few job
gains could be attributed to the enterprise zone program. Firms fre-

quently bring their workers with them from other parts of Baltimore. The companies, none of which are retail businesses, have virtually no contact with area residents and have little impact on the surrounding neighborhoods. In concluding her assessment of the zone Jennifer Pitts argues that "enterprise zones in their current form may actually be more of a hindrance than a help," by engendering false hopes among neighborhood residents. "Enterprise zones can't address the deepest problems of the ghetto: welfare dependency, teenage pregnancy and broken families, drug addiction, crime, and men and women who are not only unemployed but also unemployable.... There is a danger that the idea [of zones] will come to be seen as a relatively painless panacea, allowing legislators and voters to continue without a real strategy for coping with the desolation of the inner cities."

SOURCE: Drawn from Jennifer Pitts, "Twilight Zone," *New Republic,* 7 and 14 September 1992, 25–28.

THE LOCAL RESPONSE TO FEDERAL ASSISTANCE. — We noted earlier that federal aid is a mixed blessing; the outside money is welcome, if not desperately needed, but the red tape, delays, and changing federal requirements frequently frustrate city officials.

Other common complaints about federal programs concern the need for improved communication between federal and local personnel, more timely information on new programs, and knowledge about similar programs administered by different federal agencies.[22] Even though certain programs have been simplified, many local officials still view the federal grant process as "complex, overly detailed, slow and cumbersome, and generally less effective than it should be."[23] In fact, virtually every municipal official can relate a favorite horror story involving some federal grant program.

CASE STUDY

RED TAPE IN FLINT

BRIAN RAPP, a former Flint, Michigan, city manager, and Frank Patitucci, director of community development for that city, offer the story of a ten-year delay in completing a downtown freeway because of the need to process an environmental impact statement (EIS). Even though the final freeway link had undergone intensive local planning and had prompted major public and private development decisions, the new requirement for an EIS brought things to a halt. The U.S. Department of the Interior objected to the route because it would take small pieces of five city parks. The department preferred an alternative that, according to Rapp and Patitucci, would require "the further acquisition of 1,191 residences, 71 commercial properties, 16 churches, a hospital, a fire station, two private clubs, and 133 vacant parcels," all at a cost of an additional $26 million. The Department of Transportation was concerned about the effect of freeway noise on several hundred nearby homes. Originally, the freeway had been set for completion in 1968; by 1975 the issues still had not been resolved.

Rapp and Patitucci sum up their complaints with federal red tape in the following words:

> Perhaps the most important consequence of overregulation is excessive administrative costs. If the man-hours required to understand and cope with the labyrinth of federal reporting requirements and accounting procedures could be devoted to simply running the program, the performance of most local governments could be improved immeasurably.

SOURCE: Adapted from Brian Rapp and Frank Patitucci, *Managing Local Government for Improved Performance* (Boulder, Colo.: Westview Press, 1977), 223.

Here we might note that localities are not as helpless in the face of federal grant requirements or mandates as they might seem. A great deal of bargaining and negotiation commonly occurs among levels of governments; federal enforcement efforts are often weak; and cities can frequently shape grant programs to suit local needs, regardless of federal intent. As public administration scholars Jane Massey and Jeffrey Straussman point out, some grant requirements provide the recipient with a range of compliance choices or allow different levels of compliance. Local governments then do not simply comply or fail to comply with grant mandates; instead they choose the method and/or degree of compliance.[24] We have more to say about federal and state mandates on local governments later. Before we examine the relationship between state governments and their legal offspring, we might see what advice David Osborne of *Reinventing Government* fame has to offer with respect to overhauling the intergovernmental system.

REINVENTING INTERGOVERNMENTAL RELATIONS

DAVID OSBORNE says that Bill Clinton believes in reinventing government: "He talks the language of *Reinventing Government* and Total Quality Management. And as governor of Arkansas, he not only talked the talk, he walked the walk." What advice does Osborne offer the president? He feels he could "set state and local government free by cutting through the morass of rules and red tape that surround Washington's $160 billion in annual grants to state and local government." How? By consolidating the close to 500 grants-in-aid programs into fifteen to twenty performance-based block grants called "challenge grants." Osborne acknowledges the current fourteen block grants but laments the fact that money is distributed without regard to quality. "Wasteful, ineffective, state and local programs get the same priority as the most innovative, cost-effective approaches." Challenge grants would be competitive block grants distributed on the basis of both need and quality. The feds would establish broad guidelines, objectives, and performance measures and then state and local governments would compete for the grants based on need, quality of proposed strategies, and eventually results.

How could such a proposal make it through Congress, which likes to take credit for the distribution of federal largesse? Osborne suggests that President Clinton use the same model as the one used for closing military bases. Appoint a "federalism czar" to head a "New Federal Compact Commission." After the commission offers recommendations, the Congress would have thirty days to vote the recommendations up or down as a group, without amendments. What do you think?

SOURCE: David Osborne, "The Way to Help Governments Is to Set Them Free," *Governing,* January 1993, 65.

THE STATES AND THE CITIES

Like parents and their children, states and cities have had a love-hate relationship for years. States provide financial support for urban areas, but they are also the source of limitations and constraints. As legal creatures of the state, cities are subject to a number of potential controls and regulations. The most famous rule of law upholding total state sovereignty was promulgated by Judge John F. Dillon in the late 1860s. Dillon's rule says in effect that cities owe their origins to and derive their powers solely from the state, which has the right to abridge and control those powers. Under this rule cities have only those powers expressly granted to them by the state constitution or legislature, or those powers that can be fairly implied from those specific grants of authority. Although this narrow perspective of municipal powers still prevails in some states, other state courts have taken a more liberal view of the powers of a municipal corporation, especially where the state constitution provides for a home-rule charter. We examine the impact of home rule and the legal limitations that still surround city government in chapter 2. Suffice it to say here that cities remain very much subject to state control in a variety of ways.

Although federal grant programs receive more attention, states actually provide more money to cities than does the national government. By the late 1980s state assistance as a proportion of municipal general revenue had increased to about 20 percent. (In 1960 it was only 16 percent.) Most of this financial aid, however, is channeled into specific functional areas, with education, welfare, and highways big winners. Across the states, more than half the money is allocated to education alone.[25]

With the growing emphasis on decentralization and with the loss of federal funds, states are being asked to do even more to help their cities. How have states responded? Do they have the capacity to meet the challenge? Capacity means more than money, of course; it means management skills and political will too.[26]

During the early years of the Reagan budget cuts, some states stepped in to help fill the gap. Most states, however, made only modest efforts to replace lost federal funds.[27] Moreover, by the middle 1980s, as states began to grapple with their own budget shortfalls, state aid to localities slowed down.[28] State fiscal problems have continued through the 1990s. And Steven Gold, director of the Center for the Study of the States, sees no relief ahead; he thinks the 1990s will continue as a "decade of red ink" for the states.[29]

What the state gives, it can take away. Local officials fear that as state governments try to find ways to balance their budgets, cities may be the losers. Events in California and Illinois provide plenty of reasons for such concern. "As they watch their finances weaken, state governments are launching hit-and-run revenue raids on two once-sacrosanct government entities—pension funds and municipalities."[30] Governor Pete Wilson tapped the $62.4 billion California Public Employees' Retirement System for $1.6 billion in an effort to address the almost $14.5 billion

FY 1992 budget deficit. Governor Wilson also proposed taking a share of the countywide property taxes that go to special districts such as water utilities and transferring the revenue to public education. Such a step would reduce the amount California would have to contribute by $347 million. Governor Jim Edgar of Illinois has advanced a similar proposal to help offset the $1.4 billion gap in the state's $28.6 billion budget. He wants to claim $237 million in revenue from a state income tax surcharge that was targeted for state municipalities.[31]

Money will always be a problem, but not the only one. Although the managerial issue is less certain, evidence suggests that in the past few years a number of states have upgraded their policymaking, planning, and budgeting capacities. The big question may be political will. Historically, large cities in particular have not been well treated by hostile state legislatures, which often were dominated by rural areas. Reapportionment was supposed to change that. But reapportionment did not help large cities as much as many had hoped; the new controlling alliance of suburbia and rural courthouses still tends to be anticity. As former Cleveland Mayor Carl Stokes once complained, "One man–one vote hasn't changed a thing as far as the central city is concerned. Instead of the farmer and his conservatism and detachment, you now have the man from suburbia, who is conservative and detached, and sometimes as hostile to the city as the rural member."[32] Some are less pessimistic. The ACIR, for one, has increasingly urged a more prominent role for the states in the federal system. Moreover, the commission sees a change from the way states operated a quarter century ago: "The mind set of the states is different; they have lost their reluctance to change and to act."[33] John DeGrove, director of the Joint Center for Environmental and Urban Studies at Florida Atlantic University, agrees. In his judgment new pressures on state legislatures from local governments and interest groups will be immense, as the effects of the slowdown in federal assistance accumulate. He concludes:

> In spite of the negative environment produced by citizen resistance to government in general and government spending in particular, many states can be expected, in a true fiscal crisis atmosphere, to increase assumption of local functions, increase state aid in the form of general revenue sharing or categorical grants, and grant more fiscal flexibility to local governments.[34]

The remaining question is how responsive can state governments be in a period of immense fiscal strain? Management capacity and political will may prove less critical. The issue, plain and simple, may be that money is not available to help.

Thus far, we have examined federal-city and state-city relations. Before discussing interlocal relations, we might focus momentarily on federal and state mandates to local governments.

FEDERAL-CITY AND STATE-CITY RELATIONS: THE ISSUE OF MANDATES

A "mandate is a constitutional provision, statute, administrative regulation, or judicial ruling which places an expenditure requirement on a government, that requirement coming from outside the government forced to take the action."[35] In intergovernmental relations mandates flow downward, from the federal to the state and local levels or from the state to the local level.[36] Also, increasingly courts have become active in the mandate process, requiring various actions on the part of state and local governments (e.g., to address prison/jail overcrowding). Mandates are especially troublesome for local governments because they are on the receiving end of most of them, and invariably mandates seem to require the expenditure of money. Thus the burden falls disproportionately on those governments least able to absorb the shock and revenue sources are most restricted. Research by Catherine Lovell and Charles Tobin reveals that about 84 percent of federal and almost 90 percent of state mandates are procedural or "how to" in nature.[37] They stipulate what the activities associated with a program must be and the employment and working conditions of those who deliver the service. Approximately 15 percent of federal and 10 percent of state mandates inform local governments what programs they must deliver to their citizenry.

Since mandates are often imposed without a corresponding transfer of revenue, it is little wonder that mandates have emerged "as the most contentious issue in state-local relations."[38] Local officials want state governments to pay for their mandates. State leaders say they do pay, either directly or indirectly through state aid to cities.

INTERLOCAL RELATIONS

Metropolitan areas abound with local governments—counties, cities, school districts, and special districts. About 40 percent of all local governments (more than 30,000) are located in metro areas, and the average metro area contains almost 100 units of government with about 22 cities, 40 special districts, and 18 school districts. Figure 1.1, for example, shows the overlapping layers of government in Fridley, Minnesota. The relationships that exist among these jurisdictions tend to be informal and

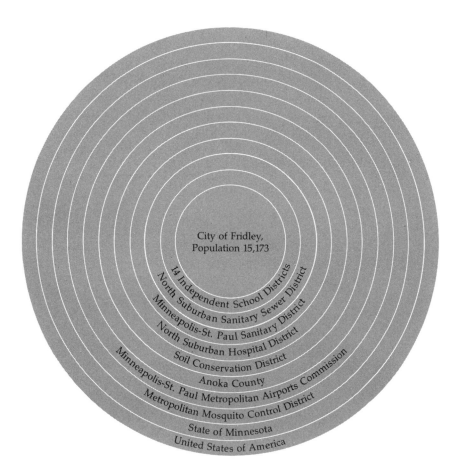

FIGURE 1.1. LAYERS OF GOVERNMENT, FRIDLEY, MINNESOTA.

Reprinted by permission of the Committee for Economic Development from *Modernizing Local Government* (New York, 1966), 12.

voluntaristic. No single political structure encompasses the entire metro area in most parts of the country. For years various groups have decried this proliferation of autonomous political units, urging in its place a more unified, centralized political structure.

Just how serious is the multiplicity of local governments in the metropolis? According to some authorities, the political balkanization of the metropolitan area contributes to the following problems:

- Municipal services are provided less efficiently because of overlapping jurisdictions, duplication of services, and lack of economies of scale.
- Political accountability is reduced because citizens are confused as to which government is responsible for which activities.
- Areawide planning is impossible.
- Fiscal disparities are created between central city and suburb.
- Great variations in service levels occur among parts of the metropolis.
- Lack of an areawide government precludes an areawide attack on problems (transportation, pollution, housing) that transcend local boundaries.
- The inability of the metropolitan area to handle its own problems compels state and federal intervention and reduces local initiatives and options.

In short, reformers blame many of the problems associated with big cities on the faulty metropolitan political structure. In an earlier period reform groups urged the creation of some form of government that would encompass the entire metropolitan area, perhaps through city-county consolidation. But in this country far-reaching structural changes almost always require voter approval, and the voters over the years have not been kind to proposals drastically to reshape government in metropolitan areas. Since the late 1940s, fewer than one-quarter of the consolidation issues placed on the ballot have been approved by the voters.[39]

REORGANIZATION SUCCESSES AND FAILURES. — Why have far-reaching changes occurred in some places and not others? There is no simple answer. Perhaps voter approval can be won only under unique crisis-related circumstances. Or some contend that a crisis may be a necessary but not sufficient reason for change. A variety of other forces, in particular strong local leadership from influential segments of the community, must converge for reorganization to succeed.[40]

Which groups customarily oppose one another over the issue of metro reform? The central-city business elite, civic organizations, big-city newspapers, and reform groups often support reorganization; suburban newspapers, mayors and employees of small towns, fringe-area businesspeople, and central-city blacks often lead the opposition. Despite the endorsement of what seem to be powerful local groups, the status quo usually carries the day. In addition the confusion and distrust created by reform opponents frequently induce voters to take the traditional way out.

The adage "Better the evil that is known" and the rule of thumb "When in doubt, do nothing" are probably decisive for many voters.[41]

CENTRALIZATION VERSUS DECENTRALIZATION.—Not everyone favors increased governmental centralization in metro areas. In recent years certain groups, minorities in particular, have urged just the opposite—greater decentralization and increased citizen participation. This movement grew out of the maximum-feasible-participation requirements associated with the Johnson administration's War on Poverty. In general, traditional metro-centralization proposals omit any consideration of what many feel is an equally important need—providing a mechanism for individuals to exercise a greater degree of control over certain services and facilities serving their neighborhood.

Support for metro decentralization also comes from scholars who, committed to the public-choice tradition, favor competition in public service. They suggest that the fragmented metropolis is analogous to a market system in which cities compete with one another for customers by offering appropriate packages of urban services. Presumably residents can select the particular community in the metropolitan area that most nearly provides the public services they need. Municipalities then are forced to compete by offering attractive services and low tax rates.

Decentralization offers other advantages, according to critics of metro reform:

- Services provided by smaller units frequently receive higher citizen evaluations than those offered by larger jurisdictions.[42]
- Economies of scale are not universally achieved with greater size. In fact, certain services may be less costly when offered by smaller units.[43]
- The existence of a large number of local governments may provide greater citizen access to political authority and thus reduce feelings of apathy, isolation, and anomie.[44]

Antireform arguments are not just hypothetical. Case studies, particularly from the Los Angeles area, demonstrate how well a multinucleated metropolis can work.

CASE STUDY

LOS ANGELES COUNTY

IN the mid-1950s the Lakewood Plan was established in Los Angeles County. The plan allows small, newly incorporated cities to contract with the county government for various urban services. A range of services, including police and fire protection, is available. The most commonly purchased services, however, are election management, health ordinance enforcement, and emergency ambulance service. The county's contract rates must be set at full cost, including a share of the general administrative or overhead expenses, and rates are subject to annual revision. Even older cities have become interested in the county's contract services, and at present about a third of the total agreements are with older cities.

Proponents of contracting praise the "dynamism, competition, and change taking place within an understandable system geared to efficient meeting of consumer demand."[45] They especially like the separation of the unit articulating the demand from the unit producing the service. The assumption is that city administrators no longer have to be concerned with enforcing bureaucratic productiveness. Instead they can concentrate on representing consumer interests in negotiating advantageous price and service contracts. Some have noted, however, that the Lakewood Plan compels cities to accept a uniform level of service in exchange for less influence on the type of service offered. Undoubtedly, where state law permits counties to take on urban responsibilities, interlocal contracting holds considerable promise. But such agreements remain voluntaristic, with municipalities cooperating only in their own interests and only with partners of their own choosing. And these arrangements cannot offer a real solution to the more serious social and economic problems confronting so many metro areas.

SOURCE: Adapted from John Bollens and Henry Schmandt, *The Metropolis: Its People, Politics, and Economic Life,* 3d ed. (New York: Harper & Row, 1975), 302–3; Robert L. Bish, *The Public Economy of Metropolitan Areas* (Chicago: Markham, 1971), 92; John J. Kirlin, "The Impact of Contract Services Arrangements upon the Los Angeles Sheriff's Department and Law Enforcement Services in Los Angeles County," *Public Policy* 21 (Fall 1973): 553–84.

Even though city-county consolidation has not swept the country and few urban counties are similar to Los Angeles, mechanisms are available for ensuring some measure of coordination among local governments in metro areas. Before examining councils of governments as coordination mechanisms, we might discuss local governments that further decentralize administrative and political power: special districts.

SPECIAL DISTRICTS: A "SPECIAL" TYPE OF DECENTRALIZATION

They are the most rapidly growing type of government in the United States, increasing from 18,323 in 1962 to 29,532 in 1987. They represent 35 percent of all local governments.[46] They do not include towns, municipalities, or school districts. Only one of ten provides services beyond a single county (they serve a limited area) and only one of ten delivers more than one service (they serve a limited function).[47] They are highly dependent on federal aid, 26 cents of federal aid for each dollar of own-source revenue, compared to 15 cents for cities, 8 cents for counties, and 2 cents for school districts.[48] What are they? These governmental units usually are called special districts or off-budget enterprises (OBE), and they are highly criticized:

> Excessive reliance on single function special districts has led to lack of coordination in local service provision, use of public funds to further private development interests, decrease in public accountability, and decreased capability of general-purpose governments to enact effective areawide policies.[49]

Special districts provide a wide array of activities and services including cemeteries, housing and urban renewal, soil conservation, sewers, water supply, electric power, transit, drainage, and irrigation. These "shadow" governmental units operate largely outside the control of general-purpose government and public scrutiny. They allow cities to do things they could not do otherwise owing to state constraints on debt limits. Most special districts have taxing authority and some even have the ability to issue revenue bonds.

The fastest-growing OBE is the industrial development agency, which issues tax-exempt industrial revenue bonds (IRB) to finance private business ventures. The Congressional Budget Office estimated total sales of IRBs in 1975 at $1.3 billion; in 1981 the estimated amount was $10 billion.[50] In essence, such development authorities allow developmental decision making to be segregated from the general-purpose local government. Paul Kantor notes that a cluster of economic development corporations in Detroit plan and direct most public and private development in the city. Dominated by business elites, the OBEs control and develop land and issue IRBs. "In effect, Detroit has separated the planning and finance of its conversion activities from mainstream local politics and placed it in the hands of interconnecting and overlapping business and governmental directorates."[51]

A Mechanism for Coordination:
The Council of Governments

Aside from the few successful instances of genuine metropolitan reorganization, the only means of bringing about greater governmental centralization in metro areas has been through some form of voluntary cooperation. A host of interlocal agreements (special districts, contractual arrangements, and so on) characterize every large urban area, but the major development in effecting greater governmental coordination has been the creation of councils of government (COGs) throughout metropolitan America. Few such arrangements existed prior to the mid-1960s. The real impetus for their formation came with the Demonstration Cities and Metropolitan Development Act of 1966. This legislation required that a number of federal urban development grants be subject to review and comment by some areawide organization. The mandate for a form of areawide scrutiny has been expanded by further legislation and through various circulars of the Office of Management and Budget, particularly publication A-95. As a consequence, metropolitan clearinghouses have been established in all the nation's metropolitan statistical areas (MSAs), in the form of either COGs or regional planning agencies, both of which are sometimes called *regional councils*.

Though stimulated and nourished by federal requirements, regional councils are voluntary in nature. They are not true governments because they lack taxing and legislative power. Organizationally COGs consist of elected officials from member governments, primarily cities and counties in the region. In the early 1970s about 50 percent of regional councils had a one-government, one-vote arrangement, although provisions for population-weighted voting have become common.

COG Activities and Funding. —Regional councils essentially do three things: prepare plans, oversee grant applications, and provide technical assistance to member governments, especially in grant preparation. The areawide review-and-comment role has given COGs their greatest potential leverage for bringing about some measure of metropolitanwide coordination. In 1982, however, President Reagan revoked the provisions of the A-95 review process and directed each state to develop its own procedures for reviewing federally funded activities. Under this order federal agencies are still required to make every effort to accommodate state and local recommendations concerning federal programs affecting their jurisdictions. Almost every state has now implemented its own version of the review-and-comment function, in many cases essentially continuing the system in place under federal guidelines.

Most of the planning done by COGs is for physical development; water and sewer, land use, open space, transportation, and solid-waste planning are most prevalent. Some economic development planning also occurs. But COGs are notorious for avoiding politically sensitive problems that might involve social change, such as metropolitan approaches to low-income housing and school desegregation.

In the past, most regional councils received the bulk of their planning and operating funds from federal sources. That too has changed in recent years. The state and local governments in affected areas have had to come up with an ever-larger portion of their COG's budget. For example, in 1976 the regional council for the Oklahoma City metropolitan area (ACOG) received over 90 percent of its money from the federal government. By 1988 that figure had dropped to 24 percent. In fact ACOG's total budget was virtually cut in half during this period, from about $2 million to $1 million.

EVALUATING THE COGs. — How successful have COGs been in bringing about some measure of metro centralization? The assessment of COGs varies considerably. The federal COG partnership peaked in 1977; since then, COGs have been engaged in a continuing quest to redefine their role and their relationship to local governments. Even though these organizations now provide more direct delivery of services and offer more management support services than before, former COG official Charles Shannon believes they have declined in importance. In his view, COGs have served as vehicles for incremental change, but "they have not met the more fundamental tests of equitably redistributing public resources, including attendant metropolitan financing methods, nor have they fulfilled comprehensive regional planning needs. . . . Two and a half decades of search for relevance, legitimacy, and authority have yielded only crumbs and tokens."[52]

Retrenchment and redefinition of mission are the major challenges facing regional organizations today. Most supporters have abandoned hope that COGs can evolve into genuine metropolitan governments.

In every city of any size a variety of local nongovernmental forces —the media, interest groups, neighborhood associations, and individual demands—constantly affect the course of municipal government. This is the nature of local government in a democracy—responding to the voice of the people. But how well do various groups fare in the process of influencing the local polity? How much democracy really exists at the city government level?

Citizens' Influences on City Government

Citizens can make their voices heard at city hall in several basic ways. The most obvious and widely employed means is voting, but several other options are available as well: organizing or joining some group or political party and contacting city officials with complaints or requests for services.

ELECTIONS AND VOTING

The first and perhaps most significant thing we can say about municipal elections is that most Americans do not vote in them. Sad to say, the average turnout for city elections is in the distressingly low range of 25 to 35 percent. Obviously local elections are not so exciting or dramatic as national contests, and the stakes are seldom very high. But beyond this,

> the principal reason for apathy in municipal elections, in fact, is likely to be a pervasive consensus; that is, there may be widespread agreement in the community as to the kinds of persons who are wanted in public office, as to expenditure levels, and as to public policies. Under such circumstances, little incentive exists for any but the most conscientious voter or the chronic dissenter to go to the polls.[53]

What difference does voter turnout make? In a democracy elections provide a vital mechanism for controlling the political system, shaping policy alternatives, and expressing community values. But in whose interests? Not the entire community it seems. Research repeatedly shows that those who do not vote have less education and income than does the active electorate. So the lower the turnout, the more likely the election will reflect the preferences of the well-to-do. Some might argue that the politically active should have more to say about community affairs. Certainly local officials are especially sensitive to the preferences of the attentive public. Still, we should remember that the election process reveals only a partial picture of the values and preferences of the whole city.

Voter participation is affected significantly by the characteristics of the municipal election process itself. About 78 percent of cities with a population greater than 25,000 hold nonpartisan elections.[54] About 60 percent of these conduct balloting separate from national, state, and other local elections.[55] Partisan cities are twice as likely as nonpartisan cities to schedule local voting at the same time as state or national elections. Since turnout usually rises with the importance of the election, those cities holding elections concurrently with the presidential or gubernatorial contests experience higher turnout rates. An examination of municipal voting also reveals that council-manager cities have a smaller turnout than do mayoral cities, and communities with nonpartisan ballots have lower levels of voting than do those with party ballots. But the real difference lies with concurrent voting. When municipal elections are held at the same time as state or national races, form of government and ballot type do not really matter. Only when city elections are conducted independently from higher-level contests do real disparities in turnout appear.

Elections are only one means by which the citizenry affects local policy. Participation in party or group activity may represent an even more direct means of exercising influence.

POLITICAL PARTIES AND INTEREST GROUPS

As we just noted, a supermajority of city elections today are nonpartisan. But there was a day when political parties played a powerful role in local politics, sometimes as handmaiden to the local political machine. The changing social and economic character of many cities, coupled with the successful efforts of urban reformers, has dealt a death blow to most big-city machines. A major vehicle for accomplishing that objective was the introduction of nonpartisan ballots and the direct primary. The next chapter continues the story of the reform movement in more detail. Here let us just say that political parties generally do not affect the governance of most cities in any significant way. For example, a recent survey of mayors from cities of 50,000 and more across the country showed that the two major political parties were seen as less active in city affairs than were most other civic and business groups.[56]

Perhaps most ordinary citizens see the diminution of party influence at the local level as a plus. Not all scholars would agree. In political scientist Bryan Jones's words, "Political parties are the mainsprings of mass democracy."[57] Unlike most other organizations interested in public affairs, parties are committed to getting out the vote. Moreover, each party makes some attempt at addressing issues and developing some agreement on those issues among candidates running on its label. Granted, parties in this country have never been very successful in inducing elected office-holders to adhere to their platforms or programs. But many political scientists believe that the alternative is worse—elected officials pursuing the dictates of their own consciences without regard to consequences or being subjected to unconstrained group influence.

Organizing like-minded citizens or joining an active interest group represents an increasingly popular means by which citizens make their wishes known to city officials. Judging the effectiveness or influence of such groups is difficult, however. According to information gathered in the late 1960s, an overwhelming majority of city council members from the San Francisco Bay Area believed that at least one group was influential on issues coming before the council. The most frequent choice was the local chamber of commerce, followed by general civic organizations such as service clubs and the League of Women Voters. Homeowners and neighborhood associations were third in importance. Yet in general these elected officials did not view groups as important, much less indispensable, to the local political system.[58] Based on more recent survey data of local government officials, between 1975 and 1985 neighborhood groups greatly increased their influence and now are viewed as "more influential than political parties and all interest groups except business organizations."[59]

Several observations can be made about group influence. First, although business is widely acknowledged as the most powerful interest, its role differs among cities and among issues within a single city.[60] Even in large cities such as Dallas and, at one time, San Antonio and Dayton, the business element dominated city politics by promising "good government" groups that controlled the process of nominating council members. In other places, the views of businesses within a municipality conflict. Downtown business interests may oppose those whose commitments are in outlying shopping centers. Or businesses with national headquarters may not find their views compatible with those of strictly local firms. Labor, conversely, rarely commands much influence in municipal politics; its interests normally lie at the state and national levels. Finally, neighborhood groups and homeowners may appear at city council meetings with some regularity, but their concerns historically have been narrowly focused. In general, they want to discourage city policies and actions that adversely affect their particular slice of the community. "Not in my backyard" (NIMBY) is a frequent rallying cry for these groups. But this parochialism may be changing. Fewer neighborhoods are making claims on city governments; instead, they are looking to city halls for partnerships. As Jeffrey Katz reports, as of 1989 "community-based development organizations had built nearly 125,000 units of housing in the United States—mostly for low-income residents. They had developed 16.4 million square feet of retail space, offices, and other industrial development."[61] Neighborhoods are asking that city governments empower them. Instead of confrontation, neighborhood representatives seek collaboration. Government in Dayton, Ohio, for example, "runs on citizen power." Seven area councils called "priority boards" working with city officials help determine not only how Community Development Block

Grants are spent but also city-generated CD funds.[62] According to Rob Gurwitt, similar neighborhood empowerment and activities are under way in cities such as San Antonio, Denver, Phoenix, Indianapolis, Richmond, Santa Clarita (Calif.), Minneapolis, and Portland.[63]

CITIZEN CONTACTS WITH LOCAL GOVERNMENT

In the daily course of events, a number of people call, write, or visit city hall—to complain about uncollected trash, for example, or loose dogs, or an unusually large pothole in a nearby street. Or they may be seeking some sort of information—where to go to receive a health service or to inquire about employment. In the past few years, considerable attention has been devoted to the nature of these contacts with local government.

Who are these people? Two characteristics heavily influence contact with local government: social class and need. As with voting, the better-educated and more affluent citizens are the most likely to understand the system and feel comfortable contacting local officials for a variety of purposes. But need for service may be even more critical, according to several recent studies.[64] Some local agencies distribute their services in response to observed demand.[65] This demand apparently relates more to citizens' perceptions of the need for service (in the form of complaints) and more general concern for the community than to their income or education.

What do these people want? Urban scholar Elaine Sharp's study of citizen-government contacts in Kansas City revealed that citizens have quite high expectations concerning the problems local government should solve, particularly in the areas of community services and public safety.[66] Responses to the question "What do you think is the most important problem that you have in your neighborhood?" most frequently concerned what Sharp calls community services (flooding, trash piles, barking dogs); next were safety problems (crime, fear of walking the streets at night). Social problems (undesirable neighbors, unsupervised juveniles) were least often mentioned. More important, people tended to think local government should do something about these matters, especially service and safety problems. A public ethic has evolved in this country, according to Sharp, that not only encourages the translation of personal problems into demands for public service but fosters the expectation that city government is indeed responsible for resolving most of these problems. Sharp's concern is that these heightened citizen expectations may lead to disappointment and disillusionment whenever city hall fails to deliver as expected.

Finally, citizen participation in local affairs is encouraged if not mandated by a few federal programs. Consider, for example, the CDBG program. Although the federal requirements are minimal (hold public hearings), some cities have seized this opportunity to develop quite elaborate mechanisms for citizen input. Such is the case in Norman, Oklahoma, a city of about 80,000 people.

CASE STUDY

CITIZEN PARTICIPATION IN NORMAN

NORMAN has created a two-tiered arrangement to facilitate citizen participation in the CDBG program. First, a broad-based citywide policy committee was established representing various groups interested in community development. On a second level, neighborhood participation has been elicited through a series of neighborhood meetings, which have the dual responsibility of identifying neighborhood development priorities and electing two members to the citywide policy committee. Of the thirty-two members in that group, fifteen are elected—two each by the five CDBG target neighborhoods and five at an annual communitywide "dialogue" convened to discuss CDBG plans and programs. The other committee members are chosen to represent two community elements—fourteen from local public agencies (e.g., city planning commission, board of education) and three from the private development sector (e.g., realtors' association, developers' council).

At the neighborhood level, participation is achieved through a series of annual meetings. The purpose of the July meeting is to elect representatives to the citywide committee and to a five-member neighborhood planning team. Various proposed activities are considered as well. In October several neighborhood meetings review proposed project costs (furnished by city staff) and agree on neighborhood priorities. The citywide committee then receives and reconciles all neighborhood requests and makes a final recommendation for project funding to the city council. The advisory committee also meets monthly in the spring of each year to review and monitor program performance.

The Norman CDBG staff proudly proclaims that during its entire history, the city has not undertaken a single CDBG project that was not first recommended by the advisory committee. A survey of committee members indicates they are pleased with the arrangement the city has created for soliciting citizen participation. They also give high marks to the way the CDBG program has assisted low- and moderate-income families and helped arrest neighborhood blight.

SOURCE: Adapted from David Morgan and Robert England, "Evaluating a Community Development Block Grant Program: A Citizens Group Perspective," *Policy Studies Journal* 12 (December 1983): 295–304.

Summary

The social, economic, and political context in which urban managers must function is complex. Especially in larger urban areas, the world of municipal governance has grown even more complicated and demanding in recent years. With population shifts accentuating the special needs of disadvantaged groups as well as decreasing the resource base, city governments are finding it increasingly difficult to meet the seemingly endless service demands of the urban populace. With cuts in federal aid programs, some cities have had an especially tough time adjusting to the new fiscal realities. But some observers contend that by relying more on their own resources—in many instances increasing taxes or fees to maintain service levels—cities have become stronger than they were ten or twenty years ago.

The urban manager's intergovernmental environment is not by any means confined to higher levels of government. A bevy of local jurisdictions, often in competition with one another, is found in virtually every metropolitan area of any size. Questions of metro government reform —centralization or decentralization—arise periodically. The issue of decentralization leads almost naturally to a concern for how citizens can make local government more responsive. Voting and direct contacts with city officials probably represent the avenues pursued by most individual citizens, but businesses and neighborhoods are more likely to rely on group activity to influence municipal affairs.

Notes

1. Jonathan Walters, "Cities on Their Own," *Governing,* April 1991, 31.

2. Ibid., 29.

3. Ibid.

4. John Herbers, "The Cavalry Is Not Coming to Save the Besieged Cities," *Governing,* September 1990, 9.

5. Thomas M. Guterbock presents evidence to refute the view that suburbanization is primarily the result of people fleeing central-city minority

presence and crime. See "The Push Hypothesis: Minority Presence, Crime, and Urban Deconcentration," in *The Changing Face of the Suburbs,* ed. Barry Schwartz (Chicago: University of Chicago Press, 1976), 137–61.

6. Walters, "Cities on Their Own," 28.

7. Alexander Ganz, "Where Has the Urban Crisis Gone? How Boston and Other Large Cities Have Stemmed Economic Decline," *Urban Affairs Quarterly* 20 (June 1985): 449–68.

8. Quoted in Jeffrey Pressman, *Federal Programs and City Politics* (Berkeley: University of California Press, 1975), 124.

9. The discussion and statistics are drawn from Advisory Commission on Intergovernmental Relations, *A Catalog of Federal Grant-in-Aid Programs to State and Local Governments: Grants Funded FY 1989* (Washington, D.C.: ACIR, October 1989).

10. George F. Break, *Intergovernmental Fiscal Relations in the United States* (Washington, D.C.: Brookings Institution, 1967), chap. 3.

11. Congressional Budget Office, *The Federal Government in a Federal System: Current Intergovernmental Programs and Options for Change* (Washington, D.C.: Government Printing Office, 1983), 104.

12. Vincent Marando, "General Revenue Sharing: Termination and City Response," *State and Local Government Review* 22 (Fall 1990): 98.

13. Gary Enos, "CDBG Program 'Ain't Broke,'" *City & State,* 17 June 1991, 3.

14. Ibid.

15. These examples come from Neal Peirce, "CDBG Celebrates 10th Anniversary," *Public Administration Times,* 15 January 1985.

16. U.S. General Accounting Office, *The Community Development Block Grant Program Can Be More Effective in Revitalizing the Nation's Cities* (Washington, D.C.: GAO, 30 April 1981), i; see also Enos, "CDBG Program 'Ain't Broke.'"

17. Peirce, "CDBG Celebrates 10th Anniversary."

18. Marc Bendick, Jr., and David Rasmussen, "Enterprise Zones and Inner-City Economic Revitalization," in *Reagan and the Cities,* ed. George Peterson and Carol Lewis (Washington, D.C.: Urban Institute, 1986), 114.

19. Neal R. Peirce, "Enterprise Zones Open Urban Opportunities," *Public Administration Times,* 1 February 1981, 2.

20. Bendick and Rasmussen, "Enterprise Zones and Inner-City Revitalization," 119.

21. Roy E. Green and Michael Brintnall, "Reconnoitering State-Administered Enterprise Zones: What's in a Name," *Journal of Urban Affairs* 9, no. 2 (1987): 159.

22. ACIR, *Fiscal Balance in the American Federal System* (Washington, D.C.: Government Printing Office, 1967), 212.

23. Morley Segal and A. Lee Fritschler, "Emerging Patterns of Intergovernmental Relations," *Municipal Year Book 1970* (Washington, D.C.: ICMA, 1970), 13.

24. Jane Massey and Jeffrey Straussman, "Another Look at the Mandate Issue: Are Conditions-of-Aid Really So Burdensome?" *Public Administration Review* 45 (March/April 1985): 292–300.

25. See table 7.2 in Paul R. Dommel, "Intergovernmental Relations," in *Managing Local Government,* ed. Richard D. Bingham et al. (Newbury Park, Calif.: Sage, 1991), 140.

26. Taken from John M. DeGrove, "State and Local Relations: The Challenge of New Federalism," *National Civic Review* 71 (February 1982): 75–83.

27. Richard Nathan, Fred C. Doolittle, and Associates, *The Consequences of the Cuts* (Princeton, N.J.: Princeton Urban and Regional Research Center, 1983), 64.

28. Steven D. Gold and Brenda M. Erickson, "State Aid to Local Governments in the 1980s," *State and Local Government Review* 21 (Winter 1989): 15. There is also a literature explaining state aid to cities; see, for example, David Morgan and Robert England, "State Aid to Cities: A Casual Inquiry," *Publius* 14 (Spring 1984): 67–82.

29. As quoted in Penelope Lemov, "The Decade of Red Ink," *Governing,* August 1992, 22.

30. Rod Zolkos, "Guvs Eye Pensions, City Taxes: States to Grab Funds of Others," *City & State,* 1–14 June 1992, 21.

31. Ibid.

32. Quoted in A. James Reichley, "The Political Containment of the Cities," in *The States and the Urban Crisis,* ed. Alan Campbell (Englewood Cliffs, N.J.: Prentice Hall, 1970), 173.

33. ACIR, *State and Local Roles in the Federal System* (Washington, D.C.: Government Printing Office, 1982), 200.

34. DeGrove, "State and Local Relations," 77.

35. John L. Mikesell, *Fiscal Administration: Analysis and Applications for the Public Sector,* 2d ed. (Chicago: Dorsey, 1986), 413.

36. This discussion draws from Mikesell, *Fiscal Administration,* 413–15; and Dommel, "Intergovernmental Relations," 144–45.

37. Catherine Lovell and Charles Tobin, "The Mandate Issue," *Public Administration Review* 41 (May/June 1981): 318–31.

38. Janet M. Kelly, "State Mandates: Fiscal Notes Reimbursement and Anti-Mandate Strategies," *Oklahoma Cities and Towns,* 25 September 1992, 7.

39. Parris Glendening and Patricia Atkins, "City-County Consolidations: New Views for the Eighties," *Municipal Year Book 1980* (Washington, D.C.: ICMA, 1980), 70.

40. Melvin B. Mogulof, *Five Metropolitan Governments* (Washington, D.C.: Urban Institute, 1972).

41. Scott Greer, *Metropolitics: A Study of Political Culture* (New York: Wiley, 1963), 196.

42. Elinor Ostrom, Roger Parks, and Gordon Whitaker, "Do We Really

Want to Consolidate Urban Police Forces? A Reappraisal of Some Old Assertions," *Public Administration Review* 33 (September/October 1973): 423–32.

43. Elinor Ostrom, "Metropolitan Reform: Propositions Derived from Two Traditions," *Social Science Quarterly* 53 (December 1972): 474–93.

44. Thomas R. Dye, "Metropolitan Integration by Bargaining among Sub-Areas," *American Behavioral Scientist* 5 (May 1962): 11–13.

45. Robert L. Bish, *The Public Economy of Metropolitan Areas* (Chicago: Markham, 1971), 92.

46. Dommel, "Intergovernmental Relations," 148.

47. Scott A. Bollens, "Examining the Link between State Policy and the Creation of Local Special Districts," *State and Local Government Review* 18 (Fall 1986): 118.

48. Ibid.

49. Ibid., 117.

50. James T. Bennett and Thomas J. Dilorenzo, *Underground Government: The Off-Budget Public Sector* (Washington, D.C.: Cato Institute, 1983), 123.

51. Paul Kantor with Stephen David, *The Dependent City* (Glenview, Ill.: Scott, Foresman, 1988), 267–68.

52. Charles Shannon, "The Rise and Emerging Fall of Metropolitan Area Regional Associations," in *Intergovernmental Relations and Public Policy,* ed. J. Edwin Benton and David Morgan (New York: Greenwood Press, 1986), 72.

53. Charles Adrian and Charles Press, *Governing Urban America,* 5th ed. (New York: McGraw-Hill, 1977), 104.

54. Tari Renner and Victor S. DeSantis, "Contemporary Patterns in Municipal Government Structures," *Municipal Year Book 1993* (Washington, D.C.: ICMA, 1993), 68.

55. Albert Karnig and B. Oliver Walter, "Municipal Elections: Registration, Incumbent Success, and Voter Participation," *Municipal Year Book 1977* (Washington, D.C.: ICMA, 1977), 69.

56. David R. Morgan, "Municipal Expenditures and Group Influence," in *Research in Urban Policy,* vol. 3 (Greenwich, Conn.: JAI, 1988).

57. Bryan D. Jones, *Governing Urban America: A Policy Focus* (Boston: Little, Brown, 1983), 135.

58. Betty H. Zisk, *Local Interest Politics: A One-Way Street* (Indianapolis: Bobbs-Merrill, 1973), 22, 143.

59. Paul Schumaker, "Neighborhood Mobilization and Political Power: Book Review Essay," *Policy Studies Review* 7 (Winter 1987): 454.

60. Jones, *Governing Urban America,* 159.

61. Jeffrey L. Katz, "Neighborhood Politics: A Changing World," *Governing,* November 1990, 48–49.

62. Rob Gurwitt, "A Government That Runs on Citizen Power," *Governing,* December 1992, 48.

63. Ibid., 48–54.

64. See John C. Thomas, "Citizen-Initiated Contacts with Governmental Agencies: A Test of Three Theories," *American Journal of Political Science* 26 (August 1982): 504–22; Elaine B. Sharp, "Citizen Demand Making in the Urban Context," *American Journal of Political Science* 28 (November 1984): 654–70; and Michael W. Hirlinger, "Citizen-Initiated Contacting of Local Government Officials: A Multivariate Explanation," *Journal of Politics* 54 (May 1992): 553–64.

65. Bryan D. Jones, *Service Delivery in the City* (New York: Longman, 1980), 89.

66. Sharp, "Citizen Demand Making," 664–69.

Suggested for Further Reading

Banfield, Edward C. *The Unheavenly City Revisited.* Boston: Little, Brown, 1974.

Bennett, James T., and Thomas J. DiLorenzo. *Underground Government: The Off-Budget Public Sector.* Washington, D.C.: Cato Institute, 1983.

Harrigan, John J. *Political Change in the Metropolis.* 5th ed. New York: HarperCollins, 1993.

Jones, Bryan D. *Governing Urban America: A Policy Focus.* Boston: Little, Brown, 1983.

Judd, Dennis R. *The Politics of American Cities.* 3rd ed. Boston: Little, Brown, 1988.

Kantor, Paul, with Stephen David. *The Dependent City.* Glenview, Ill.: Scott, Foresman, 1988.

Newell, Charldean, ed. *The Effective Local Government Manager.* 2d ed. Washington, D.C.: ICMA, 1993.

Pressman, Jeffrey. *Federal Programs and City Politics.* Berkeley: University of California Press, 1975.

2

Urban Political Structure

Americans more than most people believe that form and organization contribute to governmental effectiveness and efficiency. Especially at the local level, groups that want governmental change often argue the need for new structure. The relationship between form and function undoubtedly has been overestimated, but local political structure does matter. The form that municipal government takes and the institutional arrangements provided for citizen input into policymaking represent part of the local "rules of the governmental game." As in any game, rules make a difference.[1] They favor some groups and put others at a disadvantage, although it is sometimes difficult to know the extent to which structures help one group as opposed to another. According to urban scholar Charles A. Adrian, the structure of city government is important "in helping to determine the content of policy, access to decision making, the image of the city held by outsiders, and the accomplishments of the goals of major interest groups."[2]

Historically, reform groups in particular have had exceptional faith in the efficacy of particular forms of governmental institutions. These groups recognized that merely "throwing the rascals out" might not be enough. If local government was to be improved permanently, basic institutions had to be changed. And so, during the latter part of the nineteenth and early part of the twentieth centuries, in the name of good government, reformers fought the battle for basic changes in urban structure, and their impact is still felt today.

The Reform Movement

The urban reform movement was largely a product of the Progressive era, when the muckrakers and others aroused public opinion with their exposures of dishonesty, greed, and corruption in public life. Unsavory politics was not confined to urban areas, of course, but the physical development of the city during the latter half of the nineteenth century provided abundant opportunities for the buying and selling of contracts for paving streets, installing lighting, and building water and sewage systems.[3] Reacting to this graft and corruption, reformers searched for ways to eliminate the excesses and to oust unscrupulous profiteers from city halls and state capitals around the country.[4]

By the last quarter of the nineteenth century, the problem of corruption had been compounded by the growth of the political machine. Through political organization, those holding office in many large cities had found it possible to perpetuate themselves in power. Now the reformers had to contend not just with corruption but with the potential for long-term control by self-perpetuating organizations dominated by political bosses.

Why were the machines so successful in a number of large cities? Most observers contend that the machine succeeded because it distributed material incentives to its backers and followers and to the voters.[5] The machine clearly did not make its appeal on issues or ideology; favors and protection—with a special human touch—were the order of the day. One of the most colorful and enlightening accounts of a machine's operation comes from the famous Tammany sage George Washington Plunkitt. Plunkitt became a millionaire during his forty-year service with the Tammany organization in New York. He had this to say about how the machine was able to gain such widespread support:

> There's only one way to hold a district; you must study human nature and act accordin'. You can't study human nature in books. . . . To learn real human nature you have to go among the people, see them and be seen. . . .
>
> For instance, here's how I gather in the young men. I hear of a young feller that's proud of his voice, thinks he can sing fine.
>
> I ask him to come around to Washington Hall and join our Glee Club. He comes and sings, and he's a follower of Plunkitt for life. Another young feller gains a reputation as a baseball player in a vacant lot. I bring him into our baseball club. That fixes him. You'll find him workin' for my ticket at the polls next election day. Then there's the feller that likes rowin' on the river, the young feller that makes a name

as a waltzer on his block, the young feller that's handy with his dukes —I rope them all in by givin' them opportunities to show themselves off. I don't trouble them with political arguments. I just study human nature and act accordin'.[6]

Now, of course, the machines have largely withered away, although not necessarily because of the reformers. This is not to suggest that the reform movement had no impact on twentieth-century urban politics. To the contrary, the reform heritage is impressive. The decline and near-demise of the political machine, however, generally is thought to have resulted from other, more fundamental influences. Banfield and Wilson, for example, indicate that voters gradually became less interested in what the machines had to offer. "The petty favors and 'friendship' of the precinct captains declined in value as immigrants were assimilated, public welfare programs were vastly extended, and per capita incomes rose steadily."[7] They emphasize the importance of the assimilation of lower-class people into the middle class, and the growing acceptance of the political ethos of that group: "The central idea of which is that politics should be based on public rather than on private motives and, accordingly, should stress the virtues of honesty, impartiality, and efficiency."[8]

Perhaps the reformers were not instrumental in bringing down the bosses and their organizations. Still, many of the changes sought by reform groups were implemented in city after city across the land.

THE GOALS AND ASSUMPTIONS OF URBAN REFORMERS

City governments perform two basic functions: they provide services and manage political conflict. To many, this second task is far less legitimate than the first. Perhaps it would be unfair to say that reformers wanted to eliminate politics from city government altogether; but clearly they felt there was no room for party politics in municipal government. Obviously a city must provide fire and police protection, water and sewage facilities, and other essential services, but none of these holds a place for the party. "There is no Democratic or Republican way to pave a street," the old saying goes. More than this, partisan politics, according to reformers, had led to abuses by the bosses and their machines, which contributed so much to corrupting the cities. It seemed impossible then to eliminate graft and corruption, to rid the cities of the machines, without freeing city government from partisan politics. The reformers' basic objective was to eradicate corruption; the means to that end was the exclusion of political parties from local public affairs.

Eliminating corruption was just one goal of the early urban reform movement. If the primary purpose of city government was to provide services, then this function ought to be performed as economically and efficiently as possible. "In the period just prior to the First War, a new concern moved toward the top of the [reformers'] agenda: rationalized management of urban government. . . . The new reforms were an admixture of the business ethic and Taylorism, the new science of managerial efficiency."[9]

The reformers found in the business corporation the ideal model for streamlining and rationalizing the municipal administrative process. The city-manager plan seemed to offer what was needed: an elected local council would choose an outside administrator on the basis of managerial experience and skill. The city government, then, not only needed rescuing from the baneful effects of partisan politics; it also needed restructuring to operate as efficiently as possible. This is not to suggest that the urban reformers were apolitical. A political economy explanation of the urban reform movement is now widely accepted.

In a classic article Samuel P. Hays dispels the myth that the reform movement was a product of the working and/or middle class. Instead, the driving force came from business and professional groups.[10] In fact, according to political scientist Dennis Judd, changes in structure and electoral rules were an attempt to undercut the political strength of lower-class groups.[11] Certainly one purpose was to curtail corruption and compel city governments to operate more efficiently. But Judd contends that upper-income and business groups sought a local political climate favorable to growth and economic development. These were not true social reformers who wanted lower utility rates, safer and more affordable housing, or additional public services to improve the lives of the poor. Instead, the structural reformers were interested primarily in more efficient government and lower taxes as a way of advancing the political agenda of the business community.

Banfield and Wilson suggest that the reform movement was concerned too that local government be more democratic.[12] The reformers felt that greater popular participation was a primary means of weakening the political machine. If only the political process at the grassroots could be opened up—removed from the smoke-filled back rooms—perhaps the people could regain control of city hall. To this end reformers pushed for the initiative and referendum, the recall, and the direct primary.

Behind these three goals—elimination of corruption, greater efficiency, and more democracy—lay a basic presupposition regarding the nature of city government. The reformers assumed that a single public interest (public regardingness) existed for the city as a whole and that this interest should prevail over competing, partial, and usually private interests (private regardingness).[13] This larger community interest presumably could be discovered and agreed on if rational, well-intended people could free themselves from narrow partisan or geographic ties. The "best" people should be elected to municipal office regardless of where they lived. Therefore at-large elections became an essential part of the reformers' search for rational, efficient local government. In addition, destroying the ward system would free council members from petty ward politics. Elected officials would no longer be required to serve as political brokers, exchanging services and favors for votes. Mutual accommodation, or logrolling, among council members would cease.

THE CHARACTERISTICS OF REFORM GOVERNMENT

A number of proposals were advanced by reformers to reorganize the structure of city government formally. Although over time reform groups focused on somewhat different governmental features, we can identify certain characteristics in the municipal reform model: an emphasis on rational decision making and on increased efficiency in providing services.

Robert Boynton contrasts the reform model of city government with a political model.[14] The *reform model* embraces council-manager government; nonpartisan ballots; at-large elections; the separation of municipal elections from state and national elections; merit systems; and the initiative, the referendum, and the recall petition process. We examine several of these features, particularly the ballot type and method for selecting council members, in the sections that follow. Here we should note that separating city from state and national elections presumably is an additional means (beyond removing party labels) of isolating local elections, thus lessening the influence of political parties and their organizations. Merit systems, of course, are the obvious answer to the spoils and patronage arrangements so crucial to the success of the political machine. Putting legislation or propositions on the ballot through a referendum petition is an attempt to make local government more responsive to the people. The same is true of the recall process, whereby a petition containing a sufficient number of names can force a new election for city council positions.

Several other structural characteristics reflect reform ideals. For example, a short ballot avoids fragmented executive authority. Also, reformers generally favor small councils to avoid potential divisiveness and cumbersome decision processes. Finally, no premium is placed on concurrent council terms: "On the contrary, overlapping terms are thought of as providing stability and continuity in decision making and are encouraged in the reform model."[15]

Boynton's *political model*—the opposite of the reform ideal—is committed to providing maximum representation for various community interests, especially those with some geographic base. The model's structural arrangements also enhance the conflict-managing capacity of city government. Its characteristics include a strong mayor-council form of government, partisan elections, ward representation, coterminous council elections, and a relatively large council. In the political model a directly elected strong mayor is responsible for taking the lead in policymaking and controlling the administrative apparatus of the city. The council is relatively large (and elected from geographic constituencies) so that all legitimate community groups are represented. And the political party is a legitimate, if not essential, mechanism for aggregating and articulating competing local interests.

As with all ideal types, Boynton's two models seldom appear in their pure forms. Still certain reform mechanisms commonly are found together. For example, 83 percent of council-manager cities use a nonpartisan ballot compared with 65 percent of mayor-council cities.[16] The same situation prevails concerning at-large versus ward representation. Among council-manager cities, 68 percent conduct at-large elections, compared to 49 percent among mayor-council communities.[17]

Reform structures, moreover, are apt to be found in certain kinds of cities. First, large cities tend to resist reform structures, with one prominent exception. As table 2.1 reveals, the largest municipalities (over 500,000 population) are not attracted to the council-manager plan (20 percent in that category), but the overwhelming majority of cities, regardless of size, now employ nonpartisan ballots. This does not mean that all city elections are free of party influence; such influence is simply more subtle. At-large elections tend to be more popular in smaller cities; cities with populations of 250,000 or more residents are more likely to use district-based electoral schemes. Finally, council-manager cities are much more common among small- to medium-sized communities, although mayor-council governments are still used in about 52 percent of cities with populations between 2,500 and 24,999 (not shown in table).

Region and type of city (central city, suburb, or independent) are also linked to reformism.[18] Sunbelt cities are more likely to employ the council-manager form of government. At-large elections are most frequently found in western cities, although about 75 percent of New England and Mid-Atlantic cities also use at-large elections. Nonpartisan

TABLE 2.1.
MUNICIPAL REFORM CHARACTERISTICS
BY CITY SIZE, 1991

Size of cities and number studied[a]	Council-manager form (%)	Nonpartisan ballot (%)	At-large elections (%)
Over 500,000 (10)	20	80	38
250–499,000 (32)	56	81	26
100–249,000 (100)	67	83	46
50–99,999 (255)	64	82	47
25–49,999 (517)	63	74	53

SOURCE: Adapted from "Contemporary Patterns and Trends in Municipal Government Structures," by Tari Renner and Victor S. DeSantis, *Municipal Year Book 1993* (Washington, D.C.: ICMA, 1993), 57–68. Copyright 1993 by International City Management Association, Washington, D.C. Reprinted by permission.

a. N varies slightly for each column. Response rate by size category (from largest to smallest): 42 percent, 80 percent, 75 percent, 76 percent, and 77 percent.

elections are likely to be used in all regions, except the Mid-Atlantic. Central cities are much less likely to use at-large elections, whereas metro status is not strongly related to form of government or ballot type.

Certain social and economic characteristics also are related to a city's form of government. Communities with a more homogeneous population find the reform model, with its emphasis on efficiency and businesslike methods, more to their liking. In particular, growing, white middle-class cities and cities with mobile populations tend to embrace the council-manager plan. Ethnically and religiously diverse, nonmobile, industrial cities lean more toward the mayor-council form.[19]

THE IMPACT OF REFORM

Except in bigger, more socially diverse cities, reformers largely succeeded in depoliticizing municipal government, an action that had several effects. First, certain reform arrangements—nonpartisan ballots, the council-manager form, and nonconcurrent elections—tend to depress voter turnout in city elections. Since lower levels of voter participation often work to the advantage of the well-to-do and middle class, reform city governments may not be as responsive to the interests of the less advantaged. Ward-based elections, in contrast to at-large systems, produce more representative city councils. African Americans, for example, are much more likely to be elected to city councils using ward as opposed to at-large elections.[20] Hispanics and Native Americans seem to do best with "mixed" electoral systems, where some council members are elected at-large and others by wards.

Reformed structures also may affect municipal policy outcomes. The classic study on this issue was done by political scientists Robert Lineberry and Edmund Fowler, who examined 200 cities of 50,000 or more inhabitants. They hypothesized that the policymaking of reformed city governments would differ from that of unreformed city governments. Indeed they found lower levels of taxation and expenditure effort among reform cities, even when the social and economic characteristics of the cities were taken into account. In addition the policies of unreformed cities were more responsive to socioeconomic cleavages in their environments. The authors conclude: "If one of the components of the middle-class reformer's ideal was to 'seek the good of the community as a whole' and to minimize the impact of social cleavages on political decision making, then their institutional reforms have served, by and large, to advance that goal."[21] Others, however, question the relationship between political structures and taxing and spending patterns in cities. Using a time-series analysis, for example, David Morgan and John Pelissero matched eleven cities that changed political structure with eleven that did not. They found that taxing and spending differences were largely unaffected by changes in city government structure.[22]

Perhaps the linkage between political structure and public policy is through representation. Unreformed political structures apparently enhance minority representation. And research shows that representation does have an impact on public policy outputs. Case studies have found, for example, that the election of black mayors has resulted in public policy differences.[23] A large systematic study by Albert Karnig and Susan Welch found that the election of a black mayor may result in some changes in municipal expenditures.[24] Other research shows a positive relationship between minority elected officials and municipal employment of minorities.[25]

In general, those who feel city governments are not as responsive as they should be, especially to low-income and minority groups, often blame the reform legacy for contributing to the problem. Much of the criticism is directed at municipal bureaucrats whose power is enhanced under reform institutions. With the passing of political machines, the governance of cities increasingly has been influenced by bureaucratic independence and expertise. So some critics fault the merit system and the professionalized civil service for depersonalizing city government and isolating it from the individual. Middle-class city dwellers do not suffer unduly from this situation; they have fewer needs for public services and are reasonably well positioned to make the system respond. Typical ghetto residents, however, have complicated social and economic problems that often require extensive governmental help. But the red tape, the delays, the innumerable offices and programs make it much more difficult for the disadvantaged to obtain that needed assistance.

The extent to which the blame for bureaucratic inertia, insensitivity, and red tape should be laid at the feet of the reformers is debatable; but the municipal reform movement did place its faith in a bureaucratic rather than a political process for identifying the public interest.[26] And although city governments now may be more efficiently run, some authorities contend that large cities in particular are poorly governed. Chief executives today lack the power to control the autonomous agencies —the islands of functional power—because reform institutions, according to critics, destroyed the informal centralizing influence of the political party. Although municipal reform may contribute to more businesslike management of a city, it does so at a price—less responsiveness to disadvantaged groups within the community and more control by autonomous bureaucrats.

Forms of City Government[27]

In the preceding section, we repeatedly referred to mayor-council government and the council-manager plan. Here we should examine the specific differences between these basic forms of municipal government.

MAYOR-COUNCIL GOVERNMENT

We can identify two variations of mayor-council government: the weak-mayor and strong-mayor forms. Essentially the two types differ in degree only, and few cities reflect the extremes of either.

The mayor-council form of government preserves the basic separation of powers between the legislative and executive branches. Historically, owing to widespread suspicion of concentrated executive power, councils were the dominant force in city government. Gradually, as cities grew and government became increasingly complex, more concentrated authority was put in the hands of the chief executive. Now most authorities favor the strong-mayor variation as a way of providing the political leadership thought to be so crucial, especially for larger cities. For smaller communities the weak-mayor form still remains popular.

WEAK-MAYOR FORM.—According to Charles Adrian and Charles Press:

> The weak-mayor plan is a product of Jacksonian democracy.... Implicit in the weak-mayor plan are the beliefs that if politicians have few powers and many checks upon them, they can do relatively little damage and that if one politician becomes corrupt, he or she will not necessarily corrupt the whole city government.[28]

A number of features distinguish the weak-mayor form:

- The council possesses both legislative and executive authority. The council may appoint several important administrative officials itself and invariably must approve the mayor's appointees.
- The mayor's appointive powers are restricted.
- A long ballot may dictate the direct election of certain key administrative officials.
- The council exercises primary control over the municipal budget, perhaps through the operation of a budget or finance committee.

Figure 2.1 illustrates the essence of the weak-mayor form. Notice that the voters elect not only the mayor and the council but also several other administrative officials. Moreover, the council has considerable appointive power itself and, of course, must consent to the mayor's choice of department heads and appointees to various boards and commissions. Clearly this arrangement establishes no single administrative head of city government. Power is fragmented, and the mayor is severely hemmed in. Adrian and Press note, however, that the "mayors are not 'weak' because

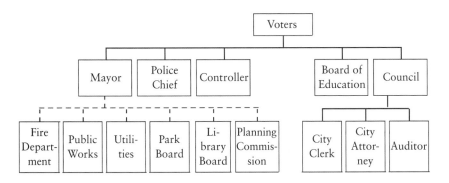

FIGURE 2.1. HYPOTHETICAL WEAK-MAYOR FORM.

- - - Council concurrence required

they lack policy-making power—they normally have a veto, can recommend legislation, and may even preside over the council. They are 'weak' because they lack administrative power."[29]

The weak-mayor plan was designed for an earlier era, when cities were smaller and government simpler. Today it seems especially ill suited for large cities in which political and administrative leadership is vital. Many of the nineteenth-century machines evolved under the weak-mayor structure because its lack of administrative centralization was an open invitation for external direction and control. Fragmented authority at the top also encourages greater bureaucratic independence. The effect of autonomy is to make city government into a series of many little governments rather than a single coordinated one. For a number of reasons, then, larger cities have searched for ways to bring about more central control of administrative activities.

STRONG-MAYOR FORM. —The strong-mayor government represents a significant departure from the fragmented executive office of the weak-mayor plan. It includes the following features:

- The mayor has almost total administrative authority, with the power to appoint and dismiss virtually all department heads without council approval.
- The mayor prepares and administers the budget.
- A short ballot restricts the number of elected administrative officials.
- Policymaking is a joint enterprise between mayor and council.

Strong mayors are likely to have a veto power that usually can be overridden only by a two-thirds or three-fourths majority of the council. Because of this strong legal position the mayor becomes the dominant force in city government, as figure 2.2 illustrates.

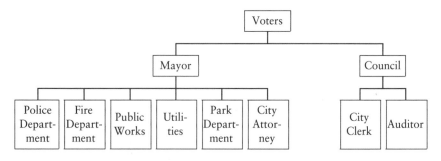

FIGURE 2.2. HYPOTHETICAL STRONG-MAYOR FORM.

The strong-mayor form is subject to criticism. First, it requires that the mayor be both a good political leader and a competent administrator, two traits not always found in mayoral candidates. In addition, much as in national government, conflict can erupt periodically between a strong, politically ambitious mayor and a recalcitrant council. A legislative-executive deadlock remains a continual threat.

In some large strong-mayor cities a new development is working to rectify the first potential shortcoming of the plan—the need to combine a good administrator and a good politician in the same office. Here a chief administrative officer (CAO) is appointed by the mayor to serve at his or her pleasure. The CAO might supervise department heads, prepare the budget (under the mayor's direction), coordinate various departments in the performance of day-to-day activities, and give technical advice to the mayor. By assigning these more mundane responsibilities to the CAO, the mayor frees time for two other major jobs: serving as ceremonial head of the city and providing broad policy leadership. The CAO remains the mayor's person because she or he is responsible only to the mayor, not to the council. It is this mayoral control that distinguishes the job of the CAO from that of the city manager.

With or without the CAO, the strong-mayor form is especially suitable to large cities with diverse populations, where strong political leadership is required to arrange compromises and arbitrate struggles for power among contending interests.

COUNCIL-MANAGER GOVERNMENT

In 1913 Dayton, Ohio, became the first city of any size successfully to adopt the council-manager form of government. Since then, with the approval and ardent support of reform groups, the plan has spread rapidly. Today a majority of cities with population over 25,000 use the form. The basic characteristics of the council-manager plan include:

- A small city council, usually five to seven people, often elected at large on a nonpartisan ballot.
- Council responsibility for making policy, passing ordinances, voting appropriations, and supervising in an overall sense the administration of city government.
- A full-time professionally trained city administrator to serve at the pleasure of the council with full responsibility for day-to-day city operations (including hiring and firing department heads without council approval).

- An executive budget prepared and administered by the city manager.
- A mayor who performs strictly ceremonial duties and has no involvement in the city's administrative affairs.

This description represents the plan as ideally conceived, and usually only slight deviations are found in actual practice. The form is shown schematically in figure 2.3. The council-manager plan departs most drastically from historical American government practice in its abandonment of the doctrines of separation of powers and checks and balances. All executive and legislative authority resides in the council alone. The manager is essentially the council's hired hand and has no direct responsibility to the citizenry. Originally reformers feared the mayor might be tempted to interfere in the administrative affairs of city government unless mayoral powers were circumscribed strictly. The solution was to make the mayor responsible to the council rather than to the people. Over time, this view has undergone modification, so that today about 60 percent of council-manager cities provide for direct popular election of the mayor.[30]

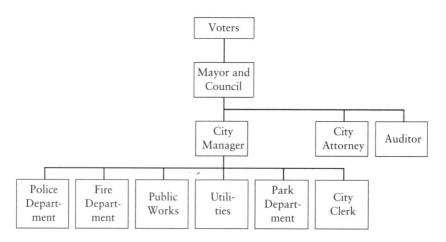

FIGURE 2.3. HYPOTHETICAL COUNCIL-MANAGER PLAN.

The council-manager plan's main attribute is its businesslike approach to city government, which presumably maximizes efficiency and technical expertise. In fact, in many places manager government has been supported by business groups, which tout, perhaps excessively, its capacity to save taxpayers' money. These groups argue that professional administration reduces waste and inefficiency and thereby effects great savings. The plan's reputation for efficiency makes it appealing to the upper- and middle-class suburbs that so many businesspeople call home. And, unmistakably, manager government has achieved considerable success among those places with little community diversity, where a high degree of consensus exists over the proper scope and function of city government.

LIMITATIONS ON THE FORM.—Despite its obvious popularity there are potential shortcomings to the council-manager form. The sharp distinction between policymaking and administration is unrealistic. We look at the policymaking relationship between manager and council in chapter 3. Here we should stress that the full-time professional manager inevitably will provide considerable policy advice to the part-time amateur council. Yet council members may not be certain just what the policy relationship should be between themselves and the manager. Citizens also may wonder who is really in charge of city affairs. Should administrative problems be brought to the mayor or to the city manager? And if a council merely rubber-stamps a manager's recommendations, then the manager—who is not directly accountable to the people—may seem to have too much power. Obviously this confusion cannot improve a government's responsiveness.

But the major potential limitation of the council-manager plan is its lack of formal provision for strong policy leadership. The council is a group of equals, the mayor is limited to a ceremonial role, and the manager presumably serves only in an advisory role. Sometimes the mayor or one of the council members emerges as a policy leader, but "more likely, the council will flounder about or turn to the manager."[31] An argument can be made, of course, that the experienced professional manager is in a better position than the council to interpret the needs of the community and thus should take the lead in policy formulation. But what does this do to the idealized role of the council? The issue is not an easy one to resolve, and we return to it in the next chapter.

CASE STUDY

SWITCHING GOVERNMENTS IN ALBUQUERQUE

ALTHOUGH more and more cities are using the manager plan, occasionally some revert to nonreform government. An interesting example took place in Albuquerque, New Mexico, a city of about

350,000 residents. In 1974 the voters, by a margin of 79 percent, replaced the five-member at-large council and city manager with a strong full-time mayor and a nine-member city council elected by wards. Apparently the change, which came after several years of study and debate, resulted in part from dissatisfaction with the performance of the city council. Power within the council had shifted repeatedly as ill-defined coalitions formed and dissolved. At one point a popular city manager was fired in large measure because of differing views on the city manager's role in policymaking.

Controversy over the manager's proper policymaking role was linked to several specific issues, especially growth and planning. Albuquerque had grown dramatically in the preceding few years, and many people were concerned that the city was in danger of losing most of its aesthetic qualities. The ousted manager had been strongly associated with the movement for planned, orderly growth in the city.

A public opinion poll conducted several days before the charter election revealed the public had several other concerns about its form of government. Respondents commented that under the council-manager structure they often did not know who could help with a problem or who was responsible for municipal affairs. Many also felt that Albuquerque had outgrown manager government and that a full-time elected mayor was needed.

SOURCE: Paul Hain, Chris Garcia, and Judd Conway, "From Council-Manager to Mayor-Council: The Case of Albuquerque," *Nation's Cities,* October 1975, 10–12.

Ballot Type

Reformers overwhelmingly won one battle. In 1910 almost no cities used nonpartisan elections. About twenty years later over half of all cities over 30,000 population used nonpartisan ballots.[32] Today, the vast majority (about 75 percent) of American cities of all sizes use nonpartisan ballots. As often happens with any reform, unanticipated side effects developed. Reform groups wanted to get the party out of municipal government as a way of destroying bosses and machine politics. Moreover parties were considered irrelevant, if not harmful, to providing services; experts and professionals should determine the service needs of the populace. But evidence now reveals that nonpartisanship had other effects, some of which are of dubious value. Before examining the consequences of removing party labels in municipal elections, we should mention that much of the research done on nonpartisan elections focuses on cities that also have other reform features, namely the council-manager plan and citywide elections. Therefore in some instances it is difficult to separate the effects of nonpartisan ballots from other influences.

Some research suggests that nonpartisan ballots give a slight edge to Republicans.[33] Recent evidence, however, indicates that this relationship is not clear-cut. Relying on surveys from about 1,000 city council members from around the nation, political scientists Susan Welch and Timothy Bledsoe report that a significant Republican bias appears only in smaller communities and in cities that have *both* nonpartisan elections and at-large balloting.[34] Nonpartisanship also tends to produce elected officials more representative of the upper socioeconomic strata than of the general populace, especially when combined with at-large elections: "When nonpartisan and at-large structures are combined, both lower income and educational level groups and Democrats are disadvantaged."[35]

Ballot type does not seem to make a difference with respect to reelection of council members. Most studies find that council incumbents overwhelmingly win reelection regardless of ballot type.[36] A 1991 ICMA survey shows that ballot type is not related to the election of women or minorities to city councils, although Hispanics fared a little better in nonpartisan elections.[37] Welch and Bledsoe report no differences in the *level* of conflict between partisan and nonpartisan elected council members. The *nature* of conflict on partisan councils versus nonpartisan was distinct, however. A "Democratic versus Republican rivalry was the most commonly cited principal source of factionalism among partisan council members, but the least commonly cited among those nonpartisan."[38]

Electoral Systems

Citywide or district elections—which should a city have? Again there is no simple answer. Proponents of at-large elections argue:

- Council members in an at-large system can rise above the limited perspective of the ward and concern themselves with the problems of the whole community.
- Vote trading and logrolling are minimized.
- The chance of domination by a machine is lessened.
- Better-qualified individuals are elected to the council.

Arguments in behalf of district elections are just the opposite. In particular, those advocating ward elections insist:

- District elections give all legitimate groups, especially those with a geographic base, a better chance of being represented on the city council.
- Ward council members are more sensitive to the small but frequently important little problems that people have (unfixed chuckholes, needed stop signs).
- Ward elections reduce voter alienation by bringing city government close to the people.

Because of the apparent strengths and shortcomings of both electoral systems, certain combinations of the two have developed. In one combination, council members are nominated by district and then elected citywide. This arrangement ensures geographic representation but also forces selected officials to think about the needs of the whole city. This combination guarantees as well that the larger community will have the dominant voice choosing representatives from each district. Blacks sometimes object to the arrangement, however, claiming it can be confusing and potentially divisive for the minority community.[39]

A second combination requires that a certain number of the council members be elected from wards, while others run at large. For example, a city might be divided into four wards with one council member elected from each ward. Then three or four additional council members would be voted on by the entire city. This combination too is open to criticism. Those officials elected at large may think they are more important than the others and in some cases may see themselves as potential rivals of the mayor.[40]

The method of choosing council members—ward or at large—does affect who is elected. As noted earlier, citywide elections tend to disadvantage blacks and other geographically concentrated minority groups. On the other hand, research shows that women do slightly better in at-large electoral systems.[41] Additional evidence indicates that ward elections provide a greater opportunity for people of lower income and education levels to be elected, regardless of race.[42] Welch and Bledsoe note that council members elected at large are better educated and are "less likely to focus on representing a neighborhood, ethnic, or party group and more likely to focus on the city as a whole."[43] They also report less conflict on councils where members are elected at large instead of from wards.[44]

The importance of electoral structure is demonstrated by a series of recent legal battles over equal representation, many of which involve ward and at-large elections.[45] In 1987 a court decision forced Springfield, Illinois, to change from an arrangement where four officials were elected at large to a mayor-council form with ten aldermen chosen by wards.[46] To avoid litigation, Tulsa, Oklahoma, decided to move from a commission form of government with at-large elections to a strong-mayor form with ward elections. Perhaps the city that has received the most public attention in recent years is Dallas. Through a series of contentious court battles, with strong racial overtones, the city's all at-large electoral system was changed in 1975 to a mixed system (with both at-large and single-member districts) and then in 1990 to an all-ward system (except for the mayor). In 1992 the council was composed of eight white, four black, and two Hispanic council members. The mayor is white. In 1993 John Ware, a black, replaced Jan Hart as city manager.[47]

Recent changes in government structures, and especially electoral systems, have been aided by legislation and a changing U.S. Supreme Court position on the issue. Originally, the Court found the issue of fair representation for minorities to be a slippery one. By a 6–3 vote, the Court in *Mobile* v. *Bolden* (1980) overturned a lower court opinion that had forced the city of Mobile to abandon its historic three-member commission form mandating at-large elections, which had never produced a black commissioner. In effect, the decision forced protesting groups to prove that at-large elections were *designed* to discriminate against minorities. That is, plaintiffs had to demonstrate that there was *intent* to discriminate. This is a heavy burden to prove against electoral systems, many of which were put in place at the turn of the century during the heyday of the reform movement.

In response to the *Mobile* decision and over the strong objection of the Reagan administration, in 1982 Congress amended the Voting Rights Act to require that courts not only look at intent to discriminate but also at the results or effects of political structures. In 1986 in *Thornburg* v. *Gingles* the U.S. Supreme Court moved beyond the judicial restraint position in the *Mobile* decision. In striking down some multimember state legislative districts in North Carolina the Court analyzed a number of factors, including

> the degree of historical discrimination; the degree of racially polarized block voting; racial appeals in political campaign rhetoric; the proportion of minorities elected to public office (although the Court made it clear that minorities do not have a right to have a fixed percentage of elected positions); and the extent to which there is responsiveness to minorities on the part of public officials in a community.[48]

Post-*Gingles* court decisions suggest that the federal judiciary is willing to enforce the High Court's more activist position.

Even where a court case is not at issue, blacks continue to try to force cities away from at-large elections, as the case study that follows shows.

CASE STUDY

Blacks in Plano Seek District Elections

In Plano, Texas (population about 111,000), a rapidly growing suburb of Dallas that has never had a black on the city council, a few years ago several African American leaders pushed to establish single-member districts to give minorities better representation. The black leaders, in speaking to a city charter review committee, argued that some ward seats should be created, along with those at large, to improve the chances of electing blacks to the council.

The mayor and some council members opposed the move. Council member Florence Shapiro said she objects to ward elections because they may lead city officials to focus too narrowly on issues. "Single-member districts cause council members to be myopic and only look at their district," she said. "The council I've been on during the last eight years has been responsive to all districts in Plano." On the other side of the issue, Cecil Starks, chairman of the Plano Minority Task Force, responded by saying, "As Plano grows and more minorities move in, at-large elections will not fulfill the needs of a diverse community."

Plano Mayor Jack Harvard commented that single-member districts are effective when there is a concentration of minorities whose needs are different from those of other residents. Most minorities in Plano, however, live throughout the city, he said. "I am totally opposed to single-member districts. They serve a purpose only if you have a segment of the city that is not represented," the mayor argued. "I don't see a need to break the city up into segments."

Ola Burton, president of the Plano Community Forum, said that the desire to see an African American elected to the council is not her only reason for supporting ward elections. Because of the city's growth, residents would be better represented under a district arrangement. "If the city were lily-white, I would feel that single-member districts would still be the most effective way," she said. "It's not just because I'm black and would like to see a black represented on the council."

In the fall of 1987, the Plano city council accepted the charter review committee's recommendation that no district seats for council elections be created. In the fall of 1993, Plano was still using at-large elections, and apparently there is no movement to change the electoral system.

SOURCE: Adapted from the *Dallas Morning News,* 10 July 1987, 15A, and telephone interview with a city official on 30 September 1993.

At-large versus district elections, which one? The court cases and the debate continue. Charles Bullock suggests that single-member districts may create nothing more than tokenism. "A single black council member, like the black caucuses in the U.S. House of Representatives and state legislatures, will not be able to institute major policy innovations without extensive support from white colleagues."[49] In *Protest Is Not Enough,* Rufus Browning, Dale Rogers Marshall, and David Tabb demonstrate, however, that black and Latino council members can successfully join with liberal whites to create coalitions. Minority incorporation results in more responsive city government.[50] Although about two-thirds of all cities were using strictly at-large elections in the early 1980s, a trend toward ward and especially mixed systems is clear.[51]

THE INITIATIVE, THE REFERENDUM, AND THE RECALL

During the heyday of machine politics, reformers searched for various ways to circumvent boss-dominated local legislatures and return control of government to the people. One way to do this was to allow citizens to petition to force a communitywide vote on various local propositions.

The *initiative* enables a legally determined number of electors, through the use of a petition, to have a charter amendment or city ordinance put on the ballot for a vote by the people. The city council is not involved in the process and cannot prevent the vote except by challenging the validity of the petition in court. The *referendum* allows a prescribed number or percentage of qualified voters, by means of a petition, to force a vote on a legislative measure after it has passed the council. If no emergency clause is attached (attesting to the urgent need to protect the public health, safety, or welfare), city ordinances often do not take effect immediately. This gives a disenchanted group an opportunity to collect signatures and bring the ordinance to a popular vote. *Recall* provides a mechanism for voters to remove an unsatisfactory council member before the official's term expires. Again a petition is required.

Proponents of direct democracy contend that these devices are essential to keep legislative bodies in check and to provide the opportunity for citizens to act directly on local policy issues. Skeptics feel that most voters are not well enough informed to vote intelligently on the kinds of matters often placed on these ballots. Indeed some referendum items are complex and esoteric, and many people simply are not interested in them. The result frequently is to turn the initiative and referendum into tools for special interests that have the time and money to take advantage of the processes. According to some critics, then, the process has deleterious effects on the normal legislative process.[52] Defenders counter that these voting procedures should not be condemned because of occasional misuse; in fact they represent an effective means to enhance citizen control of local government.[53]

Regardless of the pros and cons, a recent ICMA survey shows strong support for direct democracy. Almost 90 percent of the cities report some provision for referendum procedures. Recall elections are allowed in 58 percent of the cities. Almost half (49 percent) of over 3,700 responding cities allow initiative petitions.[54]

Home Rule and the Legal Status of the City

Despite the restricted view of municipal power reflected in Dillon's rule (see chapter 1), courts permit cities with home-rule charters to exercise a greater degree of control over strictly local affairs. Municipal home rule provided by state law or constitution allows cities to "frame, adopt, and amend a charter for their governments and to exercise all powers of local self-government, subject to the constitution and general laws of the state."[55] It may be granted to all cities or just a few, generally on the basis of population. In Oklahoma, for example, any incorporated place with a population of 2,000 or more can adopt a home-rule charter by following certain procedures spelled out in the state constitution. Among other things, a home-rule charter allows the city to determine its own form of government, type of ballot (partisan or nonpartisan), and method of electing council members (ward or at large). In effect the charter becomes the basic law, or constitution, of the city. Most states now provide for home rule, but less than half the cities of 5,000 or more operate under a home-rule charter.[56]

Does home rule really give cities greater independence? Apparently so, at least in some areas of governance. Clearly, home-rule cities are free to choose the form of government they want. Morton Grove, Illinois, for example, used home-rule authority to enact local gun control.[57] In other areas, such as finance, charter cities may have little more authority than other cities. For example, in Pennsylvania home-rule cities can set property tax rates, but the general assembly retains the power over taxation and over rates of taxation on nonresidents.[58] States always can preempt local powers or determine that state and local governments may exercise some powers concurrently. In effect, then, home-rule powers are largely subject to restraints imposed by state legislatures.[59] But administrative flexibility is only one aspect of home rule; its greatest importance may be psychological. Home rule encourages state legislators to stay out of local affairs for fear of interfering with the rights of local self-government, of violating "the principle of home rule."[60]

Traditionally, home-rule supporters have feared state encroachment. Lately, though, more concern has been expressed over federal preemption of local law. In 1985, the Supreme Court handed down a landmark decision affecting state and local governments, *Garcia* v. *San Antonio Mass Transit Authority*. By a 5–4 vote, the Court ruled that federal wage and hour standards apply to states and their local governments. The Court reasoned that the political process followed by Congress in passing laws provides sufficient protection to ensure that states and localities will not be unduly burdened. Although legislation lessened the impact of the *Garcia* ruling, critics point to other instances of federal intrusion on local affairs. Today, above all, local officials complain of unfunded federal mandates. These requirements force cities to comply with certain costly provisions of federal law. Many of these mandates relate to environmental protection, for example requirements imposed by the Safe Drinking Water Act. Even efforts to abide by provisions of the Americans with Disabilities Act passed in 1992 may impose significant costs on local governments. In general most municipal officials have little quarrel with the intent of these federal laws. They do object to being forced to comply without being provided the funds to pay for the required improvements. Although local officials are now pursuing their complaints through the political process, relief may be long in coming. As John Shannon, senior fellow at the Urban Institute, has noted: "There's an iron law: When the easy money disappears, our federal system starts pushing things down, down, down."[61] Genuine home rule will probably continue to shrink as the federal government pursues deficit reduction, and state governments contend with budgetary shortfalls.

Summary

The reform movement left an indelible imprint on local government in the United States. Many of the structural characteristics now found in most city governments were part of the reform agenda. These include the council-manager plan, nonpartisan ballots, at-large constituencies, and nonconcurrent elections. Although all cities have embraced some reforms, reform features are more likely to be found in certain kinds of cities, particularly white, suburban, middle-class cities, where greater consensus exists regarding the overall community interest.

What difference has the reform heritage made in the governing of American cities? Some suggest that even the generally acknowledged increase in honesty and efficiency in local governments cannot be attributed to the changes in structure favored by reform groups. And evidence suggests that these good-government devices generally depress voter turnout and tend to make city government less responsive to minorities and the poor. Some even insist that the reform penchant for efficiency and professional expertise has strengthened career bureaucracies to the extent that today's large cities cannot be governed effectively. Whether the reform movement alone should bear the blame for bureaucratic intransigence is arguable.

A consideration of the forms of city government and their accompanying electoral systems follows naturally from the discussion of the reform movement. The council-manager plan is now the most popular in the country for cities with a population of 25,000 and over. Mayor-council government remains more common, however, in the smallest and largest municipalities. Debates persist over the alleged advantages and disadvantages of various electoral arrangements. Nonpartisanship is pervasive regardless of city size, but the at-large electoral form has not been as overwhelmingly adopted. An interest in city government structure is more than academic. Although structure alone does not determine who gets what, certain arrangements may benefit some groups while working to the disadvantage of others.

Cities remain creatures of the state, although evidence suggests home-rule provisions have given municipalities greater freedom to frame a charter and choose their own form of government. But some worry about growing federal preemption and mandates under provision of the commerce clause of the U.S. Constitution.

Notes

1. For provocative analyses of community politics from a game perspective, see Norton Long, "The Local Community as an Ecology of Games," *American Journal of Sociology* 44 (November 1958): 251–61; and Paul A.

Smith, "The Games of Community Politics," *Midwest Journal of Political Science* 9 (February 1965): 37–60.

2. Charles R. Adrian, "Forms of City Government in American History," *Municipal Year Book 1988* (Washington, D.C.: ICMA, 1988), 3.

3. This discussion draws on Lawrence J.R. Herson, "Pilgrim's Progress: Reflections on the Road to Urban Reform," in *Political Science and State and Local Government* (Washington, D.C.: American Political Science Association, 1973), 7–9.

4. For a popular account of the reform movement, see Richard Hofstadter, *The Age of Reform* (New York: Knopf, 1955).

5. Martin Meyerson and Edward Banfield, *Politics, Planning and the Public Interest* (New York: Free Press, 1955), 69–70.

6. William L. Riordan, *Plunkitt of Tammany Hall* (New York: Knopf, 1948; originally published 1905), 33–34.

7. Edward C. Banfield and James Q. Wilson, *City Politics* (New York: Vintage, 1963), 121.

8. Ibid., 123.

9. Herson, "Pilgrim's Progress," 10.

10. Samuel P. Hays, "The Politics of Reform in Municipal Government in the Progressive Era," *Pacific Northwest Quarterly* 55 (October 1964): 157–89.

11. Dennis R. Judd, *The Politics of American Cities: Private Power and Public Policy,* 3rd ed. (Glenview, Ill.: Scott, Foresman, 1988), 108.

12. Banfield and Wilson, *City Politics,* 138.

13. Ibid., 139.

14. Robert P. Boynton, "City Councils: Their Role in the Legislative System," *Municipal Year Book 1976* (Washington, D.C.: ICMA, 1976), 67–77.

15. Ibid., 69.

16. Tari Renner and Victor S. DeSantis, "Contemporary Patterns in Municipal Government Structures," *Municipal Year Book 1993* (Washington, D.C.: ICMA, 1993), 68.

17. Tari Renner, "Municipal Election Processes: The Impact on Minority Representation," *Municipal Year Book 1988* (Washington, D.C.: ICMA, 1988), 14.

18. This discussion is drawn from Renner and DeSantis, "Contemporary Patterns in Municipal Government Structures," 57–68.

19. Robert Alford and Harry Scoble, "Political and Socioeconomic Characteristics of American Cities," *Municipal Year Book 1965* (Washington, D.C.: ICMA, 1965), 82–97. Also see Thomas Dye and Susan MacManus, "Predicting City Government Structure," *American Journal of Political Science* 20 (May 1976): 257–71.

20. Richard L. Engstrom and Michael D. McDonald, "The Election of Blacks to City Councils," *American Political Science Review* 75 (June 1981): 344–54.

21. Robert Lineberry and Edmund Fowler, "Reformism and Public Policies in American Cities," *American Political Science Review* 61 (September 1967): 716.

22. David Morgan and John Pelissero, "Urban Policy: Does Political Structure Matter? *American Political Science Review* 74 (December 1980): 999–1006.

23. See William Nelson and Phillip Meranto, *Electing Black Mayors* (Columbus: Ohio State University Press, 1976).

24. Albert K. Karnig and Susan Welch, *Black Representation and Urban Policy* (Chicago: University of Chicago Press, 1980).

25. Peter K. Eisinger, "Black Employment in Municipal Jobs: The Impact of Black Political Power," *American Political Science Review* 76 (June 1982): 380–92; Kenneth R. Mladenka, "Blacks and Hispanics in Urban Politics," *American Political Science Review* 83 (March 1989): 165–91.

26. Jon Ellertson, "The Responsiveness of Local Government," in *Law and Order Reconsidered,* Report of the Task Force on Law and Law Enforcement to the National Commission on the Causes and Prevention of Violence (Washington, D.C.: Government Printing Office, 1969), 115.

27. In addition to the mayor-council and council-manager forms of government, a small percentage of cities use the commission form (about 2 percent) and town meeting form (about 5 percent). See Renner and DeSantis, "Contemporary Patterns and Trends in Municipal Government Structures," 59.

28. Charles Adrian and Charles Press, *Governing Urban America,* 5th ed. (New York: McGraw-Hill, 1977), 153.

29. Ibid., 154.

30. Renner and DeSantis, "Contemporary Patterns and Trends in Municipal Government Structures," 64.

31. Heywood T. Sanders, "The Government of American Cities: Continuity and Change in Structure," *Municipal Year Book 1982* (Washington, D.C.: ICMA, 1982), 181.

32. Susan Welch and Timothy Bledsoe, *Urban Reform and Its Consequences: A Study in Representation* (Chicago: University of Chicago Press, 1988), 8.

33. Willis D. Hawley, *Nonpartisan Elections and the Case for Party Politics* (New York: Wiley-Interscience, 1973), 33.

34. Welch and Bledsoe, *Urban Reform and Its Consequences,* 49–50.

35. Ibid., 53.

36. Eugene C. Lee, "City Elections: A Statistical Profile," *Municipal Year Book 1963* (Chicago: ICMA, 1963), 78.

37. Susan A. MacManus and Charles S. Bullock, "Women and Racial/Ethnic Minorities in Mayoral and Council Positions," *Municipal Year Book 1993* (Washington, D.C.: ICMA, 1993), 78–79.

38. Welch and Bledsoe, *Urban Reform and Its Consequences,* 78.

39. William J.D. Boyd, "Local Electoral Systems: Is There a Best Way?"

National Civic Review 65 (March 1976): 136–40, 157.

40. Ibid., 139.

41. MacManus and Bullock, "Women and Racial/Ethnic Minorities in Mayoral and Council Positions," 78.

42. Timothy Bledsoe and Susan Welch, "The Effect of Political Structures on the Socioeconomic Characteristics of Urban City Council Members," *American Politics Quarterly* 13 (October 1985): 467–83.

43. Welch and Bledsoe, *Urban Reform and Its Consequences*, 42, 77.

44. Ibid., 102.

45. See Renner, "Municipal Election Processes," 13–14.

46. This discussion is drawn from "At-Large Voting Under Attack," *Governing*, November 1987, 8. See also "Election System Shot Down," *City & State*, 5 November 1990, 10.

47. For an in-depth discussion of the controversy, see Richard Engstrom, "Councilmanic Redistricting Conflicts: The Dallas Experience," *Urban News*, Fall 1992, 1–13.

48. Renner, "Municipal Election Processes," 14.

49. Charles S. Bullock, "Symbolics or Substance: A Critique of the At-Large Election Controversy," *State and Local Government Review* 21 (Fall): 91.

50. Rufus P. Browning, Dale R. Marshall, and David H. Tabb, *Protest Is Not Enough* (Berkeley: University of California Press, 1984), 166.

51. Sanders, "Government of American Cities," 185–86; see also Renner and DeSantis, "Contemporary Patterns and Trends in Municipal Government Structures," 61.

52. Stanley Scott and Harriet Nathan, "Public Referenda: A Critical Appraisal," *Urban Affairs Quarterly* 5 (March 1970): 313–28.

53. George S. Blair, *Government at the Grass-Roots*, 2d ed. (Pacific Palisades, Calif.: Palisades, 1977), 85–86.

54. Renner and DeSantis, "Contemporary Patterns and Trends in Municipal Government Structures," 69.

55. Adrian and Press, *Governing Urban America*, 138.

56. Alan Klevit, "City Councils and Their Functions in Local Government," *Municipal Year Book 1972* (Washington, D.C.: ICMA, 1972), 17.

57. Bernard H. Ross, Myron A. Levine, and Murray S. Stedman, *Urban Politics: Power in Metropolitan America*, 4th ed. (Itasca, Ill.: F.E. Peacock, 1991), 82.

58. See Charles Hoffman, "Pennsylvania Legislation Implements Home Rule," *National Civic Review* 61 (September 1972): 390–93.

59. See, for example, the discussion in Samuel Gove and Stephanie Cole, "Illinois Home Rule: Panacea, Status Quo, or Hindrance?" in *Partnership Within the States: Local Self-Government in the Federal System*, ed. Stephanie Cole (Urbana, Ill.: Institute of Government and Public Affairs, University of Illinois; Philadelphia: Center for the Study of Federalism, Temple University, 1976), 158–61. The authors conclude that home rule has

made some difference, but after five years the changes have not been dramatic (p. 167).

60. Adrian and Press, *Governing Urban America,* 142.

61. Steven D. Gold, "Passing the Buck," *State Legislatures,* January 1993, 37.

Suggested for Further Reading

Browning, Rufus P., Dale Rogers Marshall, and David H. Tabb. *Racial Politics in American Cities.* New York: Longman, 1990.

Clavel, Pierre. *The Progressive City.* New Brunswick, N.J.: Rutgers University Press, 1986.

Gluck, Peter, and Richard Meister. *Cities in Transition.* New York: New Viewpoints, 1979.

Riordan, William L. *Plunkitt of Tammany Hall.* New York: Knopf, 1948 (originally published 1905).

Welch, Susan, and Timothy Bledsoe. *Urban Reform and Its Consequences: A Study in Representation.* Chicago: University of Chicago Press, 1988.

PART TWO

Making and

Implementing

Urban Policy

3

Urban Policymaking

We are in the midst of a new age of skepticism regarding government. People are reassessing what government can or should do. We seem to be asking, "Can existing laws and policies be made to work better, to be more responsive to the people's needs?" This more modest, realistic assessment of the role of government brings with it the realization that we do not know as much as we should about how government works, how things get done, and what effect governmental action has. As a result, we find practitioners and academics alike searching for a more systematic basis for understanding the causes and consequences of governmental activity.

We begin with a general discussion of the policymaking process. Then we examine the role of the principal urban policymakers, looking at how policy is made at the local level and how the process demands certain characteristics from urban leaders.

The Nature of Urban Policy

At the outset we should define the phrase *public policy*. James Anderson offers this description of public policy: "A purposive course of action followed by an actor or set of actors in dealing with a problem or matter of concern."[1] He goes on to add that public policies are those developed by governmental bodies and officials. The question arises as to whether deliberate inaction by government constitutes policy. Most would answer yes[2]—if an identifiable attempt has been made to induce the government to deal with an issue or problem and no response is forthcoming. A conscious stance of no action thus can be considered as endorsing or perpetuating existing policy.

How does policymaking differ from decision making? The two phrases often are used synonymously, but a difference of scope or degree does exist. In a narrow sense decision making is choosing among competing alternatives; policymaking goes beyond this to include, in David Easton's words, "a web of decisions and actions that allocate values."[3] A policy, then, is a series of decisions that creates a comprehensive set of standards or guidelines for dealing with a subject. The line between basic policy and less comprehensive tactical or programmatic decisions may be difficult to draw in practice. But we can make the following distinction: "For those (actions) which have the widest ramifications and the longest time perspective, and which generally require the most information and contemplation, we tend to reserve the term policy."[4] In short, we think of policy as the response of a political system to the various pressures and forces produced by its environment.[5]

Although descriptions of the policy process vary widely, considerable agreement exists on one basic point: policymaking is not a highly rational, scientifically based enterprise. Instead, it is essentially political in nature. This is not to suggest that policymaking cannot be improved or that systematic analysis has no place in that effort. We know that governments at all levels expend considerable resources to improve their capacity to make informed choices; they hire analysts, retain consultants, and fund all kinds of sophisticated research in the quest for more effective policies. Sometimes the results influence major policy decisions significantly, as, for example, when a benefit-cost analysis results in the decision to go forward with a large public works project.

Many times, however, the attempt to ensure more rational choices through analysis goes for naught, as a host of obstacles and unintended consequences interfere with the successful resolution of the problem. For example, as economist Anthony Downs notes, as soon as we build a major expressway it quickly fills up with cars, so we seem no better off than before. This occurs not because of bad planning, he argues, but because of a very rational response made by rush-hour drivers. This unintended consequence is so automatic that Downs formulated what he calls the Law of Peak-Hour Traffic Congestion: "On urban commuter expressways, peak-hour traffic congestion rises to meet maximum capacity."[6]

Political economist Charles Lindblom says we are of a mixed mind about rational policy and the influence of politics. "On the one hand, people want policy to be informed and well analyzed. On the other hand, they want policymaking to be democratic, hence necessarily political."[7] This conflict is evident, for example, in policymaking for economic development. Some contend that an effective development policy can be produced only through extensive fact gathering, planning, and analysis, with the final decisions resting in the hands of a small elite group with close ties to the business community. Others worry about the lack of popular participation in such an approach. Later in this chapter we hear more from Paul Peterson, a contributor to this debate. He believes economic development policymaking is so vital to a community's well-being that the local leadership will restrict the process to a few dominant interests, thus minimizing conflict among competing groups. First, though, we need to consider the steps in the policymaking process.

THE PROCESS OF MAKING POLICY

Even though policymaking may not be highly rational, we still can identify several steps or stages in the process. Briefly these policy stages are as follows:

1. *Issue creation.* What gives rise to the problem? How does the issue get defined as a public matter?
2. *Agenda building.* How does the issue reach public decision makers? Who participates in the agenda-building process and how? What keeps problems off the public agenda?
3. *Issue resolution.* How do public officials respond to demands for problem resolution? How is the final policy choice made?
4. *Policy implementation.* Who is involved? How is policy affected at this final stage of the process?

ISSUE CREATION. — Political issues are created in various ways. Roger Cobb and Charles Elder emphasize the interaction of an initiator and a triggering device as the first step.[8] The most common case is where a person, organization, or group perceives an unfavorable distribution of resources and seeks government help to redress the imbalance. Such initiators may then search for allies or turn to the media in the hope of publicizing their cause. They may benefit from the help of a friendly officeholder who, for various self-serving reasons, wishes to adopt and push the cause of the aggrieved party. The critical step in issue creation may well be publicizing the issue—bringing the proposed solution to the problem to the attention of both those who are already aware of the problem and those who will be concerned once they learn about it.[9]

Triggering devices are largely unanticipated events that create the problem requiring government response. External events may give rise to a situation that stimulates a response by an affected group. Technological change, a natural disaster, or an unexpected human event (a riot or a sudden upsurge in violent crime or even a major court decision) can serve as a triggering mechanism. The point is that an event and an initiator, such as an affected group, must converge to create a public issue.

An example of issue creation at the local level took place in the late 1950s in Oklahoma City. Certain groups in the growing metropolitan area became apprehensive about uncontrolled development outside the city limits. They decided that government action would be required to resolve the problem, in the form of annexation of the newly developing territory. One of the most ambitious annexation drives ever undertaken by any city in this country followed. It made Oklahoma City the largest city (in land area) in the United States until the 1967 merger of Jacksonville and Duval County in Florida. Such massive annexation could not have been accomplished without lenient state laws governing the process. But why Oklahoma City? The answer is simple: The Oklahoma City Chamber of Commerce devised a comprehensive annexation plan and sold it to the city council. The chamber had decided Oklahoma City should have more direct control over land development. It also was concerned that Oklahoma City not become hemmed in by suburban communities. The chamber clearly called the shots; such a controversial effort could never have taken place without the group's support.

AGENDA BUILDING. — How does a problem or issue reach the public agenda, where some official response is expected? Not only must the issue be perceived as a legitimate concern by certain groups or powerful interests; it also must be seen as an appropriate target for government action. This may seem simple enough, but in fact one of the most effective strategies by those wanting to avoid official action is to argue that the issue lies outside the scope of government authority.[10] For example, those opposed to mandatory seatbelt or motorcycle helmet laws usually insist that these matters of presumably personal safety should not be dictated by government policy.

Two factors seem especially important in determining who gets access to the public agenda. First, local officeholders have enormous discretion over which issues are considered officially; they are not merely passive arbiters of problems brought to them by others. Elected officials, especially at the local level, frequently arrive at their own conclusions regarding the nature of local problems. As we discuss further later, city council members tend to see themselves not as politicians expected to respond to the pressures of group demands but rather as nonpolitical "trustees" or "volunteers" who have been elected to pursue their own views of the public interest.

A second key factor in whether issues are placed on the public agenda is the nature of the proposing group. Some organizations have far easier access to public officials than do others. As might be expected, the more politically powerful or prestigious the group, the more likely its concerns are to find their way onto the action agenda. Elected officials also are much more likely to grant access to groups with whom they share values and interests. Not uncommonly, the politically powerful groups and the groups with views similar to those of council are one and the same. Business interests in particular are likely to fall in this category, for their commitment to growth and investment is often viewed as being in the interest of the larger community as well. If the business is large and important enough, it may virtually force public action in its behalf, as the case study that follows illustrates.

CASE STUDY

DETROIT AND GENERAL MOTORS

IN July of 1980, the city of Detroit announced its intent to prepare a 500-acre site on the Detroit-Hamtramck border for the construction of a General Motors assembly plant. The impetus for this project was an offer in April 1980 from GM Chairman Thomas Murphy to Detroit Mayor Coleman Young: GM would construct a new plant in Detroit if the city would find and prepare a site of about 500 acres, rectangular in shape, accessible to freeways and a main rail line. The site had to be ready in two years. The plant would replace two old plants in Detroit that were scheduled for a 1983 closing. Murphy estimated that 6,000 jobs would be lost if the new plant was not built in Detroit.

Mayor Young's response was immediate. The Detroit economy was hurting, and the loss of the GM plant would be disastrous. But the scope of the project was staggering. The city couldn't do it alone—participation would be required of hundreds of people in city, county, state, and federal agencies along with the private sector. GM's deadlines and threats of relocation created a genuine sense of crisis and contributed to a feeling of urgency that was used to expedite the project. Two city officials in particular, Mayor Young and economic development director Emmett Moten, became extensively involved at every important step. They acted as "fixers" or entrepreneurs in assembling staff and financial resources and co-ordinating the entire effort. Continually emphasizing GM's threats and deadlines and equating delay with failure, Young and Moten expedited action and cleared hurdles that normally would have taken months if not years. In the end, 3,500 people and more than 100 businesses and institutions were relocated, 1,500 residential and commercial structures were demolished, and structural steel for the plant was put in place; production began as scheduled in 1985.

By almost any measure, the project was successful. GM got what it wanted, and the city was able to rebuild its tax base and save a large number of private-sector jobs. The project demonstrated that under certain conditions governments can act expeditiously in pursuit of well-defined objectives. But there were costs, some substantial. The total public-sector cost was estimated at over $200 million; plus GM extracted an agreement from the city for reduced property taxes over a thirty-year period. High acquisition and relocation costs were incurred as well. Even more important were the "political costs." First, the necessity of fast action allowed for only minimal citizen participation. Second, the extensive reliance on quasi-public and private agencies in implementing the project reduced public-sector authority and accountability. GM literally dictated many components of project policy. The giant company not only determined key elements of the plan but also set deadlines that mandated certain procedures for carrying out the project procedures that resulted in financial and political costs to the city.

SOURCE: This case is taken from Lynn Bachelor, "Evaluating the Implementation of Economic Development Policy: Lessons from Detroit's Central Industrial Park Project," *Policy Studies Review* 4 (May 1985): 601–12.

ISSUE RESOLUTION.—Here is where some final outcome occurs. Does the issue become resolved with the adoption of a new policy or modification of an existing one? Or is the matter disposed of in some other way, say, formally rejected, passed to some other level of government, or postponed for some time? How are these decisions made? Because decision making is considered in some detail in the next chapter, at this point we only sketch briefly the process by which such choices might be made.

Charles Lindblom argues that policy is determined largely on the basis of interaction among contending interests. How does one group or interest gain the upper hand (in other words, exert sufficient control or influence to achieve its objectives)? Lindblom enumerates several ways:[11]

- *Persuasion.* In many instances, one participant may be able to show another why the desires of the former will benefit the latter. We should not underestimate the power of persuasion.[12]
- *Threats.* Although not commonly used, threats may be resorted to by some groups. A threat may be as simple as telling officials that if they take a particular course of action, the group will feel compelled to oppose their reelection or some action that they support.
- *Exchange.* The adopting of a mutually beneficial arrangement is a widely used political tactic. Officials frequently engage in "logrolling," supporting another's project or proposal in direct exchange for that person's support of one's own project. Money is perhaps the most common medium of exchange, even in politics—not for bribes as such, but to buy influence or services. As the GM case shows, money in the form of mammoth organizational resources can work miracles.
- *Authority.* Although public officials can rarely command that something be done, they occupy positions of considerable authority, which can be an important resource. Their positions can enhance persuasive power and provide access to jobs and money, which others want.
- *Analysis.* The use of systematic analysis also can be listed among those influences shaping the final decision. It may provide just the ammunition needed by one side or the other to push its case. Certainly a well-conceived, accurate, and timely study may tip the scales on a closely contested issue. As Lindblom says, analysis is an indispensable element in politics: "It becomes a method of exerting control."[13]

POLICY IMPLEMENTATION.—Here is where administrators and the bureaucracy enter. Policy is inevitably modified, molded, and influenced by administrative implementation. We address bureaucratic behavior more completely later in this chapter. But we should note at this point that in large public organizations the bureaucracy has immense power. Lindblom puts it this way, policymaking "rests overwhelmingly in the hands of the bureaucracy."[14] The discretion of administrative officials in determining how policy is carried out is enormous. Moreover, administrators are frequently the source of much of the analysis and advice that informs the policy choices made by legislators and the chief executive.

Policy implementation may also be affected substantially by the need for coordination among fragmented agencies or with other governments or even the need to bargain with employee groups to secure the cooperation needed to ensure policy success. The case study on New York's sanitation department illustrates such implementation problems.

CASE STUDY

THE NEW YORK CITY SANITATION DEPARTMENT

IN the late 1960s the head of New York City's sanitation department became convinced that adopting a new truck with a larger mechanical container would reduce the manual chores required in picking up garbage and trash. The mayor agreed. A short time later, at a press conference in a Brooklyn parking lot, the mayor and sanitation officials watched as a borrowed truck did its work for the television cameras. The mayor made a speech and shook a lot of hands. Then the trouble began. The department's chief medical officer and union representatives challenged the safety characteristics of the new vehicle. The Bureau of Motor Vehicles expressed concern over the size of the truck. Once that was settled, the purchasing department held things up: it too was concerned with the truck's size. By this time the mayor's office had lost interest in the whole thing and was deep into the next political campaign. The final implementation of the plan, promised for 1969, came in 1972.

SOURCE: Erwin C. Hargrove, *The Missing Link: The Study of the Implementation of Social Policy* (Washington, D.C.: Urban Institute, 1975), 28–30. The case came originally from Jerry Mechling, "The Roles of Policy Analysis in Large Public Organizations: A Case Study of the New York City Environmental Protection Administration 1968–1971," Ph.D. dissertation, Princeton University, 1974.

Even though a series of policymaking stages can be identified, community policies seldom are made in a neat, methodical way. In fact, some see policymaking as chaotic, characterized primarily by a pattern of government reaction to a series of ever-changing external forces.

REACTIVE POLICYMAKING

Political scientist Douglas Yates has developed a rather complete description of urban policymaking that emphasizes its nonsequential and disorderly nature.¹⁵ His basic point is that, given the level and range of demands placed on big-city officials and the instability in the local political environment, the prospects for orderly agenda setting, planning, and implementation are very slim. Why? Yates insists that a number of structural characteristics of urban government create a distinctive situation that makes comprehensive, systematic policymaking impossible. Without listing all of these characteristics we might note that Yates emphasizes service delivery as the basic function of urban government. Services are tangible, visible, and even personal in their impact; in many instances they can be divided so that people in need receive more than do others. But citizens and an array of community organizations constantly press their service demands on the mayor and the urban bureaucracy, neither of which has the formal power or the resources to respond effectively to all these demands.

This lack of administrative authority stems largely from the presence of independent boards, other jurisdictions, and bureaucratic autonomy. The problem was reflected vividly in an exchange between Senator Robert Kennedy and Mayor Sam Yorty of Los Angeles following the early period of urban riots. Here is the way a city manager relates the story:

> Back in 1967 when Senator Robert Kennedy held hearings in Los Angeles on the plight of U.S. cities, he berated Mayor Sam Yorty at length for the sorry state of affairs in that city. The mayor protested vigorously. "The Mayor doesn't run the city," he said. "Blame the city council; they pass the budget. Blame the county; they run welfare. Blame the Metropolitan Transit District; they run the buses. Blame the Air Pollution Control District, the Airport Commission, the Chamber of Commerce, the banks and the businesses, the Teamsters and the *L.A. Times,* but don't blame me, I'm just the Mayor." And he was right. The mayor doesn't really run the city. Neither does the city manager. No one does and everyone does.¹⁶

Yates goes on to stress how fragmented authority creates chaos in urban policymaking. He calls this unstable political free-for-all *streetfighting pluralism,* which he defines as "a pattern of unstructured, multilateral conflict in which many different combatants fight continuously with one another in a very great number of permutations and combinations."¹⁷ Because the demands from this unrestrained battle are not filtered, channeled, assigned priority, or otherwise mediated by formal political representatives, they create a constant stream of new and often bewildering issues for urban decision makers. In effect urban policymaking becomes a reactive procedure by which the official leadership sets its agenda in response to the most dramatic problem and the loudest complaint. Yates compares the situation with a penny arcade shooting gallery, where the player has more targets than can be hit and they keep popping up all the time from all directions.

The reactive model purports to describe politics in such major cities as Boston, Detroit, Cleveland, Chicago, and New York. In small or medium-sized cities, where fewer groups are involved, events are less pressing, and the degree of uncertainty and instability is lower, the model may not fit as well. But even in a slower-paced community, policies are likely to be essentially reactive. We have several accounts of how community decisions are reached in less hectic environments. One of the best is the analysis of the social and political life in Levittown, New Jersey, by sociologist Herbert Gans, who lived there as a participant-observer for two years.

| CASE STUDY |

POLICYMAKING IN LEVITTOWN

HERBERT GANS suggests that most elected officials want to minimize conflict and controversy. They prefer a situation in which precedent can rule and no new policies are needed. Still, new problems do arise, and decisions must be made. In these instances, he claims, the policymaking process is governed by four criteria:

- Government is normally passive; it waits for issues to come to its attention.
- Government avoids or postpones decisions that cannot be resolved without conflict.
- Government gravitates toward policies with immediate payoffs, avoiding those that produce mainly long-run effects.
- The policymaking process is structured so that, whenever possible, all elected officials are free, or feel free, to reach the decision dictated by their consciences and by their desire to benefit the community.

What were the consequences of this policy process in Levittown? According to Gans, municipal services were provided satisfactorily, but most decisions, other than housekeeping ones, benefited influential interest groups that were closely allied with the city's government. Still, Gans believes that many policies were remarkably responsive to the rest of the citizenry. Perhaps there is no inconsistency here. We would not expect important groups constantly to demand local governmental action solely in their benefit. Many community issues were of little concern to powerful interests; but when a prominent group, the Levitt organization in this instance, wanted or did not want certain things done, local officials usually were responsive. Of course the development of Levittown by a single builder, the Levitt Company, undoubtedly gave that organization an unusual amount of community influence. Although Levittown itself may be an unusual case, the policymaking process described by Gans surely has a wide application.

SOURCE: Herbert J. Gans, *The Levittowners: Ways of Life and Politics in a New Suburban Community* (New York: Pantheon, 1967), 333–34.

A CHALLENGE TO REACTIVE POLICYMAKING. —The Yates model of urban policymaking, with its emphasis on fragmentation and street-fighting pluralism, has been challenged in Paul Peterson's book *City Limits*. Peterson agrees that many of the most visible actions taken by city governments are settled by bargaining and compromise among contending interests. But these *allocational policies* are not the most vital actions taken by the city. Above all, he says, the city is committed to protecting and promoting its economic well-being. To that end it must pursue what Peterson calls *developmental policies*—decisions designed to further growth and expansion, for example. These issues are not subject to the ordinary pull and tug of pressure politics. Instead they tend to be settled through highly centralized decision-making processes dominated by business and professional elites. Conflict is minimized, and the process is closed to outsiders. The result is a quiet drama "where political leaders can give reasoned attention to the longer range interests of the city, taken as a whole."[18]

The quest to improve the city's economic base may lead to measures that have adverse consequences for certain groups. For example, Peterson asserts that *redistributive policies* designed to benefit the poor do not promote the long-term economic welfare of the community. Therefore he believes local officials should avoid them. Redistribution, he feels, should be dealt with at the national level, not by city governments. But won't local groups, such as minorities or the poor, raise such a ruckus that city officials must deal with them? Not necessarily, according to Peterson. He insists that political party and group activity is so limited at the local level that community elites are largely free to concentrate on the city's economic growth. In effect Peterson's model postulates that when a community's most vital interests are at stake, local policymakers act to further the long-term good of the city.

Perhaps we can better understand the process of policymaking if we examine the roles of those who officially are charged with formulating urban policy—the executives, the councils, and the bureaucrats.

Chief Executives

Whatever our definition of the policymaking process, the urban chief executive, whether mayor or city manager, invariably plays a prominent role in the procedure. These officials work hard and long hours: mayors in mayor-council and commission cities work an average of sixty-six hours a week and city managers report an average workweek of about fifty-six hours.[19] As a number of authorities have observed, we have developed from a legislative era into an executive one. Much of the growth of executive power has come reluctantly and despite our traditional fears of executive authority. But with cutbacks in federal funds and the demand for cities to become more entrepreneurial, strong executive leadership has become indispensable.

MAYORS

Despite the call for greater leadership, few mayors have the formal authority and resources necessary to deal with the enormous tasks facing them.[20] Still, the office remains a logical focal point for those who demand more leadership. Limited resources, however, mean that the skills and the leadership tactics mayors employ must be conditioned accordingly. We noted earlier that presidential power was based on persuasion. American mayors also must persuade, but with far fewer political resources at their command.

In the discussion of strong-mayor and weak-mayor council forms of government, we mentioned that some mayors have considerably more formal authority than do others. A mayor's powers are most restricted, of course, in the council-manager system. Here the mayor's office is largely ceremonial. Under most mayor-council plans, the chief executives are not officially members of the legislative body and cannot vote except to break a tie. A large-scale (about 5,000 cities) 1991 ICMA survey, for example, reports that in mayor-council plans mayors are members of the council in only 35 percent of the cities.[21] In 60 percent of the cities they can vote only to break a tie and cannot vote on any issue in another 17 percent of the cities. Mayors in council-manager cities, in contrast, ordinarily are members of the council (82 percent of the cities) and cast votes on all issues (73 percent of the cities). Mayors in both forms of government generally preside over council meetings. But veto power is rare among council-manager mayors (12 percent of cities), whereas a majority (56 percent) of mayors in mayor-council communities have that power.

Based on the same 1991 survey, Susan MacManus and Charles Bullock provide a profile of American mayors.[22] Most are male (87 percent), white (96 percent), do not face term limits (95 percent), and serve for either four (45 percent) or two (37 percent) years. Regardless of gender, race, or ethnicity, mayors are more educated than the populations they represent. Finally, in 1991 the average nationwide salary for a mayor was about $10,000.[23] In cities with more than 500,000 residents, however, the average salary is approximately $80,000.

THE PREREQUISITES OF MAYORAL LEADERSHIP. — Formal authority is only the foundation of the resources essential to mayoral leadership. A number of other institutional characteristics are also necessary:[24]

- Adequate financial and staff resources within the city government
- City jurisdiction over key policy areas—education, housing, redevelopment, and job training
- Mayoral jurisdiction within the city government in important policy fields
- A full-time salary for the mayor along with sufficient staff for policy planning, speech writing, and so on
- Vehicles for publicity, such as friendly newspapers or television stations
- Political support groups, including a party, that can be mobilized to support the mayor's goals

As the list suggests, a mayor's capacity for leadership can be affected substantially by institutional barriers. But the personal qualities of the mayor are often of equal or greater importance: the pluralistic, dispersed nature of local government demands political leaders who can accumulate personal influence to supplement their limited formal authority.[25] Terrell Blodgett points to former mayors Henry Cisneros of San Antonio and Harvey Gantt of Charlotte, who were considered strong leaders without strong administrative powers. He concludes: "Today's city or citystate leadership can not be one of power but rather one of consensus building and facilitation."[26]

MAYORS AND EXECUTIVE-CENTERED COALITIONS. — In spite of the many formal constraints limiting what mayors can do and irrespective of individual differences in initiative and imagination, the leadership role of mayors has expanded in recent years. In particular, several authors depict the mayor as the head of an "executive-centered coalition"[27] that represents a "new convergence of power" in the city. Robert Salisbury portrays the mayor of a large city as the head of a relatively new coalition that includes two principal groups: locally oriented economic interests and the municipal bureaucrats who possess technical and professional skills.[28] To the extent the coalition succeeds, Salisbury suggests, it is because of the mayor's leadership. Salisbury is not oblivious to the constraints on mayoral power; in fact, he depicts the situation as a classic example of power not being commensurate with the responsibilities of an office. He does conclude, however, that if things are going to get done in big cities, mayors will have to take the lead.

How can mayors mobilize the coalition? The words of Robert Dahl describing New Haven's Mayor Richard Lee fit perfectly:

> It would be grossly misleading to see the executive-centered order as a neatly hierarchical system with the mayor at the top operating through subordinates in a chain of command. The mayor was not at the peak of a pyramid but rather at the center of intersecting circles. He rarely commanded. He negotiated, cajoled, exhorted, beguiled, charmed, pressed, appealed, reasoned, promised, insisted, demanded, even threatened, but he most needed support and acquiescence from other leaders who simply could not be commanded. Because the mayor could not command, he had to bargain.[29]

Some mayors do these things better than others, of course, and these personal skills seem to be more essential in large complex urban environments than in small homogeneous communities.

CITY MANAGERS

In council-manager cities the mayor has extremely limited formal power and is forced to exercise political leadership through facilitating and coordinating the work of others. The original theory of the plan implied that the city council collectively would provide the initiative and leadership in policy formulation. A full-time professional administrator, the city manager, would then be employed to conduct the daily administrative activities of city government under the overall guidance of the council. In this way the administration of city government would be divorced from politics and policymaking, a task that would be left primarily if not solely to the elected mayor and council. Indications are that the plan has never, even in its early stages, worked in this idealized fashion. In recent years overwhelming evidence has shown the prominent role now being played by the city manager in policy initiation and formulation.

Public administration scholar John Nalbandian argues that today's complex urban environment compels city managers to become involved in community politics.[30] As appointed officials, though, managers had best avoid direct involvement in local elections. Their political role takes another form. And it extends beyond merely advising the council. Modern city managers have become full-fledged brokers, building coalitions and negotiating compromises among competing groups.

WHO ARE THEY?—Local public managers are an elite group, one that is unusually homogeneous with respect to race, sex, education, and experience. A 1989 ICMA survey finds that most are male (95 percent), white (99 percent), and married (89 percent).[31] The typical manager has served in his present position for 5.4 years and spent a total of 10.1 years as a local government executive. Most managers have served in only one city (44 percent) or in two or three cities (42 percent). Ninety-one percent of all local managers hold at least a bachelor's degree (up from 69 percent in 1971), and 63 percent have a master's degree (up from 27 percent in 1971). Not only have they more schooling, but that schooling has shifted substantially from preparation in engineering to preparation in social sciences and management. Finally, city managers are paid relatively well. In 1991 the average city manager earned about $61,000. In cities over 50,000 population the city manager is more likely to earn $90,000 to $110,000.[32]

WHAT DO THEY DO?—According to the official position of the ICMA, four essential responsibilities rest with city managers:[33]

- Formulating policy on overall problems
- Preparing the budget, presenting it to the council, and administering it when approved by the council
- Appointing and removing most of the principal department heads in city government
- Forming extensive external relationships to deal with overall problems of city operations

In addition, most city charters charge managers with the responsibility for executing policy made by the city council.

The managers' duties, according to Deil Wright, can be grouped into three basic categories: managerial, policy related, and political.[34] Executing policy, budgeting, and controlling bureaucracy through appointment and removal are the key elements of the *managerial role*. The *policy-related role* involves managers' relationships with the council and mayor. We examine these relationships in more detail later. Here we should note that a 1989 survey of managers around the country revealed that 99.8 percent always (75.3 percent) or sometimes (24.5 percent) participate in the formulation of municipal policy.[35] Part of this involvement in policy-making occurs because more than four out of five (81 percent) managers report that they almost always set the council's agenda. In the *political role*, the manager is called on to negotiate not only with officials at other levels of government, particularly the state and federal level, but also with a bevy of nongovernmental groups and individuals throughout the community.

In Wright's survey of city managers in forty-five large cities, the managers were asked to indicate how they in fact allot their time among the three basic roles and how they would like to allot their time. The results are shown in columns 1 and 2 of table 3.1. Even managers in large cities see themselves operating chiefly as administrators, although only 46 percent rank this role first in their preference among the three categories. Most managers apparently want to spend more time interacting with the council and the larger public.

Recent evidence suggests this may be happening. Twenty years after the Wright study, research by Charldean Newell and David Ammons finds that the gap between what city managers do and what they want to do has narrowed.[36] Data in column 3 of table 3.1 show that the 142 city managers devote about half their time to administrative activities, 32 percent to the policy role, and 17 percent to the political role. Column 4 shows how the sample of city managers in cities with 50,000 or more population would prefer to spend their time. Differences in time devoted to specific roles and preferred allocation are negligible.

Even in an urban world less chaotic than the one depicted by Yates's model of street-fighting pluralism, city managers must play a complex policy role perhaps undreamed of by their early predecessors. In fact, many see the manager engaging in behavior traditionally reserved for elected politicians. The manager, in the words of James Banovetz, must operate as a "catalyst in the formulation of urban policy, 'brokering' or compromising and satisfying the multitudinous and conflicting demands made by special interest groups."[37] Perhaps Camille Cates Barnett (who holds M.P.A. and Ph.D. degrees), city manager of Austin, Texas, is pro-

TABLE 3.1.

TIME DEVOTED TO SPECIFIED ROLES AND
PREFERRED ALLOCATION OF CITY MANAGERS
IN 1965 AND 1985

	1965 (N = 45) Wright Study		1985 (N = 142) Ammons & Newell	
	Column 1	Column 2	Column 3	Column 4
Role	Actual (%)	Preferred (%)	Actual (%)	Preferred (%)
Management (administrative activities	60	46	50.8	50.7
Policy (council relations)	21	26	32.2	32.1
Political (community leadership)	16	19	17.0	17.2
Other	3	9		

SOURCES: Deil S. Wright, "The City Manager as a Development Administrator," in Robert T. Daland, ed., *Comparative Urban Research: The Administration and Politics of Cities*, 202–48, copyright © 1969 by Sage Publications, Inc. Reprinted by permission of Sage Publications, Inc. Charldean Newell and David N. Ammons, "Role Emphases of City Managers and Other Municipal Executives," *Public Administration Review* 47 (May/June 1987): 250. Reprinted with permission from *Public Administration Review* © by the American Society for Public Administration (ASPA), 1120 G Street NW, Suite 700, Washington, D.C. 20005. All rights reserved.

totypic of the new breed of city managers. She admits that she is a "facilitator" and "negotiator" and notes, "I think it's abdicating for a manager not to tell people what she thinks. But you don't ever want to upstage your council people."[38]

MAYOR-MANAGER RELATIONS

The relationship between mayor and manager has been the subject of considerable attention among urban scholars and practitioners. The original council-manager plan envisioned a modest role for the mayor at best. This probably was unrealistic. Even in many smaller communities mayors have been known to exercise considerable influence on a host of municipal affairs. In fact, a classic study of several small communities in Florida published in the early 1960s revealed that an activist mayor, especially one popularly elected, can pose a threat to a manager's tenure.[39] More recent research by Gordon Whitaker and Ruth Hoogland DeHoog confirms this finding.[40] In addition, they aver that contrary to some findings, conflict is a frequent cause for turnover among city managers. They argue that city managers should better understand the role of conflict in community politics and be better trained in conflict resolution techniques. Still, with cooperation, the relationship between mayors and managers can and should be mutually beneficial. James Svara, for example, contends that the mayor in the council-manager plan plays a unique role, albeit it ambiguous, in city affairs.[41] Svara creates a seven-category mayoral leadership typology based on combinations of twelve roles (activities) mayors in North Carolina perform. He concludes that the mayor is the "stabilizer" in the council-manager plan: "He will be more or less central, more or less public, more or less assertive as conditions warrant. . . . Effective [mayoral] leadership is built upon strengthening the other participants in the governing process rather than controlling or supplanting them."[42]

Finally, David Morgan and Sheilah Watson draw on a national survey to analyze the way in which mayors and city managers often work together.[43] They find that in large cities, especially, the two officials often form teams or create partnerships. The mayor took the lead in most cases, though. Among smaller communities mayor-manager collaboration also appeared but with somewhat less frequency. Here, city managers were a bit more likely to emerge as the dominant leader of the mayor-manager team. Finally the authors comment on the prevalence of what they call "caretaker" governments. In about a third of all cities, neither the mayor nor the manager possessed abundant power regardless of the frequency with which they interacted. Consequently, neither official has sufficient authority to affect municipal policy decisively. Large council-manager cities, however, had far fewer caretaker regimes than did smaller communities.

Regardless of leadership and mayor-manager typologies, as the case study that follows demonstrates, sometimes city managers simply must move on to the next position.

CASE STUDY

THE RESIGNATION OF THE DALLAS CITY MANAGER

ELGIN CRULL had worked for the city of Dallas for fourteen years, six as city manager. He had acquired a reputation as a person who ran things honestly, efficiently, and cheaply—just what the council wanted. The situation began to change when J. Eric Jonsson, a wealthy industrialist, was appointed to fill a vacancy on the council and then was chosen to serve as mayor.

Jonsson and Crull were quite different. Jonsson was cosmopolitan, oriented to the outside world; he was interested in big ideas and projects. In running for election on his own, Jonsson promoted a proposal he called "Goals for Dallas," which would bring in the "best minds" to help pinpoint and solve the city's problems. Overwhelmingly elected (73 percent of the vote), Jonsson regarded the victory as a popular mandate to carry out the Goals for Dallas program. Crull, a native of Dallas, was a local—he dealt with problems internal to the city, and he did not support Goals for Dallas. He was sure the program would lead to expensive projects and solutions of doubtful value.

After the election, the mayor and manager were on a collision course. Conflict erupted over Crull's opposition to an administrative assistant for the mayor. Jonsson also felt the manager exerted too much policy control through the budgetary process. The showdown finally came at an informal meeting of the council and, as reported by Bruce Kovner, went like this:

Jonsson: We ought to tell the city manager what services we want and he'll tell us how much it will cost. If he tells us what the budget is to be, he's making policy. We need to look ahead ten years. We need a ten-year cash-flow picture for basing a capital improvements program.

Crull: The public doesn't understand long-term programs.

Jonsson: Elgin, you are no longer running the old farm. This city is a big business. We are exploring and we need your help. But we find a kind of passive resistance on your part. You're always telling us how not to do it.

The handwriting was on the wall. Crull resigned, presumably for financial reasons—he became a bank executive—and was unanimously praised by the council for his long service.

SOURCE: Adapted from Bruce Kovner, "The Resignation of Elgin Crull," in *Urban Government*, rev. ed., ed. Edward C. Banfield (New York: Free Press, 1969), 316–21.

The City Council

Although the need for executive leadership remains crucial, representative government mandates an active policymaking role for the legislative branch. Who are these people at the municipal level? And what are they doing?

A large-scale 1991 ICMA survey of cities allows for a better understanding of American council members.[44] Four out of five are male. Seventy percent of all survey cities, however, report at least one female council member. Most council persons are white (92.5 percent). Blacks (5 percent) fare best in central cities with mayor-council governments, larger councils, and in cities in the Deep South that have large black populations.

Fifty-nine percent of survey cities elect council members using at-large elections, compared to 11.7 percent for ward or district elections and 29.3 percent for mixed elections. Blacks fare better in district and mixed-election cities whereas women fare slightly better under at-large formats.

Few (4.2 percent) jurisdictions set term limits for council members. Most councils meet either once (20 percent) or twice (67 percent) a month. About 30 percent of councils have staff assistance, with staff assistance positively correlated with city size.

Although skeptical about drawing a profile of the "typical" city council person, Susan Welch and Timothy Bledsoe offer the following description:

> He is a forty-seven-year-old white male, a lawyer or other professional by occupation, with an education beyond four years of college. His family income is well above average, the modal income range being in the "over $45,000" per year category. He has served on the council about three-and-a-half years and spends roughly twenty hours each week on council-related activities (of which nine hours is devoted to constituent service). In return for his labors, he receives a salary of $4,400 per year from the municipality.[45]

Council members usually are not active in party politics before their election, and the office is sought to "help solve problems and help people."[46]

Most council members in council-manager cities of the Bay Area, for example, do not consider themselves politicians. Over half (52 percent) insist that the "job is not in any way a matter of politics," although 39 percent recognize that the council position does require political skill. This anti-political or nonpolitical orientation is tantamount to assuming that "governing the city is no different than running a business. The managerial, administrative ethos replaces the political one."[47] This apolitical perspective may cause council members to gloss over community disagreements and to assume that the community should be governed by adherence to some general public interest. This tendency to hold one's self above politics is part of a voluntaristic norm that reduces the responsiveness of local elected officials to the public. We should observe, however, that in larger mayor-council cities, the job of council member is considerably more political.

Council members, like city managers, feel their positions require a concern for broader issues, particularly as a result of the constantly changing actions of state and national governments. As the pressures and challenges of complex government are felt by part-time amateur council members, they must respond by depending more heavily for guidance on their chief executive, professional staff, and municipal bureaucracy.

COUNCIL-MANAGER RELATIONS

Almost from the beginning, the correct relationship between manager and council has been the subject of debate. Although in theory the council-manager government appears to support the almost total separation of policy and administration (the so-called politics-administration dichotomy), even the plan's early proponents saw the need for managerial involvement in policymaking. Today the debate essentially centers on the proper spheres of responsibility of the council and the manager. James Svara offers one of the most intriguing efforts to sort out this relationship.[48]

Drawing on field observations in five large North Carolina cities in addition to other studies, Svara developed a dichotomy-duality model of policy and administration in council-manager cities. He divided the basic governing responsibilities into four categories: mission, policy, administration, and management. Then he used a curved line to graphically depict the typical division of responsibility between council and manager in each area. The basic model is shown in figure 3.1.

Mission refers to the organization's broadest goals and most basic purposes. It encompasses such matters as the scope of services provided, levels of taxation, and fundamental policy orientations (stance on such issues as growth vs. amenities, charter changes, or the need for annexation of additional land area). As the figure reveals, mission remains the overwhelming responsibility of elected officials. The manager is not powerless even here, of course—she or he will make recommendations, undertake studies, and engage in planning—but mission lies predominantly in the council's sphere.

Policy refers to middle-range issues and problems, the redistribution questions in Peterson's formulation. The annual budget certainly reflects

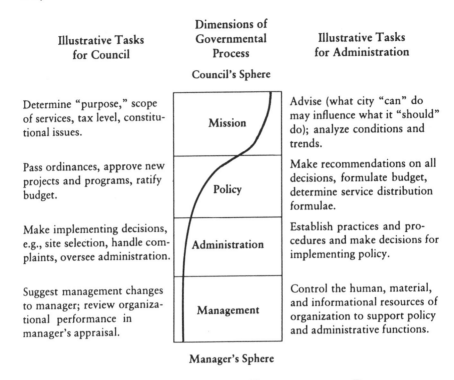

Illustrative Tasks for Council	Dimensions of Governmental Process	Illustrative Tasks for Administration
	Council's Sphere	
Determine "purpose," scope of services, tax level, constitutional issues.	**Mission**	Advise (what city "can" do may influence what it "should" do); analyze conditions and trends.
Pass ordinances, approve new projects and programs, ratify budget.	**Policy**	Make recommendations on all decisions, formulate budget, determine service distribution formulae.
Make implementing decisions, e.g., site selection, handle complaints, oversee administration.	**Administration**	Establish practices and procedures and make decisions for implementing policy.
Suggest management changes to manager; review organizational performance in manager's appraisal.	**Management**	Control the human, material, and informational resources of organization to support policy and administrative functions.
	Manager's Sphere	

FIGURE 3.1. BASIC DIVISION OF RESPONSIBILITY BETWEEN
CITY COUNCIL AND CITY MANAGER.

From "Dichotomy and Duality: Reconceptualizing the Relationship between Policy and Administration in Council-Manager Cities," by J.H. Svara, *Public Administration Review*, 1985, 45, 228. Reprinted with permission from *Public Administration Review*, © by the American Society for Public Administration (ASPA), 1120 G Street NW, Suite 700, Washington, D.C. 20005. All rights reserved.

these mid-range decisions—which programs or services to expand or cut, whether to contract out to the private sector, or whether to undertake a new service responsibility. Notice in figure 3.1 that the curved line almost bisects this sphere, although slightly more space is given to the manager. Indeed the city manager is expected to play a prominent role here, proposing and recommending a variety of policy measures. The council, of course, must ratify the budget, pass ordinances, and approve new service initiatives. But in many cities the initiative for such activities lies with the city manager.

As we move downward to the areas of administration and management, the manager's sphere naturally expands. According to Svara, administration refers to the specific decisions and practices employed to achieve policy objectives. The governing body still has some influence here. It may choose to specify the specific administrative techniques to be used, or it may intervene in service delivery, perhaps in response to constituent demands or to ensure that some special need of a council member's ward is met.

Finally, at the bottom of the figure we come to management, where we expect to find little council involvement. These are the very immediate actions taken by the city manager to control and allocate the organization's human and material resources. The council may play an oversight role here, offering suggestions or passing along citizen complaints, but the boundary between elected officials and administrators in the management arena is usually fairly clearly defined and widely acknowledged.

As figure 3.1 suggests, a dichotomy of sorts does exist, but only at the mission and management levels. In between, in policy and administration, considerable sharing of responsibilities is called for. Svara readily admits that this schematic does not apply to all council-manager cities. He identifies several variants to the model—the strong-manager model, where the line is shifted to the left, and the "council incursion" model, where the council frequently moves more prominently into the administrative sphere. In general, however, the model shown in figure 3.1 represents a reasonably typical, if not ideal, arrangement by which councils and city managers both divide and share responsibility for the basic tasks of urban governance and management.

Another approach to understanding the way in which councils and managers interact with each other is to ask each group about its views of this basic relationship. Ronald Loveridge's survey of almost sixty cities in the San Francisco Bay Area found considerable divergence in views between managers and council members regarding the managers involvement in policymaking. As a whole, managers tended to see themselves as policy activists: "A composite self-image emerges of a strong political executive, expected to exert policy leadership on most demands or issues before the city agenda."[49] Councillors held the opposite view: above all, the manager should be a staff assistant or adviser to the council. Loveridge concludes that considerable potential for conflict exists between manager and council because of their different views of the manager's policy role.

Perhaps this conflict is less likely today than in the past. In a recent national survey city council members were asked to indicate whether various officials or groups were a *very important* source of policy leadership.[50] Table 3.2 shows the results. The finding that city council members rate the city manager as almost a partner in policy initiation stands in stark contrast to the old politics-administration dichotomy. Apparently council members now more readily recognize the "contributions to the council's policy decisions that managers have always made."[51] Nevertheless, managers are more likely to act boldly (1) in safe, less controversial policy areas; (2) where policy proposals have the implicit approval of the council; and (3) in policy areas consonant with community values and the perceived wishes of important interest groups and leadership cliques. Tactically managers recognize the need for considerable behind-the-scenes policy activism based on consultation, advice, and persuasion through informal, primarily face-to-face, contacts.

TABLE 3.2.

PERCENTAGE OF COUNCIL MEMBERS IN COUNCIL-MANAGER
CITIES WHO RATE VARIOUS OFFICIALS AND GROUPS AS
A VERY IMPORTANT SOURCE OF POLICY INITIATION

Official or group	Percentage of council members rating group as very important
Council	73
Manager	72
Mayor	45
Staff	38
Boards and commissions	30
Interest groups	17
State or federal governments	17
Other	3

SOURCE: Adapted from James H. Svara, *A Survey of America's City Councils* (Washington, D.C.: National League of Cities, 1991), 78. Reprinted by permission.

City managers often find themselves thrust into the policy arena by the failure of mayors and councils to play their idealized leadership roles.[52] And there are other reasons for the prominent policy role of the manager:

- The full-time nature of the manager's job compared with the part-time involvement of council members
- The manager's experience and/or specialized training in problem solving

- The staff specialists, technicians, and department heads available to assist the manager
- The manager's role in preparing the city budget
- The manager's position at the apex of an information network, which allows the manager to channel, control, and veto options offered by others

But limits do exist on the city manager's domination of municipal policy. First, most managers are cognizant of the need to keep their councils satisfied. Likewise they recognize that councils usually frown on too much policy activism. Second, even in the management profession the dominant feeling is that managers should not publicly espouse a view contrary to a stated council position. Finally, in large council-manager cities, city managers frequently must share their policy role with the mayor. As noted earlier, Morgan and Watson report that mayor-manager "governing coalitions" were frequently found in larger cities. To the extent such a situation prevails, these council-manager cities are not so different from mayor-council cities that employ a full-time professional administrator (CAO).

Bureaucrats and Policy

As we observed earlier, bureaucrats—the city staff and operating departments—participate prominently in policymaking, both in its formulation and in its implementation. Some authorities have even argued that "perhaps the paramount role performed by public bureaucracy is involvement in public policymaking."[53] Bureaucrats have become key policy figures for several reasons. First, they are the source of much of the technical and highly specialized information so essential for making decisions. Second, legislative bodies increasingly find it necessary to write laws in terms broad enough to permit flexibility in their application. This obviously increases the authority of those who implement the laws—the bureaucrats. Finally, many bureaucrats, especially at the urban level, are in constant contact with the public in a variety of situations in which judgment and discretion are necessary to resolve problems, disputes, and complaints.

One study of bureaucratic participation in policymaking in Los Angeles illustrates the role of the bureaucracy in policy initiation. Political scientist Harry Reynolds found that almost a quarter of the legislation introduced before the Los Angeles council emanated directly from city departments.[54] Most of these measures arose in response to special needs and problems experienced by bureaucrats in the everyday performance of their administrative duties. Reynolds also discovered that many bills originating from other sources, particularly citizens' groups, reflected considerable consultation between their sponsors and interested city departments. Much the same was true of legislation spawned by interest groups. All of this was done with the complete acceptance of the city council. In short, bureaucrats are likely to be an indispensable source of policy initiation.

Most observers would probably agree, though, that bureaucrats have their major effect on policy during the implementation phase. We can identify two principal means by which they exert their influence: (1) through the development of decision rules that guide administrative behavior and (2) through the exercise of discretion in dealing with people at the street level.

BUREAUCRATIC DECISION RULES

First, to understand how and why bureaucrats develop decision rules —devices to simplify and expedite decision making and reduce uncertainty—we must understand something about the psychological needs of bureaucrats themselves. In a study of bureaucratic decision making in the city of Oakland, Levy, Meltsner, and Wildavsky observe that, like most of us, bureaucrats want to work within a relatively secure, stable organizational environment. To keep their relationships as predictable and orderly as possible, bureaucrats rely on what the Oakland study calls the *Adam Smith rule*. This decision rule, with its laissez-faire orientation, says that when a "customer makes a 'request,' take care of him in a professional manner; otherwise, leave him alone."[55] Bureaucrats employ the Adam Smith rule, coupled with a heavy reliance on professional standards, as a way of routinizing and stabilizing the decision-making process.

Levy and his colleagues demonstrate how bureaucratic decision rules affect the operation of several city departments, beginning with libraries. The Adam Smith rule would dictate that new acquisition funds be allocated to those branches with the highest circulation. The more books the patrons take out, the more money their branch receives. In the street department the rule would require that money be spent to repair streets primarily on the basis of complaints received. On the surface these decision rules sound reasonable and defensible. But, as the Oakland study points out, they often harbor a hidden allocational bias. In the case of libraries, certain low-circulation branches, particularly those serving the poor and minorities, failed to obtain the resources to provide new materials to serve the changing needs of their customers. In the street department, evidence suggested that concentrating resources on heavily traveled roads tended to benefit well-to-do commuters (including those living outside Oakland). Poorer citizens were left with few street improvements.

BUREAUCRATIC DISCRETION

Some public employees also affect policy implementation through the exercise of discretion in their daily dealings with the public. Michael Lipsky calls these people *street-level bureaucrats,* a phrase that would apply to the officer on the beat, the classroom teacher, and the welfare caseworker.[56] Lipsky argues that these bureaucrats operate under considerable stress owing to inadequate resources, threats (physical and psychological) or challenges to their authority, and ambiguous job expectations. Accordingly they develop mechanisms or defenses for reducing job-related stresses. Unfortunately for many of those with whom these officials interact (especially low-income and minority groups), their stress-reducing efforts often take the form of routinized responses to client or public demands. For example, stereotyping and other forms of racial and class bias may come to play a significant part in bureaucratic behavior.

James Q. Wilson illustrates the problem more specifically. We know African Americans make up a disproportionate percentage of the lower class. Because lower-class individuals are more likely to be associated with street crime, police officers, whether racially prejudiced or not, are more inclined to treat blacks as potential lawbreakers. Black skin, Wilson contends, remains "a statistically defensible (though individually unjust) cue that triggers an officer's suspicion."[57] Another bureaucratic defensive device is to attribute responsibility for all actions to the clients, or to assume that the clients are so victimized by social forces that they cannot be helped by the service being offered.

At the street level no group exercises more discretion than the police officer on the beat. As the president's crime commission acknowledged in the 1960s: "Law enforcement policy is made by the policeman."[58] The reason is simple: officers are confronted with so many offenses that they cannot arrest everyone involved; instead they use their discretion, particularly in matters of maintaining order. Wilson describes how this process operates in two cities where police employ somewhat distinctive styles or strategies. The *watchman style* is permissive: the police are likely to respond to less serious crimes as though maintaining order, not enforcing laws, is their principal function. The *legalistic style* is less permissive: less serious incidents are more likely to result in arrests.

POLICE DISCRETION

IN Oakland police officers walking the downtown beat often stop and investigate people who appear to be drunk. In one instance a patrolman stopped at a downtown park and politely asked two men, one white and one black, for their identification. Their fumbling about and rather incoherent muttering clearly suggested the pair had been drinking. The officer then asked them to walk a straight line, heel to toe. Neither could. After they failed another sobriety test, the patrolman patted them down, put them in the back of his car, completed two arrest reports, and called for a paddy wagon. Neither man had been creating a disturbance, and when spotted neither was in any apparent danger. This is how the officer explained his action:

> We have to bring them in to cut down on the strong-arms.... Did you see the other guy with the hole in his head? He had gotten himself half killed the other night and just got out of the hospital. Those drunks get rolled down when they don't have any money. We have to bag 'em to keep that sort of thing from happening.

In contrast, the usual policy among communities with watch-man-style departments is to avoid arresting drunks if possible. This is easiest, of course, when inebriates can look after themselves. A senior officer explained the policy in Newburgh, New York: If the person is dressed properly and is not disturbing anyone, and the officer knows where he or she lives, the police take the drunk home. Or occasionally they take the individual to the station without arrest and call the person's home. Obnoxious drunks, especially those who get rowdy in the business district or quiet residential areas, are arrested.

SOURCE: Adapted from James Q. Wilson, *Varieties of Police Behavior* (New York: Atheneum, 1971), 119–26.

Two basic problems arise from the use of defensive psychological mechanisms. First, their distortion of reality can make street-level bureaucrats less effective in performing their jobs. Second, stress-reducing oversimplifications make bureaucrats easy targets for the various groups unhappy with the performance of city government. Minority groups, African Americans, or even gay groups are especially likely to protest the actions of street-level bureaucrats who operate on the basis of stereotype. Surprisingly, these front-line employees are largely unaware of their reliance on such devices and may defend their actions vehemently. Lipsky concludes that there is validity in both positions, but he is pessimistic about the possibility of reducing bureaucracy-client antagonisms. He feels that the stress on city bureaucrats is unlikely to diminish. Thus these groups will continue to rely on defensive behavior, often without realizing it.

Summary

Public policymaking at any level will always remain something of a mystery. So many potential groups can be involved and external conditions can vary so greatly that the process can be extraordinarily difficult to comprehend. And yet, as with any other enigmatic but important process, we continue to try. In this chapter we considered the basic stages of community policymaking, emphasizing the political nature of the process. No matter how much we crave rational and efficient policy, the nature of democratic policymaking—with its heavy reliance on bargaining, negotiation, and compromise—virtually guarantees a messy process whose outcomes seldom satisfy everyone. Some scholars even offer formal descriptions of policymaking that stress the reactive role played by public officials and agencies, a process that one expert calls street-fighting pluralism. Others contend that where policy affects the city's most fundamental interests, business elites dominate the process to promote the economic well-being of the community.

No matter what form it takes or what impact it has, policy is made by people. At the urban level the official policymakers include the chief executives, city councils, and bureaucracies. Policy initiation and leadership must come from somewhere, and increasingly the chief executive, whatever the form of government, is playing a more visible and vigorous policy role. Executive leadership often emerges because legislative bodies, especially those composed of part-time amateurs, find it difficult both to acquire the expertise and to devote the time necessary to cope with increasingly complex issues. The career civil service also plays a prominent role in policymaking and policy implementation. Understanding the various ways in which bureaucratic influence operates has become increasingly important.

Notes

1. James E. Anderson, *Public Policymaking,* 2d ed. (Boston: Houghton Mifflin, 1994), 5.

2. Thomas R. Dye, *Understanding Public Policy,* 2d ed. (Englewood Cliffs, N.J.: Prentice Hall, 1975), 1.

3. David Easton, *The Political System,* 2d ed. (New York: Knopf, 1971), 130.

4. Raymond E. Bauer, "The Study of Policy Formation: An Introduction," in *The Study of Policy Formation,* ed. Raymond Bauer and Kenneth Gergen (New York: Free Press, 1968), 2.

5. This approach to understanding policymaking owes a great debt to the work of political scientist David Easton. See his *A Framework for Political Analysis* (Englewood Cliffs, N.J.: Prentice Hall, 1965), and *A Systems Analysis of Political Life* (New York: Wiley, 1965).

6. Anthony Downs, *Urban Problems and Prospects* (Chicago: Markham, 1970), 176.

7. Charles E. Lindblom, *The Policy Making Process,* 2d ed. (Englewood Cliffs, N.J.: Prentice Hall, 1980), 12.

8. Roger Cobb and Charles Elder, *Participation in American Politics: The Dynamics of Agenda-Building* (Boston: Allyn and Bacon, 1972), 84–85.

9. Robert Eyestone, *From Social Issues to Public Policy* (New York: Wiley, 1978), 89.

10. Cobb and Elder, *Participation in American Politics,* 86.

11. Lindblom, *The Policy Making Process,* 48–49.

12. Richard E. Neustadt, *Presidential Power* (New York: Wiley, 1964).

13. Lindblom, *The Policy Making Process,* 28.

14. Ibid., 68.

15. Douglas Yates, *The Ungovernable City* (Cambridge, Mass.: MIT Press, 1977).

16. Frank Aleshire and Fran Aleshire, "The American City Manager: New Style, New Game," *National Civic Review* 66 (May 1977): 239.

17. Yates, *Ungovernable City,* 34.

18. Paul E. Peterson, *City Limits* (Chicago: University of Chicago Press, 1981), 109.

19. David N. Ammons and Charldean Newell, *City Executives* (Albany, N.Y.: State University of New York, 1989), 61.

20. Jeffrey L. Pressman, "Preconditions of Mayoral Leadership," *American Political Science Review* 66 (June 1972): 511–24.

21. Statistics come from Tari Renner and Victor S. DeSantis, "Contemporary Patterns and Trends in Municipal Government Structures," *Municipal Year Book 1993* (Washington, D.C.: ICMA, 1993), 57–69.

22. Statistics come from Susan A. MacManus and Charles S. Bullock III, "Women and Racial/Ethnic Minorities in Mayoral and Council Positions," *Municipal Year Book 1993* (Washington, D.C.: ICMA, 1993),

70–84.

23. Victor S. DeSantis, "Salaries of Municipal Officials for 1991," *Municipal Year Book 1992* (Washington, D.C.: ICMA, 1992), 79–100.

24. Pressman, "Preconditions of Mayoral Leadership," 513.

25. Alexander L. George, "Political Leadership and Social Change in American Cities," *Daedalus* 97 (Fall 1968): 1197.

26. Terry Blodgett, "Beware the Lure of the 'Strong Mayor,'" *Public Management,* January 1994, 11.

27. The term is from Robert A. Dahl's *Who Governs?* (New Haven: Yale University Press, 1961), 200–214.

28. Robert H. Salisbury, "Urban Politics: The New Convergence of Power," *Journal of Politics* 26 (November 1964): 775–97.

29. Dahl, *Who Governs?* 204.

30. John Nalbandian, "Tenets of Contemporary Professionalism in Local Government," *Public Administration Review* 50 (November/December 1990): 654–62.

31. Statistics come from Tari Renner, "Appointed Local Government Managers: Stability and Change," *Municipal Year Book 1990* (Washington, D.C.: ICMA, 1990), 42–52.

32. DeSantis, "Salaries of Municipal Officials for 1991," 79–100.

33. Laurie Frankel and Carol Pigeon, "Municipal Managers and Chief Administrative Officers: A Statistical Profile," *Urban Data Service Reports* (Washington, D.C.: ICMA, 1975), 3.

34. Deil S. Wright, "The City Manager as a Development Administrator," in *Comparative Urban Research: The Administration and Politics of Cities,* ed. Robert T. Daland (Beverly Hills: Sage, 1969), 218.

35. Renner, "Appointed Local Government Managers," 51.

36. Charldean Newell and David N. Ammons, "Role Emphases of City Managers and Other Municipal Executives," *Public Administration Review* 47 (May/June 1987): 250.

37. James M. Banovetz, "The City: Forces of Change," in *Managing the Modern City,* ed. James M. Banovetz (Washington, D.C.: ICMA, 1971), 42.

38. As quoted in Alan Ehrenhalt, "The New City Manager Is," *Governing,* September 1990, 43–45.

39. Gladys Kammerer, Charles Farris, John DeGrove, and Alfred Clubok, *The Urban Political Community* (Boston: Houghton Mifflin, 1963), 197–98.

40. Gordon Whitaker and Ruth Hoogland DeHoog, "City Managers Under Fire: How Conflict Leads to Turnover," *Public Administration Review* 51 (March/April 1991): 162.

41. James H. Svara, "Mayoral Leadership in Council-Manager Cities: Preconditions versus Preconceptions," *Journal of Politics* 49 (February 1987): 224.

42. Ibid., 225.

43. David R. Morgan and Sheilah S. Watson, "Policy Leadership in

Council-Manager Cities: Comparing Mayor and Manager," *Public Administration Review* 52 (September/October 1992): 438–45.

44. This discussion draws data from MacManus and Bullock, "Women and Racial/Ethnic Minorities in Mayoral and Council Positions," 70–84; and Renner and DeSantis, "Contemporary Patterns and Trends in Municipal Government Structures," 57–69.

45. Susan Welch and Timothy Bledsoe, *Urban Reform and Its Consequences* (Chicago: University of Chicago Press, 1988), 22.

46. Raymond Bancroft, *America's Mayors and Councilmen: Their Problems and Frustrations* (Washington, D.C.: National League of Cities, 1974), 28. Information comes from a 1973 survey of 512 council members with an overall return rate for both mayors and council members of 25 percent.

47. Kenneth Prewitt, *The Recruitment of Political Leaders: A Study of Citizen Politicians* (Indianapolis: Bobbs-Merrill, 1970), 101.

48. James H. Svara, "Dichotomy and Duality: Reconceptualizing the Relationship between Policy and Administration in Council-Manager Cities," *Public Administration Review* 45 (January/February 1985): 221–32; see also William Browne, "Municipal Managers and Policy: A Partial Test of the Svara Dichotomy-Duality Model," *Public Administration Review* 45 (September/October 1985): 620–22.

49. Ronald O. Loveridge, *City Managers in Legislative Politics* (Indianapolis: Bobbs-Merrill, 1971), 24.

50. James H. Svara, *A Survey of America's City Councils* (Washington, D.C.: National League of Cities, 1991), 78.

51. Ibid.

52. Charles R. Adrian, "A Study of Three Communities," *Public Administration Review* 18 (Summer 1958): 208–13.

53. James Medeiros and David Schmitt, *Public Bureaucracy* (North Scituate, Mass.: Duxbury, 1977), 4.

54. Harry W. Reynolds, Jr., "The Career Public Service and Statute Lawmaking in Los Angeles," *Western Political Quarterly* 18 (September 1965): 621–39.

55. Frank Levy, Arnold Meltsner, and Aaron Wildavsky, *Urban Outcomes* (Berkeley: University of California Press, 1974), 229.

56. Michael Lipsky, "Street-Level Bureaucracy and the Analysis of Urban Reform," *Urban Affairs Quarterly* 6 (January 1971): 391–409.

57. James Q. Wilson, "Dilemmas of Police Administration," *Public Administration Review* 28 (September/October 1968): 412.

58. President's Commission on Law Enforcement and Administration of Justice, *The Challenge of Crime in a Free Society* (Washington, D.C.: Government Printing Office, 1967), 10.

Suggested for Further Reading

Ammons, David N., and Charldean Newell. *City Executives*. Albany: SUNY Press, 1989.

Anderson, James E. *Public Policymaking: An Introduction*. 2d ed. Boston: Houghton Mifflin, 1994.

Harlow, Leroy F. *Without Fear or Favor*. Provo, Utah: Brigham Young University Press, 1977.

Loveridge, Ronald O. *City Managers in Legislative Politics*. Indianapolis: Bobbs-Merrill, 1971.

Peterson, Paul E. *City Limits*. Chicago: University of Chicago Press, 1981.

Yates, Douglas. *The Ungovernable City*. Cambridge, Mass.: MIT Press, 1977.

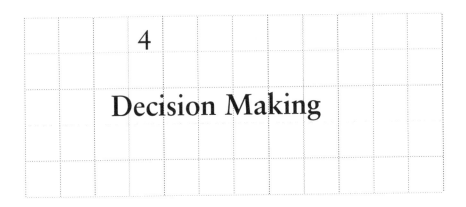

4

Decision Making

Decisions, decisions. Organizations face a never-ending round of decisions, and their chief executives inevitably play a major part in the decision process. Students of management frequently list decision making as one of the basic managerial functions, along with planning, organizing, directing, and controlling.[1] In fact, decision making is the core process; it ties the other functions together. There is even widespread agreement that, above all, managers are judged by the decisions they make.

Decision making is no less crucial to urban managers. In council-manager government especially, managers play an indispensable role in the decision process. Not only are urban managers held accountable by elected officials for a range of decisions affecting the internal affairs of the municipal government, they also actively initiate, guide, and shape a variety of decisions that formally are made by the council. Making the best possible decisions may contribute more than any other function to an urban manager's ultimate success.

A good deal has been written about the decision process, and a number of techniques have been suggested over the years to improve decision making. In fact, several scholarly disciplines—business administration, sociology, political science, and public administration—evidence a concern for how decisions are made within an organizational setting. Obviously we cannot review all the theories and issues found in the disparate literature; instead we concentrate on the four approaches most commonly found in the areas of political science and public administration: the rational-comprehensive approach, incrementalism, mixed scanning, and the garbage-can model. Because the rational approach is the most widely advocated, especially by economists, we examine some of the issues and problems associated with the model and several of the aids to rational decision making that have been developed.

Approaches to Decision Making

To some extent each of the four basic approaches to decision making —rational, incremental, mixed scanning, and "garbage can"—purports to describe reality, to represent reasonably how decisions actually are made. At the same time each approach has its normative overtones, especially the rational-comprehensive approach.

THE RATIONAL-COMPREHENSIVE APPROACH

The rational-comprehensive, economic, or classical approach to decision making is widely known and accepted. This is the way management textbooks say decisions should be made. Observers and even participants in decision making frequently hold up the rational model as an ideal against which the actual decision process should be compared and evaluated.

Rational decision making is often described as a process requiring sequential action. For instance, a decision might be made using the following steps:

1. Recognize the problem.
2. Agree on facts and overall objectives.
3. Identify alternative solutions, analyze the alternatives, and assess the consequences (both short- and long-term) flowing from each.
4. Choose.
5. Implement.
6. Evaluate.

In actuality, the decision-making process is rarely this orderly. Yet adherents to the rational approach in general do subscribe to the belief that executive decision making can be improved through careful fact gathering and precise analysis. For example, Brian Rapp and Frank Patitucci, former Flint, Michigan, officials, offer a step-by-step decision-making process that a strong mayor might pursue to improve municipal performance.[2] You assume the role of mayor here.

Step 1: Identify opportunities. You ask your staff to prepare a list of opportunities for improving city government, based on information and ideas generated during your campaign for office. You instruct the staff to look at the causes underlying observed conditions and estimate the consequences if changes are not made. Three weeks later staff members present you with the results of their preliminary study.

Step 2: Determine responsibility. The staff identifies improvements, but you are surprised to find that many of them may not be within the mayor's power to effect. Various external groups, ranging from civic organizations to the state or federal government, may be extensively involved, either as a financing source or as a possible veto threat. You decide to concentrate on those that you believe you can change.

Accordingly, you ask the staff to indicate for each item whether the mayor's responsibility is direct or indirect. Other possible participants—city council, municipal unions, private business leaders—are to be identified as well. You realize, of course, that you cannot really command others' cooperation; persuasion, negotiation, and compromise will be required.

Step 3: Order opportunities according to their impact on performance. Next, the various opportunities or needed changes are placed in order of priority on the basis of their potential impact on municipal performance. This can be done by answering the simple but important question "So what?" You instruct the staff to group activities into three basic categories of impact: significant, moderate, and low.

Step 4: Reorder priorities on the basis of available resources. Reviewing the prioritized list, you recognize immediately that, given resource limitations, many of these identified opportunities just cannot be implemented. Hence you must distinguish between what is desirable and what is doable. Working with staff, you reorder the problems based on your perception of which have the best chance of being implemented.

Step 5: Develop an action plan. Now that the final list is complete, you ask your staff to convert those in the top category ("most significant" and "most doable") into specific action plans. Each plan should answer certain questions: "What objectives are to be achieved? When are they to be achieved? What results will be produced? What resources will be required to produce these results? Where will these resources be found? Who will be held accountable for converting resources into results?"[3]

As Rapp and Patitucci suggest, a decision to adopt a new budgetary system or to develop a downtown mall will have little effect unless you know the steps required to complete it, how much it will cost, who will be responsible, and when it will be finished.

STRATEGIC PLANNING. —The decision scheme outlined above clearly reflects an attempt to decide rationally what needs to be done and how to go about doing it. In practice this process may occur rather informally, depending on the style of the decision maker and the complexity or magnitude of the problem. Some contend, however, that important decisions should be made in a more consciously systematic fashion, one that relies heavily on a formalized planning process.

In general, planning is figuring out what you want to do and how to do it. At the municipal level, planning is often associated with decisions related to land use and zoning. Historically, city planning departments prepared comprehensive or master plans. These documents formed the basis for subsequent decisions relating to the community's economic base, transportation network, and capital needs, in addition to decisions affecting land use and zoning. Such all-encompassing plans have been criticized for their static nature, their relatively narrow focus on physical development, and the difficulties that arise in their implementation. As a result, in recent years interest has grown in planning as a process rather than as the production of a comprehensive document. Some call this policy planning, but the term most frequently used is *strategic planning*. Developed in the private sector, and in particular by General Electric in the late 1950s and early 1960s, strategic planning is "a disciplined effort to produce fundamental decisions and actions that shape and guide what an organization (or other entity) is, what it does, and why it does it."[4] The management technique is based on systems theory. That is, the "organization's objectives and steps to achieve those objectives are seen in the context of the resources and constraints presented by the organization's environment."[5]

As you might expect, strategic planning involves specific, sequential stages of action:[6]

1. Identify the mission of the organization.
2. Establish a set of goals and priorities to be achieved.
3. Assess the organization's environment, including those individuals and groups whose support is crucial.
4. Develop a set of measurable objectives for goal attainment.
5. Devise various strategies or action plans for achieving the objectives.
6. Agree on a timetable for implementation.
7. Create an information system to monitor and evaluate progress.

Space limitations preclude a detailed consideration of each of these steps, which are quite similar to those enumerated as part of the rational approach to decision making. In fact, this ordered process bears a striking resemblance to the discrete stages of conducting a formal program analysis, which is the subject of the following chapter. Several points should be made about strategic planning specifically, however. Disagreement exists about how the process should take place. Public administration specialist Robert Denhardt thinks most cities lack sufficient internal expertise to conduct strategic planning without help. He suggests bringing in an outside consultant.[7] Others agree. Local government officials should not make a large investment in the technique unless they have sophisticated managerial capabilities.[8] Denhardt also favors creating a planning group of some sort to carry out the process. Depending on the scope of the goals being considered, this group might be composed of high-level city staff or extend beyond city government to include representatives of business, finance, labor, and neighborhood associations. Todd Swanstrom echoes similar sentiments.[9] He laments the elitist/technical nature of the process that seems to produce an economic growth bias. He argues that strategic planning often overlooks the values of democratic participation and the need for checks and balances.

Strategic planning in the business sector proceeds somewhat differently. Most companies place the basic responsibility for the process with line managers. A survey of business executives revealed that goals are set primarily through a bottom-up participatory process rather than dictated by top management. As Texas Instruments' Patrick Haggerty insists: "Those who *implement* the plans must *make* the plans."[10] All authorities agree on one point, however—strategic planning must be action-oriented.

Preparing the plan may be the easy part. Research on private firms by Daniel Gray, head of a Boston-based consulting firm, indicates that most executives believe the planning concept to be sound. But problems arise in implementation.[11] Some 87 percent of a large group of business leaders expressed disappointment and frustration with their strategic planning efforts. Gray attributes much of the difficulty to preimplementation factors, including poor preparation of line managers, vaguely formulated goals, an inadequate information base, poor oversight, and inadequate linkages between strategic planning and other management-control systems, particularly the budget. In the public sector, one cannot forget politics. Indeed, political scientist John Gargan insists that planning proposals must be "technically feasible, fiscally feasible, and politically feasible."[12] Since strategic planning ultimately involves value judgments about the use of scarce resources, disagreement, conflict, and political battles may be unavoidable. Unless the implementation process takes into account political realities, the best-laid plans may never become reality.

How well has strategic management fared at the local level? The following case study provides an assessment based on a few communities' experiences.

| CASE STUDY |

STRATEGIC PLANNING IN ACTION

"STRATEGIC planning is the new game in town, and no self-respecting manager wants to be left out of the action."[13] Indeed, the list of cities engaging in strategic planning is impressive—Dayton, Cleveland, Dallas, Fort Worth, San Antonio, Pittsburgh, Philadelphia, Phoenix, San Francisco, Long Beach, Sunnyvale (Calif.), Virginia Beach, Roanoke, Greensboro (N.C.), to name but a few. Moreover, a number of case studies suggest that the process has resulted in significant benefits.

A. In the early 1980s in Cincinnati, Kevin Shepard, the city's internal auditor, and city manager Sylvester Murray instituted strategic management in a number of areas: administration; economic development; employment; personal and property safety; housing, health, and human services; environmental resources; and recreation. Within each "mission" area, using the principles of strategic planning, twenty-five "critical indicators" were developed that would measure program success. The project provided Murray and other top city officials "a more accurate idea of how city agencies [were] . . . functioning." Strategic planning proved especially beneficial for Cincinnati's economic development program.

B. According to city manager Richard Helwig, when Dayton, Ohio, hired a New Jersey consulting firm in 1976, it became the first major city in the country to employ strategic planning. The payoffs were worth the initial $15,000 investment. The plan saved the city approximately $300,000 annually through consolidation of activities, extension of water lines to suburban communities (to enhance revenue), and economic development activities.

C. Defiance, Ohio, a city of about 18,000 residents, completed its first strategic plan in 1988. Results exceeded expectations. According to city administrator Mike Abels, "For the first year (in the five years) I have been with Defiance, we have enacted a budget incorporating fundamental change, have done so with no acrimony between administration and council, and have passed the budget before the first of January. This, in large part, was due to . . . our strategic plan."

SOURCES: For *A:* "Cincinnati Measures Service Success," *Public Administration Times,* 1 April 1985. For *B:* Elizabeth Voisin, "Cities Map Strategies, Set Blueprints for Change," *City & State,* September 1985, 14. For *C:* James L. Mercer, "Strategic Planning Pays Off in Goals, Dollars," *City & State,* 25 September 1989, 10.

Strategic planning obviously involves an attempt to formalize a rational approach to decision making. But just how rational can the process be when problems are complex, information is scarce, time is limited, and various competing interests have a stake in the outcome? Even two of the most ardent supporters of strategic planning as a form of "anticipatory government" note its limitations. In their book *Reinventing Government,* Osborne and Gaebler note: "Strategic planning is the antithesis of politics. It assumes a thoroughly rational environment—something that never exists in government."[14]

Charles Lindblom has argued for some years that the rational approach to decision making suffers from a number of limitations:[15]

- Human intelligence or problem-solving capacity is too limited to encompass all of the options and potential outcomes of the alternatives generated by the synoptic approach.
- Information is not adequate to assess all options accurately.
- Comprehensive analysis requires too much time.
- Comprehensive analysis is too expensive.
- Facts and values cannot be neatly separated as required by the comprehensive approach.

Lindblom also insists that real decision makers recognize many of these shortcomings and invariably search for simpler, more realistic ways to solve problems.

INCREMENTALISM

Lindblom goes beyond a critique of the rational-comprehensive approach to offer an alternative decision-making theory variously called incrementalism, muddling through, and successive-limited comparisons. Briefly, the essential features of Lindblom's muddling through include the following:[16]

- Goals are not isolated and determined before analysis begins. Goal determination and analysis are closely intertwined, even simultaneous. The means often affect the ends, and vice versa.
- Decision makers usually consider only a limited number of alter-

natives—ordinarily only those that differ marginally from existing policy.

- All consequences, even of the more restricted options, are not evaluated. All consequences cannot be known, and the time and effort required for comprehensive assessment normally is unavailable.
- Since means and ends are inseparable, problem redefinition is continuous; analysis is never-ending, and policy is never made once and for all but remade endlessly.

Incremental problem solving enormously reduces the range of investigations undertaken by decision makers. It also greatly reduces the cognitive strain of comprehensive evaluation. Its basic assumption is that many public policy problems are too complex to be understood, much less mastered. Therefore managers must search for a strategy to cope with problems, not to solve them. If an issue is not resolved with the original solution, or if a new problem arises from the initial effort, it is dealt with at a later point.

Lindblom offers several arguments in behalf of the incremental approach. First, nonincremental decisions may be unpredictable in their consequences, especially if they represent a significant departure from existing policy. Second, errors are much easier to correct when decisions are successive and limited. Finally, incremental decisions are likely to be more acceptable politically than are the far-reaching changes that can result from comprehensive analysis.

Lindblom recently presented a reassessment of incrementalism entitled "Still Muddling, Not Yet Through."[17] In it he offers some modifications and refinements but continued support for the basic approach. He now suggests a continuum of decision-making constructs, ranging from "grossly incomplete analysis" on one end to "synoptic analysis" on the other. He continues to insist that comprehensive or synoptic analysis is unattainable. But he now contends that decision makers can aspire to something he calls "strategic analysis," which he defines as any calculated or thoughtfully chosen set of stratagems to simplify complex problems (that is, to shortcut comprehensive, "scientific" analysis). Figure 4.1 depicts Lindblom's continuum.

Lindblom insists that decision making can be improved by moving toward strategic analysis and away from ill-defined makeshift problem solving. Yet even for complex problems, he thinks the use of formal analytic techniques—systems analysis, operations research, or computer modeling—should be focused on strategies rather than used as attempts at rational comprehension.

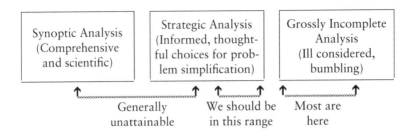

FIGURE 4.1. LINDBLOM'S CONTINUUM FOR
DECISION MAKING.

The case study that follows illustrates the nature of incrementalism at work at the municipal level.

CASE STUDY

WHAT TYPE OF STREET LIGHTS?

INCREMENTAL decision making is based on the "pluralist theory" of who governs. Basically, pluralists argue that politics, and the resulting allocation of government goods and services, is the product of the interaction of competing groups in the city. Politics is thus a process of bargaining and compromising to reach an equilibrium among competing interests. Sometimes decisions are "rational" as measured by the value of efficiency, sometimes they are not. The following case illustrates how efficiency was maximized incrementally over time with respect to street-light services in San Diego. One must remember, however, that the vote could just as easily have been 6–3 to use high-pressure sodium lamps and maximize a value other than efficiency.

In 1983 council members in San Diego voted 5–4 to convert 10,000 street lamps from mercury-vapor lights to high-pressure sodium lamps. The new technology was less expensive and more energy efficient. Nine months later, in a 6–3 vote, the council decided to modify the earlier proposal and replace high-pressure sodium lamps with low-pressure sodium lamps, once again on the assumption that the new lamps were less expensive and more energy efficient.

Although these decisions may seem purely rational (i.e., they maximize efficiency), the "real politics" of the issue pitted researchers at the Palomar Observatory, home of the second-largest optical telescope in the world, against a well-organized group of residents in the Rancho Bernardo area of the city. The former group argued that the "light pollution" generated from the high-pressure lamps would significantly impair the work of the observatory and could eventually "blind" it. On the other hand, residents complained that the low-pressure lamps produced a low-intensity light that looked like "bug lights," made people look like walking cadavers, and increased crime hazards.

The council reached an equilibrium among competing interests in favor of the pro-observatory group and those wishing to maximize efficiency. The competition, however, made the issue a highly political and contentious one.

SOURCE: This case was adapted from one presented in Robert J. Waste, *The Ecology of City Policymaking* (New York: Oxford University Press, 1989), 98–99.

Decision makers in municipal government quickly learn that a variety of influences and interests affect a decisional outcome. Could a democracy run any other way?

A few years after Lindblom's attack on rationalistic decision making, sociologist Amitai Etzioni offered a widely cited critique of incrementalism.[18] Etzioni agrees with Lindblom that rational decision making has its limitations, but he contends that incrementalism does as well. First, decisions made as an outcome of a give-and-take among numerous groups of necessity reflect the interests of the most powerful. The demands of the underprivileged and politically unorganized are usually underrepresented. Second, incrementalism does not provide any guidance or direction for organizational innovation or change: it is action without direction. Etzioni writes that even incrementalists recognize that the approach is not applicable to a large or fundamental decision, such as a declaration of war. And he insists that the number and role of far-reaching decisions are significantly greater than incrementalists admit.

Others agree with Etzioni that incrementalism does not provide a sufficient basis for making fundamental change. Yehezkel Dror, for example, asserts that incrementalism works best when[19]

- The results of present policies are satisfactory.
- There is a high degree of continuity in the nature of the problems.
- There is a high degree of continuity in available means for dealing with the problem.

MIXED SCANNING

Etzioni proposes an alternative to the rational and incremental approaches—*mixed scanning*—that incorporates elements of both. He uses the analogy of a person with two cameras, one with a broad-angle lens to capture the big picture and a second with a telephoto lens that can zero in on the details overlooked by the first. Etzioni does not reject incrementalism's concern for minor changes at the margin. He does insist that periodically, at least, an all-encompassing scanning should be undertaken to avoid straying too far from some wanted objective.

In Etzioni's recent defense of mixed scanning he identifies quite a few instances in which the approach seems to operate. One example he mentions is the court system, where higher courts (like higher executives) reserve for themselves the fundamental decisions and expect the lower courts to practice incrementalism.[20] Mixed scanning bears some resemblance to the way in which America's well-run companies are managed. In *In Search of Excellence,* Thomas Peters and Robert Waterman, Jr., identify certain core values that animate successful firms. In general these values not only substitute for long-range planning but also provide an organizing framework within which considerable autonomy, flexibility, and experimentation is encouraged.[21] The big picture guides fundamental decisions; autonomy and flexibility are used in routine matters.

Mixed scanning is an attempt to combine the best features of both rational and incremental decision making. Yet it remains essentially a compromise between the rational and incremental approaches, with few guidelines for how and when it should be employed.

THE GARBAGE-CAN MODEL

A model that moves beyond Lindblom's incrementalism reflects a more negative side of nonrationality. The garbage-can model of decision making contends that the rational model and even incrementalism depict a decision-making world that is unrealistically coherent and orderly. According to this model, the rational and incremental models err in assuming too much certainty and knowledge in decision making. In reality, most decision-making situations are plagued with ambiguities of all sorts: objectives are unclear; organizational preferences are not ordered; causality is obscure; attention and participation of key actors are uncertain; and outcomes are unknown.[22]

In metaphorical terms, the garbage-can model views

a choice opportunity as a garbage can into which various problems are dumped by participants. The mix of garbage in a single can depends partly on the labels attached to the alternative cans; but it also depends on what garbage is being produced at the moment, on the mix of cans available, and on the speed which garbage is collected and removed from the scene.[23]

Cohen, March, and Olsen, the organizational theorists who developed this model, call the situation "organized anarchy"[24] and contend that decisions are made essentially in three ways:[25]

- By oversight, without any attention to existing problems and with a minimum of time and energy
- By flight (or avoidance), postponement, or buck-passing
- By resolution, which occurs generally only when flight is severely restricted or when problems are relatively minor or uncomplicated.

According to the garbage-can model, oversight and flight dominate organizational decision making. Jay Starling agrees. His analysis of decision making in Oakland offers considerable support for this approach.[26] Starling observes that decision makers discard the tactics of avoidance and delay only when forced to by great need or compelling circumstance. Then they generally make only a limited response, based on routine, past experience, and training. Even these more active tactics often include selecting courses of action that are ambiguous to outsiders, readily reversible, or both.

One final word about this model. The name does not imply that decisions made are "garbage" or necessarily bad; even successful organizations make decisions in this rather haphazard way. Instead, the garbage-can model may merely reflect the nature of large-scale organizational culture, which in turn

is intangible, rarely written down or discussed but still a potent force in shaping and controlling [organizational] behavior: it is an observable and palpable phenomenon, reflected in the shared philosophies, ideologies, myths, values, beliefs, assumptions, and norms of the organization.[27]

How might the garbage-can model look in action? The case study that follows is illustrative.

TUNNELS TO NOWHERE

IN the fall of 1962, New York Mayor Robert Wagner, Jr., received a report from his staff that subway trains in Queens were too crowded. Wagner agreed and endorsed an expansion of the New York subway system, but no funds were available to begin construction.

Then in the mid-1960s, when Governor Nelson Rockefeller was searching for New York City votes to support a $2.5 billion transportation bond issue, he grabbed at the only capital project lying on the shelf of the NYC Transit Authority. Far from being a well-designed program, it was a haphazard wish list compiled by transit planners who had had nothing to build for more than thirty years. The bond issue carried, and suddenly some $600 million became available to the newly constituted Metropolitan Transportation Authority (MTA), a regional mass transit body. The planners and engineers, not used to so much money, let their imaginations run wild. An elaborate addition to the system was planned at a projected cost of $1.3 billion. But those estimates turned out to be "laughably low" because planners had no idea how much such a large-scale project would really cost. Within three years the price tag had ballooned to over $3 billion, while the original plan for thirteen routes and fifty-two miles was scaled back to eleven routes and thirty miles of track. By late 1974 only four miles of subway were under construction.

In the same year the New York City fiscal crisis hit. When the city realized the fiscal mess it was in, Mayor Abraham Beame halted construction of the Second Avenue subway, leaving abandoned tunnels all along eastern Manhattan. Total cost to the city at that point: $99.6 million. Total use: zero.

Why hadn't more been accomplished? According to journalist Harrison Rainie, one answer could be found in the buck-passing and wrangling within the MTA. The three major staff components of the authority—project planning, design, and construction—did not communicate well. As the project advanced through each phase, the work fell under the responsibility of a different engineer. The lack of communication contributed to long delays and soaring costs. In addition, as building progressed, the job of overseeing the work became harder. There were just not enough bodies to both check the existing 250 miles of subway and monitor the new construction. Consequently a kind of "antiturf" battle developed. The MTA bureaucratic wars were devoted almost exclusively to avoiding new responsibilities. Finally, the MTA was forced to assign the engineers responsibility for overseeing maintenance. But they were not up to the job. A large number were graduates of nonaccredited engineering schools, and many were foreigners with so little command of English that they had trouble communicating with the contractors. "From top to bottom, the engineering department was staffed with people out of their league," said one New York transit expert. "They enjoyed the comfort and safety of the civil service and they were constitutionally incapable of making waves or asserting themselves, especially in cases of manifest trouble."

Why wasn't anything done sooner? Why didn't the bad news reach the bosses earlier? Partly because no one pressed to find out the project's status. Each time officials with the power to shut it down sought an accounting, the engineers, seeking to avoid embarrassment and minimize risk, predicted the problems could be ironed out. Even the federal government, which had poured more than $800 million into the project, did not ask how its money was being spent until 1984. When federal mass transit administrator Ralph Stanley finally asked the staff "How did this happen?" he was incredulous at the response. "If you can believe it, they couldn't tell me," he said. Apparently grant managers insisted that they were responsible only for shoveling out money; they did not feel it was their job to question local priorities. Federal payments to the MTA were finally suspended in late 1985.

Rainie provides the following assessment of a project that spent $1.23 billion to create two huge tunnels and a half-dozen holes across New York City without serving a single passenger. "The overriding moral of this tunnel tale is the importance of accountability. At every stage someone was saying, 'It's not my problem.' From the maintenance crews to the federal officials, the buck didn't stop anywhere."

SOURCE: This case is adapted from Harrison Rainie, "Tunnels to Nowhere," *Washington Monthly*, March 1986, 43–48.

Decision-Making Tools

Decision making is rarely a highly rational process: "Decision-making is not a science but an art. It requires, not calculation, but judgment."[28] Still, as Etzioni and others suggest, analysis may help. Indeed, a wide body of business management literature is devoted to the tools and techniques that assist managers in making better decisions. Many of the tools are complex, but we might briefly review several techniques that are applicable to both public and private decision making.

QUANTITATIVE AIDS

Both payoff matrices and decision trees are simple graphic displays that lay out alternative decisions and likely outcomes.

THE PAYOFF MATRIX. —The *payoff matrix* is a way of displaying choices and results when a decision is simple. For example, assume a city is planning to construct a new swimming pool. How big a pool should it build? Prospective swimmers would want it as large as possible, but too big a pool would cost the city more than necessary. Although this type of facility is rarely expected to pay its way, taxpayers should not be expected to provide too large a subsidy. But a small pool, though cheaper to build and operate, would not meet demand. Using a payoff matrix, we can depict the choices and the results of those choices. Here we have just two choices: building a large pool or building a small one. The payoff matrix (figure 4.2) shows the four possible outcomes based on the two choices and the two levels of use. If a large pool is built and heavily used, everyone will be satisfied; if a large pool is built and usage is low, the city will incur excessive costs. If a small pool is built and usage is low, again everyone will be satisfied; but if a small pool is built and used heavily, the swimmers will not be happy and the city will not receive as much revenue as it would have if it had built the large pool.

Possible outcomes

	Low Usage	High Usage
Large pool	Swimmers happy; income low, costs high	Swimmers happy; income high, costs high
Small pool	Swimmers happy; income low, costs low	Swimmers unhappy; income low, costs low

Choice

FIGURE 4.2. A PAYOFF MATRIX.

THE DECISION TREE. — As a part of formal decision theory, decision trees are based on *utility theory,* which assigns numerical values to decision-makers' preferences, and *probability theory,* which assigns numbers in accordance with the likelihood that certain events will occur in the future.[29]

We can see how they work by adding some financial data to our swimming pool problem. First we must consider the probabilities associated with the use of the pool. Assume the city manager consults with the park and recreation director. Together they arrive at estimates of usage based on the potential growth of the area to be served and the usage of other city pools. They might use such terms as *probably* and *less than likely* in their estimates, but they also might use more precise terms: a 60 percent *likelihood* or a 40 percent *chance.*

By applying numerical probability to the swimming pool decision we can create a decision tree (figure 4.3). There are still two basic choices: building a large pool at $300,000 or building a small one at $150,000. Customarily, decision points in a tree diagram are represented by boxes. The circles, or nodes of the tree, depict chance events. Probabilities for each event are shown along the lines of each branch of the tree. In this case the manager and the recreation director estimate the probability of high usage with a large pool at .6, a 60 percent chance. If a small pool were built, they figure the chances are 70 percent that low

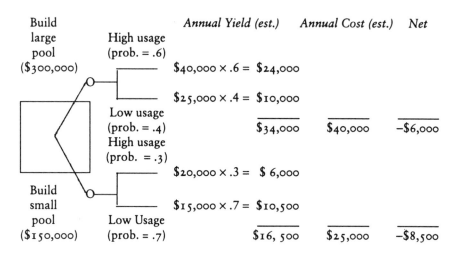

FIGURE 4.3. A SIMPLE DECISION TREE.

usage would result. But what about costs and anticipated revenue under these various conditions? We can find this information to the right of the tree in figure 4.3. For example, with a large pool the income from high usage is estimated at $40,000, whereas that from low usage is estimated at only $25,000. But the probabilities of usage must be taken into account to obtain the total estimated financial yield, as follows:

$$(\$40,000 \times .6) + (\$25,000 \times .4) = \$34,000.$$

Applying the same procedure to the decision to build a small pool produces the following:

$$(\$20,000 \times .3) + (\$15,000 \times .7) = \$16,500.$$

Notice that the probabilities, as well as the estimated revenue, are different for the small pool decision. When the estimated annual costs are figured in, we obtain the following:

	Revenue	Cost	Net
Large pool	$34,000	$40,000	−$6,000
Small pool	$16,500	$25,000	−$8,500

In this case the manager would recommend to the council that the large pool be built because it should lose less each year than the small pool.

For purposes of illustration, we kept this example quite simple. We could have added a middle option, in pool size and in usage. With each additional option the branching extends considerably.[30]

Decision trees have obvious limitations: probabilities are only estimates based on human judgment, and quantifying individual preferences is always a tricky business. Still the form can help decision makers be more precise in their calculations and think more carefully about a series of options and possible consequences. As James Vaupel argues, "The phrase 'an 80% chance,' even if it only means 'roughly an 80% chance,' conveys much more information than a sloppy, ambiguous term like 'probably,' which can mean anything from a 51% chance to more than a 90% chance."[31]

The payoff matrix and decision tree are only two of the quantitative techniques designed to help decision makers. The next chapter discusses other mathematical tools used in the more formal modes of analysis. But we should keep the potential usefulness of quantitative aids in perspective: "Many, perhaps most, of the problems that have to be handled at middle and high levels in management have not been made amenable to mathematical treatment, and probably never will."[32]

NONQUANTITATIVE AIDS

THE DELPHI EXERCISE. — The delphi technique combines two methods used by executives to gather information: the committee system and the use of experts. The delphi originated as a tool for forecasting future events. It generally requires the use of a panel of experts who are asked to respond anonymously to a survey instrument that includes a series of questions and statements regarding a particular problem. When the questionnaires are returned, the responses are tabulated by a steering committee. The committee then tries to clarify responses by editing existing items and adding new items to the list.[33] Then a second and usually a third wave of questionnaires are sent to the experts to get a greater consensus on the options being considered. In some cases one best recommendation is sought; in other instances only a ranking of options is desired. The whole idea is that experts may consider possibilities they had not thought of previously at the same time that they benefit from the views of other authorities. The questionnaires can be mailed or sent via a computer terminal. Preserving the panel's anonymity presumably avoids some of the negative consequences of committee activity, such as the bandwagon effect or the dominance of the group by one or two strong-willed vocal people.

CASE STUDY

REVISING NORMAN'S COMPREHENSIVE PLAN: THE DELPHI PROCESS AT WORK

IN the spring of 1978 the city of Norman, Oklahoma, undertook a delphi exercise in connection with a major revision of the city's comprehensive land-use plan. The basic purpose of the delphi was to gather information to assist a citizen's task force in defining and narrowing the issues to be dealt with by the city planning staff.

First the staff sponsored a series of special one-day seminars over a period of several months to raise basic questions about Norman's social, economic, and physical future. Seventy-five participants were involved, representing all the boards and commissions (park board, planning commission), the social and service organizations (Kiwanis Club, League of Women Voters), the business community, the development-related industries (including engineers and architects), and the general public (a small group chosen by the mayor and city council members).

After the seminars, the planning staff prepared a five-page instrument containing a number of housing- and development-related questions. Some of the questions that were included in the delphi instrument are shown below. The questionnaire, along with a stamped self-addressed envelope, was sent to each person who had participated in the seminars, including the mayor and council members. The first mailing produced a response rate of about 72 percent. Those not responding were dropped from subsequent mailings. The project called for four separate mailings. The director of the project, senior planner Larry Tom, added several more questions based on general comments written in by participants on the first round. The second questionnaire also included a tabulation of the first set of responses.

The planning staff expressed some disappointment at the rate of return from the first several rounds of questionnaires. Still, Tom felt the exercise provided useful information. The planning department also sponsored a random-sample communitywide survey that covered many of the same issues addressed by questions in the delphi. The staff thus had results of two information-gathering efforts that could serve as citizen and leader input into the plan preparation process.

Sample Questions Used in the Delphi Exercise

How important would it be for the city to establish policies that would

1. Provide housing for low and moderate income families.

Not important							Important	
1	2	3	4	5	6	7	8	9

2. Provide fiscal impact analysis of alternative development proposals.

1	2	3	4	5	6	7	8	9

3. Commit activity and funding to the revitalization of Norman's Central Core.

    1   2   3   4   5   6   7   8   9

4. Commit activity and funding to the conservation of older, stable neighborhoods.

    1   2   3   4   5   6   7   8   9

5. Commit activity and funding for the development of a growth guidance system.

    1   2   3   4   5   6   7   8   9

6. Encourage new commercial and industrial development in Norman.

    1   2   3   4   5   6   7   8   9

SOURCES: This case is taken from interviews and information obtained from Norman's senior planner, Larry Tom, in May 1978.

THE SCENARIO. —Scenarios essentially are attempts to picture some future state of events through the use of a written narrative. They require projections of existing trends and predictions of future occurrences in whatever areas decision makers want to explore. Scenarios might be prepared by a group of experts and offered in several different versions. Sometimes the devices are used in connection with other analytic techniques, particularly of a quantitative nature. Scenarios might work in this way:

> Scenarios could be used in developing and analyzing transportation policies or transportation systems. Starting with various philosophical assumptions and introducing technological, social, political, economic, and physical factors and events, alternative urban futures could be developed.... These environments might depict the preferred or optimal urban future, the worst possible future, or both, and numerous other futures in between. Various policies and systems could then be tested in terms of their effectiveness in achieving the optimal future.[34]

WRITTEN GUIDELINES. —Another nonquantitative aid to decision making is the use of formal guidelines or outlines to assist in structuring the problem. In the 1960s, when he was mayor of Milwaukee, Henry Maier devised a form to serve as a handy decision-making tool for chief executives or as a useful reporting form for their staff and assistants. The form addresses the following issues:[35]

- Available facts must be identified and gathered. The answer to the question "What has occurred?" leads to the question "Why has this happened?"
- Following problem identification and fact gathering, assumptions may be made based on judgment and intuition.
- Resources must be evaluated to find a means for solving the problem.
- Based on fact, assumption, and available resources, alternatives are considered, each built on a hypothesis (if this occurs, the result should be . . .).
- Before a selection is made, each alternative is examined for potential implementation problems and the political conflict it may create.

Figure 4.4 (pages 138–39) depicts the actual form developed for use in the Milwaukee mayor's office. According to Maier, its greatest value was in paring down the vast amount of time and effort required to gain a clear perspective on all the facets of a particular problem. In his words, "The system has passed the only test that ought to be made of it; it has proved a successful guide in the decision-making process."[36]

Most of the more advanced techniques for assisting urban decision makers can be used only in fairly large cities. Still smaller communities are encountering these tools when they bring outside consultants in to work on major problems. Most of these decision-making aids, both quantitative and nonquantitative, were developed either in defense-related enterprises or in the private sector. Some are more suitable for the local public sector than are others. But regardless of their value, public managers are likely to be seeing more of them in the future.

Summary

Decision making is a complex activity, whether it takes place at the individual, organizational, or community level. Is it a rational process? This question has been addressed by a number of theorists from various disciplines. As a result we have several models that purport to describe how decisions really are made. The rational-comprehensive approach, incrementalism, mixed scanning, and even the garbage-can model all have their defenders, and each has certain attractive features. Perhaps, as the incrementalists argue, most decisions do come about by virtue of habit, inertia, muddling through, or whatever. But even the father of incrementalism, Charles Lindblom, agrees that governmental decision making can and should be improved.

And help is available. A variety of tools, quantitative and nonquantitative, have been developed over the years to assist those who want to make decisions more rationally. The payoff matrix and the decision tree help decision makers put alternatives into a more systematic perspective. Nonquantitative aids, such as the delphi exercise, scenario writing, and written guidelines, offer ways of approaching decisions that can provide useful information to public officials.

STAFF REPORT   OFFICE OF THE MAYOR
(Note: Where space is insufficient   CITY OF MILWAUKEE
  attach an appendix.

1. PRELIMINARY ANALYSIS

A. Problem Identification: Date of report _____
   Suspend judgment until presentation is   Common Council file # _____
   complete and you are sure you grasp the   Analyst _____
   whole problem and have identified the   Target date for action _____
   real problem, rather than the apparent one. Originator _____

B. Description: Problem Situation and Its History (Outline):
   1. Make your summary brief, accurate, and clear.
   2. Use words that define the problem exactly; make sure there is no ambiguity
   in the terms used.
   3. Include what is known; point out what is unknown and must be found out.

C. Scope of Analysis (Financial, Legal, Organizational, Administrative Questions):
   1. It may be necessary to group factors as:
   a. Factors controllable by you.
   b. Factors subject to control of others.
   c. Factors subject to chance.
   2. Ask yourself such questions as: What is the budgetary impact? What are the
   potential beneficial or nonbeneficial effects on tax and other revenues? What
   legislation exists or may be required? What existing agencies can handle the
   problem? What administrative plans have been made on the project or proposal?

D. Facts Assembled (Financial, Legal, Organizational, Adminis-	Relative Weights		
trative, etc.; give source):	1*	2*	3*

   1. When you cannot check facts directly, be sure you thoroughly
   question the source. (The complete Report Guide lists a num-
   ber of sources for factual material, such as municipal reports,
   legal guides, department reports, libraries, checking to see
   what is done in other cities.)
   2. According to your opinion of their relative importance, assign
   relative weights to the various facts you have gathered.
   3. Does it appear that there is an overriding decisive factor in
   your analysis? If so, what is the consequence of its presence?

E. Assumptions:
   1. Ask yourself: What have I assumed to be true in this situation? Is it true? How do I
   know? What other assumptions may be true? What can I do to test their reliability?
   2. Challenging what is believed to be true about a problem that has not been solved is
   often the quickest way to find the reason why it has not been solved.
   3. Errors of assumption include assuming facts that aren't so, inferences that aren't
   logical, universal opinions that are incorrect.
   4. The skilled problem solver has to develop an automatic skepticism, especially
   about "obvious" answers and dogmas.

F. Alternative Solutions and Consequences:
   1. Standard practice for all problem solving is to list all the possible alternatives
   before making a decision.
   2. When you are faced with a problem that offers only an unpalatable solution, if
   you can find one other possible solution or alternative, you have changed the
   problem in a fundamental way.

*1. Most important. 2. Very important. 3. Important.

3. *If the problem turns out to be a true dilemma, which is the lesser-evil course?*
4. *Consideration of consequences, secondary or direct, is a big part of problem solving. Set up criteria to test results. Sometimes probable success is easily demonstrated. Sometimes it can be demonstrated only by elaborate technical proof. Sometimes it can be judged by opinion only. Yet you have not thought out your attack on a problem until you have estimated what the consequences of each effort to solve it will be.*

11. EVALUATION

	Alternative #			Relative Weights
	1*	2*	3*	

A. Public Relations (Groups or Individuals Affected):
  1. *Evaluation is the product of the analyst's judgment and the result of opinion research involving respective groups.*
  2. *Estimate the relative effect of the various alternatives on various groups involved: also, list the groups according to the way you rate their comparative importance.*
  3. *Typical groups to be considered are: (a) Those with immediate pecuniary or economic interest; (b) Those with immediate legislative interest; (c) Those with broad civic or community interest; (d) The general public.*

B. Official Relations (Groups or Individuals Affected):
  1. *Have you sounded out sentiment of those officially involved such as the Common Council, city, county, state, or federal departments or agencies which may be affected?*
  2. *How does this decision accord with previous decisions by those concerned?*
  3. *If a reversal of policy of others is involved, is the issue significant enough to warrant the change?*
  4. *Have you listed and weighted opinions of those involved?*
  5. *Which alternatives will involve the greatest net gain or the least net loss in our official relations?*

C. Press:
  Have you consulted previous news stories on this matter? What editorial positions have been taken, either recently or in the past?

D. Recommendation:
  A recommendation is essentially "a counsel as to a course of action." It should be held to essentials and be clear and definite and based on conclusions supported by your prior analysis.

E. Action Advised:
  1. *List the procedural steps that should be taken to carry out the above recommendation.*
  2. *Include such things as the timing of the announcement of the decision, the manner of its announcement, and the order in which the steps should be taken.*

FIGURE 4.4. FORMAL GUIDE FOR DECISION MAKING USED BY THE MAYOR'S OFFICE IN MILWAUKEE.

*1. Most important. 2. Very important. 3. Important.

SOURCE: From *Challenge to the Cities*, by H.W. Maier. Copyright 1966 by Random House, 156–59. Reprinted by permission.

Notes

1. Burt K. Scanlon, *Principles of Management and Organizational Behavior* (New York: Wiley, 1973), 5.

2. The following comes from Brian W. Rapp and Frank M. Patitucci, *Managing Local Government for Improved Performance* (Boulder, Colo.: Westview Press, 1977), chap. 16.

3. Ibid., 329.

4. John M. Bryson, *Strategic Planning for Public and Nonprofit Organizations* (San Francisco: Jossey-Bass, 1988), 5.

5. Robert B. Denhardt, "Strategic Planning in State and Local Government," *State and Local Government Review* 17 (Winter 1985): 175.

6. These stages of the strategic planning process are modified from John J. Gargan, "An Overview of Strategic Planning for Officials in Small to Medium Size Communities," *Municipal Management* 7 (Summer 1985): 162.

7. Denhardt, "Strategic Planning in State and Local Government," 176.

8. Gregory Strieb, "Applying Strategic Decision Making in Local Government," *Public Productivity and Management Review* 15 (Spring 1992): 341.

9. Todd Swanstrom, "The Limits of Strategic Planning for Cities," *Journal of Urban Affairs* 9, no. 2 (1987): 139.

10. Quoted in Thomas J. Peters and Robert H. Waterman, Jr., *In Search of Excellence* (New York: Warner Books, 1982), 31.

11. Daniel H. Gray, "Uses and Misuses of Strategic Planning," *Harvard Business Review* 64 (January–February 1986): 89–97.

12. Gargan, "An Overview of Strategic Planning," 166.

13. Richard V. Robinson and Douglas C. Eadie, "Putting Strategic Planning to Practical Use in Cleveland Heights, Ohio," *Ohio Cities and Villages*, October 1983, 13.

14. David Osborne and Ted Gaebler, *Reinventing Government* (Reading, Mass.: Addison-Wesley, 1992), 235.

15. Charles E. Lindblom, *The Intelligence of Democracy* (New York: Free Press, 1965), 138–43. Copyright © 1965 by The Free Press, a division of the Macmillan Company.

16. These characteristics are adapted from ibid., 143–48; and Charles E. Lindblom, "The Science of 'Muddling Through,'" *Public Administration Review* 19 (Spring 1959): 79–88.

17. Charles E. Lindblom, "Still Muddling, Not Yet Through," *Public Administration Review* 39 (November/December 1979): 517–26.

18. Amitai Etzioni, "Mixed-Scanning: A 'Third' Approach to Decision-Making," *Public Administration Review* 27 (December 1967): 385–92.

19. Yehezkel Dror, "Muddling Through—'Science' or Inertia?" *Public Administration Review* 24 (September 1964): 154.

20. Amitai Etzioni, "Mixed Scanning Revisited," *Public Administration*

Review 46 (January/February 1986): 8–14.

21. Peters and Waterman, *In Search of Excellence,* chap. 12. The authors refer to this phenomenon as "simultaneous loose-tight properties," or simultaneous centralization and decentralization.

22. Harold Gortner, Julianne Mahler, and Jeanne Nicholson, *Organization Theory* (Chicago: Dorsey Press, 1987), 263.

23. Michael Cohen, James March, and Johan Olsen, as quoted in Harold Gortner, Julianne Mahler, and Jeanne Nicholson, *Organization Theory* (Pacific Grove, Calif.: Brooks/Cole, 1989), 263.

24. Michael Cohen, James March, and Johan Olsen, "Garbage-Can Model of Organizational Choice," *Administrative Science Quarterly* 17 (March 1972): 1–25.

25. Michael Cohen and James March, *Leadership and Ambiguity* (New York: McGraw-Hill, 1974), 83–84.

26. Jay D. Starling, *Municipal Coping Strategies* (Beverly Hills: Sage, 1986), 22–27.

27. Florence Heffron, *Organization Theory & Public Organizations* (Englewood Cliffs, N.J.: Prentice Hall, 1989), 212.

28. Theodore C. Sorensen, *Decision-Making in the White House* (New York: Columbia University Press, 1963), 10.

29. Jack W. Lapatra, *Applying the Systems Approach to Urban Development* (Stroudsburg, Pa.: Dowden, Hutchinson and Ross, 1973), 46.

30. See John F. Magee, "Decision Trees for Decision Making," *Harvard Business Review* 42 (July–August 1964): 126–38.

31. James W. Vaupel, "Muddling Through Analytically," in *Improving the Quality of Urban Management,* ed. Willis Hawley and David Rogers (Beverly Hills: Sage, 1974), 187–209.

32. Herbert A. Simon, *The New Science of Management Decision,* rev. ed. (Englewood Cliffs, N.J.: Prentice Hall, 1977), 63.

33. Kenneth L. Kraemer, *Policy Analysis in Local Government* (Washington, D.C.: ICMA, 1973), 127.

34. Ibid., 131.

35. Henry W. Maier, *Challenge to the Cities* (New York: Random House, 1966), 155.

36. Ibid., 161.

Suggested for Further Reading

Bingham, Richard D., and Marcus E. Ethridge, eds. *Reaching Decisions in Public Policy and Administration: Methods and Applications.* New York: Longman, 1982.

Duchane, Steve. *A Practical Guide to Designing Strategic Management Planning in Municipalities.* Owosso, Mich.: Crest Printing, 1985.

Etzioni, Amitai. *The Moral Dimension.* New York: Free Press, 1988.

Kraemer, Kenneth L. *Policy Analysis in Local Government.* Washington, D.C.: ICMA, 1973.

Lindblom, Charles E. *The Intelligence of Democracy.* New York: Free Press, 1965.

Mills, Warner, Jr., and Harry Davis. *Small City Government: Seven Cases in Decision Making.* New York: Random House, 1962.

Simon, Herbert A. *The New Science of Management Decision.* Rev. ed. Englewood Cliffs, N.J.: Prentice Hall, 1977.

5

Analysis for Urban Decisions

Urban managers are problem solvers above all. Dealing with problems means making tough choices among alternative solutions. Resources are limited, time is crucial, alternatives may be hazy, and objectives may be ill defined, but decisions must be made. The process is often reactive, erratic, and unpredictable—muddling through versus a rational choice among clearly defined options. Both public and private managers have long searched for ways to improve the management process by making more effective decisions. A variety of aids have been developed: systems analysis, operations research, computer simulation, and benefit-cost analysis, to name a few. And there has been a growing consensus that some of these methods and techniques can be employed profitably by urban managers.

Program Analysis and Other Systematic Approaches

Program analysis represents one method for improving public decision making. By providing a means of systematically comparing alternatives in the light of their costs and consequences, program analysis helps decision makers choose a course of action. As a process, program analysis is quite similar to a variety of analytic approaches that go by slightly different names. For example, *systems analysis, policy analysis,* and *operations research* are closely related to what we call *program analysis.*

The purpose of most analysis is to provide a scientific basis for choosing among the alternative actions confronting decision makers.[1] Its proponents believe that much of the confusion and uncertainty associated with organizational decision making can be reduced by using systematic or even scientific methods of problem solving. Policy analysis and program analysis are the two phrases most commonly used to describe this process in the public sector. Although the two terms are sometimes used interchangeably, *policy analysis* is more often applied to fairly broad or complex problems involving a variety of external interests and groups. Revising the city's general planning document would be an example of policy analysis. *Program analysis* is more limited in scope, referring to a narrower problem with fewer external actors. Deciding where in the city to build three government-subsidized rental houses might be a problem for program analysis. The phrase *operations research* comes from the business world. Operations researchers are concerned with questions of pure efficiency, as they seek to identify the optimum choice from a specific set of given alternatives.

We also might mention that program analysis is not the same as program evaluation. *Analysis* attempts to project what may happen at some future time if certain choices are made. *Evaluation* assesses how effectively a particular program has met its intended objectives; evaluation comes after an activity has been implemented. Finally, we might make the distinction between public management and organization theory/behavior. Organization theory is more conceptual in nature. This field of inquiry focuses on organizational design and process issues and attempts to understand individual and group behavior in organizations. Chapter 8 is devoted to this topic. In contrast, public management is more applied and concerns "how to" manage complex organizations. This chapter is devoted to public management.

The Analysis Process

Any form of analysis involves a series of steps. Although these steps might not be followed unfailingly in every instance, generally the analysis procedure includes the following:[2]

1. Clearly defining the *problem* or need
2. Stating the specific *objectives* being sought
3. Identifying those *constraints* that could limit the proposed courses of action
4. Identifying and describing the key features of the various *alternatives* for attaining the objectives
5. Devising appropriate *selection criteria* for choosing among the alternatives

6. *Analyzing* the alternatives; *selecting* the best alternative according to the accepted criteria
7. *Implementing* the selected alternative
8. *Evaluating* the results and determining the extent to which the objectives have been attained; providing *feedback* to previous steps and revising if necessary

Figure 5.1 displays these components in schematic form. As the figure shows, the analysis process is closely related to the rational-comprehensive decision-making model outlined in the last chapter. Before turning to a detailed examination of them, we should look at an illustration of how program analysis worked in an actual case.

The mayor of a large city asked his chief administrative officer to look into complaints about the city's emergency ambulance service.[3] The *problem* was to provide more effective medical attention to persons requiring the services of an ambulance on an emergency basis. The *objective* was substantially to reduce both the ambulance response time and the time needed to bring patients to the hospitals. A major *constraint* was the mayor's time limit, which restricted the magnitude of the changes that could be considered and eliminated such far-reaching alternatives as establishing a dense network of first-aid stations and instituting preventive health measures.

The *alternatives* included adding more ambulances, establishing more ambulance locations, and reorganizing the service so that ambulances would be deployed in the areas of highest demand. The *selection criterion* was to find the lowest-cost alternative that would still meet the objective. Since the problem involved a complex relationship among hospital locations, ambulance locations, the geographic distribution of emergency calls, and the frequency of calls, a mathematical model of the system was constructed. This allowed the analysts to modify various components of the system and observe the effects of these variations.

The study concluded that the *selection of one alternative* could reduce response time by 20 percent at a modest increase in cost. This alternative was chosen and gradually *implemented*. Data were collected and *evaluated* carefully to determine whether the expected benefits were indeed being realized. Necessary alterations became *feedback* to earlier steps in the process.

DEFINING THE PROBLEM

Defining the problem may seem to be the easiest part of the analysis. But this is seldom so. Just as in decision making, where often the most diffi-

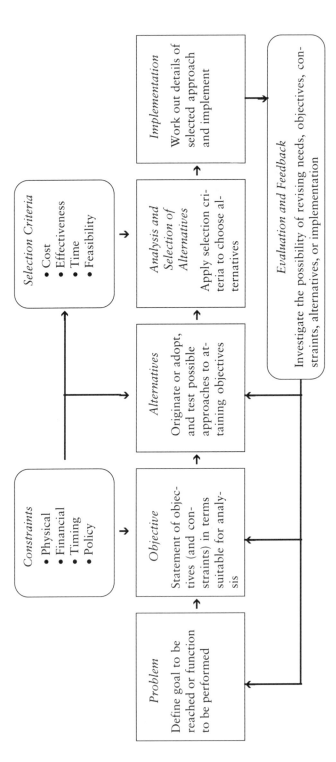

FIGURE 5.1. COMPONENTS OF ANALYSIS.

SOURCE: Adapted from "Introduction to Systems Analysis," by J.K. Parker, Appendix C to *Applying Systems Analysis in Urban Government: Three Case Studies* (Report prepared by the International City Management Association for HUD, March 1972), p. 5. Reprinted by permission.

cult task is to secure consensus concerning the goals or objectives of a program, the most difficult step in program analysis may be defining the need to be met. Three experimental studies involving the ICMA demonstrate that urban officials have a tendency to generalize problems, making it difficult to state needs in specific enough form for analysis purposes.[4] Where local government does not have staff expertise in program analysis, outside experts may have to be employed to assist in defining the problem.

Because the task of problem formulation is difficult and obviously crucial to what follows—a solution to the wrong problem cannot be of much help—an issue paper may be prepared. An *issue paper* is as complete an assessment of all that is currently known about the problem or issue as the readily available data allow.[5] It might include the following kinds of questions:

- What are the sources of the problem? What forces are contributing to it?
- What is the magnitude of the problem? How many people or groups are affected? What will the problem's dimensions be in the future?
- Which specific groups (clientele) are affected by the problem? If other than the general public, what are the special characteristics (age, minority status, geographic location, income, education level) of the affected groups?
- Which other groups or agencies, particularly public, are working on the problem?
- Does the problem have political overtones?

An issue paper can go beyond problem definition to include objectives, evaluation criteria, alternatives, and recommendations for follow-up action. But its primary purpose is to present the carefully thought through dimensions of the problem, stating them in terms amenable to analysis.

Whether or not an issue paper is prepared, a problem must be defined as specifically as possible. For example, the generalized problem that a community has too little housing for low- and moderate-income families might be stated in more specific terms as the goal or objective of constructing 1,500 standard-quality renter housing units each year.[6] Or if the general problem is a rising crime rate, the objective might be to reduce serious juvenile crimes by 20 percent within a two-year period.

We should make two other points about problem definition. First, it is essential that the problem be one that is under the control of the city government. Although this may sound obvious, it is not always taken into account. For example, the general problem of unemployment in the city may not be something the city government by itself can realistically undertake to correct. Second, problem definition is a responsibility of top management and should not be left to technical specialists. This is not to say that analysts cannot help; experienced analysts can be of considerable value to decision makers in narrowing and identifying a problem. But the final definition must rest with top officials.

The following are examples of issues or problems that could be treated successfully with program analysis:[7]

- What is the most effective way of deploying limited police personnel? By geographic location? By time of day? By reported crime incidence?
- How many fire stations are needed? Where should they be located?
- What mix of health treatment programs is needed to serve a particular clientele?
- What specific equipment and routing should be used in the collection and disposal of solid waste?
- What type and size recreation facilities should be provided, and where should they be located in the community?

STATING THE OBJECTIVES AND CONSTRAINTS

In the second step the problem or need is converted into a set of measurable objectives that, when met, presumably will solve the problem. Statements of public objectives are likely to be vague and conflicting.[8] Objectives must be specific enough to be measurable, ordinarily in quantitative terms. Some possible objectives include

- Reducing traffic fatalities by 10 percent
- Reducing the average response time of a fire company by 10 percent
- Increasing the reading comprehension level of students finishing elementary school by 20 percent
- Reducing the number of complaints of missed garbage collection by 30 percent

Clear, straightforward formulations of objectives, like those above, develop from analysts' experience or from extensive discussion with decision makers and others knowledgeable about the topic.

It is very important that objectives do not predetermine which alternative will be used to deal with the problem. Whether means and end can be effectively separated in complex problems is debatable; still, an objective should say nothing about the means to be used in achieving the end.

At this point in the analysis more specific attention to the needs of client groups is necessary. If program analysis is to be sensitive to the political environment, which may well determine just how effective its outcome will be, particular attention must be paid to those who will benefit and those who potentially stand to lose from the program effort. Jacob Ukeles, former director of the Mayor's Management Advisory Board in New York City, refers to this as *client analysis*. He argues that groups should be differentiated by the degree to which they are likely to be affected by a decision: "Trade-offs are constructed on the basis of the net benefits and losses to the most highly impacted groups."[9] Among other things, this focus on the differential effects of programs may bring to the analysts' attention groups that are not particularly vocal in the political arena. Client analysis should be a continuous process, and it should begin in earnest at the point of specifying objectives. Citizen surveys, discussed in the next chapter, can serve as a useful aid in collecting information from clients.

Constraints also must be considered at this stage. Such things as time, financial, and physical limitations, as well as the restrictions imposed by past policies, must be taken into account. How much time is available, both for the analysis and for the implementation? What kinds of personnel needs will be required? What is the budget, again both for the analysis and for the problem resolution? Will new or remodeled physical structures be necessary? Do past municipal policies or commitments limit this particular administration? All of these considerations must be fed into the analysis at the time the objectives are established.

GENERATING ALTERNATIVES

Various potential courses of action must be developed within the existing constraints. How do analysts develop alternatives? There are a number of possible sources: guidance from top officials, brainstorming, consultation with other municipalities that have faced the same problem, discussion with governmental departments knowledgeable in the area, suggestions from interested community groups, professional literature, and suggestions from vendors and suppliers. For example, suppose the objective is to reduce juvenile car theft. Analysts might develop alternatives not only from the police department but also from officials in the courts, in the welfare department and other social service agencies, and in the school system, and from juveniles themselves.[10]

DEVELOPING SELECTION CRITERIA AND ANALYZING ALTERNATIVES

After a sufficient number of alternatives have been generated, each must be evaluated using appropriate criteria. This is a fairly straightforward step, which involves assessing each alternative's probable performance against each criterion and comparing the alternatives with one another on the basis of performance against the criteria.

So criteria must come first. At least four broad criteria are found in any analysis program: effectiveness, costs, time, and feasibility.

EFFECTIVENESS. — To gauge effectiveness we must devise measures that reveal how well an alternative achieves a program's objective. For example, does it increase the health and safety of citizens? Does it improve the condition of the streets? Does it increase citizens' satisfaction with recreational opportunities? In developing measures of program effectiveness, an analyst may select workload measures of physical capacity or change: tons of garbage collected, number of clients served, number of hospital beds filled, acres of park land. These indicators can be useful as a first step in assessing governmental performance, but they provide little or no information about effectiveness—how well a program's objectives are being met or how satisfied citizens are with public facilities and activities.

Following are some potential measures of urban service effectiveness.[11]

Public safety measures: average police response time; crime rates; crime clearance rates; number of traffic accidents, injuries, and fatalities; average response time for first-arriving fire company; and fire loss, including dollar value of property, injuries, and fatalities
Public health measures: communicable disease rate; infant mortality rate; air-quality standard
Public works measures: missed garbage collections per total collections; cleanliness of streets; smoothness of streets
Leisure and recreation measures: circulation of library books and number of persons participating in recreational programs per 1,000 population

Some of these criteria are better than others at measuring the degree to which real program objectives are met. For example, for ambulance, fire, and police services, response time often is used as a measure of effectiveness.

Costs. —Estimates of cost are essential in evaluating alternatives. This sounds simple: just add up the costs of personnel, materials, and overhead. Unfortunately, however, analysis incorporates several kinds of costs—opportunity costs, indirect costs, and capital versus operating costs, to name a few. There are several guidelines for figuring the costs of an alternative:[12]

- Separate capital from operating expenses. Where capital costs are necessary, these may have to be prorated over a period of several years.
- Identify both direct and indirect costs. Indirect costs are easy to overlook, but expenditures for staff support, fringe benefits, maintenance, and usage of space should be included in the total cost.
- Omit sunk costs—costs that have been previously incurred. In this regard analysis differs from strict cost accounting.
- Consider funds required over a multiyear period to obtain a complete picture of an alternative's cost commitment.
- Indicate the source of funding. An alternative may be paid out of several identifiable sources, such as state or federal project grants. Some types of funds are easier to obtain than others.

Opportunity costs and external costs are important. The use of resources in a particular way precludes their use for some other purpose. Thus foregone opportunity costs must be estimated. Finally, various alternatives may have cost consequences beyond what is spent by the city government. A particular proposal to construct a new street might bring neighborhood deterioration, for example. Unfortunately, negative consequences are difficult to anticipate and thus frequently are omitted in cost considerations.

Combining Benefits and Costs. —Before an assessment of options is complete, some effort could be made to relate costs to benefits. If dollar figures can be assigned to all costs and all benefits, a benefit-cost ratio can be calculated. Often, genuine benefit-cost analysis is beyond the capability of most city staffs because it requires a greater knowledge of applied economics than these staffs have (see below).

TIME AND FEASIBILITY.—The final two criteria for evaluating alternatives are time and feasibility. Time can be thought of as a cost, of course. Beyond that, some options may take considerably longer to meet the objective than will others. This is especially important if public officials are under pressure to produce quick results.

Considering feasibility means carefully assessing potential veto points along the way to implementation. For example, who has to agree to this proposal? Which groups will oppose the alternative? Will the city council buy this solution? Which political pitfalls await this option? The best solution imaginable is of no value if it cannot be implemented. The political feasibility of a project is so important to its success that we consider it in a separate subsection at the end of this section.

IMPLEMENTING THE SELECTED APPROACH

Whenever possible, a pilot implementation of a preferred alternative should be tried before the solution is adopted on a continuing or permanent basis.[13] Where this is not feasible, the alternative should be implemented on a careful, planned basis with constant monitoring and evaluation. Implementation does not follow automatically once a policy has been formulated; it is often a difficult and frustrating process that is full of pitfalls.

Analysis can help uncover potential pitfalls by identifying the issues and problems that may affect the implementation of a selected alternative.[14]

- How many agencies (internal and external to the city) must participate or cooperate to ensure successful implementation?
- Does the selected alternative visibly affect certain clientele groups in an adverse way? (Is there a cutback in services, for example?)
- Does the alternative threaten the power or privileges of important officials? Are employees' jobs threatened? If so, what reaction might be expected from employees' organizations?
- Are there complicated legal questions?
- To what extent has public debate galvanized opinion for or against the alternative?[15]

Some authorities suggest that municipalities prepare an implementation feasibility analysis. Analysts often fail to appreciate the potential implementation difficulties that may arise when a new program is undertaken. The problems of implementation are not overstated; the lack of concern for implementation feasibility is a primary cause of unsuccessful program analyses.

Evaluating and Providing Feedback

One of the final steps in the analysis process is the careful, continuous evaluation of the implemented alternative. Is the program alleviating the original problem? Analysis does not stop with implementation; it is a dynamic process that requires ongoing assessment of consequences. The feedback arrows in figure 5.1 graphically convey this notion. In fact, an iterative approach is a basic characteristic of analysis for policy decisions: "If none of the alternatives originally considered can achieve the goals, further alternatives must be sought and, if that fails, the goals must be reexamined and possibly lowered."[16]

Program Analysis and Political Feasibility

Although feasibility was identified as one of the critical criteria for evaluating alternatives, the preceding discussion did not do justice to its enormous significance. At first glance, it may sound simple enough to consider who might or might not support a given policy option or what group might have enough power to block a particular course of action. But the history of program analysis clearly reveals otherwise; the primary reason many programs never see the light of day is not technical quality but lack of political feasibility. Arnold Meltsner, a specialist in the study of policy analysis, argues that one of the difficulties in considering political feasibility is the lack of a convenient methodology. He offers a three-step approach, as follows.[17]

Determining the Relevant Environment. —The analyst begins by defining a policy space or policy issue area. An issue area goes beyond what the need or problem is to include those publics and actors that dominate this area. If the issue area is economic development, for example, community financial interests certainly have to be taken into account. Or if the city is interested in private collection of solid waste, the most salient affected group clearly is those municipal employees who might lose their jobs.

Organizing Political Information. —Meltsner recommends the paper-and-pencil scenario as an organizing device. As we noted in the last chapter, preparing a scenario of the future is more an art than a science. It requires speculation and conjecture based on the best knowledge available. The task can be made easier, however, by developing a set of basic categories about which information is needed: actors, motivations, beliefs, resources, sites, and exchanges.

Actors are those individuals, groups, and coalitions most likely to be affected by and interested in the policy problem. At first, perhaps three groups appear: friends, enemies, and fence sitters. Soon the dynamics of the process push fence sitters to take sides. Some, of course, have much more to gain or lose than others, but it may not be easy to determine just how strong the concerns of particular actors are.

What are the *motivations* of the various policy actors? What do they really want? What will they settle for? What will it take to mobilize a fence sitter? The problem here is that clever political actors don't tip their hand. The more an actor can mask his or her policy preferences, the better his or her bargaining position in many cases.

Closely related to an actor's motivations are *beliefs, values,* and *attitudes.* People perceive the political world through a particular frame of reference or belief system. Such beliefs may be encapsulated in a few dominant words, such as "local control" or "the advantages of competition." For example, a general view that economic development leads to more or better jobs is pervasive among business leaders and may be used by certain groups to push subsidies or tax breaks for development.

Almost every policy actor possesses something another actor may want. These are considered *resources* and are used to satisfy another actor's motivations. Resources range from the material (e.g., a job with higher wages) to the symbolic (e.g., appointment to a prestigious committee). Information and even political skill might be among the resources available to some policy activists. The analyst must try to determine which specific resources the skillful actor may use to gather support and build coalitions.

Meltsner mentions the site for the final decision as another important element in political analysis. By site he means not only the arena (e.g., city council committee) but also the location in time. As discussed in chapter 1 with the rise of off-budget enterprises in development policy, the decision arena might be a quasi-official body of some sort or even a private group, rather than the city government. At times, even a meeting with an agency head would constitute a critical site.

Finally we come to *exchanges.* The analyst must predict or estimate likely outcomes based on all the information available. In particular, he or she must identify the possible areas of agreement or conflict so that alternative proposals that will achieve the requisite political support can be considered. From this perspective, developing alternatives implies anticipating the sorts of coalitions that are likely to form around a particular option. These coalitions are built mostly through a series of exchanges —side payments, tradeoffs, or policy modifications. The analyst tries to ascertain what exchanges might be needed to produce a certain outcome. Which group wants what? How much will this group accept? How much political support from certain actors is critical for success? There is nothing exact here; the analyst must rely on experience and judgment, while hoping that most of the relevant facts have been collected.

INTEGRATING POLITICAL KNOWLEDGE. —The third and final step in the assessment of political feasibility is to incorporate the knowledge of the political process in the analysis itself. How should this be done? Much depends on the local situation, of course, but two general possibilities exist. The analyst may make a decision based on quantitative or economic reasoning and then modify that answer in the light of political considerations. The more difficult but also probably more effective strategy is to introduce politics at each stage of the analysis. Thus the analyst would consider political feasibility in problem definition, in identification of alternatives, and in the recommendation of preferred policy alternatives.

RESISTANCE TO CHANGE

As former city official and political scientist David Ammons notes: "An analyst who has devoted hundreds of hours to a project only to see his recommendations rejected is sure to feel disappointment."[18] As someone who has been there, Ammons suggests that disappointment is natural, but warns that failure should not lead to discouragement. Resistance to analysis will always come from

- Persons benefiting from current policies
- Persons benefiting from current operational inefficiencies
- Persons who fear new technologies or new operational methods
- Persons who are or feel incapable of applying or understanding the results of analytic techniques
- Persons who dominate the decision-making process through charisma or brokering abilities and prefer not to have that dominance threatened by the introduction of a new element in the process.[19]

No one said it was going to be easy. Change never is, and change lies at the heart of analysis.

Analysis at Work

Based on a 1988 survey of senior municipal officials—city managers, finance directors, and chief administrative officers—Gregory Streib and Theodore H. Poister provide information about perceived need for management improvement in cities.[20] The 400-plus respondents were asked to rate a number of management tools regarding the amount of improvement needed. The areas mentioned in need of "great improvement" most often were associated with the analysis process. More specifically, these officials identified management areas in need of considerable improvement: (1) revenue base, 56 percent; (2) information management, 40 percent; (3) planning capability, 38 percent; (4) staff development, 34 percent; and (5) analytical capabilities, 34 percent. Clearly analysis is needed to run the modern city.

Fortunately, an abundance of analytical tools are available to decision makers to help manage urban America.

APPLICATIONS

Analysis does not have to be highly sophisticated to be useful. All too often students of urban management and practitioners steer clear of analysis because they have heard terms such as beta coefficients, the linear model, factor analysis, time-series analysis, and so on. Yes, a number of statistical techniques can take a while to master. On the other hand, there are many more that can be mastered fairly quickly with a bit of patience and practice. The case study that follows provides an example of analysis in action.

CASE STUDY

CALCULATING A "STAFFING FACTOR"

MANY of the services provided by local governments are not limited to a 40-hour-per-week operation. The municipal pool may be open 56 hours per week. Police and fire services must be provided around-the-clock, 168 hours a week. How many employees are needed to fill a *position* to provide extended-hour or uninterruptable service, taking into account vacations, sick leave, holidays, and so forth. In order to determine the number of employees needed, a "staffing factor" must be calculated. The staffing factor is the number of employees needed to provide full coverage of a position.

You are a policy analyst in the parks and recreation department. The city manager wants to know how many lifeguards are going to be needed to staff the new indoor municipal pool. You are told that there must be two lifeguards on duty at all times and that the pool will be open 8 hours per day, 7 days a week, year-round. A full-time lifeguard will receive 1 week of paid vacation and 5 days of sick leave per year. Part-time lifeguards will receive the same benefits, but prorated on the basis of number of hours worked. To avoid overtime pay, the assumption is that no employee will work more than 40 hours per week. How many lifeguards do you need?

The first step in the calculation of the staffing factor is based on the formula

$$E = P - A$$

where E = the number of hours actually worked by the average employee (i.e., effective hours), P = the number of paid hours per employee per year, and A = the average number of hours of paid absences per employee per year (vacation, sick leave, etc.). In the example above, P = 40 hours per week × 52 weeks per year = 2,080. A = 40 hours of vacation and 40 hours of sick leave = 80. $E = P - A = 2,000$.

The second step uses E above to calculate the staffing factor:

$$\text{Staffing Factor} = \frac{Hours\ per\ year\ of\ operation}{E}$$

From information supplied to you, hours per year of operation = 8 hours per day × 7 days a week × 52 weeks a year = 2,912.

$$\text{Staffing Factor} = \frac{2,912}{2,000} = 1.45$$

In order to staff one of the lifeguard positions, one full-time and one approximately half-time employee, or an equivalent combination of part-time employees, will be needed to provide extended, uninterrupted service. But because two lifeguards must be on duty at all times, you need the equivalent of 2.90 employees, or

$$\text{Staffing Factor} = \frac{Hours\ per\ year\ of\ operation}{E}$$

16 hours per day × 7 days a week × 52 weeks = 5,824 hours.

$$\text{Staffing Factor} = \frac{5,824}{2,000} = 2.90$$

SOURCE: This case is adapted from information and formulas provided by David N. Ammons, *Administrative Analysis for Local Government: Practical Applications of Selected Techniques* (Athens, Ga.: Carl Vinson Institute of Government, University of Georgia, 1991), chap. 16.

Earlier in this chapter we mentioned that "opportunity costs" should be considered when evaluating various alternatives. When one allocates X dollars to project Y, those dollars cannot be spent on project Z. How does one measure opportunity costs? Although not a perfect measure, one way of measuring opportunity costs, particularly for developmental policies where the city has funds to invest, is to compare the return or benefit from a project to the city with the return on the funds if they had been otherwise invested, say, in a pension fund. At a minimum, the true cost of a multiyear project must be calculated. It is not true, for example, that a $100,000 project that generates $10,000 per year will pay for itself in ten years.

MORE ADVANCED APPLICATIONS

Two areas of municipal service where analytic techniques seem to work well are in locating fire stations and improving equipment-dispatching practices. A report prepared for the Department of Housing and Urban Development (HUD) claims that over fifty communities have used analysis to tackle problems involving station siting and dispatch policy.[21] In some instances cities achieved cost savings by eliminating certain fire units; in other instances changes in response areas and in dispatching systems led to significant improvements in operations. A guide prepared by HUD for fire chiefs and local government executives lists other advantages of analysis for the firefighting service:

- Proposed changes are easier to sell to the council and the public when you have available a well-prepared analysis with statistics, computer printouts, and charts.
- Computer models allow analysts to respond to skeptics and opponents who propose alternative plans.
- If a city is using productivity bargaining—tying pay increases to gains in productivity—analysis can help identify areas where increased productivity is wanted.
- Analysis is a way of pretesting ideas safely and inexpensively before proposing them publicly.

The HUD publication acknowledges certain risks in the process: criticism from those who oppose change, tough political fights, potential legal complications, and the need to hire outside consultants. An example of political opposition occurred in Trenton, New Jersey, where one fire union official wrote to the local newspaper:

What happens if the firehouse that houses the engine which responds to your neighborhood is closed? Who are you going to hold responsible when your child, mother, father, wife, or husband perishes in a fire because two bright men with their pencils and computers say that the equipment we have is too much for a city of this size and the manpower too great?[22]

Despite reservations and even considerable resistance from firefighters, analysis is being used to reduce fire units and relocate stations. One successful application took place in Wilmington, Delaware.

CASE STUDY

WILMINGTON'S FIRE STATION PROBLEM

In the early 1970s a decision was made by the city of Wilmington, Delaware (population 80,386), to suspend construction on several new planned fire stations pending a reassessment of their locations. An analysis was undertaken by a project team led by the director of program analysis in Wilmington's Department of Planning and Development. This provided an opportunity to field-test a deployment technique developed by the New York City Rand Institute that required the use of two separate computer-based models. One, the Parametric Allocation model, uses only a limited amount of data regarding the available firefighting resources to determine how many fire companies should be located in each region of the city. The other, the Firehouse Site Evaluation model, uses the coordinates of incident locations, travel times, and various potential places within the region to identify the best coordinates for a new station. In this case over a hundred different potential fire company locations were compared using the siting model.

The program analysis determined that at least one fire company could be eliminated, making it possible to close an old station. The project team further recommended that five of the seven remaining engine companies be moved to new firehouses as they were built. The mayor (the city has a strong-mayor form) accepted the recommendations and directed that negotiations with the firefighters' union proceed with the hope of eliminating two fire companies. An eight-member negotiating team was formed, headed by an assistant city attorney who was an experienced labor negotiator. No layoffs were proposed; reductions were to be made by attrition (seventeen current vacancies in the fire department would also be frozen). The elimination of the two fire companies was presented along with other pay and benefit proposals as a package to be accepted or rejected as a whole. Although the city proposed a compromise of a one-company reduction, the proposal was rejected by a vote of the union.

After further negotiation and subsequent rejection by the firefighters, the city acted unilaterally to eliminate one engine company. This step removed the final point of contention from the contract, and a settlement was reached quickly.

Within a year or so following the cut, the commissioner of public safety, the fire chief, and most firefighters agreed that the move had produced no negative effects. It was estimated that the elimination of the engine company would save the city about $240,000 a year, not including pension costs.

SOURCE: Adapted from Warren E. Walker, *Changing Fire Company Locations: Five Implementation Case Studies* (Washington, D.C.: U.S. Department of Housing and Urban Development, 1978), 25–40.

Analysis does not always work so well. Especially where objectives are less well defined and the problem cuts across different agencies, achieving good results from systematic analysis can be difficult. The case study that follows involves an analysis of drug-abuse treatment options in Miami-Dade County, Florida.

CASE STUDY

DRUG-ABUSE TREATMENT OPTIONS IN MIAMI

THIS relatively complex analysis was initiated by the county manager's office of Metropolitan Dade County, Florida. The project team consisted of members of the Community Improvement Program Office (a staff office to the manager) and consultants from the Urban Institute. The general problem: how to treat hard-drug users most effectively. Drug education and other preventive measures were excluded from the study because little was known about their effectiveness and because time was too limited. Instead the analysis focused on the county's treatment program (primarily Methadone detoxification and maintenance) and the programs in four private treatment centers.

At the outset it was discovered that none of the programs had well-articulated objectives, standard criteria for evaluation, or satisfactory data on their operations. Two primary effectiveness criteria were finally established: (1) the number of person-months free of heroin use and (2) the number of persons and person-months free of the use of any addictive drugs, including Methadone. Notice that the number of people completing treatment was not included as a criterion—graduation did not ensure rehabilitation.

The identification of alternatives was prominently shaped by the gap between the estimated number of addicts and the number enrolled in existing programs. Essentially three different degrees of expansion of existing programs were considered.

Program costs turned out to be difficult to estimate primarily for two reasons: some costs of the programs were not charged against them, and some specialists' services were being shared with other programs. Future costs were also tricky to develop.

Estimating program effectiveness was the most difficult task. It included four phases:

1. Estimating the magnitude of the problem (need assessment)
2. Evaluating existing treatment programs
3. Collecting effectiveness information from similar jurisdictions
4. Estimating the likely effectiveness of each alternative

Because of the diversity of organizations and approaches involved, the most time-consuming part was evaluating existing county programs. Also, problems arose in obtaining the needed data on current programs, including evidence of continued drug use, arrests, dropout rates, and length of time in the program. Two programs would not even release patients' names, and locating former patients for follow-up data proved especially difficult. Finally the analysts developed costs and estimated effectiveness for a period of five years for a number of combinations of treatment program expansions. The analysis did not recommend one treatment program over another; instead it provided three basic alternatives (low, medium, or high costs) for various combinations of current programs.

As it turned out, the county did not formally act on any of the alternatives, for reasons that were unspecified in the original report. Apparently the additional costs of program expansion may have been instrumental in the decision. Still, one recommendation that involved identifying and treating addicts processed through the county jail formed the basis for a new treatment diversion program as a substitute for prosecution.

The authors of the report commented on the importance of soliciting the cooperation of the agencies affected by the analysis. Early drafts of the report, for example, contained certain errors and assumptions that could have been checked had agency personnel participated as part of the analysis team. Also, the authors felt that the analysis would have been expedited had agency personnel been actively involved in collecting and analyzing cost and effectiveness data for their own programs.

SOURCE: Adapted from Harry Hatry, Louis Blair, Donald Fisk, and Wayne Kimmel, *Program Analysis for State and Local Governments* (Washington, D.C.: Urban Institute, 1975), 127–38.

BENEFIT-COST ANALYSIS

Although few municipalities except the very largest are likely to undertake a formal, full-blown benefit-cost study, it is not unusual for this type of analysis to appear in studies done by outside consultants. And the method has long been applied to certain large-scale public improvements, especially water resource projects. So local public managers need to know something of what is involved in producing a benefit-cost study. In essence the analysis calls for the calculation of a ratio that reflects the relationship between all foreseeable benefits and all known and estimated costs. If the benefits exceed the costs, presumably the project is worth pursuing; if not, a strong argument can be made against the undertaking.

Although in theory benefit-cost analysis seems functional, in practice it generates a number of problems. At least two basic limitations are generally acknowledged.[23] First, the process can become subjective, especially where a number of intangible benefits accrue to the proposal. Omit these potential benefits and the ratio may be badly biased; include them and you risk being arbitrary. Analysts, then, must use common sense in deciding what to include, especially as potential benefits. A second problem relates to the issue of who pays the costs and who receives the benefits. It is very difficult to incorporate allocational and distributional considerations in benefit-cost analysis. For example, if a proposal involves a redistribution of income, a straightforward summation of costs and benefits does not reveal the true impact of the project.

A quick example involving deregulation illustrates some of these problems.[24] In 1981 the National Highway Traffic Safety Administration

(NHTSA) announced it intended to either eliminate the front-bumper crash standard for automobiles or lower it from 5 miles per hour to 2.5 miles per hour. As a justification the agency cited benefit-cost studies showing that scrapping the bumper standard would save consumers about $65 over a ten-year period, the result of increased gas savings from lighter cars. But the NHTSA's calculations omitted, among other things, an almost certain rise in auto insurance premiums if such a change were made. According to one insurance company, the $65 supposedly saved with lighter bumpers would end up costing $110 in increased insurance premiums over a five-year period.

The moral of this story, and the appropriate caveat for local decision makers, is that benefit-cost studies must be scrutinized carefully to ensure that all possible benefits and costs are included in the analyses. There may be occasions, of course, where such studies provide useful information.

CASE STUDY

A Benefit-Cost Analysis of the Supported-Work Experiment

In 1972 New York City began an important policy innovation in the personnel area, the *supported-work social experiment*. Sponsored by the Vera Institute of Justice, the experiment involves the voluntary use of ex-addicts and ex-offenders to deliver public goods and services in the city.

In 1974 about 1,400 people were in the program. Most were hired by a private nonprofit organization set up by Vera and funded partly by federal, state, and local agencies and through work contracts arranged with the city. Those participating in the program were paid about $100 a week. All ex-addicts were required to have been enrolled in a drug treatment program for at least three months before joining the operation. Anyone who had worked for twelve months during the two years prior to entry was not eligible.

The program has two goals. The first is obvious: to increase future employment prospects for participants. The second is to provide the city with valuable public goods and services. The fifty different projects undertaken by the experiment include painting curbs for fire zones and constructing wooden traffic barriers for the police department. The economic value of these activities can be estimated roughly by determining what the city had been paying for these services in the past.

In the mid-1970s Lee Friedman, who was responsible for economic studies at the Vera Institute, did a benefit-cost analysis of the two supported activities. Data were gathered on 120 sample participants. Friedman actually calculated two benefit-cost ratios, one a social benefit-cost figure and the other a taxpayer ratio. The second one was thought to be more politically realistic, since it compared how much taxpayers gave up to operate the program with what they received from it. The taxpayers' benefit-cost ratio is shown below. For each person-year, Friedman estimated the program was worth $6,920. Most of this came from the value of the goods and services produced by the participants. The other categories of benefits—welfare reduction, increased taxes collected, and the savings from crime reduction—were calculated primarily by comparing program participants with a control group of similar individuals not included in the experiment. In this sense the supported-work effort was a true social experiment. The costs associated with conducting the program were $6,131 for each participant, mostly participant salaries and benefits. So the ratio of benefits to costs was 1.13, meaning, of course, that benefits exceeded costs by 13 percent.

The supported-work experiment has been successful and is now being tried in thirteen other cities. It also provides a good example of how benefit-cost calculations can assist in evaluating the usefulness of a social program.

Benefits:
1. Public goods and services	$4,519
2. Welfare reduction	1,797
3. Increased income taxes collected	311
4. Savings from crime reduction	293
Total	$6,920

Costs:
1. Supported-work costs	$6,131

Benefit-cost ratio: 1.13

SOURCE: Adapted from Lee S. Friedman, "An Interim Evaluation of the Supported Work Experiment," *Policy Analysis* 3 (Spring 1977): 147–70.

Management Information Systems and Computers

Accurate analysis demands accurate information. But not only is information costly; it also is not easily available. Obtaining reliable, continuous, and systematic information for problem solving requires a conscious effort to develop an information-gathering process or system.

Electronic data processing (EDP) and automated data processing (ADP) generally refer to the same thing: the use of computers to process certain kinds of information. At a higher level we have information systems, of which there are two basic types: the urban information system (UIS) and the management information system (MIS). The UIS essentially represents a data bank of wide-ranging information covering the city (or metropolitan area) as a whole. Its purpose is largely to assist in planning and community development. The system might include a variety of census data, some at the block level, and a multitude of items collected by the city on a geographic basis.

A type of UIS that is growing in popularity is the geographic information system (GIS). A GIS is a computerized mapping system that aids in spatial analysis. "When you consider that at least 80 percent of the information collected by local governments relates back to a particular location, the management promise of GIS comes into sharper focus."[25] In Brevard County, Florida, a GIS is used to display parcels of land, roads, water and sewer lines, zoning, and topography. In addition, county officials can use the GIS for other management purposes. A point on the map can be accessed; and the road maintenance schedule can be determined. Decision makers employ the GIS technology to optimize school bus routes, for fire substation siting, to redraw political boundaries at reapportionment time, and to map the outbreak of diseases. In South Carolina a GIS is being used to guide decisions concerning economic development activities, where to build roads and extend water and sewer lines, and so forth. Eventually, the GIS will be accessible to local governments in South Carolina through work stations. While GISs are costly and are often plagued by technical and political problems (see below), they hold considerable promise for the future.

The second major type of information system, the management information system (MIS), is a tool for internal decision making and control. In the early 1980s, for example, the city of Dearborn, Michigan, installed a microcomputer system called Public Services Network. It incorporates twelve terminals located in agencies that handle requests for service. When the operator keys in particular information, the system routes the problem to the proper agency, eliminates duplicate requests, and permits the aggregation of data that reveal how much time was spent on each request. Thus at budget time Dearborn's deputy director of public works was able to say, "Mr. Mayor, of the 40,000 requests for service that we received, 27 percent went to Parks. And we can say unequivocally, last year we spent $100,000 for tree removal and $50,000 for utility maintenance."[26]

Another way of distinguishing among information systems is by their level of sophistication.[27] At the base, or first level, is the use of automated data-processing techniques to perform routine repetitive administrative tasks—utility billing, payroll calculations, property accounting, and licensing, for example. The second level of sophistication includes support for planning and control of real-time internal management operations—scheduling, dispatching, allocating, and monitoring traffic control and emergency vehicle usage. The emphasis here is on a rapid response capability, which requires an on-line, real-time computer application. A third level of usage is for strategic planning and scheduling. This level involves simulation models and perhaps the software capacity to perform the program evaluation review technique (PERT) and the critical-path method (CPM), techniques designed to manage and control large-scale projects over a long period of time.

APPLICATIONS

Computer usage in local government is quite widespread. Kenneth Kraemer and Alana Northrop, for example, report that city governments use computers for 450 different computer applications. The average city has about eighty such applications operational.[28] Based on a 1988 survey of about 5,000 city officials in forty-six leading-edge cities in computer usage, Kraemer and Northrop found that usage was highest in core administrative departments—finance, budgeting, and personnel—and in revenue-related departments such as treasury, assessment, and utilities. Among line departments, the most frequent computer users were libraries, police, and public works.[29] Most applications, especially in small cities,[30] were still at the base level: payroll, utility billing, accounting, and tax assessment. Computer use at higher levels in small cities was far less common,[31] although the literature contains a growing number of examples of microcomputer applications. The small community of Olathe, Kansas, for example, uses six microcomputers plus a large mainframe to develop an information system for its public works department, including a vehicle management system (which tracks vehicle costs by month and operating cost per mile and provides a lifetime repair history, among other functions), a sanitation commercial route balancing system, and a pavement evaluation system (which tracks street pavement conditions by block).[32]

Another example of EDP use at the second level of application is the use of computerized refuse vehicle routing in Fort Lauderdale, Florida.[33] The key to this operation is the Census Bureau's geographic base file, DIME (dual independent map encoding), which gave the city ready access to a street network file. The DIME file had to be verified and updated, but the city manager reported it to be an excellent tool for supporting computer-based packages. The manager also indicated that this computerized system was expected to improve routing, equalize crew workloads, and generally ensure more efficient refuse service.

CASE STUDY

Police Computer Applications in Tulsa

In recent years, city officials in Tulsa, Oklahoma (1990 population 367,302), have looked at innovative approaches to problem solving, many of which have involved the computer. A number of applications have been made in the police department. A primary installation includes a sophisticated information retrieval component known as the Tulsa Regional Automated Criminal Information System (TRACIS), which permits on-line inquiries for criminal offense data. The system is heavily used; operators, working twenty-four hours a day, six days a week, respond to an average of 22,000 requests each week. One feature of the system, the Quick Record Check, provides a short rundown on a car or person, giving stolen vehicle information and current warrants and arrest records. If an officer is following a suspect car, for example, the license plate number can be called in for a check that reveals all the information about the vehicle.

Another computer application, the Arrest Detail Screen (ARDET), provides a complete arrest background and an MO file, which lists the suspect's identifiable characteristics and special methods of operation, the type of weapon used, witnesses, and what was said. With up to 800 burglaries reported monthly in Tulsa, ARDET receives plenty of use.

Interfaced with the TRACIS system is an automated microfiche retrieval system. This unit can store up to 200,000 master files filled with crime information, mug shots, fingerprints, and arrest records. FBI and Oklahoma State Bureau of Investigation rap sheets are also in the system.

A Computer Assisted Dispatch System (CADS), involving two minicomputers, is used to dispatch police calls, handle complaints, and keep tabs on officer activity. When a call comes in, the description and location of the offense appear on the dispatcher's screen. Because the dispatcher always knows the location of each unit, he or she can send the closest available car to answer the call. With about 900 incoming calls a day, the automated dispatching system is essential. CADS also includes information from the city's 911 emergency telephone system. When a citizen calls the 911 number requesting fire, police, or ambulance assistance, a single button transfers the call directly to the dispatcher's screen.

In addition to their obvious functional benefits, the police department's computers have the advantage of allowing detailed analyses of high crime areas, analyses that may suggest the need for more intensive police coverage. In all, the department has come to rely heavily on the computer as a vital tool for decision making, management, and control.

SOURCE: Adapted from Carole H. Hicks, "The Broad Scope of Computer Usage in City Government," *Current Municipal Problems* 7 (1980–81): 191–96.

ASSESSING THE VALUE OF COMPUTERS

Underlying the interest in information systems is the assumption that management can make more rational decisions if a volume of information is readily at hand. How has this worked in practice?

Many local officials apparently like computers. Among computer users in 46 representative cities, about two-thirds have reported that the quality of services is either excellent or good.[34] Still, with over a quarter of municipal computer users rating their systems as fair or poor, there is considerable room for improvement. James Danziger, an authority on public-sector computing, believes that the computer's potential for aiding local government is high.[35] He nonetheless lists several ways in which the presumed advantages of computerization have failed to materialize. Based on a study of computer applications in twelve cities and counties around the country, he finds little evidence that EDP saves money, for example. This has been so primarily because anticipated reductions in staff generally have not happened. Danziger also suggests that EDP can stimulate the collection and storage of large amounts of data that no one really needs. And finally he indicates that a reliance on EDP can increase the tendency of supervisors to evaluate subordinates' performance more on quantitative than on qualitative grounds. Such a practice could actually reduce the quality of service. Danziger concludes with a call for more systematic inquiry on the part of social scientists to specify more clearly the consequences of particular computer applications under various conditions.

Responding to the call for more systematic research, Alana Northrop and colleagues assess the payoffs from computerization using a longitudinal study (1976 to 1988) of thirty-seven leading-edge cities in the United States. Their findings suggest that the payoffs of computerization have been "slow to be realized."[36] Nevertheless, compared to 1976, municipalities have been computerized: "By 1988, cities were experiencing the most payoffs in the areas of fiscal control, cost avoidance, and better interaction with the public.... A minimal level of payoffs were observed in nonfiscal management control and planning decisions. Some cost savings were cited as were payoffs in increased availability of information."[37]

Barry Bozeman and Stuart Bretschneider, authorities on the applications of management information systems, offer several guidelines to public users of MIS.[38] First, MIS planning should proceed incrementally, primarily because of the need to be sensitive to external control and political change. Second, public use of information technology should be designed to anticipate extraorganizational linkages. Otherwise MIS can become a small fiefdom of knowledge used by insiders to pressure top management. Third, the MIS chief should not report to the highest level in the organization. Top officials' concern with political cycles and quick results can undermine the long-term objectives of the system. Fourth, MIS should not generally be used to enhance managerial control. Such efforts will likely meet with resistance, which may diminish the value of MIS as a managerial tool. The fifth guideline echoes Danziger's position: MIS should not be justified on the basis of labor savings. Although sometimes sold that way, such systems have not been shown to bring significant labor-reduction benefits. Finally, MIS planning must be sensitive to staffing problems. Public agencies often do not fare well in competing with the private sector for highly trained specialists. Staffing will not take care of itself; personnel agencies must be aware of the special problems of recruitment and retention in the area of MIS.

Computer applications in the public sector will no doubt continue to grow, but many politicians and old-line bureaucrats still view computers and information systems with skepticism. Politicians have little interest in information systems because it has yet to be shown that these systems enhance the political control or leverage of political leaders.[39] In Houston, for example, creation of a GIS was in part hampered by the city council. "Elected to two-year terms, the council members 'never looked beyond the current year's operating budget.'"[40] Also, "it's equally important that the project show early results, because no politician wants to pay for a project that won't bear fruit during his or her term in office."[41] Oklahoma City is another case of where development of a GIS proceeded too slowly. The process was begun in the 1970s, but so many problems arose that in 1988 a consulting team was finally called in to "straighten things out."[42]

Why are lower-level officials distrustful of MISs? Economist Anthony Downs offers an answer that takes into account the power shifts caused by automated data systems.[43] First, lower- and intermediate-level officials tend to lose power to higher-level officials, especially staff, because an enormous amount of information flows to the top. Second, those who actually control automated data systems gain power at the expense of those who do not. Each operating department recognizes this and at least initially fights for its own computer system. In fact, with the growing use of microcomputers, the 1980s saw a big emphasis on decentralizing municipal computing. Still, most cities have retained a single central computing unit, and there is some evidence that the pendulum is swinging back toward more centralization, at least among large municipalities and business organizations.[44]

The Contributions and Limitations of Analysis

Experience with a variety of local government analysis efforts over the years has taught various lessons about conditions that affect the success of analysis:

- Commitment from top management is crucial.
- Financial support is needed; analysis is often expensive and usually requires the use of outside consultants.
- If consultants are used, the user organization must be prominently involved with the project.
- The selection and definition of the problem are extremely important. But even top-level officials frequently have trouble identifying quantifiable objectives and defining constraints.
- Projects that are narrowly defined and have few social and political implications are more likely to be successful.
- The availability of quality data especially over time is always problematic.

- Internal resistance may well develop from a fear of unwanted change.
- A basic conflict inevitably develops between the analyst's concern for a complete study and the decision maker's need for immediate results.

Because of these many limitations and constraints, skeptics often charge that analysis is not as helpful as it could be. As former Cincinnati city manager William Donaldson put it, "The core problem in municipal government is not knowing what to do but being able to *do* it ... the ability to implement is a much more difficult skill to acquire than having the ideas in the first place."[45] Donaldson's observations clearly point up how crucial implementation is in making program analysis work. What factors seem to contribute to successful implementation?

Richard Lehne and Donald Fisk assessed the results of ten analyses of local government operations. They wanted to establish whether these studies had any impact on local decisions and, if so, under what conditions. Findings suggest that the potential success of these analyses was determined largely by two sorts of influences: bureaucratic and technical.[46] The most important bureaucratic influences were the decision makers' interest and the immediacy of the decision. If a problem required prompt solution and top officials were vitally concerned, an analysis was likely to have greater effect. Certain technical considerations also were important: study timing, implementation considerations, and a well-defined problem. If a study appeared opportunely (e.g., during the budget cycle), addressed the problems of implementation, and focused on a narrowly defined situation, it was more likely to influence decisions than was a study lacking these characteristics.

Other institutional issues also influence the effectiveness of analysis.[47] First, the sole responsibility for analysis probably should not be placed in operating departments. These departments might be tempted to consider only alternatives that are in their self-interest. But those operating agency personnel who have considerable expertise in their field should be involved in the analysis, perhaps as members of an analysis team. What about city size? Any city with a population of 100,000 or more should consider creating a small central staff for program analysis. This office could also perform program evaluation. The central staff would need to effect a continuing and close relationship with the budget office—in some places management analysts actually are assigned to the budget office. No matter what its size, the central staff should report directly to the chief executive or have ready access to that office.

Should outside consultants be used? Smaller cities or large cities in which analysis has not been done previously may find external help indispensable. Outside firms may produce better results, but the studies are likely to cost more. Also, outsiders may not be in a city long enough to grasp the complexities of a situation and to deal with the problems of implementing their recommendations.

Some have argued for institutionalizing analysis in local government through the budgetary process.[48] This presumably would link analytic work more closely to the actual decision-making process; otherwise the use of analysis may be sporadic, chancy, and fragmented. An analysis-budgeting nexus can be an effective means of providing local decision makers with continuing analytic support for dealing with a broad range of local problems.

ANALYSIS, INFORMATION SYSTEMS, AND COMPUTERS IN PERSPECTIVE

Several problems and limitations associated with analysis, information systems, and computers have already been mentioned, and there are others as well. First, analysis and computers cannot replace judgment, eliminate value conflicts, or preclude the bargaining and compromises associated with the political process. As one practitioner writes:

> The ultimate solutions and decisions to most complex urban problems involve value judgments. They require decisions as to which problems are assigned what priority, as to the level of taxes that can and should be levied, and as to the allocation of available fiscal resources to such problems. There is no question that management science is helping governments concerned with their urban problems to identify and define them better.... However, the final decisions about such problems involve judgments as to what is "best" for the people. Under our form of government, these are political decisions, and despite the development of management science they will remain so.[49]

Despite problems and limitations, analysis and computer applications (technology) will play an increasing role in the urban future. Muddling through is not enough. If local governments are to be "reinvented," then much of that transformation will be influenced by analysis and the technology of today and tomorrow—the computer. So many of the key themes that Osborne and Gaebler discuss in *Reinventing Government*[50] require analysis and automation. An example may illustrate this point.

A prominent theme in *Reinventing Government* is "customer-driven" government. Citizens are the customers of local governments; as such, city officials must consider their needs, demands, and preferences. Computer technology is helping to build a better bridge of understanding between government and the citizenry. St. Charles, Missouri; Norwich, Connecticut; South Orange, New Jersey; Holden, Massachusetts; Torrance, California; Grand Junction, Colorado; and other cities use a software package known as "City Manager." This automated complaint management system lets city departments use personal computers to record, refer, and track complaints using personal computers. The cost of the software is only about $1,200.[51]

Owing in part to the efforts of Public Technology Inc. (PTI), a Washington, D.C., based nonprofit research and technology consulting organization, new developments in computer technology make possible a "well-connected" community. One innovation used in Kansas City, Missouri, and Hillsborough County, Florida, allows citizens to access local government data such as city council agendas; agency names, addresses, and telephone numbers; and procedural information via computers located in popular public access areas. According to the president of PTI, Costis Toregas, "Local Governments have just begun to realize the value of the information they gather as part of their duties and the needs of their citizens as consumers of this information."[52]

Summary

Analysis is a response to the demand for more than an incremental approach to urban decision making; it is based on the rational-comprehensive decision-making model. No matter what it's called—systems analysis, policy analysis, or program analysis—each operates with basically the same procedure. The problem must be defined, objectives must be stated clearly, constraints must be identified, alternatives must be proposed in the light of appropriate selection criteria, analysis and selection must take place, and the solution must be implemented. And the process does not end here. The implemented program must be evaluated, with feedback leading to revision where necessary.

Case studies show that the use of systems analysis in municipal decision making has not been as successful as one would hope. Why? Analysis often falters for political, bureaucratic, and technical reasons. Also, the structure of municipal governments may be working against the process. Possibly the entire analysis function should be separated from operating departments. This would free the procedure from departmental prejudices and resistance.

What should we conclude about the place of analysis in urban management? Several points seem worth noting. First, good analysis is hard to do. Given the severe limitations of data and methodological tools and the complex environment in which analysis must take place, there are more reasons to expect urban analysis to fail than to expect it to succeed.[53] Second, analysis is likely to be more successful under some conditions than under others: basically, the easier the problem, the greater the chance of success. Third, political feasibility is particularly critical for public-sector analysis. The crucial factor in successful implementation may be the analyst's skill in deciphering the complex political environment in which problem solving takes place.

But analysis should not be abandoned. We know how fragmented and disjointed the urban policymaking process can be. Although much of this may be unavoidable, anything that can give decision makers a larger, more comprehensive picture is needed. And the systems approach represents a step in this direction. On a more immediate note, the continuing pressure on public officials to get more results for the dollar surely demands that some problems be attacked on a rational, systematic basis. Analysis and computer technology are the tools required to foster change, to reinvent government.

Notes

1. Richard Rosenbloom and John Russell, *New Tools for Urban Management* (Boston: Graduate School of Business Administration, Harvard University, 1971), 6–7.

2. These steps are modified slightly from John K. Parker, "Introduction to Systems Analysis," in *Applying Systems Analysis in Urban Government: Three Case Studies* (Report prepared by the International City Management Association for HUD, March 1972), Appendix C, pp. 4-10; and E.S. Savas, "Systems Analysis—What Is It?" *Public Management* 51 (February 1969): 4.

3. This example comes from Savas, "Systems Analysis," 5.

4. *Applying Systems Analysis,* 3.

5. E.S. Quade, *Analysis for Public Decisions* (New York: American Elsevier, 1975), 69.

6. Adapted from Carter Bales and Edward Massey, "Analyzing Urban Problems," in Rosenbloom and Russell, *New Tools for Urban Management,* 280.

7. Taken from Harry Hatry, Louis Blair, Donald Fisk, and Wayne Kimmel, *Program Analysis for State and Local Governments* (Washington, D.C.: Urban Institute, 1975), 16–17.

8. Quade, *Analysis for Public Decisions,* 103.

9. Jacob Ukeles, "Policy Analysis: Myth or Reality," *Public Administration Review* 37 (May/June 1977): 227.

10. Parker, "Introduction to Systems Analysis," 7–8.

11. For a lengthy list of local public-service measures, see Robert Lineberry and Robert Welch, Jr., "Who Gets What: Measuring the Distribution of Urban Public Services," *Social Science Quarterly* 54 (March 1975): 700–712. Also see Harry Hatry, Louis Blair, Donald Fisk, John Greiner, John Hall, Jr., and Philip Schaenman, *How Effective Are Your Community Services?* (Washington, D.C.: Urban Institute and ICMA, 1977).

12. Bales and Massey, "Analyzing Urban Problems," 286–87.

13. Parker, "Introduction to Systems Analysis," 9.

14. Quade, *Analysis for Public Decisions*, 259.

15. Adapted from Hatry et al., *Program Analysis*, 100–101.

16. Quade, *Analysis for Public Decisions*, 20.

17. This section is adapted from Arnold J. Meltsner, "Political Feasibility and Policy Analysis," *Public Administration Review* 32 (November/December 1972): 859–67.

18. David N. Ammons, *Administrative Analysis for Local Government: Practical Application of Selected Techniques* (Athens, Ga.: Carl Vinson Institute of Government, University of Georgia, 1991), 156.

19. Ibid., 4.

20. Gregory Streib and Theodore H. Poister, "Established and Emerging Management Tools: A 12-Year Perspective," *Municipal Year Book 1989* (Washington, D.C.: ICMA, 1989), 51–53.

21. Jan Chaiken and William Bruns, *Improving Station Locations and Dispatching Practices in Fire Departments: A Guide for Fire Chiefs and Local Government Executives* (Washington, D.C.: U.S. Department of Housing and Urban Development, 1978), 5.

22. Quoted in ibid., 7.

23. Michael J. White, Ross Clayton, Robert Myrtle, Gilbert Siegel, and Aaron Rose, *Managing Public Systems: Analytic Techniques for Public Administration* (North Scituate, Mass.: Duxbury, 1980), 292.

24. This example comes from "Tales from the Cost-Benefit Wonderland," *Consumer Reports*, June 1981, 338.

25. Boyce Thompson, "The Dazzling Benefits (and Hidden Costs) of Computerized Mapping," *Governing*, December 1989, 43; for further discussion and analysis of GISs, see Jeffrey L. Brudney and Mary M. Bowen, "Do Geographic Information Systems Meet Public Managers' Expectations?" *State and Local Government Review* 24 (Spring 1992): 84–90.

26. Quoted in Steven Vignet, "Computers and Productivity," *Public Productivity Review* 8 (Spring 1994): 76.

27. Kenneth Kraemer et al., *Integrated Municipal Information Systems: The Use of Computers in Local Government* (New York: Praeger, 1974), 50–51.

28. Kenneth L. Kraemer and Alana Northrop, "Curriculum Recommen-

dations for Public Management Education in Computing: An Update," *Public Administration Review* 49 (September/October 1989): 447–48.

29. Ibid., 449.

30. Donald F. Norris, "Computers and Small Local Governments: Uses and Nonuses," *Public Administration Review* 44 (January/February 1984): 70–78.

31. James N. Danziger, "Evaluating Computers: More Sophisticated EDP Uses," *Nation's Cities* 13 (October 1975): 31–32.

32. William A. Ramsey, "Local Government Microcomputer Information Systems," *Public Administration Review* 44 (January/February 1984): 68–69.

33. Robert H. Bubier, "Modern Refuse Vehicle Routing," *Public Management*, August 1973, 10–12.

34. James Danziger, Kenneth Kraemer, Debora Dunkle, and John L. King, "Enhancing the Quality of Computing Service: Technology, Structure, and People," *Public Administration Review* 53 (March/April 1993): 161–69.

35. James N. Danziger, "Computers, Local Governments, and the Litany to EDP," *Public Administration Review* 37 (January/February 1977): 28–37.

36. Alana Northrop, Kenneth L. Kraemer, Debora Dunkle, and John Leslie King, "Payoffs from Computerization: Lessons Over Time," *Public Administration Review* 50 (September/October, 1990): 512.

37. Ibid.

38. Barry Bozeman and Stuart Bretschneider, "Public Management Information Systems: Theory and Prescription," *Public Administration Review* 46 (November 1986): 475–87.

39. Garry D. Brewer, "Systems Analysis in the Urban Complex: Potential and Limitations," in *Improving the Quality of Urban Management*, ed. Willis Hawley and David Rogers (Beverly Hills: Sage, 1974), 155.

40. Thompson, "The Dazzling Benefits (and Hidden Costs) of Computerized Mapping," 44.

41. Ibid.

42. Ibid.

43. Anthony Downs, "A Realistic Look at the Final Payoffs from Urban Data Systems," *Public Administration Review* 27 (September 1967): 204–10.

44. Danziger, Kraemer, Dunkle, and King, "Enhancing the Quality of Computing Service: Technology, Structure, and People," 161–69.

45. William V. Donaldson, "Donaldson on Policy Analysis," *The Bureaucrat* 10 (Fall 1981): 57.

46. Richard Lehne and Donald Fisk, "The Impact of Urban Policy Analysis," *Urban Affairs Quarterly* 10 (December 1974): 115–38.

47. Hatry et al., *Program Analysis*, 15–24.

48. Harry Hatry, "Can Systems Analysis Be Institutionalized in Local Governments?" in *Systems Analysis for Social Problems*, ed. Alfred Blum-

stein, Murray Kamras, and Armand Weiss (Washington, D.C.: Washington Operations Research Council, 1970), 61. For the opposing point of view, see Aaron Wildavsky, "Rescuing Policy Analysis from PPBS," in *Public Expenditures and Policy Analysis,* ed. Robert Haveman and Julius Margolis (Chicago: Markham, 1970), 461–81.

49. Reprinted from Matthias E. Lukens, "Emerging Executive and Organizational Responses to Scientific and Technological Developments," in *Governing Urban Society: New Scientific Approaches,* ed. Stephen Sweeney and James Charlesworth (Philadelphia: American Academy of Political and Social Science, monograph no. 7, 1967), 121. Copyright © 1967, by the American Academy of Political and Social Science. All rights reserved.

50. These themes are found as chapter titles in David Osborne and Ted Gaebler, *Reinventing Government* (Reading, Mass.: Addison-Wesley, 1992).

51. Len Strazewski, "City Manager Software Tracks Town Complaints," *City & State,* 26 February 1990, 17.

52. Len Strazewski, "Good Connections," *City & State,* 10 February 1992, 11–12.

53. Brewer, "Systems Analysis," 179.

Suggested for Further Reading

Ammons, David N. *Administrative Analysis for Local Governments.* Athens, Ga.: Carl Vinson Institute of Government, University of Georgia, 1991.

Behn, Robert D., and James W. Vaupel. *Quick Analysis for Busy Decision Makers.* New York: Basic Books, 1982.

Busson, Terry, and Philip Coulter, eds. *Policy Evaluation for Local Government.* Westport, Conn.: Greenwood, 1987.

Hatry, Harry, Louis Blair, Donald Fisk, and Wayne Kimmel. *Program Analysis for State and Local Governments.* 2d ed. Washington, D.C.: Urban Institute, 1987.

Patton, Carl V., and David S. Sawicki. *Basic Methods of Policy Analysis and Planning.* Englewood Cliffs, N.J.: Prentice Hall, 1986.

White, Michael J., Ross Clayton, Robert Myrtle, Gilbert Siegel, and Aaron Rose. *Managing Public Systems: Analytic Techniques for Public Administration.* Lanham, Md.: University Press of America, 1986.

6

Urban Service Delivery

To this point we have discussed urban decision making in general and how analysis works within that process. But urban policymaking does not stop with decision making. Decisions are only a prelude to further action by the city government—the development of programs and the delivery of services. Providing services always has been a major function of local government, and recent years have brought an even greater concern with service delivery as city officials have been forced to cut programs or find ways to operate more efficiently.

Urban service delivery is not particularly exciting. After all, collecting and disposing of solid waste, repairing streets, and providing water do not represent highly dramatic events in the life of a city. But some of the most vital services provided by any level of government are the responsibility of municipalities, and these activities consume a great deal of urban managers' time and attention. Cities are more concerned than ever with issues of service efficiency and accountability, as they find themselves caught between strong opposing pressures. Municipalities must respond to all the problems that arise out of an advanced state of urbanization just when they face shrinking resources, severe fiscal limitations, and public resistance to higher taxes.

In this chapter we look at several characteristics of service delivery, beginning with certain basic issues that cities must confront in providing even routine services. As we see, more is involved than just economy and efficiency. It is impossible to improve services if there are no measures of current output. How do cities assess their service performance? How do cities implement and evaluate new programs?

The Issues

Authorities almost unanimously agree on four urban service goals: efficiency, effectiveness, equity, and responsiveness.

Efficiency involves maximizing output from a given amount of input or resources. How much does it take to obtain the result we want? Efficiency is a process-oriented concept that assesses how inputs are converted into outputs; it says nothing about the degree to which goals are achieved or about citizen reaction to the service being provided.[1] *Effectiveness*, in contrast, is concerned with objectives; it reflects the extent to which goals are being met. It is a result-oriented concept focusing on how nearly the wanted outcome is being fulfilled without regard for the cost involved or resources used.[2]

The assessment of what municipalities do must involve both efficiency and effectiveness; we return to the question of maximizing both in a later section.

EQUITY

Levy, Meltsner, and Wildavsky present three ways of looking at equity.[3] First there is *equal opportunity,* in which all citizens receive the same level of service. Second is *market equity,* in which citizens receive services roughly proportional to the amount of taxes they pay. A third approach is *equal results,* in which an agency allocates its resources so that people are in an equal condition after the money is spent. Applied to the street department, equal opportunity requires the agency to spend about the same amount of money to repair or resurface streets in all sections of the city. Market equity allocates street maintenance resources in accordance with the taxes paid by each neighborhood. Equal results demands that areas of the community with substandard streets receive more attention until those streets are on a par with others in the city.

Levy and his colleagues suggest that these standards can be arrayed on a rough scale, with each requiring more resource redistribution than the previous one. Unquestionably the equity standard people adopt plays a crucial role in their judgment of agency performance. Generally speaking, most people today believe in the concept of equal opportunity. Market equity is a more conservative definition of equity, with equal results being more change oriented or liberal in nature.

In their analysis of schools, streets, and libraries in Oakland, the investigators Levy, Meltsner, and Wildavsky found differing equity outcomes by service area. Partly because of federal aid, the schools had moved a bit beyond equal opportunity to some equality of results. The street department, in contrast, had not quite reached equal opportunity, leaning more in the direction of market equity. And the libraries tended even more toward market equity. The authors concluded that the more an agency relies on the Adam Smith rule (which states that the frequency of demand determines the level of services), the more the resource distribution process approaches market equity. In libraries, for example, the authors found that new funds were allocated to branches with the highest circulations. "The initiative lies with the customer, as library patrons 'vote' with their cards. The more books they take out, the more money their branch receives."[4]

Services are distributed in response to a number of influences, and some neighborhoods are likely to receive more than others. But is there evidence that low-income and minority groups are systematically deprived in the allocation of service resources? Findings are mixed. In a study of parks and fire protection in San Antonio, it was reported that the "underclass hypothesis" did not fare well.[5] That is, parks and fire protection services were not systematically biased against the poor. What about schools? Some studies suggest public schools in black and low-income neighborhoods receive less money, employ less-qualified teachers, and have poorer facilities. Others have found that certain federally funded compensatory programs provide such schools with more resources than middle-class schools have. A similarly mixed situation has been reported regarding distribution of recreational facilities.[6] Recreational resources favor wealthy neighborhoods in some places; in others the poor seem to benefit more. In short, service delivery patterns produce what Robert Lineberry has labeled "unpatterned inequalities":[7] "who gets what varies from service to service [and city to city]."[8]

Whether or not maldistribution of services is intentional, certain groups have gone to court in an effort to produce changes in service distribution. If it can be shown that discriminatory service provision is the result of racial discrimination, the courts may grant relief. In *Hawkins* v. *Town of Shaw* (1971), the Fifth Circuit Court of Appeals held that Shaw had systematically deprived its black citizens of equal protection of the law by distributing unequally a number of urban services. Other similar suits have produced mixed results.[9] Service maldistribution apparently has to be quite severe for the courts to intervene, and racial bias almost undoubtedly has to be shown.

How might a city investigate questions of service equity? The city of Savannah, Georgia (population about 145,000), has developed a program to measure the equity of municipal services, as illustrated by the case study that follows.

Measuring Service Equity

Recognizing that neighborhoods in Savannah differ considerably in living standards, city manager Arthur Mendonsa began a program to address variations. Called the Responsive Public Services Program, it has two purposes. The first is to provide the city with a set of measures that reflect important differences in the quality of life by neighborhood. The second is to make a systematic effort to close the gap between neighborhoods by providing more public services to those areas with unusual needs.

The city was divided into twenty-eight planning units or neighborhoods, and the following conditions were measured in each:

- Level of crime—the number of basic property and violent crimes (e.g., burglary, robbery, car theft) per 1,000 population
- Level of fires—the number of structure fires per 1,000 population
- Cleanliness—ratings of lots, streets, and alleys on a cleanliness scale ranging from 0 to 5
- Water service—leaks per mile and the number of developed properties without water service or with water pressure problems
- Sewer service—sewage blockages per mile and the number of properties without sewer service
- Housing—percentage of dwelling units classified as substandard
- Recreation services—facilities needed to bring the area into compliance with city standards
- Drainage conditions—the number of structures that experience flooding on a two-year and ten-year storm frequency and the number of street segments closed on the same storm frequency
- Street conditions—miles of unpaved streets and surface condition of streets measured on a scale from good to bad

Differences among neighborhoods on these measures are not minor, as shown by the following examples:

- The lowest neighborhood crime rate was 5.6 per 1,000 inhabitants; the highest was 320 per 1,000 inhabitants.
- The lowest neighborhood fire rating was 0; the highest was 7.47 per 1,000 inhabitants.

- The lowest water leak rate was 0.4 leak per mile; the highest was 22.7 per mile.

The objective of the program is to bring inadequate neighborhoods up to an acceptable level compared to the city as a whole (neighborhoods are surveyed every two years). To help correct some of the deficiencies, the city has done the following for substandard neighborhoods:

1. Cleanliness—increased the frequency of street sweepings and stepped up environmental code enforcement
2. Water service—instituted a program of replacing water-line laterals and begun planning for water system capital improvements to eliminate pressure and flow problems
3. Street conditions—initiated an ongoing street paving (or re-paving) program
4. Level of fires—instituted an intensive fire prevention inspection program
5. Level of crime—set up crime prevention programs including a special patrol effort

City manager Mendonsa admits that in the quest for equity, "we may have to provide unequal levels of service in order to produce equal benefits from the services." For example, the city sweeps some streets once a week, others once every two weeks, others once every four weeks. The object, of course, is to produce equal levels of street cleanliness.

SOURCE: Adapted from Arthur A. Mendonsa, "Yardsticks for Measuring the Success of Service Programs in Savannah," *State and Local Government Review* 18 (Spring 1986): 89–92.

RESPONSIVENESS

Responsiveness, the fourth issue in service delivery, concerns the degree to which citizens' preferences and demands are met. Determining such preferences can be difficult. Most citizens do not contact city agencies about service delivery. For example, a study conducted in the early 1970s in Milwaukee found that only a third of the whites and 6 percent of the blacks sampled had made contact with city government officials.[10] Over a decade later, political scientist Michael Hirlinger reports a contacting ratio of 64.2 percent in Oklahoma City. He notes, however, that "the overall contacting rate is considerably higher than most of the previous citizen contacting studies,"[11] which is usually in the range of 30 to 40 percent.

Are citizens satisfied with city services? Most survey data suggest yes, although variations exist, by class and service area especially. A recent meta-analysis (a study that empirically examines a large number of quantitative studies) by Thomas Miller and Michelle Miller provides some details.[12] They analyzed 261 citizen surveys administered over a ten-year period across the country. They standardized the various survey results on a scale of 0 to 100, with 0 for very bad, 25 for bad, 50 neutral (neither good nor bad), 75 for good, and 100 for very good. For eight categories of community services the average adjusted score was 67.2 percent, close to the 75 percent benchmark score of "good." For services evaluated by sixty or more jurisdictions, the three best rated services were fire (81 percent), library (79 percent), and trash collection (78 percent). The three worst rated services were animal control (60 percent), street repair (58 percent), and planning/zoning (57 percent).

Most research reveals that people want more services but are reluctant to pay more taxes.[13] One reason for this contradictory response is that many citizens feel they are not receiving real value for their tax dollars. A more general explanation of the disparity between wanting more services and lower taxes has to do with the separation of payment of services from service delivery. As long as they do not pay directly for each service, most people prefer more services. They still want lower taxes because the connection between taxes and services remains indirect. Some authorities contend that the use of service charges (user fees) or even greater reliance on the private sector to deliver municipal services can help illuminate the link between services and their cost.

Research suggests that, at least in big cities, service delivery varies in its response to public demands. Large-city service delivery has become quite regularized, dominated by bureaucratically determined decision rules. These rules can take several forms. We mentioned the Adam Smith rule, by which the frequency of demand determines the level of certain services. In the same Oakland study that gave rise to this rule, it was found that professional norms and technical considerations also are important in shaping bureaucratic response in certain service areas. Another consideration affecting how municipal bureaucrats handle requests for service is how difficult the problem is. As shown in a study of service delivery in Houston, the simpler the problem, the more likely it is to be satisfactorily handled.

SERVICE DELIVERY IN HOUSTON

IN Houston, some demands for municipal service are more likely to generate a response than others. For example, 80 percent of stray-animal complaints are responded to satisfactorily because the rabies-control department relies primarily on citizen contacts to initiate its service. A majority of water-related complaints receive a satisfactory response as well. The water department depends heavily on citizen-initiated contacts because many of the problems can be resolved quickly without a large commitment of resources.

But many other citizen demands are largely ignored. For example, street repairs, traffic problems, and sewer and drainage matters account for nearly half of all contacts initiated with the Houston city government. Yet only 21 percent of these are satisfactorily resolved. This low level of responsiveness has nothing to do with class or race discrimination. Here responsiveness is a function of the seriousness of the problem. Only one of every ten drainage complaints is handled adequately (even though they represent 22 percent of all contacts) because flooding is such a major problem throughout Houston that the city cannot do much about it. Essentially the same is true of street, traffic, and sewer demands. The vast number of complaints in these areas overwhelms the limited municipal resources available to deal with the problems. For instance, two-thirds of sewer-line complaints are ignored because the city's antiquated sewage system, coupled with the lack of drainage facilities, presents almost insurmountable obstacles for the relevant department.

No evidence was found to indicate that Houston's bureaucrats are guilty of race or class bias in responding to citizen contacts; both black and white and rich and poor areas receive an equal level of response. Instead, responsiveness is directly related to the type of demand. Minor grievances (broken water lines, missed garbage pickups, roving dogs) are effectively handled; those service problems requiring massive commitments of municipal resources are not.

SOURCE: Adapted from Kenneth R. Mladenka, "Citizen Demands and Urban Services: The Distribution of Bureaucratic Response in Chicago and Houston," *American Journal of Political Science* 25 (November 1981): 693–714.

Although bureaucrats are not oblivious to citizens' demands, they do not assess those demands in a very sophisticated fashion. They use what Robert Lineberry calls a *body count approach* to consumption measurement.[14] Ordinarily this involves the tabulation of gross totals —tons of garbage collected, number of dogs picked up, number of books circulated, and so on. These raw demand indicators, however, reveal very little about actual citizen preferences.

Lineberry goes on to argue that an even more important reason why bureaucracies are not very responsive is that they are monopolies. This raises the issue of alternative service delivery arrangements. Are there alternative ways of providing urban services that might produce more competition in service delivery and thus better services? Some say yes. For example, competitive government is one of the key themes in Osborne and Gaebler's *Reinventing Government:* "The issue is not public versus private. It is competition versus monopoly."[15] Especially in an era of cutback management, the search for cost-effective ways of providing services has been stepped up. In particular, more attention is now being given to contracting with the private sector and to using intergovernmental agreements. We deal with some of the alternatives to traditional service delivery in the next chapter, where efforts to increase municipal productivity are discussed. At this point, however, we need to consider the measurement of service quality.

Measuring the Quality of Urban Services

A few years ago, city administrators were asked to identify three means by which the delivery of city services and programs could be improved. The most commonly cited means (by 58 percent of the 264 respondents) was the "utilization of output or performance measures to determine adequacy of service."[16] If we are seriously interested in questions of service quality, equity, and distributional impact, we must be able to measure the outputs of city agencies and programs.

The private sector uses a variety of accepted measures of performance—profit, sales, return on investment and so on. Public enterprise is not so fortunate; far fewer commonly accepted measures of performance tell managers, political leaders, and citizens how municipal service is faring. Brian Rapp and Frank Patitucci suggest two reasons for the general absence of municipal performance measures. First, much of what cities do to improve the quality of community life is intangible. Second, political leaders resist the establishment of measures that might be used by constituents to hold them accountable for the actions of city government. Yet these two practitioners contend that "the absence of accepted performance measures makes it impossible to establish achievable objectives which, in turn, are the basis of setting priorities, allocating resources, organizing personnel, and evaluating program implementation."[17] The authors go on to insist that the lack of accepted measures makes it difficult to determine which investment—for example, more police, more street cleaners, or more garbage collectors—will provide the greatest return on the tax dollar or give citizens the greatest satisfaction.

Of course cities do rely on some kinds of urban service indicators. First are *input measures,* which specify the level of resources committed to a particular activity. In the police service these might include the number of full-time officers assigned to an area or the number of patrol cars available during a period of time. In the field of public works, input measures could take the form of tons of asphalt used, cubic yards of concrete poured, or gallons of paint sprayed. Input measures are often criticized because they may bear little relation to output or level of performance. Yet they are useful to administrators who need to show that all neighborhoods are receiving approximately equal resources (or treatment). They can prove valuable, then, when issues of equity arise.

Second, and closely related to input measures, are *workload indicators,* probably the most widely used measures of service delivery. These are often reported in gross form—the body count measures Lineberry talks about—to indicate the sheer quantity or volume of service provided. Simple workload measures (tons of garbage collected, number of arrests, gallons of water treated) tell us very little. If we create a ratio, however, we obtain more information: the number of cases cleared per number of arrests or the number of books circulated per 10,000 population. Most *efficiency measures* are also ratios: they relate the amount of service output to the input required to produce it. Efficiency measures often take the form of amount of output per worker-hour (the number of tons collected per worker-hour) or per dollar expended (the number of gallons per dollar). Efficiency measures are a useful way to compare performance over time or even between jurisdictions, where comparable information is available.

But efficiency measures do not indicate the extent to which the goals and objectives of a program are being met. For this we use *effectiveness measures,* or *service quality/outcome measures,* like police call response times or the frequency of preventive police patrols. These measures also can reflect the extent to which unintended adverse consequences occur or gauge the degree of public satisfaction with services.

Measures of productivity also can be used to assess service adequacy. Generally, productivity embraces both efficiency (number of tons of garbage collected per person-hour) and effectiveness (number of citizen complaints about refuse not collected). Productivity measures, then, are not distinct from the other two measures; they attempt to include them both. An emphasis on productivity encourages a jurisdiction to use multiple measures, rather than a single indicator, to evaluate service quality.

In a flow chart, the measurement process might look like the following:

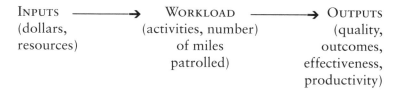

INPUTS ⟶ WORKLOAD ⟶ OUTPUTS
(dollars, (activities, number) (quality,
resources) of miles outcomes,
patrolled) effectiveness,
productivity)

PERFORMANCE MEASURES

Most authorities recommend that cities rely heavily on available information, at least in their initial effort to improve effectiveness measuring and reporting. This has the obvious advantage of minimizing costs and the paperwork burden associated with information gathering. But it is unlikely that existing departmental records are sufficient to provide the range of measures needed. In particular, indicators of quality, including citizen satisfaction, are not apt to be readily available. At the same time it is important to recognize that performance measurement can become burdensome if we do not exercise some selectivity in choosing measures. Obviously every aspect of a program cannot be measured, but more information may be available for measurement purposes than is generally recognized. Harry Hatry discusses four sources of performance information: inspection of physical features, community sample surveys, linked records, and recategorization of existing data.[18]

INSPECTION OF PHYSICAL FEATURES. — The inspection of physical features may be used to supplement input measures or workload indicators. For example, in addition to calculating tons of waste collected, a city might evaluate street cleanliness. Washington, D.C., has tested procedures for doing this. Trained observers inspect randomly selected streets and alleys within the city. These inspectors rated street cleanliness against a set of photographs depicting different degrees of cleanliness.

For street maintenance programs, the traditional measures of miles of road repaired and complaint data can be supplemented by using a roughometer, a device that indicates the degree of smoothness of a street's surface. In one community, roughometer readings are compared with the degree of comfort as rated by a test group of citizens.

These measurements obviously are imprecise gauges of quality. Yet they do represent imaginative attempts to go beyond the usual indicators of physical output—indicators that are quite remote from the quality of services experienced by ordinary citizens.

COMMUNITY SAMPLE SURVEYS.—For gauging consumer satisfaction, the level of citizen participation, and public perception of employee courtesy, random sample citizen surveys are almost indispensable. In a later section we consider in more detail how these surveys are conducted; here we simply comment on their value as a means of assessing service performance. Surveys can point out distortions in the picture that local officials receive if they rely exclusively on complaint records or personal contact with interest groups or selected citizens. Surveys also can identify the proportion of service users and nonusers, as well as the reasons for nonuse.

LINKED RECORDS.—Hatry discusses the possibility of tracing governmental clients through one or more agencies to assess the effects of several related services. He suggests, for example, that more data linkages among the police, the courts, and the correctional system would benefit all parties. Linked records were used in a study of neglected and dependent children in Nashville. The flow of children was traced from the point of entry, through various short-term holding facilities, to the courts. The data were used to evaluate delay times as well as the apparent quality of care.

RECATEGORIZATION OF EXISTING DATA.—If data are categorized in certain ways (by geographic subdivision, by economic class, by educational background), it may be possible to identify the impact of the program on selected neighborhoods or other clientele groups. This allows the service agency to address more specifically the needs of targeted groups. Collecting service data by geographic area is a must for efforts to improve equity, as the Savannah case presented earlier illustrates.

Performance measures are widely used in law enforcement, partly because the police have long supplied crime-related information to federal and state agencies. Also, of course, police actions are generally written up in report form, which facilitates data collection. Table 6.1 depicts several crime-control effectiveness measures taken from a joint Urban In-

TABLE 6.1. EXAMPLES OF EFFECTIVENESS MEASURES FOR POLICE CRIME CONTROL.

Overall objective: Promote the safety of the community and an atmosphere of security, primarily through the deterrence/prevention of crime and the apprehension of offenders; provide service in a fair, honest, prompt, and courteous manner to the satisfaction of the citizens.

Objective	Quality characteristic	Specific measure	Data collection procedure
Prevention	Reported crime rate	Number of reported crimes per 1,000 population, by type of crime.	Data generally available, though with well-known definitional and collection problems. Numerous ways of grouping crimes exist. A suggested grouping is (a) violent crimes, (b) major property crimes, and (c) any other crime that has a direct victim (such as minor vandalism).
	Households victimized	Percentage of households victimized by one or more crimes.	Reasons for underreporting also would be solicited. True crime rates may be roughly estimated by scaling up the reported rate using the percentage unreported.
	Property loss	Dollar property loss from crime per 1,000 population.	Data from basic incident reports (though dollar values are not always explicitly estimated today).
Apprehension	Crimes solved	Percentage of reported crimes cleared, by type of crime.	Already in general use.
	Property recovery	Percentage of stolen property that is subsequently recovered; (a) percentage of vehicles (and their value) recovered; (b) percentage of value of other property recovered.	Often available today. "Value recovered" preferably should have damages subtracted out.

Continued . . .

TABLE 6.1. — CONTINUED

Objective	Quality characteristic	Specific measure	Data collection procedure
Responsiveness	Response times	Percentage of emergency or high priority calls responded to within x minutes.	Data already available in many departments today from dispatcher information.
Feeling of security	Citizen fear	Percentage of public feeling safe/unsafe walking in their neighborhood at night.	Survey of a representative sample of citizens.
Overall citizen satisfaction	Citizen/user satisfaction with overall performance	Percentage of citizens/users rating police overall performance as excellent/good/fair/poor, and by reason of dissatisfaction/satisfaction.	Survey of a representative sample of citizens. Preferably, citizens without firsthand contact should be distinguished from those with firsthand contact.

SOURCE: Adapted from *Measuring the Effectiveness of Basic Municipal Services*. Urban Institute and International City Management Association (Washington, D.C., 1974), 40–44. Reprinted by permission.

stitute–ICMA report. The table specifies (1) the overall broad objective; (2) more specific objectives (prevention, apprehension, responsiveness, and so on); (3) the quality characteristics derived from the specific objectives (crimes solved or property recovered, for example, as part of the apprehension objective); (4) the specific measure that might be used to represent the level of effectiveness (the percentage of reported crimes cleared, for example, as a measure of crimes solved); and (5) the suggested data collection procedure. An enlarged version of the report, called *How Effective Are Your Community Services?* was issued recently. It includes not only crime-control measures but also similar effectiveness measures for solid-waste collection, recreation services, library services, fire protection, transportation, and water supply.[19]

As table 6.1 reveals, many important measures of effectiveness (e.g., victimization rates and citizens' feelings of safety and overall satisfaction) are not readily available from existing records. They must be gathered using citizen surveys. In general, measures of service quality are more difficult to obtain than are measures of output efficiency.

Using Measurement Data

Measuring the quality and effectiveness of municipal services can be useful in the following areas: program planning and budgeting, management operations, program analysis and evaluation, establishing performance targets, establishing employee incentive programs, and improving citizen feedback for governmental decision making.[20]

Program Budgeting. — Effectiveness measures are indispensable to program budgeting, and this may be their principal use in cities that employ such budgeting systems. These measures can reveal which service areas are not meeting objectives and help identify problem areas or areas that deserve high priority for resource allocation.

Service effectiveness data by themselves may not indicate why conditions are below expectations or what to do in those cases. Analysis of these data, however, can point the way toward remedial action. In particular, citizens' ratings of various services—recreation, library, and transit, for example—may reveal that facilities are not being used because people are not aware of them. This can prompt a city to consider ways to increase awareness.

Management Operations. — Effectiveness data can be an important supplement to other information used by administrators for making decisions and allocating resources. These data must be collected more frequently when they are to be used for operational purposes rather than for annual program planning and budgeting. Where performance measures are available on a weekly or monthly basis, they can help identify problems, modify priorities, or bring about reassignment of personnel. For example, street cleanliness ratings could be used to help establish assignments of street-cleaning crews and equipment. Or if daily water-supply tests reveal an excessive content of dangerous chemicals, personnel can be assigned to take immediate action. Where information is available by service district, the relative performance of district personnel can be monitored and changes made where necessary.

PROGRAM ANALYSIS AND EVALUATION. — *Program analysis* focuses on alternative courses of proposed governmental action; *program evaluation* concentrates on the effects of current programs. For both processes performance data are mandatory. We should observe, however, that regular effectiveness measurement does not replace the need for either of these activities. Instead, it is an essential ingredient in carrying out analysis and evaluation.

ESTABLISHING PERFORMANCE TARGETS. — One way to ensure that effectiveness measures make a difference in municipal operations is to establish performance targets. These targets allow management to monitor continuing progress toward specific objectives; they give employees a goal; and they may even encourage innovation. Performance targets might be incorporated into a formal Management by Objectives (MBO) system in which objectives are set and progress is determined by using a set of efficiency and effectiveness measures (see chapter 8).

ESTABLISHING EMPLOYEE INCENTIVE PROGRAMS. — Performance measures can become a significant part of employee incentive programs for managerial and nonmanagerial personnel (see chapter 9). It is important that these measures be comprehensive so that employees are not encouraged to emphasize certain activities at the expense of others. For example, police officers might stress the issuance of citations to the exclusion of more qualitative aspects of the job if appropriate performance measures are not included in an incentive system. One of the more interesting and controversial employee incentive programs was developed in the city of Orange, California. Monetary incentives were given to police officers on the basis of reductions in the city's crime rate.[21] Although the overall reported crime rate did decline, we might wonder whether the program did not encourage the police to make fewer arrests.

IMPROVING CITIZEN FEEDBACK.—Performance measures can stimulate more and better citizen feedback in two ways. First, the collection of certain qualitative information virtually requires citizen surveys. If collected properly, this information should be far more representative of community feelings than complaint data or the limited personal observations of employees and officials. Second, the nature of the information is much clearer to the average citizen than are the commonly used workload measures. And an increased understanding of what government does could prompt more citizen involvement in local public affairs. This notion obviously assumes that performance indicators will be a featured part of any annual progress report made to the citizenry by city officials.

The city of Phoenix (like Sunnyvale, California; Dallas, Texas; and Dayton, Ohio) has been measuring service performance for a number of years, using a variety of techniques. The case study that follows describes some of the tactics Phoenix has tried.

CASE STUDY

PERFORMANCE MEASUREMENT IN PHOENIX

FROM 1970 to 1977, Phoenix, Arizona, began applying traditional industrial engineering principles to measuring and improving performance. Stopwatch analysis and other direct observations were used to establish work standards for 60 percent of all city activities, complete with weekly and monthly reports. This effort, coupled with a version of program budgeting, paid big dividends. Phoenix officials estimated that more than $25 million was saved during this period, and service effectiveness was enhanced.

Beginning in 1977, the city shifted from industrial engineering productivity efforts to organizational development activities (see chapter 8). Quality circles were introduced, and periodic surveys of the workforce were instituted to gauge employee satisfaction. In 1982 Phoenix implemented a performance review system, borrowed from Dallas, as a way of assigning more definite responsibility for job performance. In large bureaucracies, the individual worker's contribution to the organization's output may be unclear or ill defined. Individual contribution may be lost. To encourage first-line supervisors and employees to overcome this problem, the city implemented, on a pilot basis, a system to

• Develop clear individual work elements and job standards.

- Periodically clarify and renegotiate those job standards.
- Use work components and job standards to build objective performance measures.
- Develop ongoing communication to help the employee succeed.

This performance review system generated abundant paperwork, so over the next two years one of the two affected departments (urban development and housing) streamlined the process and cut the number of forms by half. The other department, streets and traffic, abandoned the approach and returned to traditional engineered work standards.

One other aspect of the Phoenix approach is worth noting. In March 1986, city manager Marvin Andrews decided that Phoenix needed to improve its departmental monthly reporting system. The reports were often page after page of statistics and columns of numbers without the benefit of an abstract or summary. There was too much information in too much detail to be very useful. The manager wanted a monthly reporting system that focused only on key activities, those that most reflected individual department performance. It had to be brief and easy to read and reflect output measures rather than workload or input measures.

To implement the reporting system, a three-member staff team asked department heads, "If you were the Phoenix city manager, what information would you need to run the city?" The usual response was, "What we're giving him now, in our present monthly reports." This was not the answer the team wanted. As a result the team turned to a newly installed strategic planning process. All city departments were developing mission statements, establishing objectives, analyzing internal and external conditions, and setting priorities. The team decided to use those "vital few" objectives each department identified as its "bottom line" in the new monthly reporting system. This new procedure is now undergoing a six-month shakedown period, but expectations are high that the outcome will be favorable to its continued use.

SOURCE: Adapted from Lance L. Decker and Patrick Manion, "Performance Measurement in Phoenix: Trends and a New Direction," *National Civic Review* 76 (March–April 1987): 119–29.

PROBLEMS IN USING PERFORMANCE MEASURES

Political scientist Michael Lipsky's work on urban bureaucracy leads him to question the usefulness of performance measurement.[22] He argues, first, that job performance, especially of street-level bureaucrats who exercise much discretion in their work, is extremely difficult to measure. Objectives are ambiguous if not conflicting, and too many external influences affect performance. Second, he says it is not even apparent that measured increases or decreases signal better or worse performance. Crime statistics illustrate this difficulty best. Do increases in arrest rates represent improved police performance, or do they reflect deteriorating police performance in the face of increased criminal activity?

Third, Lipsky notes that bureaucrats change their behavior in response to what is being measured. This phenomenon was first highlighted by sociologist Peter Blau. He observed that employment counselors shifted their attention to the more easily employed at the expense of those more difficult to place when a system was implemented that evaluated performance on the basis of placement rate (the practice is called "creaming"). Lipsky insists that such behavior takes on the property of a general rule: Behavior in organizations tends to drift toward compatibility with the ways the organization is evaluated. Finally, he asserts that too many measures do not really reflect service quality. In fact, he says emphasis on quantity or even efficiency may have adverse consequences for service quality. Lack of concern for service quality can produce a "debasement of service," a situation that may infuriate the public if workers are given pay raises based on falsely credited productivity improvements.

If Lipsky's arguments are correct, should a city abandon all efforts to measure urban services? Probably not, but local officials certainly should keep these issues in mind as they consider whether and how to institute performance measurement. At the least, great care must be taken in fashioning a measurement program designed for municipal personnel whose positions allow great discretion and latitude in judgment.

IMPROVING PERFORMANCE MEASUREMENT

Based on a thorough study of eighteen medium-sized and large city and county governments, political scientist John Hall offers five suggestions for managers who want to institute or improve an efficiency or effectiveness measurement system:[23]

- Introduce the system gradually to a few departments each year, giving priority to receptive agency heads or those who have a potential use for the data.

- Involve department heads and their staffs in the selection of measures and data uses, but with direction from central staff analysts.
- Allow the central staff adequate time to set up a system involving extensive participation, as well as to monitor and follow up data on an ongoing basis.
- Consider the selection of measures as a negotiating process with the departments, in which central staff analysts must balance the desire to institute the best measures possible with the need to understand agency views and to establish credibility with agency personnel.
- Explore various data display formats, and develop imaginative graphics and supporting narratives. Be selective in choosing the measures to send to various levels of management. (This tends to increase the data's understandability and usefulness to local officials.)

Hall notes that city councils, if they get involved at all, frequently oppose measurement systems on cost grounds. He suggests that council members be kept informed of how data are being used, and that when the council wants to see these data, they be presented in an easy-to-understand format.

Implementing and Evaluating Urban Programs

The delivery of urban services or the implementation of urban programs is considerably more than a smooth, automatic, rational process. Or, in the words of Charles Fox:

> The rational-comprehensive or classical model of policy implementation is simple, clear, and elegant. Democratically elected officials make unambiguous policy choices. Policies are then handed over to a hierarchically structured agency. Specific instructions are formulated at the top of the pyramid and passed down the chain of command to the line personnel, who carry them out without discretion. Most observers know that this ideal is unachievable in reality. Still . . . it is a backdrop against which the real world policy implementation is often measured. The further away from the ideal an implementation process is, the more likely will it be judged wanting.[24]

The best-laid plans of urban policymakers often are modified if not derailed by compromises, tradeoffs, and power plays among those responsible for actual program performance. As we saw in chapter 3, good planning and good intentions are not enough; attention also must be paid to how services or programs actually are carried out. Periodic interviews with department heads and staff, periodic written reports, and of course complaints all provide essential guidance on program or service effectiveness. But these traditional modes of monitoring and evaluating are sporadic and unsystematic. Especially when new programs have been initiated or in areas where costs have increased disproportionately, a more regularized approach to assessing performance is needed.

Basically there are two kinds of evaluation: monitoring and program evaluation. The first of these, sometimes called *performance monitoring* or *process evaluation,* is concerned with regularly examining the general effectiveness of programs in major areas, such as public safety, health, and recreation. Monitoring attempts to identify general program-related changes, but does not try to indicate what part specific governmental activities play in producing observed effects. In other words, monitoring does not separate program impacts from changes that may have resulted from nonprogram efforts, such as those by private groups.

Program evaluation goes further. It attempts to identify how the condition of both the citizens and the community have changed as a result of a specific government program or set of activities. It seeks out both intended and unintended consequences, good and bad. The process goes as follows:[25]

1. Determine the program objectives.
2. Translate the objectives into measurable indicators of achievement.
3. Collect data on the indicators for those who participated in the program (and for an equivalent group who did not participate).
4. Compare the data on participants and the equivalent nonparticipants.

Once the data are in hand, managers can gauge program effectiveness and make knowledgeable recommendations concerning program continuation, modification, or even termination. Although the procedure seems simple, we see shortly that the whole process can be beset with a variety of unexpected problems. First, however, we should examine the different ways evaluation can be performed.

EVALUATION DESIGNS

Evaluation implies comparison. The major purpose of any program comparison is to identify those changes that can be reasonably attributed to the program itself. Ideally, of course, we would like to compare what actually has happened with what would have happened had the program not been in effect. Impossible, of course. The next-best procedure is to separate out the program's effects from other extraneous influences that might have produced some observable change.

Before we can discuss evaluation design, we again must consider program objectives and evaluation criteria. First, like program analysis and service delivery assessment, evaluation demands that objectives and criteria be put in measurable form. Second, evaluation criteria must focus on those things the program is intended to affect. Workload measures, indicators of physical capacity, and clients served are insufficient if not inappropriate. Third, unintended consequences, especially negative side effects, must be considered explicitly. Fourth, more than one objective and more than one evaluation criterion should be specified. Finally, dollar costs always should be included as one criterion. With these requirements in mind, we can consider evaluation designs.[26]

BEFORE-AND-AFTER PROGRAM COMPARISON. —This is the easiest, cheapest, most common, and most unreliable of the evaluation designs. Essentially it measures program activity at two points: one immediately before and one at some appropriate time after program implementation. No explicit provisions are made to control for outside influences. As Urban Institute researchers Hatry, Winnie, and Fisk suggest, other plausible explanations for any observed change may exist, including abnormal weather conditions, other public or private programs with coincidental objectives, and special characteristics of the target population not originally recognized. To the extent possible, a good evaluation design should take these things into account; the before-and-after design cannot.

Despite its limitations, the before-and-after program comparison design may be the only practical approach when personnel and time are limited. For example, Washington, D.C., used a before-and-after design to evaluate Operation Clean Sweep, an intensive, one-time effort to remove litter and other solid waste in nine neighborhood service areas. Neighborhood cleanliness was assessed before and after the operation by trained observers using a series of photographs matched to a cleanliness rating scale. A before-and-after citizen survey was also undertaken to determine whether residents noticed any difference in cleanliness. City officials felt that no major external changes had affected the area under consideration, so the before-and-after design seemed a valid approach. Even though the city was disappointed by the lack of major improvements in street cleanliness (a decision was made not to continue the program), the evaluation itself was judged a success.

TIME TREND PROJECTION. —This design compares actual postprogram information with estimated projections based on preprogram observations made over a period of time. The approach uses statistical methods, including linear regression, to derive projected program values that are then contrasted with actual results.

> Crime or accident statistics, for example, may rise or fall for individual years, but when years are considered together a trend may be apparent. Comparison of data from one preprogram year with postprogram data may be influenced by extremes and thereby be misleading.[27]

Clearly this design is superior to the single comparison of the before-and-after approach, but it still lacks the explicit control necessary to assess as accurately as possible the real impact of a given program.

COMPARISON WITH OTHER JURISDICTIONS OR POPULATIONS. —This design identifies a comparable city or a comparable population within the same community in which the program is not operating. The approach was used by the state of Connecticut to assess the effects of a crackdown on highway speeding. Following the program's implementation, the automobile fatality rate in Connecticut was compared with fatality rates in neighboring states. The evaluation showed that some influence unique to Connecticut had caused a decline in fatality rates relative to those of neighboring states.

Although this design incorporates some controls for outside effects, it still falls short of being an ideal approach. Also, finding comparable jurisdictions or populations is always a problem.

THE CONTROLLED EXPERIMENT. —Hatry, Winnie, and Fisk call this the Cadillac of program evaluations. Undoubtedly controlled experiments are the most powerful design of all; they are also expensive and difficult to perform. The program's essential feature is the selection of at least two groups: a control group and an experimental group. Members of the population (or probability samples thereof) are assigned randomly (that is, scientifically) to produce two groups that are as much alike as possible. The experimental group receives the program "treatment"; the control group does not. Postprogram performance is then measured and compared. This design is probably most effective where individuals undergo a specific treatment program in an area such as employment training, corrections, rehabilitation, health, or drug or alcohol abuse. Various quasi-experimental designs, in which true experimental conditions are approximated but not quite met, also can be used.[28]

A few years ago a police patrol project using a quasi-experimental design was undertaken in Kansas City, Missouri. The police department established three areas in which the amount of patrol activity would vary. In one area no routine patrol activity whatsoever was performed; police responded only on call. In a second area patrol functions were expanded considerably, to double or triple what they had been. In the third locale patrolling was maintained as before. At the end of the experiment no significant differences in crime rates were reported for the three areas, "nor was there any appreciable difference in citizen attitudes, reported criminal victimization, citizen behavior, police behavior, or even traffic accidents."[29] Obviously the results called into question a variety of long-standing assumptions concerning the effectiveness of certain police activities.

Why don't more cities undertake controlled experiments? Experiments are not easy to conduct; costs are usually high; and the necessary expertise is not readily available. And other problems inhere, according to Carol Weiss:

> In practice, evaluation can seldom go about the business so systematically. The constraints of the field situation hobble the evaluation—too few clients, demand for quick feedback of information, inadequate funds, "contamination" of the special-treatment groups by receipt of other services, dropouts from the program, lack of access to records and data, changes in program, and so on.[30]

Even getting those involved to agree to a random assignment of population can present problems. Practitioners often want to assign people to treatment groups on the basis of their professional knowledge and experience. Generally they want to put those who need the program services most into the experimental group, not leaving the process to chance. And this essentially defeats the purpose of the experiment.

Hatry, Winnie, and Fisk identify a fifth approach to evaluation: comparisons of planned and actual performance. Although we can hardly call this a design, they argue that it is a useful approach in the absence of any other evaluation method. In fact, they contend that comparisons of actual results with planned or targeted results still are surprisingly rare.

Where the preferred experimental design is not feasible, Hatry, Winnie, and Fisk recommend the use of the first three designs in some combination. They also suggest the regular and extensive use of the last approach as a supplement to the other evaluation designs.

EVALUATING PROGRAM EVALUATION

Good program evaluations at any level of government remain uncommon.[31] We can touch on only a few of the reasons here, but significant impediments still lie in the way of achieving useful evaluation results. The cost and time involved surely rank high as reasons for the lack of comprehensive program evaluation in local government. Beyond that, Pamela Horst and her associates discuss three reasons why evaluations are ineffective.[32]

Program implementers have great difficulty stating clear, specific, measurable objectives. When asked for a statement of goals, they tend to answer in terms of services offered, number of people served, and so on. But to program evaluators, who want the intended *consequences* of a program, these are not valid program objectives.[33]

Beyond definition and measurement problems, serious difficulties arise in connecting program objectives to program effects and consequences. Different assumptions are made in different locales about what form program intervention can take and how it relates to the intended outcome. For example, the operating assumptions of one halfway house or therapeutic community may bear no resemblance to those of other institutions that go by the same name.

Finally, Horst suggests that some managers often feel that sound evaluation presents a clear and present danger. The status quo is comfortable. Old ideas and timeworn practices die hard, and some managers hesitate to support evaluation if it appears likely to disrupt existing organizational arrangements.[34]

These very real possibilities lead Horst and her colleagues to recommend a *preassessment of evaluability*. A determination should be made as to whether a major evaluation effort is warranted. In effect, the three root causes of ineffective evaluation should be raised in question form:[35]

- Are the objectives, program activities, anticipated outcomes, and expected impact sufficiently well defined as to be measurable?
- Are the assumptions linking expenditure to implementation, outcome, and impact sufficiently logical to be tested?
- Does the person in charge of the program have sufficient capacity and motivation to act as a result of evaluation findings?

Evaluation can make important contributions to the overall assess-

ment of urban policy, but not all program evaluations provide useful results. Figuring out what can be profitably evaluated remains the tough
task of imaginative administrators.

Citizen Surveys

Community surveys can generate useful information about citizens' perceptions, preferences, and needs for a variety of urban services. Responses to questions regarding service delivery and program effectiveness
can be particularly valuable for policy analysis and program evaluation.
Another basic reason for using surveys comes from city manager Thomas
Dunne.[36] He argues that the public increasingly wants local government
to do less *for* them and more *with* them. Therefore people must be given
opportunities to be heard beyond the customary public hearings and advisory committees. Dunne tells how his city has used citizen surveys in
connection with the preparation of the municipal budget. (Respondents
were asked a series of questions about their preferences for different levels of expenditures and city services.) Douglas Watson, city manager of
Auburn, Alabama, tells a similar story. In Auburn there is institutionalized use of citizen surveys in the budgetary and policymaking process.[37]

Figure 6.1 shows some typical survey questions. Many of these
questions deal with people's perception of service adequacy, although
some extract factual information (the library-card question). A number
of the questions are crime related; others elicit demographic data. This
background and neighborhood information can provide the means for
in-depth analysis of survey data. A number of surveys, for example, have
found that blacks consistently give urban services lower ratings than do
whites. This is especially true for police protection.

1. In general, would you rate the St. Petersburg Bus Service available
   to you and members of your household as Excellent, Good, Fair,
   or Poor?
2. Do you or any other member of this household have a library
   card for the St. Petersburg library? Yes, No, or Don't know.
3. How would you rate the pool, park, and recreational opportunities in your neighborhood? Excellent, Good, Fair, or Poor.
4. In the past 12 months, did the collectors ever miss picking up
   your trash and garbage on the scheduled pickup day? (*If yes,
   ask:*) How many times would you say this occurred? ( ) No, never
   missed; ( ) Yes, 1 or 2 times; ( ) Yes, 3 or 4 times; ( ) Yes, 5 or 6
   times; ( ) Yes, __ times; ( ) Don't know or don't remember.

5. Turning now to police protection and public safety, how safe would you feel walking alone in this neighborhood at night? Very safe, Reasonably safe, or Not safe at all.
6. Would you rate the speed of the St. Petersburg Police in responding to calls as Excellent, Good, Fair, or Poor?
7. Would you say the streets in your neighborhood do *not* need *any* repair, need *some minor* repair, or need *major* repair?

FIGURE 6.1. TYPICAL QUESTIONS IN A CITIZEN SURVEY.

SOURCE: From *Measuring the Effectiveness of Basic Municipal Services,* Urban Institute and International City Management Association (Washington, D.C., 1974), 105–12. Reprinted by permission.

The case study that follows shows how survey analysis can help decision makers allocate resources.

CASE STUDY

A CITIZEN SURVEY IN ELYRIA

IN the summer of 1979 a limited survey of citizen attitudes was undertaken in Elyria, Ohio (population about 60,000), by a Chicago-based consulting organization, Public Administration Service. The survey was only one component of a larger study of the operations and management of the Elyria Police Department. Citizen opinions were to be used to supplement information from police records, interviews with officials, and observations of police activities.

The survey was conducted by telephone, with each interview lasting an average of fifteen minutes. A random sample of local telephone numbers was generated by a computer using a process called random digit dialing. The survey was administered by Elyria senior citizens trained in telephone interview techniques and in the use of the survey instrument itself. Calls were made in the evenings and on the weekends to avoid biasing the results by contacting too few people who were employed during the day. In all, 492 citizens were interviewed, a response rate of 58 percent. A 42 percent refusal rate seems high, but the authors indicate that the actual respondents were reasonably representative of the larger community based on census characteristics.

The survey included a series of questions about respondents' perceptions of local crime trends and their feeling of personal safety. In general respondents felt that crime was "staying about the same" both in the city at large and in their particular neighborhoods. And although most residents felt relatively safe walking after dark in their own neighborhoods, many were reluctant to walk alone at night in downtown Elyria. The results changed, however, when the data were disaggregated by neighborhood and by income level. In effect, less affluent respondents and those living in poor neighborhoods were most fearful for their safety. By using statistical techniques (two-way analysis of variance), the researchers determined that neighborhood was more important than income. On this basis the authors suggest that law-enforcement decision makers in Elyria can justify a mixed strategy of concentrating enforcement resources in certain neighborhoods and special responsiveness to the poor, with perhaps more emphasis on the former strategy.

SOURCE: Adapted from Charles Hale and Jeffrey Slovak, "Citizen Surveys as Tools for Public Decision Making," *Current Municipal Problems* 7 (1980–81): 438–45.

CONDUCTING THE SURVEYS

A prime consideration in conducting a survey is the degree of accuracy wanted. Survey consultants (likely to be necessary if a city has never undertaken a survey) can provide ready guidance on the degree of accuracy (based on sampling error) resulting from surveys of varying sizes. Sampling precision actually depends on two variables: sample size and the percentage responding to a particular question. For example, if 400 people were included in the sample, under the most demanding conditions the sampling error would be plus or minus 5 percent, with a 95 percent confidence level. Thus if half the respondents answered yes to a particular question, with a sample of 400 the real value in the larger population would be between 45 and 55 percent yes (95 times out of 100). Again, under the most statistically demanding conditions, a sample size of 800 would yield a sampling error of plus or minus 3.5 percent, with 95 percent confidence. Depending on the decision maker's need for accuracy, a sample of between 400 and 800 should be adequate for most communities, regardless of size.

Cost inevitably looms as a major consideration in doing sample surveys. For this reason, cities should consider either a telephone survey or a mail questionnaire. Neither is likely to be as satisfactory as a personal interview, but both can be done less expensively. Most telephone surveys now use random digit dialing. Done properly, with a relatively simple, short questionnaire, the method can yield good results.

SURVEY LIMITATIONS

It is important to guard against several problems that can arise in conducting and using surveys. First, an opinion poll should not focus on complex issues about which citizens lack information. In one city the small budget for tree management was eliminated after citizens ranked forestry lowest on a selected list of services. Windstorms later blew down a number of trees, and citizens were in an uproar when they discovered that forestry crews had been eliminated.

Second, the questionnaire should offer a range of possible alternatives or responses. In one survey blacks were asked: "If there were no obstacles, financial or social, would you prefer to live in a black community or in a predominantly white suburb?" Those conducting the survey finally recognized that an important category was missing. A follow-up survey included another choice: an integrated neighborhood. The results were enormously different: the large majority for a black community in the first poll shifted to a smaller majority for an integrated community in the second survey.

Third, the survey should be designed and worded very carefully to minimize the chance that the poll will be misunderstood, or even abused. One community in the Southwest used a citizen survey to justify the construction of a nuclear power plant, yet the words *nuclear* and *atomic* did not appear in the questionnaire.[38] Even technically well-done surveys, though, can be deliberately misconstrued by those who want to use only part of the results to support their particular point of view.

Finally, those who will be deciding the issue should be committed to making use of the survey. Polls are of no value if official decision makers do not use the results.

Two final comments on citizen surveys seem warranted. First, some research indicates that subjective (i.e., citizen) service evaluations do not correspond well with more objective measures of service quality.[39] So citizen surveys should not be used as substitutes for various objective indicators of municipal performance. Second, as we saw earlier, studies show that citizens' attitudes toward taxes and services are generally contradictory. People often provide positive assessments of most services and want at least the present level continued. But they don't want to pay more taxes. It goes without saying that no one likes taxes, so survey questions asking about service levels and tax rates must be very carefully drafted if the information is to be of much value. To the extent possible, explicit tradeoffs between taxes and services should be forced through the questionnaire design. For example, when General Revenue Sharing was eliminated, the city of Anderson, South Carolina, used a citizen survey to pose directly the question of whether taxes should be increased or garbage service reduced from twice to once a week. The results favored a lower service level, so the city switched to once-a-week pickup.

In all, the potential advantages of using communitywide surveys seem to outweigh the risks. In no other way can public officials derive reasonably accurate, systematic information about how citizens think their city government is performing. In the absence of the market mechanisms of price and competition, democratic governments are under special obligation to make their operations as sensitive to the public will as possible. And elections alone are not sufficient for that purpose.

Summary

Dealing with service delivery involves more than just improving efficiency and economy. A greater interest in equity has found its way onto the local agenda. Equity in turn leads to questions of responsiveness. Among other things, we are learning that the urban bureaucracy, through the operation of frequently unobtrusive decision rules, has a lot to do with how services are distributed and the extent to which delivery appears responsive to citizens' needs. Many authorities are pessimistic about the capacity of the bureaucracy to modify its behavior in the absence of incentives of the sort normally associated with private enterprise. Somewhat naturally, therefore, an interest has developed in finding alternative delivery mechanisms, among them contracting to private concerns for certain services. How far this trend will go remains to be seen, but it does reflect the growing interest in finding ways to solve the more services–less resources quandary. The next chapter deals with alternative service delivery in greater detail.

Improving service is impossible unless a municipality collects reasonably good information on the level and quality of services that are currently available. Most cities collect a variety of data, but usually not in usable form. Gross measures of work accomplished do not really tell us very much. We must standardize such data, being sure that the criteria are appropriate to the program.

How can urban managers determine whether programs are being implemented as planned? We know that employees for a variety of reasons do not always carry through as directed. Therefore administrators often find it necessary to undertake special efforts to monitor and evaluate program performance. Evaluation designs are of several sorts. The cheapest and easiest to perform, the before-and-after design, is also the least reliable. The best design, the controlled experiment, unfortunately is the most costly and difficult to undertake. Authorities in this area urge that if a controlled experiment cannot be done, combinations of the less desirable designs—before-and-after comparison, time trend, and comparison with other jurisdictions—be used instead.

Citizen surveys increasingly have proved their worth in providing data about the public's perceptions of municipal services, although such surveys should not be substituted for objective service measures. These efforts are not cheap, sometimes are misunderstood, and some experts question the cognitive ability of citizens to assess service delivery accurately. Nevertheless, citizen surveys furnish information that public decision makers can obtain in no other way: "In a society committed to democratic norms, the views of the citizenry—no matter how (ill) conceived—are significant in themselves!"[40] Continual program monitoring, program evaluations, and citizen surveys can help a city government make more informed judgments about the quality and effectiveness of urban services.

Notes

1. David Greytak, Donald Phares, with Elaine Morley, *Municipal Output and Performance in New York City* (Lexington, Mass.: D.C. Heath, 1976), 11.

2. Ibid.

3. Frank Levy, Arnold Meltsner, and Aaron Wildavsky, *Urban Outcomes: Schools, Streets, and Libraries* (Berkeley: University of California Press, 1974), 16–17.

4. Ibid., 233.

5. Robert L. Lineberry, "Equality, Public Policy and Public Services: The Under-Class Hypothesis and the Limits to Equality," *Policy and Politics* 4 (December 1975): 67–84.

6. George Antunes and Kenneth Mladenka, "The Politics of Local Services and Service Distribution," in *The New Urban Politics,* ed. Louis Masotti and Robert Lineberry (Cambridge, Mass.: Ballinger, 1976), 160.

7. Robert L. Lineberry, *Equality and Urban Policy: The Distribution of Municipal Public Services* (Beverly Hills: Sage, 1977), 142.

8. Kenneth R. Mladenka, "Citizen Demands and Urban Services: The Distribution of Bureaucratic Response in Chicago and Houston," *American Journal of Political Science* 25 (November 1981): 708.

9. See Daniel Fessler and Christopher May, "The Municipal Service Equalization Suit: A Case of Action in Quest of a Forum," in *Public Needs*

and Private Behavior in Metropolitan Areas, ed. John E. Jackson (Cambridge, Mass.: Ballinger, 1975), 157–95.

10. Peter K. Eisinger, "The Pattern of Citizen Contacts with Urban Officials," in *People and Politics in Urban Society,* ed. Harlan Hahn (Beverly Hills: Sage, 1972), 50.

11. Michael W. Hirlinger, "Citizen-Initiated Contacting of Local Government Officials: A Multivariate Explanation," *Journal of Politics* 54 (May 1992): 558.

12. This discussion is from Thomas I. Miller and Michelle A. Miller, "Standards of Excellence: U.S. Residents' Evaluations of Local Government Services," *Public Administration Review* 51 (November/December 1991): 503–13.

13. Wayne Hoffman, "The Democratic Response of Urban Governments: An Empirical Test with Simple Spatial Models," in *Citizen Preferences and Urban Public Policy,* ed. Terry N. Clark (Beverly Hills: Sage, 1976), 51–74.

14. Lineberry, *Equality and Urban Policy,* 163.

15. David Osborne and Ted Gaebler, *Reinventing Government* (Reading, Mass.: Addison-Wesley, 1992), 76.

16. Thomas Thorwood, "The Planning and Management Processes in City Government," *Municipal Year Book 1973* (Washington, D.C.: ICMA, 1973), 29.

17. Brian Rapp and Frank Patitucci, "Improving the Performance of City Government: A Third Alternative," *Publius* 6 (Fall 1976): 73.

18. Harry Hatry, "Measuring the Quality of Public Services," in *Improving the Quality of Urban Management,* ed. Willis Hawley and David Rogers (Beverly Hills: Sage, 1974), 50–54.

19. Harry Hatry et al., *How Effective Are Your Community Services?* 2d ed. (Washington, D.C.: Urban Institute and ICMA, 1991).

20. The following sections are adapted from *Measuring the Effectiveness of Basic Municipal Services* (Washington, D.C.: Urban Institute and ICMA, 1974), 9–15.

21. See Paul D. Staudohar, "An Experiment in Increasing Productivity of Police Service Employees," *Public Administration Review* 35 (September/October 1975): 518–22.

22. Michael Lipsky, *Street-Level Bureaucracy* (New York: Russell Sage Foundation, 1980), 48–51 and 171.

23. John R. Hall, Jr., *Factors Related to Local Government Use of Performance Measurement,* Report to the Department of Housing and Urban Development (Washington D.C.: Urban Institute, 1978), vii–viii.

24. Charles J. Fox, "Biases in Public Policy Implementation Evaluation," *Policy Studies Review* 7 (Autumn 1987): 129; see also other implementation symposium articles in this issue of *Policy Studies Review.*

25. Carol Weiss, *Evaluation Research* (Englewood Cliffs, N.J.: Prentice Hall, 1972), 24–25.

26. The following sections draw on Harry Hatry, Richard Winnie, and Donald Fisk, *Practical Program Evaluation for State and Local Government Officials,* 2d ed. (Washington, D.C.: Urban Institute, 1981), chap. 3 and app. A.

27. Ibid., 31.

28. See Donald Campbell and Julian Stanley, *Experimental and Quasi-Experimental Designs for Research* (Chicago: Rand McNally, 1963).

29. Jeffrey Henig, Robert Lineberry, and Neal Milner, "The Policy Impact of Policy Evaluation: Some Implications of the Kansas City Patrol Experiment," in *Public Law and Public Policy,* ed. John Gardiner (New York: Praeger, 1977), 226.

30. Weiss, *Evaluation Research,* 16.

31. For a good overview of current issues and problems in policy evaluation, see the three articles in *Policy Studies Journal* 16 (Winter 1987–88): 191–241; and Terry Busson and Philip Coulter, *Policy Evaluation for Local Government* (Westport, Conn.: Greenwood Press, 1987).

32. Pamela Horst, Joe Ray, John Scanlon, and Joseph Wholey, "Program Management and the Federal Evaluator," *Public Administration Review* 34 (July/August 1974): 301.

33. Weiss, *Evaluation Research,* 26.

34. Ibid., 114.

35. Horst et al., "Program Management," 307.

36. Thomas G. Dunne, "Citizen Surveys and Expenditure Controls," in *Managing Fiscal Retrenchment in Cities,* ed. Herrington J. Bryce (Columbus, Ohio: Academy for Contemporary Problems, 1980), 22.

37. Douglas J. Watson, Robert J. Juster, and Gerald W. Johnson, "Institutionalized Use of Citizen Surveys in the Budgetary and Policy-Making Processes: A Small City Case Study," *Public Administration Review* 51 (May/June 1991): 232.

38. Gregory Daneke and Patricia Klobus-Edwards, "Survey Research for Public Administrators," *Public Administration Review* 39 (September/October 1979): 421.

39. See, for example, Brian Stipak, "Citizen Satisfaction with Urban Services: Potential Misuse as a Performance Indicator," *Public Administration Review* 39 (January/February 1979): 46–52. For an opposing view, see Jeffrey Brudney and Robert England, "Urban Policy Making and Subjective Service Evaluations: Are They Compatible?" *Public Administration Review* 42 (March/April 1982): 127–35.

40. Brudney and England, "Urban Policy Making and Subjective Service Evaluations," 129.

Suggested for Further Reading

Busson, Terry, and Philip Coulter, eds. *Policy Evaluation for Local Government.* Westport, Conn.: Greenwood Press, 1987.

Epstein, Paul D. *Using Performance Measurement in Local Government.* New York: Van Nostrand Reinhold, 1984.

Hatry, Harry, Louis Blair, Donald Fisk, John Greiner, John Hall, Jr., and Philip Schaenman. *How Effective Are Your Community Services?* 2nd ed. Washington, D.C.: Urban Institute and ICMA, 1991.

Hatry, Harry, Richard Winnie, and Donald Fisk. *Practical Program Evaluation for State and Local Government Officials.* 2d ed. Washington, D.C.: Urban Institute, 1981.

Jones, Bryan D., with Saadia Greenberg and Joseph Drew. *Service Delivery in the City: Citizen Demand and Bureaucratic Rules.* New York: Longman, 1980.

Levy, Frank, Arnold Meltsner, and Aaron Wildavsky. *Urban Outcomes: Schools, Streets, and Libraries.* Berkeley: University of California Press, 1974.

Lineberry, Robert L. *Equality and Urban Policy: The Distribution of Municipal Public Services.* Beverly Hills: Sage, 1977.

Miller, Gary J. *Cities by Contract: The Politics of Municipal Incorporation.* Cambridge, Mass.: MIT Press, 1981.

7

Productivity Improvement and Cutback Management

Today more than ever public managers are expected to do more with less. Fiscal austerity, regardless of the cause, means that urban administrators must search for ways to provide services as inexpensively as possible.

There is always hope, of course, that local taxpayers will understand the city's plight and acquiesce to either tax increases or additional charges for services. But in many places that hope is unrealistic. Thus, the pressure to contain costs and improve productivity is relentless. What, then, can local public managers do?

Figure 7.1 shows possible sequences of events after a municipal revenue dropoff. The figure depicts three options: reduce services, improve productivity, or find new revenue. Obviously the three are not mutually exclusive; indeed, a city may find it essential to pursue all three simultaneously. In this chapter we look at two of these issues, productivity improvement and cutback management, both part of the cost containment effort that has so preoccupied municipal officials during the past decade.

Productivity Improvement

What is productivity? In the previous chapter we suggested that productivity incorporates both efficiency and effectiveness. To improve productivity, then, we have to offer more or better services from the same resources or the same quantity or quality of services from fewer resources. A majority (53.9 percent) of local government administrators surveyed defined productivity as "the efficiency with which resources are consumed in the effective delivery of services." Another 17 percent chose

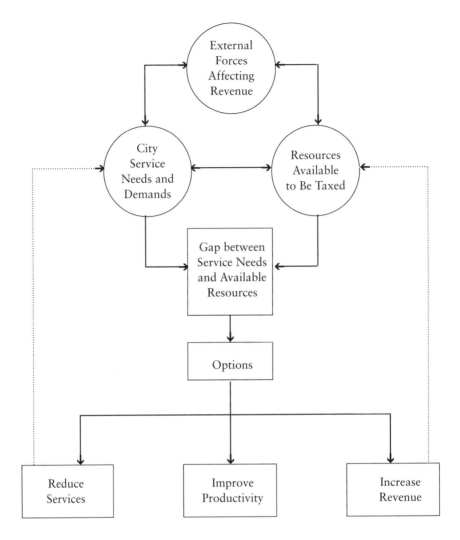

FIGURE 7.1. RESPONSE OPTIONS FOR MANAGING
MUNICIPAL RETRENCHMENT.

SOURCE: Adapted from the City of Alexandria, Virginia, 1979 Annual Report as shown in *Managing Fiscal Retrenchment,* ed H.J. Bryce (Columbus, Ohio: Academy for Contemporary Problems, 1980), 4.

this definition: "the use of any of a wide assortment of progressive techniques or improvements that seem to work better in a given case."[1] Improving productivity obviously extends beyond cutting costs, which often occurs without concern for program effectiveness. Yes, we can reduce library costs by shortening hours, but this will not improve productivity. But if we use volunteers to keep libraries open—thus maintaining service levels while cutting costs—we increase productivity.[2]

How widespread are municipal productivity improvement programs? In 1978 a General Accounting Office study of productivity in a group of 139 cities found that 66 percent had "self-identified" programs to enhance productivity.[3] Only 21 percent, however, used their programs as a primary strategy to control rising costs; instead, most relied on "budgetary belt tightening." About a decade later, Gregory Streib and Theodore Poister reported a decline in productivity improvement programs as a management technique.[4] Based on survey data gathered from a large number of city officials, productivity improvement programs were used in about 42 percent of responding cities in 1976, 67 percent in 1982, and 54 percent in 1988. The decline was attributed to lack of staff capabilities in smaller jurisdictions, costs associated with many programs, inability to measure benefits/results of programs, and implementation difficulties.

For purposes here, we discuss four broad approaches to improving productivity:

- Reorganizing, consolidating, or revising existing structures, programs, or procedures
- Improving employee performance
- Applying improved or advanced technologies
- Developing alternatives to existing service delivery arrangements

The first three of these approaches involve improvements within the municipal organization itself; the last one often involves external entities —private contractors or even other governmental jurisdictions.

Reorganization, Consolidation, or Revision

Historically, government reorganization has focused on strengthening the capacity of the chief executive to control and direct subordinate agencies. The assumption is that if administrative agency officials (i.e., bureaucrats) are forced to follow more closely the policy dictates of the chief executive, they will be less able to pursue their own policy goals, use discretionary authority, and the like. In its ideal form the council-manager plan, for example, allows the manager to appoint without council approval most, if not all, major department heads. This arrangement departs significantly from the traditional weak-mayor form, with its multiple elected city officials and required council approval for most mayoral appointments. Partly because of the rapid spread of the city-manager plan, municipal government has gone much further than either state or county government in concentrating authority in the hands of a single chief executive.

Modern administrative reformers tend to follow certain "principles" to enhance chief executive power. Political scientist Douglas Fox lists four of them:[5]

- Authority should be concentrated in the chief executive and in top appointed department heads.
- Similar functions (e.g., water maintenance and sewer maintenance) should be integrated in the same department.
- Multimember boards and commissions should be replaced with single administrators.
- Central staff agencies (e.g., personnel and budget) should report directly to the chief executive.

Each of these principles helps achieve the fundamental purpose of reorganization: to strengthen the chief executive by concentrating political and administrative authority and accountability in that office.

Thus far we have discussed reorganization as a process of enhancing executive power primarily to ensure bureaucratic responsiveness. Given the public's historic antipathy to executive power, reorganization efforts, which usually have to be approved by a legislative body, are generally sold not on political grounds but as a way to save money. Yet some authorities contend that consolidation as a form of reorganization has been oversold. Although its proponents hold that reorganization can reduce employment and save money, most empirical research finds little if any savings.

One area where consolidation still sparks an interest, though, is in the field of public safety. Despite typically strong opposition, especially from fire departments, a few cities have managed to bring about a degree of consolidation of their police and fire departments. Johnson City, Tennessee, is a case in point.

CASE STUDY

POLICE AND FIRE CONSOLIDATION IN JOHNSON CITY

IN 1979 Johnson City (population about 45,000) became the first city in Tennessee to combine police and fire operations under a new Public Safety Officer (PSO) program. On 1 January forty-eight public safety officers began patrolling the city in six newly established zones. Twenty-five of the officers had been hired for the PSO program; the other twenty-three were traditional fire or police personnel who had requested cross-training to qualify for PSO service. Each officer had to complete more than 300 hours of police and fire training that included study of first aid and rescue techniques.

Before it went into effect, citizen response to the controversial new program was predictably skeptical. But the high visibility of PSO patrols has generated considerable support. And more important, genuine improvements in service delivery have been achieved. Based on a comparison of first-quarter statistics for 1978 and 1979, the police chief proudly announced a reduction in burglaries of 46 percent and a decline in property loss of 44 percent. "We feel that this drastic reduction in burglary statistics is a clear indication of the success of the visibility factor of the PSO patrols," the chief stated. Emergency response time was also down dramatically, from an average of over five minutes to just under two minutes.

The quality of fire service has been upgraded as well. PSO involvement in firefighting had generated the most controversy prior to program implementation. Now the fire chief reports he is "100 percent for the PSO program." "When you get there," he added, "the fire is either under control or completely out." When the PSOs arrive at the scene of a fire, they make a quick assessment of the situation and radio what they see. If the fire is small, the officers try to suppress it using extinguishers carried in the trunks of their cars. If it is a working fire, the officers immediately don firefighting equipment and, if no rescue operation is necessary, stand by to assist the arriving firefighters.

The PSO program achieved two immediate objectives: a significant reduction in emergency response time and a decrease in the fire department workweek from seventy-two to fifty-six hours. In all, the city manager proclaimed, "The effectiveness of this program has even surpassed our greatest hopes."

SOURCE: Adapted from Judy Moss, "Johnson City Merges Police, Fire Functions," *Current Municipal Problems* 6 (1979–80): 342–45.

Reorganization and service consolidation represent major program changes; less sweeping revisions might include more economical use of personnel, improvements in scheduling and work standards, or perhaps even doing away with rules, policies, and procedures. In an effort to use personnel more economically, Fremont, California, has "civilianized" more than a third of its police force.[6] In New Rochelle, New York, community service workers handle about 30 percent of all calls to the police department, including emergency medical calls, general complaints, and other requests for assistance. In Miami some three dozen public service aides (PSAs), ages eighteen to twenty, respond to thousands of nonenforcement calls that would otherwise occupy regular police officers. And more than two-thirds of the PSAs have gone on to become full-fledged officers (some in other cities), reducing departmental recruitment costs. The PSAs are paid about half what a regular uniformed officer receives, but the police department insists they perform 75 percent of an officer's duties.

Scheduling changes are often imposed on sanitation departments in hopes of boosting productivity. In Wilmington, Delaware, city practice allowed garbage collectors to go home when their route was completed, regardless of the number of hours worked.[7] Then it was discovered that most five-member truck crews were finishing their rounds in twenty-two hours a week, although they were paid for forty. The city reduced the crew size, increasing the average time of route completion to thirty-two hours, and cutting the number of workers by 40 percent.

Revising work standards can be an effective way to do more with less. Harrisburg, Pennsylvania, for example, created a vehicle maintenance center (VMC) by consolidating separate departmental garages.[8] Flat-rate work standards were introduced. These standards, prepared and published by private companies, are revised annually. They constitute standard times for performing various automotive and truck repairs (for example, a brake adjustment on a 1990 Chevrolet half-ton pickup), including the time needed to find the necessary tools and to drive the vehicle to and from the repair bay. The work standards were implemented gradually and informally over a twelve-month period. Although management did not consult with either employees or union officials before introducing the standards, no resistance or objections arose. Most employees perceived the standards simply as a managerial device for determining labor costs.

Finally, David Osborne and Ted Gaebler in *Reinventing Government* argue that perhaps the best way to improve productivity in public organizations is to make government mission-driven, not rule-driven: "Rule-driven government may prevent some corruption, but at the price of monumental waste."[9] They cite General George S. Patton's dictum, "Never tell people how to do things. Tell them what you want them to achieve and they will surprise you with their ingenuity."[10] In short, Osborne and Gaebler suggest establishing clear organizational goals and objectives. Then individuals should be turned loose with a minimum of rules and regulations to bind them. What about accountability in such a system? Accountability comes in the form of performance standards, which we discuss in chapter 8.

IMPROVEMENTS IN EMPLOYEE PERFORMANCE

A second basic approach to enhancing productivity focuses on improving employee performance, either by creating incentives that entice employees to put forth greater effort or by finding more efficient methods (technologies) of task performance. We examine the second strategy in the next section; here we look at the first, motivation.

What is the relationship between motivation and productivity? Daniel Yankelovich, who heads his own social research firm, has been interested for some time in the changing work ethic in America. He points to a Gallup study done for the U.S. Chamber of Commerce. It concluded that large reservoirs of potential exist among workers, and that managers can draw on these reservoirs to improve performance and increase worker productivity.[11] It seems that workers have the potential to be more productive. And as many surveys show, they are willing to be more productive; yet most admit they do not work as hard as they could. Why not?

According to Yankelovich, the fundamental reason is the existing reward system. Two factors seem to be involved here. First there are the financial rewards. Again Yankelovich cites the Gallup survey: when workers were asked who they thought would benefit if they improved their productivity, only 9 percent felt they, the workers, would; most assumed that consumers, managers, or even stockholders would reap the benefits. Clearly, then, one reason employees do not work harder or more effectively is because they see little chance of personal gain from the effort. The second factor is psychological: how workers are treated on the job. Again in the Gallup survey, when people were asked if they would work harder and do a better job if they were more involved in decisions relating to their work, 84 percent replied affirmatively. According to Yankelovich, the fundamental problem of productivity in our society lies "in the deeply flawed reward system, both psychological and financial, that now rules the American work place."[12] So our motivational incentives take two forms: monetary and nonmonetary.

MONETARY INCENTIVES. —Efforts to improve productivity must take into account the human element. Money continues to have a powerful effect on human behavior, as it should. Public-sector employees should be rewarded for hard work. Thus we find a growing interest in using monetary incentives as a means of increasing motivation and stimulating greater output on the part of municipal workers.

Osborne and Gaebler argue fervently in *Reinventing Government* that individuals and especially groups of employees should receive bonuses based on their performance.[13] They also believe that public employees should be allowed to keep productivity or budgetary savings. In Visalia, California, for example, employee groups get to keep 30 percent of productivity savings. In the same city, mechanics decided they needed new tools, but no revenues were available. After cutting energy consumption in the shop by 30 percent through various cost-saving activities, the mechanics were allowed to keep budgetary savings and buy their new tools.

NONMONETARY INCENTIVES. — Programs involving nonmonetary incentives are designed to meet employees' needs for growth and development on the job or for more leisure time. A recent five-year study released by Families and Work Institute, a New York-based nonprofit organization, adds to the growing evidence that workers are less willing to sacrifice for work and are putting more emphasis on their personal lives. "Workers are most willing to work hard and care about the success of their company [and the quality of their work] when they have good relationships with their supervisors, do not have to choose between work and their personal responsibilities and feel they have an opportunity to advance. . . ."[14] Employers can enhance productivity and loyalty, according to the research, by providing workers with flexibility, control, and a quality working environment. Specific programs that might be included under nonmonetary incentives include job enrichment, quality circles, flexible work schedules, performance targeting, and dependent-related activities.

Job enrichment encompasses a variety of ways to make work more interesting for workers and improve the quality of organizational life. Included in this category are (1) *team participation*, to encourage cooperation and provide a more comprehensive view of the work process; (2) *job redesign*, to give the employee greater control over how a task is done or responsibility for completing an entire piece of work rather than one segment of a task; and (3) *job rotation*, to give the worker the broad experience that can increase understanding of the interrelatedness of various parts of the organization and to reduce boredom.[15]

The *quality circle* (QC) stresses employee involvement. It assumes that people will contribute useful suggestions for improving work methods and be more concerned about the quality of their work if they directly participate in decisions affecting their jobs. The QC concept, generally attributed to the Japanese, has spread in American industry as well as the public sector. As we discuss in the next chapter, quality circles, or their equivalent, are an integral component of Total Quality Management (TQM), which in the vernacular of *Reinventing Government* allows organizations to be "customer-driven."

Flexible work schedules are growing in popularity. "Today more than 20 percent of the total labor force is engaged in flextime, job-sharing, or permanent part-time work."[16] Flextime allows workers to set their own hours within a framework that meets the needs of the organization. These programs are particularly useful to individuals in meeting the needs of their dependents or in general to give workers more control of their lives. Research suggests that flextime has positive effects such as increasing morale and productivity and at the same time reducing absenteeism and tardiness.[17]

Performance targeting essentially involves making explicit to workers, either individually or as a group, the type and level of performance expected from them over a specific time period.[18] Performance targeting is customarily incorporated into more comprehensive systems for directing and evaluating employee performance such as Management by Objectives (MBO) or TQM, which we consider in more detail in the next chapter. Here suffice it to say that performance targeting helps motivate employees to perform more efficiently or effectively by providing them with specific targets, objectives, or quotas to meet.

Dependent-related activities are growing in importance. Some experts estimate that between the years 1985 and 2000, about *two-thirds of new entrants into the American workforce will be women.* (Only about 15 percent will be nonminority males).[19] New issues are associated with the changing demographics of work. Discounted child-care programs, dependent-care accounts that set aside pretax dollars for child care, parental leave, and cafeteria-style benefits programs are important to both males and females, but especially females. A mother who is divorced, for example, might choose additional days of paid leave instead of health insurance if her children are covered under their father's health policy.[20]

TECHNOLOGICAL IMPROVEMENTS

Many authorities believe that substantial increases in municipal productivity are likely to come primarily from increased use of new technologies. In a survey of city officials "advanced technology" was ranked as the most promising productivity strategy.[21] Historically, of course, it is through technology that the great gains in output have been achieved in industry and agriculture. Municipalities represent fertile ground for the application of new technologies because most city functions are labor intensive. At the same time many operations involve the use of hardware and equipment that lend themselves to change and innovation. For example, over a three-year period in the mid-1970s, the city of Milwaukee reported the following budgetary savings from the introduction of new equipment and technologies:[22]

- The bureau of engineers in the public works department saved $325,000 by installing a new system in which television cameras are used to examine sanitary sewers for points of surface-water infiltration. Leaks discovered are sealed with a spraying technique from inside the sewer.
- Electric pumps automatically activated by high storm-water levels were installed at twenty-nine locations at a cost of $167,000, creating estimated annual savings of $50,000 by eliminating the need to dispatch emergency crews with portable pumps.
- The police department increased its revenue $1 million a year by computerizing warrant preparation and adding a special warrant division.

Over the last several decades a number of equipment improvements have been made in the areas of firefighting and solid-waste collection. Although these improvements often result in cost savings and productivity gains, they may also produce labor-management tension when workers perceive technological change as a threat to their jobs. Such was the case in the summer of 1974 in the city of Little Rock, Arkansas.[23] New labor-saving procedures and equipment were introduced without employee involvement. Previously a four-member crew had operated from each truck, picking up garbage at the rear of each house. In 1974, based on recommendations from outside consultants, management unilaterally adopted a new side-loading truck, the Shu-Pac, that could be operated by a single person, the driver. Sanitation workers, angry that this drastic change was made without consulting them, refused to use the new trucks. Communications between labor and management virtually ceased. In August 1974 the workers went out on strike. The dispute was eventually resolved, and sanitation department improvements resulted in annual savings of over $366,000. Still, city officials learned a valuable lesson in the politics of technological innovation.

Regardless of potential conflict, as the case study that follows suggests, technological change is often hard to stop once started.

THE DIFFUSION OF TECHNOLOGY

SCOTTSDALE, ARIZONA, often viewed as one of the most innovative cities in the United States, is credited in 1969 with pioneering the use of the cost-efficient, high-tech, side-loading garbage truck discussed previously. The vehicle requires only a driver, who is never required to leave the truck. The cost of a unit is about the same as the more traditional truck requiring a crew of two to three workers (up to about $100,000). The vehicle has an AM-FM radio, is air-conditioned, and the driver is provided with a cassette so she or he does not have to stop and write down locations where loose garbage is sighted. In Scottsdale, use of the technology has meant tremendous cost savings. While the city has increased its population by 50 percent in the past ten years (to about 120,000), the garbage collection crew has remained at forty-eight employees.

In Mesa, Arizona, the new garbage truck can collect refuse from 1,200 homes a day, compared to 800 under the old system. The city expects to save $1 million annually by using the trucks citywide.

City officials in Ontario, California, expect big savings from the new garbage collection technology as a result of fewer disability claims. There also is less need to hire substitutes for injured sanitation workers.

The fully automated truck is catching on quickly, especially in nonunion western cities. As many as 100 cities are buying the trucks.

SOURCE: Elizabeth Voisin, "Trash Pickup No Chore," *City & State*, October 1987, 30.

ALTERNATIVE SERVICE DELIVERY

A fourth and final way to increase productivity is to find alternatives to city-operated service monopolies. The rationale for developing alternatives to municipal monopolies is simple: Economists have long argued that monopolies are inefficient and unresponsive; competition, on the other hand, allegedly forces producers to operate as efficiently as possible to stay in business. The basic idea behind alternative service arrangements, then, is to stimulate greater productivity by introducing competition into the local public sector. Indeed, Osborne and Gaebler are convinced that a pivotal factor in the process of reinventing government is competitive government, or injecting competition into service delivery.[24]

Although E.S. Savas identifies as many as nine alternative delivery arrangements (including franchises, subsidies, vouchers, voluntary service, and self-help),[25] a recent analysis of patterns in the use of alternative service delivery approaches among cities and counties by the ICMA shows that only two options are used extensively across the full range of municipal services: contracting to the private sector and entering into intergovernmental agreements.[26] The ICMA study found that franchises are used infrequently and primarily for public utilities (gas or electric). Subsidies are used most often for health and human services, with programs for the homeless being the most common. Public safety (e.g., neighborhood watch) and health and human services (e.g., programs for the elderly) were the two service areas where volunteers were used most frequently. Given their widespread use, attention here focuses on contracting and intergovernmental agreements.

Contracting out has a number of advantages, according to its proponents. Perhaps the most important is that it purportedly results in cost savings. After all, the greatest impetus for governments to consider alternative service delivery mechanisms in the first place is fiscal stress.[27] Private-sector services cost less because competition and the profit motive presumably bring operating efficiencies. In a recent study by Touche Ross and Company (an international accounting and consulting firm), for example, 74 percent of over 1,000 city and county officials cited cost savings as an advantage of contracting out.[28] Similarly, a large-scale study of contracting for a variety of local services—from street maintenance to payroll processing—in the Los Angeles area found service costs were significantly lower where the services were privately delivered.[29]

Contracting also allows a municipality to procure specialized services not otherwise available, to avoid large start-up costs, and to have greater flexibility in adjusting program size (without worrying about negotiating with recalcitrant municipal employees). Given these advantages, it is little wonder that state and local governments are estimated to contract out over $100 billion annually.[30]

There are disadvantages too. Some argue that, in the long run, privatizing increases costs, since a profit is involved and the private contractor must pay taxes too. Also, historically, the awarding of government contracts has been plagued with charges of kickbacks and corruption. The process of deciding whether or not savings will occur from contracting is not an easy task. Frequently governments use line-item budgets, which show objects of expenditures instead of activities performed by governmental units. If information about how much it costs to provide a particular public service is not available, a city cannot make accurate cost comparisons of private vendors. Also, before contracting, the full costs of a public service should be determined, including indirect costs, contract administration costs, opportunity costs, and so forth. Fortunately help is available to city officials in determining these costs. In a recent article in the *Municipal Year Book*, public administration expert Lawrence Martin offers a methodology for comparing the costs of government versus contract service delivery.[31] Drawing up contracts can be a tricky business as well, and there is always the possibility that important details may be left out. Then contracts must be monitored, of course. But from a practical point of view two disadvantages loom largest: strong opposition from municipal employees who fear job losses and forfeiture of fringe benefits (even if they are hired by the private contractor) and the loss of management control over direct operations.[32]

Pros and cons aside, some services lend themselves more readily to contracting than do others. In general, the services that appear to be the best prospects for contracting out are those that

- Are *new*, which avoids problems with city employees.
- Have *easy-to-specify outputs* (e.g., solid-waste collection), which makes contract preparation and monitoring easier.
- Require *specialized skills* (e.g., engineering or law) or *specialized equipment*, which smaller cities in particular cannot afford on a regular or permanent basis.
- Involve *large numbers of low-skill workers* (e.g., solid-waste collection and janitorial services), since these areas appear to hold the most promise of cost savings because of pay and benefit differentials between the public and private sector.

Contracting to the private sector does not have to be an all-or-nothing proposition, as the case study that follows shows.

CASE STUDY

PRIVATE CONTRACTING IN MINNEAPOLIS

IN 1971 Minneapolis was forced to make a change in its method of collecting solid waste. Before that year, municipal forces picked up only wet garbage from all city households, while a number of private haulers collected rubbish and trash. Because of a change in the state law, the city decided to switch to a combined collection system for all solid waste. The big issue was who would provide the service. After considerable study, the council opted for an arrangement that called for the existing city department to serve part of the community and a newly formed private company, composed of several dozen existing haulers, to handle the remaining areas.

The city was divided into districts assigned essentially at random to the corporation and the city department. The territory covered by the private company was comparable to that served by the city force. A five-year contract was awarded to Minneapolis Refuse (the private corporation), with payment to be renegotiated annually, based on the number of households served. The contract carefully specified the service expected, including service frequency and complaint-handling procedures, and required bond guaranteeing performance. The city closely monitored the private corporation and kept very detailed records on the work of the city department, which enabled the city staff to make an accurate comparison of the relative cost and effectiveness of the two operations.

How did the two competing service entities compare during the first few years of the contract?

- Cost per ton was lower for contract collection than for municipal service.
- Until the fifth year, cost per household was lower for the private firm; the city gradually closed the gap over the life of the contract.
- Citizen satisfaction, based on telephone complaints, was about equal for the two services.
- Perhaps most important, *the number of tons collected by city crews increased and the rate of increase in cost per ton for municipal collection dropped sharply after competition was introduced.*

In his study of the Minneapolis experience, E.S. Savas concludes by pointing out the virtues of competition: "It seems clear that a healthy competitive climate exists, a climate which tends to produce explicit and open reporting, increased productivity, and more cost-effective service delivery for the citizens." As noted earlier, the same message about the virtues of competition is being preached over fifteen years later by Osborne and Gaebler in *Reinventing Government.*

We should note the special circumstances under which the Minneapolis arrangement developed. The service was not previously dominated by a municipal monopoly; it had been divided between a series of noncontract private haulers and a city force. So no major economic or political dislocations were produced by the new system, which undoubtedly made the transition much easier.

SOURCE: Adapted from E.S. Savas, "An Empirical Study of Competition in Municipal Service Delivery," *Public Administration Review* 37 (November/December 1977): 717–24.

Solid-waste collection seems particularly well suited to private contracting; fire protection does not. This is not to say that contracting out of firefighting services is impossible. Witness the well-publicized success story of Scottsdale, Arizona.

CASE STUDY

PRIVATIZING FIRE PROTECTION IN SCOTTSDALE

IN Scottsdale, a private company, Rural-Metro, supplies fire protection to residents of the city and several other communities in the Phoenix area. Rural-Metro has a complement of full-time, around-the-clock personnel at Scottsdale fire stations. But the company requires fewer employees (59) than would a traditional municipal department because of the availability of cross-trained city employees (35), called wranglers, who double as part-time emergency firefighters. Judy Weiss, administrative manager for community services, Marc Ranney, parks support services manager, and Carlos Ramirez, city equipment operator, are examples of wranglers. The wranglers receive extra pay (from $9.24 to $15.34 per hour) to be available on a standby basis every fourth week. This arrangement has helped Scottsdale achieve an estimated 47 percent savings over the costs of a city-operated force. Part of the cost reduction also results from the Rural-Metro company's construction of most of its own apparatus, which is often nonstandard and thus considerably cheaper than conventional equipment.

SOURCE: Adapted from Roger S. Ahlbrandt, Jr., "Implications of Contracting for a Public Service," *Urban Affairs Quarterly* 9 (March 1974): 337–58; and "City Employees Realize Fireman Dreams; Boost Public Safety," *Scottsdale Citizen,* September 1985, 12.

Despite the widely acclaimed success of Rural-Metro in Scottsdale, the traditional municipal fire service has been extraordinarily resistant to change. Part of the reason is the success firefighters have in convincing people that any change from the typical municipal operation might endanger life and property. They argue as well that homeowners may pay more for fire insurance if the community's fire-suppression capacity receives a lower rating from the national Insurance Services Office.

INTERGOVERNMENTAL AGREEMENTS. — A second basic alternative to municipal monopoly is the intergovernmental agreement or contract. Certainly there is nothing new about agreements or contracts between units of government; they have long been used as an important device to supply needed services. Some of the motivations for privatizing—potentially saving money, acquiring services needed only on a periodic basis, avoiding large initial cost outlays, and obtaining specialized services not otherwise available—also stimulate an interest in intergovernmental agreements. In chapter 1 we examined the extensive agreements between cities and the county government in Los Angeles County (the Lakewood Plan). These service arrangements developed because many of the small suburbs were unable to afford the large initial investment needed to hire and equip a municipal workforce. The county, on the other hand, had built up the capacity to provide a range of urban services. So a natural symbiotic relationship evolved. Although legal and geographic considerations obviously limit the use of intergovernmental service agreements, many cities seem to be more and more interested in them.

A 1980s survey found that about 52 percent of responding cities had entered into a formal or informal service agreement with another government.[33] A more recent survey compares the usage of intergovernmental agreements between 1982 and 1988 in seven service areas. Based on data from 1,700 cities and counties, Tari Renner notes that the use of intergovernmental agreements has remained remarkably stable over time.[34] Exceptions to the rule included substantial increases in agreements in the health and human services area and agreements for tax-bill processing. Substantial declines in agreements were recorded for solid-waste disposal and street light operation. For all seven service areas and the more than fifty specific services in those areas, the five most frequent services that local governments enter into agreements with other governments are bus system operation/maintenance (31 percent of responding cities and counties), paratransit system operation/maintenance (28 percent), operation of libraries (25 percent), tax assessment (25 percent), and hazardous waste disposal (24 percent).

The case study that follows demonstrates the benefits from interlocal contracting.

CASE STUDY

AN INTERLOCAL AGREEMENT IN GRAYSON COUNTY

IN the early 1970s the city manager of Sherman, Texas (population about 31,000), began to look for ways to reduce the costs of data processing. He decided to explore the possibility of establishing a joint computer center with the other major governmental units in the area. After a meeting with representatives of the city of Sherman, the city of Denison, Grayson County, and the independent school districts in Denison and Sherman, an outside consultant undertook a feasibility study. The study found a number of inadequacies in the existing data-handling arrangements of the five governments. Costs were too high, and dissemination of information was inadequate. The report also recognized that a joint data-processing venture, although difficult to establish, would be justified under the proper conditions.

Governing boards for all five public entities approved the idea of a joint venture, and a meeting was held in October 1973 to negotiate an interlocal agreement. The major areas covered in the agreement were policymaking for the joint center, cost distribution, management of the center, and the procedure for handling requests by other governments wanting to use the facility. The agreement calls for the center to be managed by a policymaking body consisting of five voting members, who hire a manager to conduct the daily affairs of the center. Administrative support is handled under contractual arrangement with the Texoma Regional Planning Commission. The center is financed from funds deposited annually in advance, based on the anticipated use of each member government. Requests for use by other governments are considered on an individual basis.

Very little investment was required to open the center. The start-up costs for collecting, converting, and processing the new data from each government were substantial, however. A number of new services have been added since 1973, which of course necessitated the acquisition of new hardware and the addition of new personnel. The center staff now consists of eight full-time employees. Currently all services are provided in a timely manner, with routine requests handled in no more than twenty-four hours. Data-processing costs for the five major users increased substantially during the first several years' operation, but have since leveled off. In all, the cooperating jurisdictions appear to be spending less than had been projected, and users are apparently quite satisfied with the quality of the service.

SOURCE: Adapted from Kent Myers and David Tees, *Interlocal Cooperation: Six Case Histories* (Arlington, Tex.: Institute of Urban Studies, University of Texas, 1978), 35–53.

Interlocal agreements are not suitable for every municipal function, of course. But the kind of cooperative effort that went into the Grayson Governmental Data Center holds promise for communities that face common service problems, where the service involved can benefit from economies of scale.

The Barriers to Increased Productivity

No matter how appealing or useful many productivity improvement programs seem, substantial obstacles often impede their implementation. A recent survey of small communities identified financial constraints as the most serious barrier to improving productivity.[35] Often a city must spend money to save money. A second difficulty among small municipalities is the lack of analytical capacity. Resources are just not available to purchase labor-saving equipment or to hire analysts. As one local manager from Massachusetts put it, "It's not that we don't know how to improve productivity, but rather there is so little time and so few resources to implement obvious cost-effective changes."[36]

The study cites apathy as the third most common stumbling block to improvements. Why apathy? Perhaps, as suggests Frederick Hayes, former budget director of New York City, the real reasons are that "innovations in local government involve real risks—of program failure, of raising politically influential opposition, and of causing strikes, slowdowns, or other problems of employee resistance."[37] Hayes goes on to say that the cards are stacked against productivity improvement in city governments. Few people have a direct interest in making changes, and risks and institutional inertia are difficult to overcome. In effect, because benefits are often long range and not readily apparent, the principal barriers to increased productivity are political, not technical.

Those who want to improve municipal productivity, then, have their work cut out for them. At the least three things seem essential: strong support from top management (including, if necessary, the city council), employee participation, and a favorable climate for innovation. Mark Keane, former executive director of the ICMA, cites commitment from the top as the main ingredient of a successful productivity improvement program.[38] Upper leadership must also convince middle management of the desirability of introducing new technologies and approaches. In fact, Hayes contends that middle managers may be more fearful of the changes associated with productivity improvements than are ordinary workers. This apprehension often stems from resentment of external interference, reluctance to take risks, skepticism about the possibility of constructive change, the desire to protect subordinates, and the general absence of any tradition of innovative management.[39]

| CASE STUDY |

MIDDLE-MANAGEMENT RESISTANCE TO CHANGE

INGLEWOOD, CALIFORNIA (population about 102,000), has used one-person refuse trucks for over a decade at significantly reduced costs, and with fewer injuries and greater satisfaction for personnel. Informed of the Inglewood program, the sanitation director in an eastern city using four-member crews on its trucks said he did not believe it. Having confirmed that they were in use, he opined that Inglewood's streets and contours were different from his city's. Convinced that conditions in both places were generally the same, he lamented that his constituents would never accept a lower level of service. Persuaded that the levels of service were equal, he explained that the sanitation crews would not accept a faster pace and harder work conditions. Told that the Inglewood sanitation workers prefer the system because they set their own pace and suffered fewer injuries caused by careless co-workers, the director prophesied that the city council would never agree to such a large cutback in personnel. Informed of Inglewood's career development plan to move sanitation workers into other city departments, the director pointed out he was responsible only for sanitation.

SOURCE: Adapted from *Improving Productivity in State and Local Government* (Washington, D.C.: Committee for Economic Development, 1976), 46.

Not surprisingly, attempts to change accepted practices can generate considerable employee resistance. Productivity improvements often are aimed at reducing labor costs, so people quite naturally fear for their jobs. And productivity efforts in the private sector conjure up images of work speedups, efficiency experts, and time-and-motion studies. Walter Balk, a professor of public affairs, notes another reason why employee unions resist or even actively oppose productivity programs.[40] Unions usually represent occupational groups or persons who work at similar jobs. If small groups within a unit are rewarded differentially for productivity gains, the union is placed in an awkward position because its historical objective is parity for all members of the unit. If the union accepts the differential award system, it appears to be supporting management in a move that may well be unpopular among members who do not receive rewards. So for a variety of reasons every effort must be made to keep employees informed and directly involved in productivity decisions. Equally important, if possible, is a guarantee of employment at some other city job for workers affected by productivity-related layoffs.

Even where management is committed, employees cooperate, and the climate is open to change, urban managers confront the difficult problem of measuring productivity gains.

Measuring Productivity

In chapter 6 we examined the various ways in which urban services can be measured. If a city is serious about productivity programs, the issue of measurement intrudes again. All the problems of what and how to measure come into play. Along with data on various costs, input and workload measures have to be gathered. Some of these have to be converted to efficiency measures, perhaps by developing ratios that include worker hours or costs in the denominator. And of course effectiveness indicators are essential. To carry productivity measurement to its logical conclusion, then, we may have to combine efficiency and effectiveness measures. One municipal service for which this can be done more easily than it can for others is solid-waste collection. Table 7.1 depicts efficiency and effectiveness measures that could be used for a small city sanitation department.

Developing appropriate performance measures is tough, and many cities still lack the necessary data. Especially if contracting out is contemplated, local officials must be sure that data on service costs are accurate so that genuine comparisons can be made. For example, a council member might say, "It's costing us only $10 a ton to get rid of garbage at the landfill. Why should we pay $20 a ton to a private resource recovery plant?"[41] Then a closer examination of the city's cost might reveal the omission of management time for supervising the landfill. The city's estimate also excludes vehicle repairs, service provided by another department. There are no costs for self-insurance. And city figures leave out depreciation. Sure enough, private business cannot compete with the $10 price if much of the true cost has not been taken in account. The old adage of comparing apples to apples comes into play here.

TABLE 7.1.
SAMPLE MEASURES OF SOLID-WASTE COLLECTION
PRODUCTIVITY

	Actual output 1st six months	Estab- lished target	Actual output 2d six months
A. *Efficiency measures*			
Tons collected/route/week	4.5	5.0	5.2
Tons collected/worker-hour	0.75	1.1	1.0
Households serviced/crew collection hour	80.5	109.6	101.0
Worker-hours/route	12.0	10.0	10.0
Cost/ton collected	$16.85	$15.13	$15.62
Cost/crew collection hour	$20.14	$18.10	$18.70
Cost/household services	$ .25	$ .20	$ .23
Cost/equipment hour	$ .52	$ .45	$ .50
B. *Effectiveness measures*			
Number of citizen complaints	34	50% less	22
Percentage of routes completed on time	60	75	80
Number of missed pickups	19	50% less	12
Average street cleanliness rating[a]	2.9	2.7	2.8

SOURCE: *Performance Measurement and Cost Accounting for Smaller Local Governments* (Providence: Department of Community Affairs, State of Rhode Island, n.d.), 24.

a. The rating of street cleanliness is on a scale of 1 to 4, with 4 being the cleanest.

Finally, it seems essential that multiple measures be used and that special attention be devoted to measuring the quality of service. In fact, the viability of any productivity program may well rest on this last point, as J. Patrick Wright's story of operations at General Motors shows. In the 1970s, of all twenty-two of GM's U.S. plants, the GM assembly line in Tarrytown, New York, produced the poorest-quality cars. Some dealers even refused its cars. But it had the lowest manufacturing costs at GM. So the Tarrytown plant manager, although building the worst cars in the company, was receiving one of the biggest bonuses of all assembly plant managers.[42] Enough said.

Retrenchment–Cutback Management

Improving productivity may not be enough; fiscal austerity may demand even more of urban managers. If reductions are essential, what should be cut and how? Can vital services be protected when resources decline? How will employees react to hiring freezes or layoffs? Are there ways of making existing resources go further? These are only a few of the questions that arise when retrenchment hits. There is no formula or package of responses that will suit all localities equally well. But the growing literature on cutback management offers some clues about the problems local managers might encounter and how to handle them.

Revenue slowdowns or reductions create special organizational problems. Charles Levine, an authority on cutback management, indicates that without slack resources to yield "win-win" consensus-building solutions or to provide side payoffs for losers, resistance to change grows, and organizational flexibility and the capacity to innovate diminish.[43] And personnel problems develop: there are fewer resources with which to reward creative, innovative employees; promotions are harder to come by; and there are fewer openings to attract new young talent. All is not bleak, however. An era of retrenchment can provide an opportunity not only for improving productivity but also for reevaluating the need for or at least the level of services ordinarily taken for granted. As Carol Lewis and Anthony Logalbo put it, "The growing perception of scarce resources presents a climate for creative change."[44] We look at the strategies and options pursued by some cities in the face of budget constraints; but first we should examine how cities react to fiscal stress.

REACTING TO FISCAL STRESS

Charles Levine and his colleagues undertook in-depth research on how four large urban areas reacted when confronted with the need to retrench.[45] Examining Oakland, Cincinnati, Baltimore, and Prince Georges County, Maryland, they learned that each of these administrative units initially tried to improve efficiency, delay certain expenditures, and ration services. The authors label this tactic *stretching and resisting*. Few programs, at least at the outset, were terminated. In addition, all the localities tried to persuade the state and county governments to assume certain service obligations, with some success. Where that failed, the overwhelming choice of decision makers was to lower service levels across the board, maintaining the existing service mix and site distribution. Yet postponing expenditures had a differential effect: most delays were in capital spending and maintenance and thus predominately affected public works departments.

As might be expected, the deeper the decline and the longer it lasted, the more likely local officials were to target cuts, terminate programs, and initiate layoffs (beyond attrition). This stage of the retrenchment process, in which officials are forced to eliminate programs, close facilities, and terminate employees, is called *cutting and smoothing*. Smoothing is the administrative reaction to cutting—the attempt to ameliorate the most negative consequences of reductions in the hope of producing the least disruption to programs and personnel. Officials try to dampen the antagonism and weaken the resistance of internal and external groups adversely affected by the changes.

Several other tendencies were noted in the four communities. Almost every place found some substitutes for local revenue, primarily from state and federal sources. And even where formal authority was already strong and centralized, there was an additional effort to centralize authority, especially in the area of budgetary control. Somewhat surprisingly, neither external groups nor city employees were very effective in slowing down or deflecting proposed reductions in expenditures. They conclude that those cities with more centralized control and less politicized decision making are likely to be most effective in managing the retrenchment process. In particular, the authors contend that council-manager communities often can handle cutbacks better than can cities with other forms of government.

THE PRECONDITIONS FOR ORDERLY RETRENCHMENT

Levine and his associates identified six basic preconditions to managing an organizational contraction effectively: authority, continuity, feedback, budgetary flexibility, incentives, and the capacity to target cuts.[46] Their research persuaded them that management's capacity to redirect resources and make essential changes is strongest when these conditions are present; their absence creates a deficiency that can be overcome only through painful political adjustment.

The first precondition is the *authority* to act. Without centralized managerial authority, we find splintered policymaking. This may lead to actions that are hesitant, fragmental, and inconsistent. The second requisite is *continuity* in top management. The concern here is not only with consistency but also with long-term planning. Continuity allows a retrenchment plan to unfold over several budget cycles without confusion, backtracking, and changes of direction. Third, rapid and accurate *feedback* is essential. Otherwise a city may struggle with a cost-cutting program without any clear idea about its effectiveness or about which options are likely to succeed if more cutbacks are necessary.

Developing and maintaining *budgetary* flexibility is a fourth requisite for successfully managing decline. Managers must be able to shift resources from one area to another or to substitute one factor for another (equipment for labor or part-time employees for full-time staff). Inflexibility can stymie effective reductions.

Incentives for improving performance and conserving resources are the fifth precondition for retrenchment. Without incentives—both monetary and nonmonetary—good managers may drag their feet or leave the organization altogether. And without a cadre of experienced senior managers, orderly cutbacks may be impossible. The sixth and final condition is the *capacity to target cuts* in line with some larger plan or objective. If rules or contracts prevent urban managers from targeting reductions, they are left with piecemeal across-the-board cuts. This means hiring freezes, deferred maintenance, and the postponement of equipment replacement, hardly a managed organizational response at all.

Unfortunately, according to Levine, these six prerequisites tend to be lacking in most public agencies. At this point, then, we need to see what does happen when communities are confronted with cutbacks and retrenchment.

Managing Retrenchment

From a municipal manager's viewpoint, obtaining new sources of revenue, improving productivity, or shifting the service burden to another level of government is always preferable to cutting programs and personnel. But the endless budgetary squeeze may force some places to take drastic steps; reductions may have to be made.

Politically, the easiest cuts are those made across the board. Most experts agree with Levine, however—even though such an approach seems equitable, it deprives management of the opportunity to reexamine priorities and make choices based on program needs. In fact, recent research shows that cities do not always go for the politically expedient solution. Gregory Lewis's study of 154 cities found substantial targeting of employment cuts that apparently were aimed at less efficiently performed services.[47] But how does one choose what to target? Two basic options seem possible, and they may not be mutually exclusive.

ALLIANCE BUILDING. — One approach is an alliance-building process. Cultivating support from various groups may allow local officials to implement a programmatic retrenchment process.[48] This strategy requires that groups agree on goals, objectives, and priorities. Proposed spending reductions are then considered in the light of their consequences for established priorities. Setting objectives and priorities is difficult enough in the best of times; under adverse financial conditions it requires unusual political courage and leadership skills because choosing means saying no to some groups. This is where alliance building comes in. To the extent that certain groups can be won over or their potential opposition neutralized, the retrenchment process can proceed much more smoothly.

Certain leadership tactics may prove helpful in constructing coalitions. Public administration specialist Robert Biller has identified several such tactics especially applicable to the cutback process.[49] First, separate winning from losing. Make reductions in such a way that losers feel they are being treated fairly. Then, where possible, distribute gains to winners (or nonlosers) in a different arena and at a different time. Such a two-tiered process helps to avoid pitting winners and losers directly against each other.

Second, provide general rather than specific reasons for cutbacks. Advancing particular reasons makes it easier for the opposition to mobilize. If, for example, particular program weaknesses or deficiencies are cited, opponents may respond with a proposal to fix the problem rather than accept the cuts. Offering general reasons (for example, the organization simply cannot afford the prior level of spending) makes it harder for oppositional coalitions to organize because there are no specific points to oppose.

Third, include some across-the-board cuts. If rancor and divisiveness are to be avoided, the retrenchment process must be seen as fair, with no favoritism shown. Establishing some percentage reductions along with targeted cuts increases the perception of fairness and legitimacy: "We are *all* being asked to share *some* of the burden."

GROUP PROCESS TECHNIQUES.—Another option for achieving budget reductions is to use group process techniques. What follows is a structured decision-making process city councils might rely on to determine where to make cuts.[50]

First, the council identifies a series of programs, activities, or even departmental divisions that can be eliminated or cut substantially. Such a list can be generated in various ways—by brainstorming, by requesting staff to furnish a comprehensive list, or by having each council member develop his or her own list, which is then combined with the others to create a complete listing. The use of a group process technique, such as nominal group technique (NGT) or delphi, comes next. NGT is a somewhat formalized process by which each group member secretly establishes a series of preferences or priorities, perhaps using a weighting scheme to reflect degree of importance. The staff then tallies the preferences for the entire group to consider.

At this point, staff estimates the savings associated with each possible program cut. Finally, the nominal group technique can employ specialized computer routines that allow council members to compare all possible program reductions. This step in the process probably requires assistance from a consultant. That person might serve as a moderator who discusses each program cut being considered. Using the computer, the moderator can offer a series of paired comparisons of all proposed program reductions. The facilitator moderates discussion of each paired comparison: "Should A be cut before B?" "Should A be cut before C?" and so on. When everyone has had a chance to speak, a vote is called for between the competing pair. As soon as the group votes on a comparison, the results are fed into the computer, which is programmed to make logical inferences from previous comparisons so that all possible pairs need not be compared. The end product is a group judgment as to the relative priority of all items. The council would not be bound by the results, of course, but would presumably use the outcome as a guide for making the final decisions on budget cuts. Such a process was undertaken in several Ohio cities and counties in the early 1980s, with the help of a consultant. The reactions of local officials to the use of group process techniques were generally positive.

RETRENCHMENT IN PERSPECTIVE

When budgets are cut, two groups suffer most: employees and service recipients. Most cities usually begin their personnel reductions with attrition, but layoffs may be unavoidable during a prolonged retrenchment. And once a city begins to terminate employees, a whole new set of problems shows up. Most union contracts require that the last hired be the first fired. This seniority principle plays havoc with affirmative action efforts and can lead to lawsuits by aggrieved minority groups and women. It becomes critical, then, to explain the situation as completely as possible to employees and to middle management. If people within the organization feel that internal actions are not consistent with external announcements or that favoritism or politics is at play, cutback management can become an adversary process clouded by cynicism, distrust, and efforts at sabotage.

Cutback management also affects service recipients. In light of the service distribution literature and various definitions of equity we discussed in the last chapter, Fredric Bolotin makes a strong argument that city officials should assess the equity of service cuts required by retrenchment across various neighborhoods.[51]

Communication is also crucial in managers' relationships with the public, the service recipients. The public relations task during a period of retrenchment is extraordinarily demanding. Many people feel that public agencies are inefficient and overstaffed, that cost cutting is simply a matter of trimming the fat or making employees work harder. When local officials must reduce services, they must be prepared to take a thoroughly documented case to the people.

Summary

Doing more with less has become a cliché in urban circles. Yet many cities have no real choice—revenues are down and the public shows little sign of wanting less service. Under these circumstances urban managers may well have to pursue one or a combination of several strategies: increasing productivity, reducing expenditures, or finding new revenue sources.

Programs to improve productivity are becoming more and more important as cities search for ways to hold down costs. Clearly the opportunity for improving organizational performance is the silver lining in the dark cloud of fiscal austerity. But strong support from the top is critical in creating the climate necessary for change. And some are beginning to recognize that a rethinking of the traditional organizational reward structure is imperative. Employees must feel that gains in productivity will also benefit them.

Managing organizational decline in the city is a new experience, and until recently few guidelines were available. Now, however, enough communities have suffered through revenue shortages that they have a much better feel for the retrenchment process. Many times, local officials deny the seriousness of the problem and delay taking effective action. If the situation fails to improve, the next step might be characterized as stretching and resisting. While searching for new revenue sources or operating efficiencies, officials may be forced to impose hiring freezes and even across-the-board service reductions. Finally, if the crisis becomes prolonged, the city may enter a cutting and smoothing phase in which deep, targeted reductions are made.

Effective retrenchment demands the authority to act, continuity in top management, timely and accurate feedback, budgetary flexibility, a functional incentive program, and the capacity to target cuts. But most of all it demands of urban managers the ability to understand the human elements at work in the process—the employees threatened by municipal change and the service recipients who are unwilling to accept increased taxation or reduced levels of service as plausible solutions to the forced cutback problem.

Notes

1. David Ammons and Joseph King, "Productivity Improvement in Local Government: Its Place among Competing Priorities," *Public Administration Review* 43 (March/April 1983): 113–20.

2. W. Maureen Godsey, *Productivity Improvement in Small Local Governments,* Urban Data Service Reports, vol. 14 (Washington, D.C.: ICMA, 1982), 2.

3. *State and Local Government Productivity Improvement: What Is the Federal Role?* (Washington, D.C.: General Accounting Office, 1978), 9–12.

4. Gregory Streib and Theodore H. Poister, "Established and Emerging Management Tools: A 12-Year Perspective," *Municipal Year Book 1989* (Washington, D.C.: ICMA, 1989), 45–46.

5. Douglas M. Fox, *Managing the Public's Interest* (New York: Holt, Rinehart and Winston, 1979), 50.

6. These examples come from Mark Frazier and Jim Lewis, "Some American Communities 'Privatize' to Cut Costs," *Transatlantic Perspective,* July 1981, 4.

7. Ibid.

8. This information is from John M. Greiner, Roger Dahl, Harry Hatry, and Annie Millar, *Monetary Incentives and Work Standards in Five Cities* (Washington, D.C.: Urban Institute, 1977), chap. 3.

9. David Osborne and Ted Gaebler, *Reinventing Government* (Read-

ing, Mass.: Addison-Wesley, 1992), 112, but see chap. 4 in general.

10. Ibid., 108.

11. Daniel Yankelovich, "The Work Ethic Is Underemployed," *Psychology Today,* May 1982, 5–8.

12. Ibid., 6.

13. Osborne and Gaebler, *Reinventing Government,* 158, 117–24; see also John M. Greiner, Harry Hatry, Margo Koss, Annie Millar, and Jane Woodward, *Productivity and Motivation: A Review of State and Local Government Initiatives* (Washington, D.C.: Urban Institute, 1981), 113.

14. Barbara Vobejda, "Survey Says Employees Less Willing to Sacrifice," *Washington Post,* 3 September 1993, A2.

15. *Employee Incentives to Improve State and Local Government Productivity* (Washington, D.C.: National Commission on Productivity and Work Quality, 1975).

16. Richard C. Kearney, *Labor Relations in the Public Sector,* 2d ed. (New York: Marcel Dekker, 1992), 243.

17. Ibid.

18. This discussion is drawn from Greiner et al., *Productivity and Motivation,* 119–20.

19. Norma M. Riccucci, "Affirmative Action in the Twenty-first Century: New Approaches and Developments," in *Public Personnel Management: Current Concerns–Future Challenges,* ed. Carolyn Ban and Norma M. Riccucci (New York: Longman, 1991), 91.

20. See Barbara Romzek, "Balancing Work and Nonwork Obligations," ibid.

21. Theodore Poister and Robert McGowan, "Municipal Management Capacity: Productivity Improvements and Strategies for Handling Fiscal Stress," *Municipal Year Book 1984* (Washington, D.C.: ICMA, 1984), 213.

22. Hayes, *Productivity in Local Government,* 62–64.

23. This information comes from James F. Lynch, "The People Equation: Solution to the Solid Waste Problem in Little Rock," in *Public Technology: Key to Improved Government Productivity,* ed. James Mercer and Ronald Philips (New York: AMACOM, 1981), 201–9.

24. See Osborne and Gaebler, *Reinventing Government,* chap. 3.

25. E.S. Savas, *Privatizing the Public Sector* (Chatham, N.J.: Chatham House, 1982), 57–58.

26. See Elaine Morley, "Patterns in the Use of Alternative Service Delivery Approaches," *Municipal Year Book 1989* (Washington, D.C.: ICMA, 1989), 42.

27. David R. Morgan, "Municipal Service Delivery Alternatives," in *State and Local Government Administration,* ed. Jack Rabin and Don Dodd (New York: Marcel Dekker, 1985), 293.

28. Irwin T. David, "Privatization in America," *Municipal Year Book 1988* (Washington, D.C.: ICMA, 1988), 45.

29. Eileen Brettler Berenyi and Barbara J. Stevens, "Does Privatization

Work? A Study of the Delivery of Eight Local Services," *State and Local Government Review* 20 (Winter 1988): 11–20.

30. Lawrence L. Martin, "A Proposed Methodology for Comparing the Costs of Government versus Contract Service Delivery," *Municipal Year Book 1992* (Washington, D.C.: ICMA, 1992), 12.

31. Ibid.

32. See Sidney Sonenblum, John Kirlin, and John Ries, *How Cities Provide Services: An Evaluation of Alternative Delivery Structures* (Cambridge, Mass.: Ballinger, 1977), 33.

33. Lori M. Henderson, "Intergovernmental Service Arrangements and the Transfer of Functions," *Municipal Year Book 1985* (Washington, D.C.: ICMA, 1985), 195–98.

34. Tari Renner, "Trends and Issues in the Use of Intergovernmental Agreements and Privatization in Local Government," *Baseline Data Report* 21 (November/December 1989): 4.

35. Godsey, *Productivity Improvement*, 7.

36. Quoted ibid.

37. Frederick O'R. Hayes, *Productivity in Local Government* (Lexington, Mass.: D.C. Heath, 1977), 13.

38. Mark E. Keane, "Why Productivity Improvement?" in *Productivity Improvement Handbook for State and Local Government*, ed. George J. Washnis (New York: Wiley, 1980), 14.

39. Hayes, *Productivity in Local Government*, 252.

40. Walter Balk, *Improving Government Productivity: Some Policy Perspectives* (Beverly Hills: Sage Professional Paper in Administrative and Policy Studies, 1975), 42.

41. This example has been adapted from David Seader, "Privatization and America's Cities," *Public Management*, December 1986, 9.

42. J. Patrick Wright, *On a Clear Day You Can See General Motors* (Grosse Pointe, Mich.: Wright, 1979), 210–11.

43. Charles H. Levine, "Organizational Decline and Cutback Management," *Public Administration Review* 38 (July/August 1978): 316–26.

44. Carol Lewis and Anthony Logalbo, "Cutback Principles and Practices: A Checklist for Managers," *Public Administration Review* 40 (March/April 1980): 185.

45. This section comes from Charles Levine, Irene Rubin, and George Wolohojian, *The Politics of Retrenchment: How Local Governments Manage Fiscal Stress* (Beverly Hills: Sage, 1981), chaps. 7 and 8.

46. Information in this section is taken from Charles Levine, Irene Rubin, and George Wolohojian, "Managing Organizational Retrenchment: Preconditions, Deficiencies, and Adaptations in the Public Sector," *Administration and Society* 14 (May 1982): 101–36.

47. Gregory Lewis, "The Consequences of Fiscal Stress: Cutback Management and Municipal Employment," *State and Local Government Review* 20 (Spring 1988): 64.

48. Jeremy Plant and Louise White, "The Politics of Cutback Budgeting: An Alliance Building Perspective," *Public Budgeting and Finance* 2 (Spring 1982): 65–71.

49. Robert Biller, "Leadership Tactics for Retrenchment," *Public Administration Review* 40 (November/December 1980): 604–9.

50. John Gargan and Carl Moore, "Enhancing Local Government Capacity in Budget Decision Making: The Use of Group Process Techniques," *Public Administration Review* 44 (November/December 1984): 504–11.

51. Fredric N. Bolotin, "Distribution of Cutbacks in Local Government Services: A Conceptual Framework," *State and Local Government Review* 22 (Fall 1990): 117–22.

Suggested for Further Reading

Ammons, David. *Municipal Productivity.* New York: Praeger, 1984.

Harney, Donald F. *Service Contracting: A Local Government Guide.* Washington, D.C.: ICMA, 1992.

Levine, Charles, Irene Rubin, and George Wolohojian. *The Politics of Retrenchment: How Local Governments Manage Fiscal Stress.* Beverly Hills: Sage, 1981.

Mercer, James L., Susan Woolston, and William Donaldson. *Managing Urban Government Services: Strategies, Tools, and Techniques for the Eighties.* New York: AMACOM, 1981.

Morley, Elaine. *A Practitioner's Guide to Public Sector Productivity Improvement.* New York: Van Nostrand Reinhold, 1986.

Savas, E.S. *Privatization: The Key to Better Government.* Chatham, N.J.: Chatham House, 1987.

Ukeles, Jacob B. *Doing More with Less: Turning Public Management Around.* New York: AMACOM, 1982.

PART THREE

Internal Management

Processes

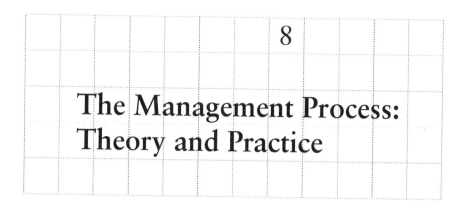

8

The Management Process:
Theory and Practice

Internal management consumes a good deal of urban managers' time and attention. Even in large cities, where external pressures and the need for policy leadership are constant, most managers spend the bulk of their time administering the municipal organization.[1]

Budgeting, planning, and personnel administration occupy a major portion of the internal management day-to-day agenda. But management involves much more than this. Managers must motivate and lead those who bear the responsibilities for providing vital city programs and services. Urban administrators must make key decisions regarding how well the municipal organization is performing. What can be done to encourage employees to do their best? Are there approaches and management strategies that will enable individual employees and the organization as a whole to perform more effectively?

These are some of the concerns addressed in this chapter. We begin with a discussion of motivation and theories of human behavior, which help managers better understand why employees perform the way they do. Next we look at leadership. What do we know about effective organizational leadership? A discussion of "managing for results" follows. The focus here is on management strategies—Management by Objectives and Total Quality Management—that facilitate accomplishing organizational goals and objectives. Finally we examine organization development. This approach to perpetuating or changing organizational beliefs and values is important in a period when all organizations, public and private alike, are asked to respond to change.

Motivation and Theories of Human Behavior

What motivates people to perform in an organizational setting? We know some of the incentives: money, security, a feeling of a job well done, praise, a feeling of being in on what is happening, promotion, and recognition. Are some of these motivators more important than others? Intuition tells us so, but empirical research offers mixed results. How we rank incentives depends largely on our theory of human nature and behavior. What are some of the approaches to understanding human behavior and what implications do they have for employee motivation?

SCIENTIFIC MANAGEMENT

The scientific study of management dates back to the latter part of the nineteenth century and was given its most systematic exposition in the works of Frederick W. Taylor. According to Taylor, careful analysis could uncover a single best way of performing any repetitive task. Jobs could be standardized and routinized. Then each employee would be selected and trained specifically to fit the needs of the jobs. Person and machine would work in glorious harmony at maximum output. Taylor recognized that workers would have to be motivated properly for this approach to operate at its full potential. Simple enough. Using a theory of "economic man," Taylor assumed people would work harder and more efficiently if they were rewarded in relation to their individual output. The more workers produced, the more money they made. Piecework was ideally suited to this philosophy of worker motivation.

We can argue about how scientific Taylor's approach was, but it did contribute significantly to improvements in work methods and processes that made the mass production and assembly-line techniques of the modern corporation possible. And although it was not long before a reaction developed to the mechanistic, dehumanizing philosophy of scientific management, we can still identify certain management practices in use today that bear a strong resemblance to Taylor's approach. The current emphasis on pay for performance is one. Productivity improvement is another. In some cities management negotiates productivity contracts with groups of employees by tying supplemental increases in wages to increased levels of productivity.

HUMANISTIC MANAGEMENT

THE HUMAN RELATIONS APPROACH.—Building on the work of Elton Mayo and Fritz Roethlisberger at the Hawthorne Western Electric plant outside Chicago, a new approach to management evolved that came to be called *human relations*. "Human Relations dethroned *Economic Man* and installed *Social Man* in his place."[2] The human relations movement stressed the importance of the informal social structure and how it affected the behavior and motivation of workers. Other needs of employees, such as approval, belonging, and group membership, were emphasized. Meeting the human and social needs of workers presumably would create a more satisfied workforce. Although some apparently saw this as virtually an end in itself, others believed that happier workers would be more productive. Undoubtedly the human relations movement did much to improve working conditions, but research shows that happy, contented workers do not necessarily work harder or produce more. Also, the early human relations approach did little to motivate employees to search for higher-order needs, such as autonomy and self-actualization.

THE ORGANIZATIONAL HUMANISTS.—In the 1950s and 1960s, the early human relations theories began to be modified. Abraham Maslow, Douglas McGregor, Frederick Herzberg, and Chris Argyris offered views of human nature that, among other things, took account of human needs in a more sophisticated way. Maslow, for example, suggested his now-famous hierarchy of needs. He based his theory on the assumption that needs are motivators of behavior only when they remain unsatisfied. Once the lower physiological needs (hunger, thirst, shelter) and security needs (both physical and economic) have been reasonably well satisfied, a higher level of needs is activated. Social needs (belonging and acceptance) occupy the next rung on the ladder. Psychological or ego needs (status, recognition, esteem) emerge next. At the top is something Maslow calls *self-actualization,* a state in which a person achieves his or her fullest potential as a human being.[3] Maslow's hierarchy implies that most employees are not motivated strictly by economic needs.

McGregor, building on Maslow's hierarchy, posited the existence of two polar management approaches: Theory X and Theory Y. Theory X, the traditional view, holds that people are basically lazy and unambitious; they want to avoid work and responsibility. In trying to motivate employees based on the assumptions of Theory X, management must use a series of carrots and sticks. It can take a hard line, devise tight controls, and push the workforce to produce more. Or, it can take the soft line and allow employees greater participation. Both strategies have weaknesses: the hard approach can generate antagonism, resistance, even sabotage; the soft approach can reduce output. McGregor challenged this conventional management theory. He suggested that even though employees often seem to respond as though Theory X were valid, this be-havior is not innate.

Theory Y postulates that people do not inherently dislike work; people exercise self-direction and self-control in pursuit of goals they deem worthwhile. Theory Y implies that if employees are indifferent, lazy, intransigent, uncreative, uncooperative, and unwilling to take re-sponsibility, management's methods of organization and control are at fault.[4] McGregor would have management create conditions under which members of an organization can achieve their own goals by direct-ing their efforts toward the success of the enterprise. Under Theory Y an organization can most effectively reach its own economic objectives if it meets the needs and goals of its members. Herzberg and Argyris also suggest that unless employees' needs for growth and development are met, they will be dissatisfied with their jobs.[5]

Maslow, McGregor, Herzberg, and Argyris have been called *organi-zational humanists*. They differed from the earlier human relations pro-ponents in emphasizing the organization as well as the individual em-ployee. Not only were these scholars concerned with providing greater opportunities for employees to gain a sense of recognition, accomplish-ment, and fulfillment from their work; they also recognized the organiza-tion's need to get the job done. They did not feel that these two goals were antithetical. Presumably managers and their subordinates can jointly set high performance goals and exercise responsible self-control in their achievement.[6]

THE HUMANISTIC APPROACH: AN APPRAISAL. —How accurately have organizational humanists captured reality? One serious flaw in mo-tivational theories is their monolithic quality. They assume that all people have a common set of needs and that those needs are shared to the same degree. Critics argue that few people want the same things, at least to the same degree. Employees want, and to some extent search for, jobs that are congruent with their individual preferences.[7]

Empirical research does not provide much support for certain key assumptions of the humanistic approach. Maslow's hierarchy of needs and Herzberg's two-factor theory, for example, have not fared well in tests.[8] Other research findings suggest that many of the basic tenets of humanistic motivational theory do not apply to lower-level employees. "Evidence indicates a two-step hierarchy: Lower-level employees show more concern with material and security rewards, while higher-level em-ployees place more emphasis on achievement and challenge."[9]

Recent research offers a more optimistic appraisal of the link between job satisfaction and job performance. Job satisfaction does contribute to lowering absenteeism and employee turnover, which helps boost productivity. Also, such participatory management techniques as Management by Objectives can contribute to gains in employee output.[10]

NEWER HUMANISTIC APPROACHES. — Two books have given humanistic management a boost. Although both go beyond a concern for motivation to embrace a range of management ideas and principles, they offer new insight into how effective organizations can accomplish more by emphasizing human values.

First, *Theory Z: How American Business Can Meet the Japanese Challenge* espouses the view that U.S. companies can improve quality and performance by adopting certain features of the Japanese approach to management. In some ways Theory Z seems to be an extension of Theory Y; for example, its essence is trust and cooperation between labor and management. According to management professor William Ouchi, Theory Z includes the following:[11]

Lifetime Employment. Although not universal in Japan, lifetime employment is offered by most large organizations. Higher-level positions are filled entirely by promoting employees within the company. If slowdowns occur, everyone—including company managers—takes a pay cut, but no one is laid off. Such actions foster a feeling of shared experience and loyalty.

Slow Promotions. Because evaluation is long term, promotions come very slowly. The fact that employees have little incentive to try to advance at someone else's expense presumably elicits a commitment to long-term goals and facilitates cooperation and openness.

Nonspecialized Career Paths. By moving among various company operations, a young manager acquires a feeling for the wholeness of the organization and a familiarity with every function, every specialty, and every office.

Consensus Decision Making. This particular approach to decision making is probably the best-known feature of Japanese management. What sometimes is not understood is how far the Japanese carry the consensus process. For every important decision, "everyone who will feel its impact is involved in making it." The process can involve as many as sixty to eighty people and can drag on for days if not weeks. There is also a deliberate ambiguity about who is responsible for what decisions. All of this is designed to further mutual sharing and commitment to organizational objectives.

Ouchi insists that at least some of these practices can be applied in the United States, and he mentions several companies that have attempted to move toward a more Theory Z-like approach, including Hewlett-Packard, IBM, Intel, certain GM plants, and Texas Instruments.

How applicable is Theory Z to the local public sector? One account of its use involves the New York City Sanitation Department's Bureau of Motor Equipment. In the late 1970s this agency faced imminent collapse. Its top management was forced to resign, and a new team was brought in with a mandate to turn things around. Among other changes, the new leadership introduced collective decision making by creating a labor-management committee that gathered information and insights from the workforce on how to improve productivity and hold down costs. Within a few years the bureau was "transformed from an organization deep in the red and unable to complete its assigned job to one which is operating so smoothly that it is actually beginning to generate an income."[12]

The second book with a prominent humanistic perspective is Osborne and Gaebler's *Reinventing Government*. Of the ten principles advanced to "reinvent" government, three are particularly humanist based and call for the empowerment of communities/neighborhoods, citizens, and government workers.[13]

Community-Owned Government. Reminiscent of the rhetoric associated with the community-control movement in the 1960s and early 1970s, community-owned government requires empowering residents, primarily at the neighborhood level. Services should be owned by the community and not the bureaucracy. Examples are abundant, from community-oriented policing to job-training centers run in part by dislocated workers to neighborhood-based community development corporations and tenant cooperatives. Why community-owned service delivery instead of using professional service agents (i.e., bureaucrats)? Osborne and Gaebler argue that (1) communities are more committed to their members than service agents are to their clients, (2) communities understand their problems better than service professionals, (3) service agents deliver services whereas communities solve problems and care, and (4) communities are more flexible and innovative since they are not bound by extensive rules and regulations like large service bureaucracies. Citizens, neighborhoods, and/or communities should be empowered, both politically and administratively, and entrusted with ownership of local services.

Customer-Driven Government. Citizens are *customers,* not clients. Government should meet the needs of the customers and not the bureaucracy. Big-name management consultants from Peters and Waterman to Drucker to Deming tell of the importance of employees being in touch with their customers. Many major corporations do so. "Hewlett-Packard asks customers to make presentations describing their needs to its engineers. All senior managers at Xerox spend one day a month taking phone calls from customers." Listening to the voice of the customer can be facilitated through various mechanisms, including customer surveys (used in Los Angeles and Orlando), community surveys (used in Dallas, Dayton, and Fairfield, California), customer councils (used by housing authorities in Louisville), and complaint tracking systems (used in Phoenix). A management technique that can facilitate customer-driven government is Total Quality Management (TQM). This management philosophy has been used for some time now in the private sector and is currently being transferred to the public sector. We discuss this innovation later in this chapter.

Decentralized Government. Like the organizational humanists of the 1950s and 1960s, Osborne and Gaebler argue for empowering workers. They cite the call of Harlan Cleveland, former dean of the Humphrey Institute at the University of Minnesota, for the "twilight of hierarchy." They argue that public institutions should move from hierarchy to participation and teamwork, "to return control to those who work down where the rubber meets the road." Decentralization can be achieved through the use of participation management, labor-management committees, no-layoff policies, and by flattening the organizational hierarchy. The last strategy is essential because the "most serious resistance to teamwork and participatory management often comes from middle managers, not unions."

Teamwork can promote entrepreneurial government. East Harlem schools are run by teams. Visalia (Calif.) and St. Paul use cross-departmental teams to develop new city projects. Teamwork brings numerous advantages:

- Cross-departmental teams allow for more complete analysis of problems because employees from different departments will have different perspectives.
- Cross-departmental teams break down "turf" walls.
- Teams build bridges and networks throughout the city administration.
- Teams often hold employees to higher standards of performance than do "bosses." Peer approval is an important evaluative reference point for most people in organizations.

Clearly management approaches that accentuate the human potential of the workforce have come a long way since the early days of the human relations school. Today's emphasis on decentralization, participation, teamwork, creativity, and entrepreneurship comports well with the long-standing view that involved workers are the key to increased productivity. Nevertheless, we still need leaders: the importance of leadership at all levels of the organization is indisputable.

Leadership

Earlier we discussed the importance of community leadership by urban executives, particularly popularly elected mayors. But leadership in city government has another dimension—the exercise of direction and supervision by management within the municipal organization itself. One observer comments that "leadership is the most important demand placed upon the urban administrator. The most saleable quality possessed by a city manager, county executive, or other similar official is his ability to coordinate, direct, and motivate others."[14] This view is widespread, but research has not been able to say what exactly constitutes effective leadership and what impact the exercise of different forms of leadership has on the achievement of organizational objectives.

THE ELEMENTS OF LEADERSHIP

Most authorities believe that leadership, at least in organizations, involves a relationship among leader, follower, and situation. Normally these elements interact in pursuit of some goal or objective. *Leadership,* then, is "the process of influencing the activities of an individual or a group in efforts toward goal achievement in a given situation."[15]

Leadership theory and practice have been influenced strongly by the approaches to human behavior discussed earlier. Scientific management emphasized the job: the leader's role was to determine how best to accomplish a given task; the needs of the organization, not of its individual members, were paramount. Under the human relations approach, the leader's task was to facilitate cooperation among employees while providing for their personal growth and development. Individual needs, not the needs of the organization, were the principal concern.[16]

Contemporary thinking recognizes the importance of both task and people. Leadership is concerned therefore both with achieving some specific goal and with developing human potential and maintaining and strengthening the work group. But how is this done? Are there some people who by virtue of their personal characteristics turn out to be better leaders than others? Are certain styles or approaches to leadership more effective than others?

LEADERSHIP TRAITS

The idea that some people are born leaders has been historically popular. For many years, the study of leadership concentrated on identifying those traits that characterize natural leaders. But empirical research has failed to validate the leadership trait approach. This is not to say that a leader's personality is of no consequence, only that efforts to distinguish leaders from others on the basis of personality traits have been largely unsuccessful. The prevailing view is that leadership is largely situation specific. One person may emerge as a leader in one case; another might rise to the top in a different context.

Still, a recent comprehensive review of the literature on leadership finds that certain characteristics seem to differentiate leaders from followers, effective from ineffective leaders, and higher-echelon from lower-echelon leaders. After citing a number of studies, Ralph Stogdill concludes:

> The leader is characterized by a strong drive for responsibility and task completion, vigor and persistence in pursuit of goals, venturesomeness and originality in problem solving, drive to exercise initiative in social situations, self-confidence and sense of personal identity, willingness to accept consequences of decision and action, readiness to absorb interpersonal stress, willingness to tolerate frustration and delay, ability to influence other persons' behavior, and capacity to structure social interaction to the purpose at hand.[17]

Stogdill insists that his findings do not represent a return to trait theory. Instead they reflect a movement away from the extreme situational approach that denies the importance of individual differences. He concludes that leadership consists of an interaction among members of a group in which the leader emerges by demonstrating his or her capacity for carrying a specific task through to completion.

LEADERSHIP STYLES

What about styles of leadership? Proponents of scientific management saw the need for hard-driving, authoritarian leaders, people concerned almost exclusively with getting the job done. Human relations advocates promoted more participative leadership styles, in which managers give maximum latitude to their subordinates. Current attempts to define leadership styles are more complex, but they still rely on the task-people dichotomy.

TASK VERSUS PEOPLE.—A well-known model of leadership styles is shown in the continuum of leadership behavior in figure 8.1 (page 255). Leaders who fall toward the more authoritarian end of the spectrum are likely to be task oriented; those who are more democratic are inclined to be group centered.

This bipolar theory has been expanded by management consultants Robert Blake and Jane Mouton in the form of a Managerial Grid, as shown in figure 8.2 (page 256).[18] Concern for production is depicted on the horizontal axis; concern for people, on the vertical. A 9 on either axis represents the maximum commitment to that orientation. The grid presents five basic positions:

- 1,1—Minimum effort toward the goal and toward sustaining the group
- 1,9—Maximum attention on group needs with little concern for output
- 9,1—Total interest in production with virtually none for the group
- 9,9—Maximum concern for both group and productivity
- 5,5—Average concern for both output and group needs

The 9,9 position encompasses not only goal orientedness but also a desire to enhance organizational effectiveness through extensive employee involvement in problem solving.

The grid approach is much more than a way of analyzing leadership style. The Managerial Grid (a phrase copyrighted by Blake and Mouton) has become a form of organization development in which seminars and team-building exercises are used to effect a total change in the organization's work climate. The authors insist that evidence is available to show that 9,9-oriented managers enjoy maximum career success.

Leadership styles vary. So what? Does a leader's style make any difference in the way employees feel or behave? Does one style or another lead to greater productivity?

THE EFFECTS OF STYLE.—Research shows that different leadership orientations can affect employees.[19]

- More participatory or person-oriented leadership tends to enhance employee morale.
- Participatory leadership tends to strengthen group cohesion.
- No particular style is consistently associated with greater productivity, although there appears to be a slight tendency for work-oriented leadership to be positively related to productivity.

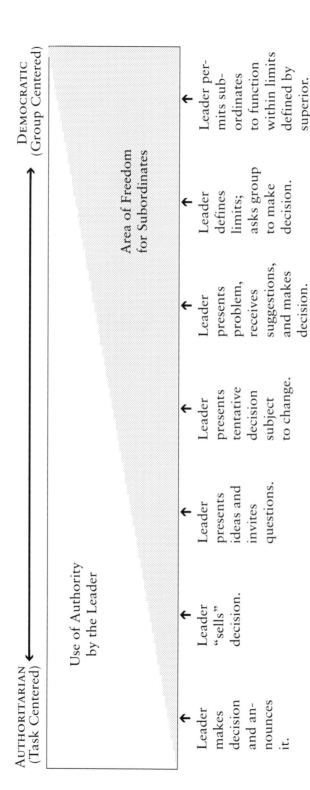

FIGURE 8.1. A CONTINUUM OF LEADERSHIP BEHAVIOR.

SOURCE: Adapted from "How to Choose a Leadership Pattern," by R. Tannenbaum and W. Schmidt, *Harvard Business Review* 36 (March-April): 96.

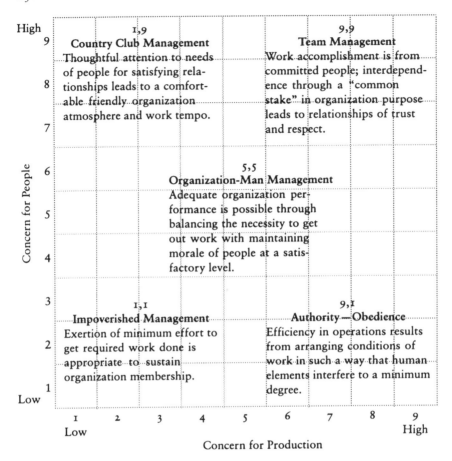

FIGURE 8.2. THE MANAGERIAL GRID.®

SOURCE: From *The New Managerial Grid*, by R.R. Blake and J.S. Mouton. Copyright © 1978 by Gulf Publishing Company, 11. Reprinted by permission.

We cannot advocate either democratic or autocratic supervision as a means for increasing employee output. But employee and group satisfaction tends to be higher with a more democratic leadership style, although several studies suggest differences by size and composition of the group. Stogdill indicates that satisfaction with democratic leadership is highest in small interaction-oriented groups; members appear to be better satisfied with autocratic leadership in large task-oriented groups.

New Directions

With the realization that leadership is a highly complex phenomenon came efforts to construct more sophisticated models of the process. Paul Hersey and Kenneth Blanchard offer an elaborate view of leadership that stresses its situational nature.[20] They identify four basic leadership styles —telling, selling, participating, and delegating—but insist that the appropriate style depends on the *readiness level* of the followers (i.e., the extent to which a follower is able and willing to accomplish a specific task). Where followers' readiness is low or moderate, leaders should tell or sell; where it is moderate to high, leaders should encourage participation or even delegate (see table 8.1). The idea is that employees with lower levels of readiness require strong task-oriented direction. As workers became more ready or more responsible, leaders can place less emphasis on the job and more on positive reinforcement and socioemotional support (relationship behavior). The highest level of employee readiness calls for delegation, a style that encourages autonomy and reduces the need for both task direction and supportive relationships.

Blake and Mouton, originators of the managerial grid, take exception to Hersey and Blanchard's leadership theory.[21] They contend that, contrary to the assumptions of the situational model, there is only one

TABLE 8.1.
LEADERSHIP STYLES AND READINESS LEVELS
OF FOLLOWERS

	Readiness level		*Appropriate style*
R1	Low readiness (unable and unwilling or insecure)	S1	Telling (high task and low relationship behavior)
R2	Low to moderate readiness (unable but willing or confident)	S2	Selling (high task and high relationship behavior)
R3	Moderate to high readiness (able but unwilling or insecure)	S3	Participating (high relationship and low task behavior)
R4	High readiness (able/competent and willing/confident)	S4	Delegating (low relationship and low task behavior)

SOURCE: Paul Hersey and Kenneth H. Blanchard, *Management of Organizational Behavior: Utilizing Human Resources,* 5th ed., copyright 1988, 180. Reprinted by permission of Center for Leadership Studies, Inc. All rights reserved.

best leadership style, the 9,9 approach. They discuss research in which a group of one hundred public and private managers were asked to choose between situational alternatives and 9,9-oriented alternatives to twelve hypothetical managerial problems involving different levels of employee maturity. For each level of maturity and for each of the twelve problems, the 9,9 responses were selected over the situational ones to a statistically significant degree.

Robert E. Quinn would strongly disagree with Blake and Mouton's "one best way" position. And although he would support Hersey and Blanchard's "situational leadership," his theory of leadership is more dynamic and fluid. Drawing on the organizational change and culture literature, Quinn in his book *Beyond Rational Management* identifies positive and negative leadership zones.[22] These zones are based on four common organizational models or cultures—human relations, open systems, rational goal, and internal process—and two axes. The vertical axis ranges from chaos (with too much responsiveness to the needs of workers and spontaneity to environmental stimuli) to rigidity (with too much control, order, and predictability). The horizontal axis ranges from belligerence and hostility (with too much emphasis on external actors and on competition) to apathy and indifference (with too much internal focus on system maintenance and coordination).

The outer negative ring in figure 8.3 (page 259) shows what happens when each of the four organizational values is carried to an extreme. The human relations model that focuses on relationship behavior becomes the irresponsible country club. Open systems theory with an overemphasis on responsiveness, gathering external support, and political expediency becomes nothing more than a tumultuous anarchy. When effort, productivity, efficiency, and authority (rational goal model) are carried to an extreme, the organization becomes an oppressive sweatshop. Finally, too much control, procedural sterility, and following the rules (internal process emphasis) can produce a frozen bureaucracy.

In contrast, the inner positive zone shows those characteristics of each organizational culture that can be used to foster caring, participative, responsive, innovative, productive, and stable organizations. The key to success, according to Quinn, is the ability of an organization to change continually and, as the inner negative circle shows, to clarify its values. No one model is correct for all times. The more fully one set of positive values is pushed to the exclusion of another set, the greater the danger the organization faces. Quinn's *situational and dynamic* theory of leadership has important implications for management. It suggests above all that managers must constantly guard against pushing one approach to the extreme. By remaining sensitive to competing organizational values, a successful leader or manager can learn to understand and adapt to constant organizational change.

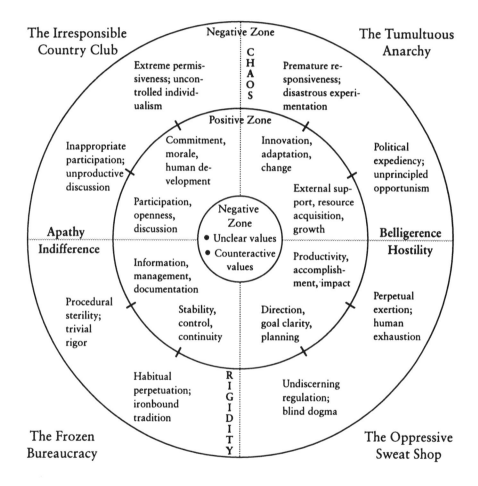

FIGURE 8.3. ROBERT QUINN'S POSITIVE AND NEGATIVE
LEADERSHIP ZONES.

SOURCE: Robert E. Quinn, *Beyond Rational Management* (San Francisco, Calif.: Jossey-Bass, 1988), 70. Copyright 1988 by Jossey-Bass, Inc., Publishers. Reprinted by permission.

Managing for Results

Managers obviously affect their organizations through the exercise of leadership. But administrators also achieve results through their decisions about departmental organization, communication and control system structure, and rewards and sanctions.[23] Organizational performance has always been a high priority, but in today's environment of high public expectations, fiscal stress, and reinventing government, managing for results is more important than ever. We cannot discuss an entire philosophy or program of management here, but we can look at two management approaches that have drawn considerable interest from public managers in the past few years: Management by Objectives and Total Quality Management. Both management approaches facilitate what Osborne and Gaebler call "results-oriented government."[24]

MANAGEMENT BY OBJECTIVES

Peter Drucker brought the phrase *Management by Objectives* (MBO) into common use in 1954.[25] One of its foremost proponents, George Odiorne, defined MBO as a "process whereby the superior and subordinate managers of an organization jointly identify its common goals, define each individual's major areas of responsibility in terms of the results expected of him, and use these measures as guides for operating the unit and assessing the contribution of each of its members."[26] Like many other management approaches, MBO originated in the private sector. But Drucker insists it is especially well suited to governmental agencies, where objectives and results are critical. He contends public service institutions are prone to the "deadly disease of 'bureaucracy'; that is towards mistaking rules, regulations, and the smooth functioning of the machinery for accomplishment, and the self-interest of the agency for public service."[27]

MBO, in one form or another, has been widely accepted in local government. A recent ICMA survey found that 62 percent of the cities use MBO and that over 40 percent of the cities rate it as a "very effective" management tool.[28] Local officials especially like the way MBO helps them in clarifying goals and assisting employees in defining the nature of their jobs.[29]

APPLYING MBO.—Although MBO can work in an autocratic setting or with "top-down goal setting,"[30] most descriptions of the process stress employee involvement—at least down to the small-group level. The heart of MBO, setting objectives, is normally a group activity. The following illustration, involving a police chief and the head of the police patrol division, shows how the system might work.[31]

1. The chief and the division head, working separately, write out in detail their perceptions of the broad goals and responsibilities of the patrol division.
2. The two officials meet face to face and compare their written perceptions of the patrol division's goals. Then they reach collective agreement on each goal and its relative importance.
3. Again the chief and the patrol head work separately, spelling out a list of tentative objectives. Both take into account the agreed-on divisional goals and responsibilities as they establish specific objectives.
4. The two meet again and agree on the specific measurable objectives to which the division will be committed.
5. Finally the chief and the division head specify completion dates for each objective. Dates can be precise (30 June) or flexible (eighteen to twenty-four months).

After the patrol division's goals and objectives are set, the patrol commander initiates the MBO process with the various sections that make up the division. Thus the process can be carried down even to the individual employee level. We might note that a somewhat common distinction is made here between goals and objectives. *Goals* specify the long-range state of affairs to which the organization aspires; *objectives* are the more immediate, specific targets that must be reached to accomplish the goals.

Once objectives and timetables have been established, the monitoring and feedback stages begin. Performance usually is assessed on a quarterly basis, at least at the departmental level. This is especially likely where the objectives are tied to a particular fiscal year. The city manager might be provided with either quarterly or semiannual reports from various departments. Table 8.2 depicts a way in which agreed-on objectives might be monitored, in this case for solid-waste collection.

The process seems orderly, but urban managers implementing MBO face several problems, not the least of which is setting workable objectives. We can identify four basic criteria by which decision makers can determine the workability of objective statements.[32] The first criterion is *significance*. Everything a city, division, or department does may not be of enough consequence to warrant inclusion in an MBO scheme. Superiors and subordinates should be able to reach agreement on those items

TABLE 8.2.
A Sample Format for Reporting Actual versus Targeted Performance for MBO: Solid-Waste Collection

Performance measurement	Actual value previous year (FY 1996)	Target current year (FY 1997)		Quality performance			
				1st qtr.	2d qtr.	3d qtr.	4th qtr.
Percentage of blocks whose appearance is rated unsatisfactory (fairly dirty or very dirty—2.5 or worse on visual rating scale)	18	13	Target	16	14	12	10
			Actual				
Number of fires involving uncollected solid waste	17	12	Target	3	4	3	2
			Actual				
Percentage of households reporting 1 or more missed collections during a year	17	12	Target	a		12	
			Actual				
Percentage of households rating overall appearance of neighborhood as "usually dirty" or "very dirty"	23	18	Target	b		18	
			Actual				

SOURCE: Adapted from *Measuring the Effectiveness of Basic Municipal Services*, Urban Institute and International City Management Association (Washington, D.C., 1974), 13. Reprinted by permission.

a. Citizen survey to be undertaken once—in third quarter.
b. Citizen survey.

worthy of inclusion. Next is *attainability*. Objectives must be realistic expressions of what a division or department can be expected to attain. If set too high or too low, objectives are of little value as a guide to organizational performance. Third is *measurability*. Objectives should be quantified as much as possible; they must be expressed in such a way that someone can make an impartial judgment about progress or lack of it. Finally, the *understandability* of objectives is important. Objectives must be clearly understood by both employees and outside groups that have an interest in what the department is doing. This means objectives must be stated in simple, nontechnical terms.

CASE STUDY

CHARLOTTE IMPLEMENTS MBO

SEVERAL years ago, Charlotte, North Carolina, implemented MBO. According to the city manager and his assistant, the procedure is divided into four steps. First, every department submits its proposed objectives for the coming fiscal year as part of the city's regular budget process. Second, objectives are reviewed and recommendations to the city manager are made by the city's budget analysis staff. Third, recommendations for objectives, as modified by the manager, are sent to the city council as part of the proposed budget for the fiscal year. Finally, after the objectives have been adopted by the council, their status is reviewed by the budget staff at quarterly intervals, with a six-month presentation made to the city council.

Objectives can be modified only after careful review and discussion with all affected parties. Success in meeting objectives is then used as a guide in formulating program recommendations for the following fiscal year and in determining the size of budgetary appropriations.

Although Charlotte has achieved some measure of success with MBO, the city's leaders learned several lessons along the way. First, MBO must have the sustained support of top management. Second, the process takes from three to five years to implement, depending on the size of the organization: "The process of getting departments to think in terms of objectives and measures of effectiveness takes time." Third, an agency or a person with clout must be named to carry out the day-to-day details of the program. And fourth, participants must be shown that management is using MBO when it makes managerial and budgetary decisions.

SOURCE: This case is based on David Burkhalter and Jerry Coffman, "Charlotte/Management by Objectives," *Public Management,* June 1974, 16.

ASSESSING MBO. — Odiorne reported on a series of object lessons derived from an application of MBO in a western state. His warnings and suggestions seem just as appropriate at the municipal level.[33] First, decentralization, or the moving of important decisions to lower levels in the organization, is not a natural occurrence in political organizations. It meets resistance from those in the bureaucracy who stand to lose power. Second, the most important reason for the failure of MBO is the tendency to treat it as a paperwork system rather than a face-to-face management process. "The logic of MBO alone won't carry it off if the system is depersonalized and mechanistic." Third, commitment is what makes MBO work, and its absence can cause it to fail. Finally, measuring objectives is not for purposes of punishing poor forecasters. Objective setting should serve the positive function of providing management with vital signs and indications of the need for adjustment.

How well has MBO performed? On the positive side several studies have found that when managers have an active role in designing and implementing MBO, it can have a significantly positive effect on the overall job satisfaction of participants. Of course better morale is not MBO's major purpose; improved performance is. And as noted previously in this chapter, a recent assessment of MBO applications shows that "when there is high commitment from top management, MBO programs result in large productivity gain."[34]

TOTAL QUALITY MANAGEMENT

Statistician W. Edwards Deming originated Total Quality Management (TQM).[35] As part of the effort to reconstruct the nation's manufacturing base, Deming was invited to Japan in 1950 to deliver management lectures. The Japanese embraced his ideas that *quality* is the common goal of all participants in an organization and that quality is a *continuous, long-term process.* The rest of the story is well known. By the early 1980s Japan had emerged as a world economic leader; and American companies began looking to TQM to raise declining rates of productivity and enhance competitiveness.

TQM can be defined as "the art of continuous improvement with customer satisfaction as the goal."[36] David Kearnes, former CEO of Xerox and later deputy secretary of education, characterizes TQM as "a race without a finish line."[37] It is important to understand that TQM, like MBO, is concerned with results. But where MBO is more concerned with measuring *outputs,* TQM focuses more on *quality* as the product of organizational effort. Traditional output methods like MBO attempt to measure *individual* accomplishments and performance. TQM stresses *teamwork* and collaborative efforts through such mechanisms as quality circles, cross-departmental/functional project teams, and matrixlike structures.

APPLYING TQM. — "The success of TQM depends on a carefully thought-out, long-range strategic plan and meticulous monitoring of statistical data."[38] A local government management system should have five key characteristics before considering TQM.[39] First, the jurisdiction should have the ability to gather hard data on current service performance (usually measured as the level and cost of services) and customers' expectations. Second, an executive-level planning group is needed to set long-term strategic goals and objectives based on a careful analysis of current service performance. These goals and objectives should not be expressed in terms of outputs or line items. Instead, targets for *service improvement* should be established. Third, a communication network should be established such that goals can be understood and acted on by all participants in the organization. Fourth, active management teams, both within and across departments, are needed. Finally, short-term ad hoc teams and more permanent teams of employees, suppliers, and even customers use data to discover and implement service improvements.

Given these management abilities, a popular method for implementing TQM is the "cascading" or top-down process, where top management members learn TQM methods and teamwork and then teach (or cascade) the next hierarchical level, and so on down the hierarchy.[40] Since cascading takes time, may not produce a consensual direction for improvement, and is long term in orientation (often the antithesis of American management philosophy), frequently TQM will require a short- and long-term component.

A four-phase "Twin-Track" model for implementing TQM is shown in figure 8.4.[41] As the figure shows, the implementation effort begins with assessment and ends with institutionalizing the innovation. Assessment primarily requires determining the current levels of service quality using hard data. This phase will probably involve citizen and employee surveys. Planning requires development of a strategic plan for service-quality improvement. Participants must analyze an array of statistical data to develop service-quality goals. Cascading TQM throughout the

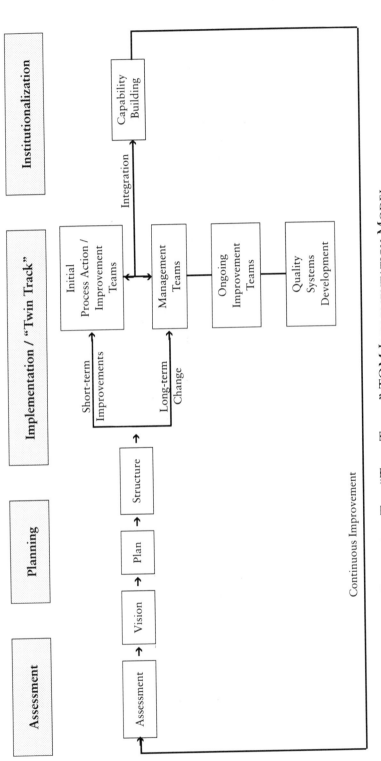

FIGURE 8.4. THE "TWIN-TRACK" TQM IMPLEMENTATION MODEL.

SOURCE: Adapted from Pat Keehley, "Total Quality Management: Getting Started." Reprinted with permission from the October 1992 issue of *Public Management* magazine, published by the International City/County Management Association (ICMA), Washington, D.C.

entire organization starts in the implementation phase. Pilot programs can be used to show quick gains, illustrating the power of the approach. TQM may also lead to new service delivery design methods and better methods for measuring service quality. As figure 8.4 shows, the purpose of the "Twin-Track" approach is to show some short-term benefits and at the same time not lose sight of the long-term goal of continuous improvement. Finally, internal capacity in areas such as training, personnel, communication, and top-level commitment are put in place so as to institutionalize TQM as a way of thinking and not just another short-lived management exercise.

ASSESSING TQM.—In many respects the jury is still deliberating about the fate of TQM in American business and government organizations. In the private sector a number of the winners of the prestigious Baldrige National Quality Award have embraced TQM and reaped the benefits of doing so, including Motorola, Westinghouse, Xerox, Cadillac, Federal Express, and IBM.[42] Conversely, others report that faced with fiscal stress, business has soured on TQM. Florida Power and Light, winner of Japan's Deming Award for quality management, slashed its programs because of complaints of too much paperwork. Despite winning a 1990 Malcolm Baldrige Award, the Wallace Co., an oil supply company based in Houston, filed for Chapter 11 bankruptcy protection.[43]

More recently, TQM has found a home in government. Writing in *Governing,* Jonathan Walters discusses how TQM is winning converts across the landscape of state and local government. He calls the movement "The Cult of Total Quality."[44] Governments such as New York City, Madison, Fort Collins (Colorado), Dallas, Austin, Palm Beach County, Sacramento County Schools, Oregon State University, Gilbert High School (Arizona), Arkansas, and North Dakota are into TQM. Sometimes the results have been spectacular. In Madison, Wisconsin, TQM in the city garage resulted in a reduction of average turnaround from nine days to three days and a savings of $7.15 in downtime for every $1 in preventive maintenance, for a total annual savings of $700,000.[45] The quality-driven approach to city government may be costly, however. For a workforce of about 700 people, Wilmington, North Carolina, had an initial training outlay of about $75,000 for TQM and continues to pay about $30,000 a year.[46]

Finally, we might note that political scientist James E. Swiss offers a strong argument that orthodox TQM will not work well in government.[47] He cites four primary impediments to the usefulness of traditional TQM. First, because TQM was originally designed for use with manufacturing operations, its focus is on products. In contrast, government primarily delivers services. Service delivery is more labor intensive, and services are often produced and consumed at the same time. Even if a service is being delivered with maximum efficiency, the behavior or appearance of the service agent can negate customer approval. In short, developing quality measures is harder to do in the public sector and reducing variation in quality is difficult with street-level bureaucrats. Second, TQM is based on the idea of delighting the customer. Although a laudable goal, defining the customer of a public agency is at best a tenuous job. Does the Food and Drug Administration serve patients with a particular disease who need a promising medicine approved, pharmaceutical interests, the health profession, or the general public? The literature in bureaucratic politics is replete with stories of how interests have coopted the long-term goals of agencies.

A third impediment is that orthodox Total Quality Management rejects the use of output-oriented techniques in favor of continuous improvement through changing inputs and work processes. Swiss argues that in recent years the public sector has made great strides in implementing such innovations as pay for performance, merit pay, program budgets, and MBO. That effort should not stop. An emphasis on inputs and process may lead to goal displacement as bureaucrats look for more money and people (inputs), as legislators look at budget line items to see what their district gets (inputs), and as an elaborate system of rules and regulations—from hiring to procurement—is established to *control* the fourth branch of government. In the public sector an output orientation *can* lead us down the road of quality and toward a long-range vision. Finally, TQM demands an almost single-minded commitment to quality, best promoted by a very strong organizational culture. The task of fostering that essential culture resides with top leadership. But in public organizations, upper-level executives (mayors and city managers) may not stay with the city for long. Turnover at the top makes the job of creating and sustaining a strong, continuous organizational culture difficult if not impossible.

Swiss concludes that "reformed TQM" can be a useful tool for contemporary city management. It "saves the orthodox principles of employee empowerment, continuous improvement, and quantitative tracking of product quality and of client reactions."[48] On the other hand, reform TQM "jettisons orthodox TQM's hostility to output goals and measurements, deemphasizes its demands for output uniformity and organizational culture continuity, and sensitizes managers to the dangers of satisfying just an immediate client."[49]

Organization Development

Over twenty-five years ago, a strategy for organizational change began to appear in the management literature. Called organization development (OD), it called into question many of the long-standing assumptions about organizations, both private and public. Above all, OD proponents were convinced that too many large organizations had ossified, had become too rigid and bureaucratic and thus unable to respond effectively to the turbulent change sweeping corporate America. In the public sector OD was seen by some observers as a way of loosening up hidebound bureaucracies, promoting greater flexibility and an improved capacity to respond to unforeseen events. In short, its adherents saw OD as a means of helping public entities change, grow, and develop into more creative, effective organizations. In some ways, TQM and the growing use of self-directed teams are related to if not outgrowths of OD's emphasis on changing organizational culture and practices.

DEFINITION, ASSUMPTIONS, AND OBJECTIVES

What is OD? According to one definition, OD is a "planned, systematic process in which applied behavioral science principles and practices are introduced into an ongoing organization toward the goals of effecting organizational improvement, greater organizational competence, and greater organizational effectiveness.[50] To survive, organizations must become more adaptable, flexible, and innovative. Changes cannot be minor or peripheral: improved organizational performance requires appropriate modifications in the appraisal, compensation, training, staffing, task, and communications subsystems—in short, in the total human resources system.[51] Such changes should result in an organization that not only performs better but also offers employees an opportunity for personal growth and development.

OD numbers the following among its objectives:

- Creating an open problem-solving climate throughout the organization
- Building trust among individuals and groups within the organization
- Increasing self-control and self-direction for people within the organization
- Developing more effective team management to permit functional groups to work more competently
- Creating better methods of conflict resolution instead of relying on the usual bureaucratic methods of top-down control[52]

OD adherents recognize the value of outside assistance in the organization's effort to remake itself. The literature speaks continually of the role of the consultant or change agent, who should be someone external to the organization. This tenet of the approach clearly affects its application.

Applying OD

Although no set procedure is followed in every instance, an OD effort might include these major stages:

Problem recognition → Data gathering →

Diagnosis → Feedback to management →

Intervention → Assessment of progress →

Continuation of the program

Several of these stages warrant detailed examination.

Data Gathering and Diagnosis. —Once top managers perceive the need for change, they usually bring in outside consultants. Consultants are likely to spend a good deal of time gathering information. They query both managers and employees about their perceptions of the group or team in which they work and the larger organization itself. Personal interviews, observations, and written questionnaires may be used. This systematic collection of information helps enhance OD's claim that it is an applied behavioral science.

Intervention Tactics. —OD practitioners recognize the enormous difficulty in achieving organizational change. Such resistance calls for stern measures. So most OD experts insist on some form of external intervention to turn the organization around. Such interventions normally involve training in one form or another or working with small groups or teams. Whether called team building or by some other similar name, these programs and techniques have essentially the same purpose: creating an open, trusting, noncompetitive environment for individuals in the group. OD clearly traces its roots to the organizational humanists.

An additional intervention strategy is goal setting and planning. At the tactical level this could include individual goal setting (which could take place much the way it does in MBO), team goal setting (which could incorporate the use of the Blake-Mouton grid system), and of course organizational goal setting.[53]

OD in San Diego

A FEW years ago, with financial assistance from HUD, the city of San Diego instituted an OD experiment in its communications and electrical (C&E) division. The project's goal was to use organization development methods to improve employee job satisfaction and productivity, along with customer satisfaction. Various OD methods were employed to improve communications and to encourage members of the organization to provide the information needed to make changes. The point was to take advantage of the knowledge and experience of the people who make the operations work and to remove obstacles to their productivity and job satisfaction.

One of the decisions top management made early in the project was that issues should be resolved at the lowest practical level, rising to the next level in the hierarchy only when lower-level personnel did not have sufficient expertise or authority. The information from client and employee surveys was forwarded to work groups, which, during team-building workshops, developed lists of problems and recommended solutions. Recommendations were not to be vague general statements, but concrete proposals about how the problems could be resolved. Division managers selected the proposals to be implemented, choosing those that offered the most promise of improving productivity. A total of 245 problems were identified; 194 were satisfactorily resolved.

The OD exercise yielded substantial documented savings and improvements. According to two of the city's OD specialists, the approach "resulted in 29 percent improved productivity, $72,763 saved in service costs, 25 percent decrease in turnover, 19.5 percent reduction in absenteeism, 57 percent lowered service times, and improved morale and customer satisfaction." An independent assessment of the project by the Stanford Research Institute called it a "notable success."

The city manager was so pleased with the experiment that he moved to institutionalize group problem solving. Six city departments are now using group problem-solving techniques, and the manager continues to appoint special groups and task forces to address selected issues through the group problem-solving process.

SOURCES: Adapted from "Improving Employee Productivity and Morale Using Organization Development Methods," in *Practical Ideas for the Government That Has*

Everything—Including Productivity Problems (Washington, D.C.: Department of Housing and Urban Development, 1979), 21–24. The last two paragraphs come from William Cain III and Richard Hays, "Doing More with Less: San Diego's OD," *Western City* 35 (October 1979): 8–10.

EVALUATING OD

Several writers have noted that public organizations face more serious problems with OD than does the private sector. Most of the difficulties relate in one way or another to the political environment.[54]

- Trust and openness may not be possible (or perceived as possible) in situations with political implications. Politicians and nonelected officials as well could find it politically embarrassing to air their dirty linen. In addition, some government operations may be considered too sensitive to be openly discussed and debated.
- Public laws and policies relating to accountability take a Theory X position regarding human nature; OD assumes just the opposite.
- Some of the practices of OD—team building and spending time on relational issues—may be viewed with skepticism if not hostility by politicians and the public.

Finally, Hersey and Blanchard contend that OD's preoccupation with interpersonal and collaborative relations relies too much on one approach.[55] They insist again that there is no one best strategy for achieving organizational change. OD should be most effective, in their opinion, in organizations where members have a relatively high readiness for change and only need someone to facilitate it.

Potential Problems with New Management Techniques

Although efforts to change, improve, and reform public organizations should never cease, potential payoffs may fall short of expectations. Public administration specialist Gerald Gabris identifies five dysfunctions that often arise from efforts to employ new management techniques.[56]

First, because a number of changes in procedures and operations are required with each of these techniques, a *process burden* may be created—more paperwork, forms, data collection, and training sessions. Line managers tend to resent these extra chores, especially if they do not anticipate any beneficial changes as a result of the new technique.

Second, new management approaches may not take into account the unique setting of the department or organization. A department of public safety may have group norms, role relationships, reporting systems, and work outputs quite different from those of a public works department. Members of cross-functional teams associated with TQM may have different frames of reference. New management systems require *adaptation* and *close monitoring.*

Gabris identifies the lack of *internal capacity* as a third potential problem. "Too often, management techniques are recommended and adopted by public organizations that lack implementation capacity."[57] He goes on to describe a small city's frustrating experiences in trying to install a performance budgeting system. Most line managers had difficulty understanding the new system and did not see how it would improve effectiveness. Training sessions took longer than expected, with the result that some supervisors felt they were being required to take too much time away from more important responsibilities. In addition, the computer needs associated with the new budgeting procedures exceeded the city's in-house computing capacity. If put in place, the system would have required contracting out for additional computer time, at costs considerably over original estimates. So, when the outside experts who recommended and designed the system departed, city officials decided to abandon performance budgeting, not because they opposed the idea but because they realized the city did not have the internal capacity to make it work.

Fourth, installing new procedures can produce *credibility anxiety.* Because employees as well as supervisors are often suspicious of new techniques, when failures occur, a ripple or spillover effect can be created, in which employees question the usefulness or credibility of changes that follow the failure.

The fifth potential problem, *unrealistic expectations,* is related to credibility anxiety. New management systems may be oversold in regard to both how much improvement can be expected and how much time changes will take. Even when local officials have been thoroughly briefed and have become convinced of a technique's value, they may expect quick results. If these are slow in coming, the resulting disillusionment can lead to abandonment of the technique or to a reduced commitment from the top that dooms it to eventual failure.

To avoid some of these dysfunctional consequences, Gabris recommends such strategies as decentralizing and sharing the burden of implementing new techniques, providing incentives for eliminating burdensome procedures, engaging in substantial preimplementation research, pretesting, implementing only one technique at a time, and acknowledging and celebrating small successes.

Summary

One of the basic issues in management theory is motivation: what motivates people to do the things asked of them on the job? Associated with different views of motivation are different theories of human behavior. Applied to management these include the scientific management approach, the human relations approach, and a less defined area called organizational humanism. Some authorities contend that organizational humanists have overestimated the extent to which many workers, especially in the blue-collar ranks, value job challenge and autonomy as opposed to material rewards. Still, the best-run companies here and in Japan operate on the basic principle that involved workers are the most productive workers.

Leadership is another provocative, complicated topic. Although few deny its importance within the organization, research is again ambiguous regarding the leadership style most likely to be effective. The task to be done, the people involved, and the context in which it all occurs may determine the style of leadership used. The consensus now seems to be that neither a democratic nor an autocratic leadership style can ensure increased productivity, although worker satisfaction does tend to be greater under more participatory leadership.

Management by Objectives is an approach that has spread throughout the public sector. Its essence is the collaborative setting of measurable objectives and the use of these objectives to assess employee performance. Many see MBO as a way of bringing about greater decentralization, thus inculcating feelings of greater personal responsibility among employees. MBO's effectiveness in improving worker performance has not been clearly established. More recently Total Quality Management (TQM) has been embraced by private-sector and public-sector organizations alike. Deming's approach to management calls for continuous improvement in the quality of products and services as defined by customers.

Organization development is another approach to management improvement. OD supporters find contemporary bureaucratic structures inadequate in the face of an increasingly complex and turbulent organizational environment. Significant change is called for, which may require the use of an outside change agent to intervene with various strategies and tactics designed to set the organization aright. OD seems to generate a positive response from supervisors and employees, but the jury is still out on its overall impact on organizational effectiveness.

Public managers still lag behind their private counterparts in making use of the kinds of information and practices discussed in this chapter.

Some of these applications, if and when adopted, undoubtedly will be modified at the local level to take account of the existing political environment. Although these approaches should continue to prove attractive to city governments, urban managers should proceed with caution. These management techniques are often oversold, and so frustration and disappointment often accompany their implementation.

Notes

1. Deil Wright, "The City Manager as Development Administrator," in *Comparative Urban Research,* ed. Robert T. Daland (Beverly Hills: Sage, 1969), 203–48.

2. George Strauss, Raymond Miles, Charles Snow, and Arnold Tannenbaum, eds., "An Overview of the Field," in *Organizational Behavior: Research and Issues* (Madison, Wisc.: Industrial Relations Research Association, 1974), 5.

3. Abraham H. Maslow, *Motivation and Personality* (New York: Harper & Row, 1954).

4. Douglas McGregor, *The Human Side of Enterprise* (New York: McGraw-Hill, 1960), 48.

5. Frederick Herzberg, *Work and the Nature of Man* (Cleveland: World, 1966); and Chris Argyris, *Integrating the Individual and the Organization* (New York: Wiley, 1964).

6. Strauss et al., "Overview of the Field," 8.

7. William Dowling, Jr., and Leonard Sayles, *How Managers Motivate: The Imperatives of Supervision* (New York: McGraw-Hill, 1971), 13.

8. Frank Gibson and Clyde Teasley, "The Humanistic Model of Organizational Motivation: A Review of Research Support," *Public Administration Review* 33 (January/February 1973): 89–96.

9. Hal G. Rainey, *Understanding and Managing Public Organizations* (San Francisco: Jossey-Bass, 1991), 124.

10. Robert Rodgers and John E. Hunter, "A Foundation of Good Management Practice in Government: Management by Objectives," *Public Administration Review* 52 (January/February 1992): 27.

11. William Ouchi, *Theory Z: How American Business Can Meet the Japanese Challenge* (New York: Avon Books, 1981), 15–36.

12. Ronald Contino and Robert Lorusso, "The Theory Z Turnaround of a Public Agency," *Public Administration Review* 42 (January/February 1982): 70.

13. This discussion is drawn from David Osborne and Ted Gaebler, *Reinventing Government* (Reading, Mass.: Addison-Wesley, 1992), chap. 2 for community-owned government, chap. 6 for customer-driven government, and chap. 9 for decentralized government.

14. James Banovetz, David Beam, Robert Hollander, and Charles Zuzak, "Leadership Styles and Strategies," in *Managing the Modern City*, ed. James Banovetz (Washington, D.C.: ICMA, 1971), 133.

15. Paul Hersey and Kenneth Blanchard, *Management of Organizational Behavior*, 5th ed. (Englewood Cliffs, N.J.: Prentice Hall, 1988), 86.

16. Ibid., 88.

17. Ralph Stogdill, *Handbook of Leadership: A Survey of Theory and Research* (New York: Free Press, 1974), 81.

18. Robert R. Blake and Jane Srygley Mouton, *The New Managerial Grid* (Houston: Gulf, 1978).

19. Stogdill, *Handbook of Leadership*, 403–4.

20. Hersey and Blanchard, *Management of Organizational Behavior*, chap. 8.

21. Robert Blake and Jane S. Mouton, "Theory and Research for Developing a Science of Leadership," *Journal of Applied Behavioral Science* 18 (1982): 275–91.

22. Robert E. Quinn, *Beyond Rational Management* (San Francisco: Jossey-Bass, 1988). This discussion primarily is drawn from chaps. 4 and 5.

23. Raymond E. Miles, *Theories of Management: Implications for Organizational Behavior and Development* (New York: McGraw-Hill, 1975), 4.

24. Osborne and Gaebler, *Reinventing Government*, chap. 5.

25. Peter F. Drucker, *The Practice of Management* (New York: Harper & Row, 1954).

26. George S. Odiorne, *Management by Objectives* (New York: Pitman, 1965), 55–56.

27. Peter F. Drucker, "What Results Should You Expect? A User's Guide to MBO," *Public Administration Review* 36 (January/February 1976): 13.

28. Gregory Streib and Theodore H. Poister, "Established and Emerging Management Tools: A 12-Year Perspective," *Municipal Year Book 1989* (Washington, D.C.: ICMA, 1989), 47–48.

29. Perry Moore and Ted Staton, "Management by Objectives in American Cities," *Public Personnel Management* 10 (Summer 1981): 223–32.

30. Odiorne, *Management by Objectives*, 140.

31. This illustration is similar to one found in Fred Pearson, "Managing by Objective," in *Developing the Municipal Organization*, ed. Stanley Powers, F. Gerald Brown, and David S. Arnold (Washington, D.C.: ICMA, 1974), 179.

32. Ibid., 180–82.

33. George Odiorne, "MBO in State Government," *Public Administration Review* 36 (January/February 1976): 28–33.

34. Rodgers and Hunter, "A Foundation of Good Management Practice in Government," 34.

35. The discussion in this paragraph is drawn from Warren H. Schmidt and Jerome P. Finnigan, *The Race without a Finish Line* (San Francisco: Jossey-Bass, 1992), chap. 1.

36. Ibid., xii.

37. As quoted in ibid.

38. John L. Larkin, "TQM Efforts Increase at All Levels of Government," *Public Administration Times,* 1 June 1991, 1.

39. Pat Keehley, "Total Quality Management: Getting Started," *Public Management,* October 1992, 10–11.

40. Ibid., 14.

41. Discussion of the model is drawn from ibid.

42. See Schmidt and Finnigan, *The Race without a Finish Line,* chap. 13.

43. Jay Mathews with Peter Katel, "The Cost of Quality," *Newsweek,* 7 September 1992, 48–49.

44. Jonathan Walters, "The Cult of Total Quality," *Governing,* May 1992, 38–41.

45. Joseph Sensenbrenner, "Quality Comes to City Hall," *Harvard Business Review,* March–April 1991, 68.

46. Walters, "The Cult of Total Quality," 41.

47. James E. Swiss, "Adapting Total Quality Management (TQM) to Government," *Public Administration Review* 52 (July/August 1992): 356–62.

48. Ibid., 360.

49. Ibid.

50. Wendell French and Cecil Bell, Jr., *Organization Development: Behavioral Science Interventions for Organizational Improvement* (Englewood Cliffs, N.J.: Prentice Hall, 1973), 3.

51. Ibid., 70.

52. These objectives are taken from Robert T. Golembiewski, "Organization Development in Public Agencies: Perspectives on Theory and Practice," *Public Administration Review* 29 (July/August 1969): 368; and Warren G. Bennis, *Organization Development: Its Nature, Origins, and Prospects* (Reading, Mass.: Addison-Wesley, 1969), 15.

53. Richard Beckhard, *Organization Development: Strategies and Models* (Reading, Mass.: Addison-Wesley, 1969), 35–40.

54. William Eddy and Robert Saunders, "Applied Behavioral Science in Urban Administrative/Political Systems," *Public Administration Review* 32 (January/February 1972): 13–15.

55. Hersey and Blanchard, *Management of Organizational Behavior,* 360.

56. Gerald T. Gabris, "Recognizing Management Technique Dysfunctions: How Management Tools Often Create More Problems Than They Solve," *Public Productivity Review* 10 (Winter 1986): 3–19.

57. Ibid., 10.

Suggested for Further Reading

Cohen, Steven, and Ronald Brand. *Total Quality Management in Government.* San Francisco: Jossey-Bass, 1993.

Hersey, Paul, and Kenneth Blanchard. *Management of Organizational Behavior.* 5th ed. Englewood Cliffs, N.J.: Prentice Hall, 1988.

Osborne, David, and Ted Gaebler. *Reinventing Government.* Reading, Mass.: Addison-Wesley, 1992.

Ouchi, William G. *Theory Z: How American Business Can Meet the Japanese Challenge.* New York: Avon Books, 1981.

Rainey, Hal G. *Understanding and Managing Public Organizations.* San Francisco: Jossey-Bass, 1991.

9

Personnel Policies and Practices

The area of personnel administration has traditionally been technical and specialized and certainly has not involved major social or political issues. Today city personnel departments are still concerned with a number of customary tasks: recruitment, examination, selection, job classification, and compensation. But recent developments and tasks given to personnel departments have propelled them into major areas of controversy, areas where federal law and court decisions are mandating a variety of changes. For example, minorities and women are challenging a host of traditional employment practices that rely on merit systems. The issue of sexual harassment is a problem the personnel office must often help the organization address. Americans with disabilities now have extended rights in the workplace. *Reinventing government* advocates also urge greater use of performance plans. Municipal unions are still a strong and vocal force to be reckoned with in city politics. Local leaders are being forced to search for ways to accommodate all these pressures, and the personnel department usually plays a critical role in each area.

We begin by considering certain basic personnel issues—how the personnel function should be organized and matters of staffing, classification, and compensation. Then we address many of the current issues and dilemmas associated with modern personnel administration, including questions about equal employment/affirmative action, sexual harassment, the new Americans with Disabilities Act, and a summary of the current use of pay-for-performance systems in local government. Finally we come to labor-management relations. How do public and private unions differ? Are their differences so pronounced as to warrant treating public unions significantly differently from those in the private sector? Collective bargaining is the mainstay of labor relations in this country today, public or private. We outline the procedures, with particular emphasis on methods of resolving labor disputes. The section ends with an examination of the controversy surrounding strikes by public employees.

Administration

ORGANIZATIONAL STRUCTURE

When cities began to establish formal personnel policies and procedures, they logically followed the example set by the national government in 1883 with the creation of the Civil Service Commission after passage of the Pendleton Act. In most cases this meant the creation of an independent civil service commission. These commissions, usually composed of three or five members, were concerned primarily with ridding the municipality of patronage politics by implementing competitive examinations for entry into city service. They also attempted to protect the municipal workforce from political interference. Elaborate regulations and procedures were created to prevent employee dismissal for political or other reasons unrelated to work performance. But as city employment expanded and new personnel problems developed, many became disenchanted with the concept of an independent board. They argued that the personnel function should be a more direct part of the top-management team.

The basic alternative to the civil service commission is the staff (central) personnel department, which is directly responsible to the chief executive. The rationale for making personnel part of the executive staff is the frequently cited "principle" that executive authority should be commensurate with responsibility. By 1962, the Municipal Manpower Commission had endorsed the concept of an executive-centered personnel system.[1] In 1970 the National Civil Service League took the same position.[2]

Accordingly, more and more cities are placing the personnel function under executive control. According to a recent survey of local government personnel structure and policies by N. Joseph Cayer, one of the foremost public personnel specialists in the United States, the most prevalent personnel organization form is the central personnel board with no separate civil service commission. Based on his 1989 ICMA-sponsored survey of all cities with populations of 10,000 or greater, Cayer found that 44 percent of responding cities use this form of organization.[3] In some places the civil service commission remains but with considerably reduced authority. Results from Cayer's survey, for example, show that about 30 percent of the cities report that an independent commission performs limited functions. Of those functions the three most frequent were acting as a grievance adjudicator (23.5 percent of the cities), over-ruling disciplinary action (25.9 percent), and reinstating employees (25.6 percent). In 11 percent of the cities the independent commission acts only as an advisory board. A true independent commission with full powers was found in only 2 percent of the cities.

THE MERIT SYSTEM

Whatever their organizational structure, most cities of any size claim to operate a merit system. Of course few cities would admit to having any other type of personnel program. Who favors patronage these days? Later in the chapter we consider how the concept of merit has changed in response to challenges by minorities and women. Here we note the traditional principles a merit system might embrace, according to the 1970 Intergovernmental Personnel Act:

- Recruiting, selecting, and advancing employees on the basis of their relative ability, knowledge, and skills
- Providing equitable and adequate compensation
- Training employees, as needed, to assure high-quality performance
- Retaining employees on the basis of the adequacy of their performance
- Assuring fair treatment of applicants and employees ... without regard to political affiliation, race, color, national origin, sex, or religious creed
- Assuring that employees are protected against coercion for partisan political purposes and are prohibited from using their official authority for the purpose of interfering with or affecting the result of an election or a nomination for office[4]

CASE STUDY

AN INDEPENDENT CIVIL SERVICE COMMISSION

THE city of Flint, Michigan, operates under a three-member independent civil service commission established by city charter. One commissioner is appointed by the city council, one by the city hospital board of directors, and one by the board of education. This group has been assigned all the major personnel responsibilities normally conducted by a city government. The commission appoints the personnel director, who supervises the staff. Under the Flint system only four positions remain exempt from civil service: city manager, director of finance, city attorney, and city clerk. In effect, Flint's city council and city manager have no control over personnel policy or administration.

Here are a few of the procedures the Flint civil service carried out in the 1970s: All positions in Flint, from dogcatcher to city engineer, were filled by promotion from within if at least two qualified employees wanted the job. When open recruitment was permitted, only minimal search efforts were undertaken—advertisements were placed in the local newspaper and in trade journals. Any recruitment beyond that had to be done by managers themselves, with no guarantee that their candidates would be hired.

When the civil service decreed that a job should be filled from within, the appointing department had to promote the person with the highest test score regardless of other qualifications. If a position was opened to outsiders as well, only a person whose test score was among the top three could be hired. This procedure placed a heavy burden on the civil service test. Test scores were graded to the second decimal place, reflecting a degree of accuracy that seems absurd given our knowledge of test validation. Moreover, certain groups could accumulate additional test points. Veterans automatically had 5 points added to their final scores, and each internal applicant received 1 point for every year of relevant experience with the city. To make the top three, then, an applicant who was not a veteran or a current employee had to score 10 to 20 points higher than anyone else.

If test scores, military experience, and years of city service were accurate predictors of job performance, the system might be justified. No evidence suggests this is true. Indeed, in the early 1970s Flint's civil service tests for several entry-level positions (including police officers and firefighters) were declared invalid by court order. Considerable evidence was accumulated to show that the city's employment practices often discriminated against applicants on the basis of race, age, sex, and cultural background.

SOURCE: Adapted from Brian Rapp and Frank Patitucci, *Managing Local Government for Improved Performance* (Boulder, Colo.: Westview, 1977), 98–101.

Some of the personnel issues raised in Flint are considered in greater detail in the next section. Certainly, on the face of it, a totally independent personnel system seems to contradict every tenet of administrative practice concerning the need for organizational control by top management.

Personnel Functions

Because personnel practices help determine the nature of the municipal workforce, they indirectly affect everything a city does.[5] Municipal personnel decisions also have a potentially important impact on the local economy. We noted in a previous chapter that any significant cutback or slowdown in municipal employment among inner cities affects minority job opportunities adversely. And because salaries loom so large in the overall city budget, personnel decisions (to add personnel, to grant pay increases) have serious consequences for revenue and tax policies (see chapter 10).

What are the areas in which personnel decisions are made? What are the basic personnel functions? Personnel departments perform a host of activities. Clearly, however, several are pivotal: staffing, position classification, compensation, and performance evaluation.

STAFFING

Historically, local governments have not been competitive with the private sector in attracting competent personnel. Usually this was blamed on low municipal salaries, so many cities felt compelled to offer attractive fringe benefit plans, including good retirement packages. The situation has changed, especially in larger urban areas. At the lower and sometimes even middle levels of employment, city governments today are more than competitive—in fact, they often pay higher salaries than does the private sector for comparable positions. At the top end the question of pay comparability is less certain: "... there is growing concern that public salaries, particularly at the highest levels of state and local government, have fallen too far behind, that good people are not entering or staying in government because of low pay."[6]

RECRUITMENT.—Traditionally, local public agencies adopted a largely passive approach to recruitment, a let-them-come-to-us philosophy. This produced a recruitment process based on having a friend or a relative who worked for the city. Remnants of the who-you-know strategy persist. But most authorities today urge public agencies to adopt a more positive, aggressive recruiting posture. In some municipalities applications are received, candidates are examined, and appointments are made all in one visit to a public personnel agency, and open continuous examinations (no closing dates) are common. In effect, the entire employment process has been speeded up as a way of making public jobs more attractive and accessible.[7]

Although cities have become more active in recruitment—with widespread advertising and the use of visiting recruitment teams—most use vigorous tactics only when the labor market is tight or very special needs arise. More often, recruitment is routine. In the mid-1970s, for example, the Oakland personnel department filled job openings primarily by using existing eligibility lists.

> If the staff member cannot fill the slot this way, he looks to past practices, perfunctorily contacts departments, and then draws up a publicity plan.... Only if the publicity effort [ordinarily a three-day newspaper ad] fails to produce enough applicants do calculations become more complex and time-consuming.[8]

To a considerable extent, personnel recruitment today involves the extra effort to make the workforce more representative, an activity we consider in more detail below.

EXAMINATION AND SELECTION. — Merit systems demand some objective measurement criteria by which to rank prospective employees. In most cities this translates into tests—unassembled and written. Unassembled tests consist of an evaluation of experience and references, an oral interview, and perhaps an effort to gauge competence by having the applicant perform some task. This form of testing has not stirred up the controversy its written counterpart has.

The traditional assumption that written tests have the capacity to identify qualified workers has come under attack from a variety of quarters.[9] Much of the criticism has erupted over the issue of test validity. The Flint case is typical. How well do employment test results correspond with job performance? That's the big question, and minority groups are the ones asking it, with good reason. Local governments still rely heavily on written examinations, many of which have not been properly validated. Moreover, the common practice is to use various components in the selection process sequentially. So applicants who lose out at the written exam stage do not receive further consideration. And the fact remains that certain minority groups often do not fare as well on written tests as do members of the majority culture.

Why are written examinations so prevalent? Many public officials think these tests have advantages in addition to their presumed objectivity.[10] They not only save a good deal of time (compared to oral exams); they also serve as a means of defense against hiring the obviously inept. At the least, officials believe written tests are valid as a basic screening device.

Yet the attacks on written tests and on the "rule of three" (requiring appointment of one of the three top scorers) have resulted in changes in traditional testing and certification practices. Although still relying on numerical scores, some jurisdictions have begun using what is called *category certification*.[11] This approach acknowledges that tests are not absolutely precise measures and that all applicants who score within a certain range on the test should be considered approximately equal. Santa Fe Springs, California, has developed a two-tiered hiring eligibility list, consisting of "outstanding" and "qualified" candidates.[12] Rankings and numerical test scores are not furnished to hiring departments because the city believes that fine distinctions among applicants should not be made on the basis of such criteria. Instead, the list of all outstanding candidates is referred to the department head, along with the satisfactory list, if necessary. This arrangement produces a much larger number of qualified candidates than does the usual rule of three, thus increasing the chances of a target group appointment (e.g., the appointment of a woman or a member of a racial minority).

Other possibilities exist as well. One would be to determine ranking on eligibility lists randomly, without regard to race, sex, ethnicity, or scores. All persons who passed would be considered eligible for hiring. Appointments could then be made from the list as is currently done, following the rule of three.[13]

Still another option is to decentralize the hiring process to the line level coupled with using methods other than written tests for hiring decisions, such as probationary appointments or assessment centers. These civil service reforms are under way in a number of states and cities: "The states of California, Minnesota and Virginia and the cities of Baltimore, Dallas, Indianapolis and San Diego, for example, have decentralized their hiring systems and have dumped the rule of three. All but Baltimore and Dallas have also moved away from written tests to evaluate job candidates."[14]

The debate over the compatibility of merit and equal opportunity remains unsettled. Civil rights groups continue to push for changes in the traditional practices that rely heavily on tests and credentials. And of course the courts have played a major role in determining just how far institutions must go in modifying practices in order to ensure equal access to all groups.

CLASSIFICATION

Many authorities believe position classification, which is based on rank-in-the-job, is the cornerstone or hub of modern personnel management. If activities were not grouped together into positions requiring similar qualifications, duties, and responsibilities, not only would there be no accurate description of the workforce, but each individual would have to be treated separately. Obviously this would create inconsistencies, especially in the area of pay. Indeed, perhaps the principal advantage of position classification has been the ability to standardize salaries.[15] The whole idea is to ensure equal pay for equal work.

Citing the advantages of classifying jobs is one thing; doing it accurately is another. Because class labels determine salary, classifications must be current. But cities seem to have a hard time keeping them up to date. Why? Departmental resistance is the primary reason. For classifications to be valid, the personnel staff must investigate the nature of every job in the organization. And in the eyes of many line agencies, the investigation is an intrusion. Supervisors tend to overclassify employees, thereby rewarding their workers and enhancing the importance of their own jobs.

COMPENSATION AND PERFORMANCE APPRAISAL

COMPENSATION. — The compensation plan typically is tied to position classification. Several positions are assigned to a particular pay grade, as is done in the federal civil service. Within each pay level there are steps, commonly five or six. The most frequent salary increment between steps is 5 percent.[16] How does an employee move up the pay ladder? Most cities claim movement upward is based on merit. The facts suggest otherwise. As Joseph Cayer puts it:

> All too often ... performance ratings are not done carefully, and employees move up the steps automatically. In fact, the employee usually expects it, and the supervisor seldom disappoints. As a result, step increases are usually "seniority" increases rather than merit increases.[17]

A 1980 survey of over 400 local governments revealed that only 20 percent of the jurisdictions provide merit increases based solely on performance; all others take length of service into account to some degree.[18]

The past few years have brought increased interest in pay-for-performance or incentive systems tied to individual or group productivity. One recent survey of U.S. firms found that 70 percent offer at least some form of performance incentive (e.g., merit raises, bonuses, commissions, group incentives, or profit sharing). "Merit pay used to go mostly to executives (often in the form of stock options) and salespeople. Today they're increasingly available to middle managers, clerical, and blue-collar workers."[19]

Cities are following suit. In a recent ICMA-sponsored survey Streib and Poister found that the use of performance monitoring and employee incentive programs has increased dramatically in American cities. Between 1976 and 1988 the use of performance monitoring as a management technique grew by more than 30 percent (67 percent of survey cities use the technique). Employee incentive programs almost doubled at 48 percent (64 percent of survey cities use the technique).[20]

CASE STUDY

PAY FOR PERFORMANCE IN LOCAL GOVERNMENT: USE AND EFFECTIVENESS

BABE RUTH understood pay for performance. In 1929, when someone pointed out that he was being paid twice as much money as President Hoover, the Babe's response was succinct: "I had a better year than he did."

In *Reinventing Government* Osborne and Gaebler devote chapter 5 to the theme of "results-oriented" government—funding outputs, not inputs. In addition, their Appendix B is entitled "The Art of Performance Measurement."[21] Despite all the recent hype, holding government workers accountable through the use of pay for performance is not a new idea. "It has been discussed, defended, and criticized for the past decade. Those who do not like it continue to say it is both costly and disruptive to group morale.... [It] is, in fact, difficult, expensive, and controversial." As city manager of Aurora, Colorado, Jim Griesemer notes, "It's not a panacea." Nevertheless, as a concept and practice, pay for performance is here to stay.

The real pioneers in the area of pay for performance are local governments. Scottsdale, Arizona, and its 1,060 city workers have been on the system since 1982. The 350-plus workers in Biloxi, Mississippi, have operated under the management tool since 1986.

In 1989 Denver, Colorado, put its entire 8,000 workforce on performance pay. In Biloxi, Steve Held, finance and personnel director, notes: "I think pay for performance, in some form, is really the only way to go. It's a true merit system...." The assistant city manager in Scottsdale, Richard A. Bowers, thinks pay for performance works well, but he also notes: "Even after years, the system needs constant review and tweaking and turning and asking people how they feel about it...." A Denver personnel director, A. Fred Timmerman, asserts: "Where's the incentive to do anything more than meet expectations if I work outstandingly all year next to someone who's just meeting expectations and we get the same raise?"

The system is not self-executing. The city of Aurora, Colorado, is on its second try with performance pay. The first round failed due to inadequate training of supervisors. In Denver, the fear of favoritism in the evaluation process is a concern. Biloxi has three separate layers of evaluations. The former city manager of Scottsdale also notes that you can't sell the innovation on the grounds of efficiency: "If you try to promote pay for performance on the basis that you're going to spend less money on your people, you are bound to fail.... What you are doing is spending roughly the same amount smarter than under the old civil service system of across-the-board increases."

SOURCE: Elder Witt, "Sugarplums and Lumps of Coal," *Governing*, December 1989, 28–33.

PERFORMANCE APPRAISAL. —Determining who gets merit pay or extra compensation for outstanding performance is not a simple matter. Personnel experts have struggled for years to devise acceptable systems for evaluating employee performance. If appraisal techniques do not measure performance, then performance pay becomes an empty process.

Most cities of any size now engage in formal employee evaluation. But the process varies somewhat between managerial employees and rank-and-file workers. Two recent studies reveal the following differences:[22]

- About three-fifths (59 percent) of cities formally evaluate managerial employees. The comparable figure for nonmanagerial employees is 86 percent.

- Managerial appraisal is more frequently associated with the allocation of rewards, whereas nonmanagerial appraisal places greater emphasis on employee communication and development.
- Managerial employees are much more likely to be evaluated using a performance-based evaluation system such as Management by Objectives (MBO). In contrast, nonmanagerial employees are evaluated primarily using rating scales, a trait-based evaluation technique.

Performance-based rating systems often rely on MBO or behaviorally anchored rating scales (BARS). These devices force the rater to select the phrase or statement that best describes how an employee might respond or behave under specific or general circumstances. Most experts agree that these approaches are superior to the more conventional rating scales, which ask a supervisor to rate a subordinate using a 5- or 7-point scale for a group of generally desirable traits, such as efficiency, loyalty, promptness, or intelligence. Many observers consider these traditional scales as too subjective and often unrelated to job performance.

In an era where reinventing government means teamwork, quality circles, and Total Quality Management (TQM), the customary performance appraisal process may have to be modified: "Traditional performance appraisals are bad simply because they tell too many people they are losers."[23] Charles Fox argues that formal appraisals should be "abolished or their use subverted."[24] He insists that TQM, mission-driven government, professionalism, and other factors make the technique a management dinosaur. Instead, he contends groups can be evaluated according to mission or task completion. Or employees can be rated as simply "satisfactory" or "unsatisfactory." Courts will accept the designations, he argues, as long as they are used fairly and consistently.

Equal Employment Opportunity

For some time now, cities have been committed to nondiscrimination in hiring. But as minority groups hasten to point out, voluntary compliance and good-faith efforts have not changed the situation very much. This viewpoint is well stated by Herbert Hill, former national labor director of the NAACP:

The record of thirty years of fair employment practice laws makes it absolutely clear that the concept of passive nondiscrimination is totally inadequate and obsolete. In practice a ritualistic policy of "nondiscrimination" or of "equal opportunity" usually means perpetuation of the traditional discriminatory patterns or, at best, tokenism. The law now requires the broad application of preferential hiring systems to eliminate the pervasive effects of racial discrimination in virtually every segment of the American economy.[25]

Although Hill says the law now mandates what he calls *preferential hiring*, the issue remains unsettled. In fact, equal employment opportunity (EEO) continues to be surrounded by a host of legal conflicts, at both the legislative and the judicial level. Most of the legal action is taking place at the national level, although the disputes of course arise from local conditions.

AFFIRMATIVE ACTION

The initial strategy for achieving equal employment opportunity was to concentrate on eliminating discriminatory personnel policies and practices. The limited achievements of this effort led to what we now call *affirmative action*. The approach mandates more than passive nondiscrimination; it requires action programs to redress employment imbalances for both minorities and women. Above all, affirmative action focuses on results, not promises and plans.

The concept of affirmative action was given the status of federal policy by executive order in the early 1960s. The approach officially reached state and local governments with the passage in 1972 of the Equal Employment Opportunity Act. The act made local governments subject to Title VII of the Civil Rights Act of 1964, which prohibits employment discrimination. The 1972 act also established the Equal Employment Opportunity Commission (EEOC). Since passage of the 1978 Civil Service Reform Act, EEOC can investigate and bring suit against private and public employers for alleged violations of Title VII.

PREFERENTIAL HIRING. —Just how far employers must go in their nondiscrimination efforts still is being vigorously debated if not legally contested. Some agree with Herbert Hill that affirmative action mandates preferential hiring practices.[26] For others, preferential hiring smacks of reverse discrimination. The use of goals and quotas remains bitterly controversial. For example, a recent *Washington Post*/ABC News poll found that overwhelmingly respondents opposed the use of racial preferences in jobs (80 percent) or in college admissions (76 percent).[27] Inevitably the courts and Congress have been forced to decide the nature and scope of preferential hiring.

THE COURTS.—Writing in early 1989, public administration expert John Nalbandian outlines the U.S. Supreme Court's position on affirmative action.[28] He argues that the Court has reached a consensus based on a two-part analytical approach: The first part examines the *justification* for taking race into consideration, "the more the impact the affirmative action has on nonwhites, the more justification is required." The second part of the approach considers the *content* of the affirmative action activity with particular attention to the consequences for nonminority employees: "The Court is concerned with limiting affirmative action tightly within the scope of the problem it is supposed to solve." In other words, "societal discrimination" may not be justification for affirmative action (AA) plans. And to the extent possible, AA plans should be tailored to bestow benefits to identifiable victims so as to mitigate the impact on innocent others.

Beginning in January 1989, the Court decided three cases that "critics say have undermined the fairness of civil rights laws."[29] In *City of Richmond v. J.A. Croson Co.* a majority of the U.S. Supreme Court (6–3) found that the minority business enterprise (MBE) set-aside program ordinance in the city of Richmond, Virginia, was unconstitutional.[30] Cities had designed such programs to ensure that minority businesses received a certain percentage of city contracts.

The second decision was in *Ward's Cove Packing Co. v. Antonio*, in which the Court ruled that showing racial discrimination through the method of adverse impact or disparate effect was no longer enough. This method had allowed employers to use statistical data to show that women or minorities were underrepresented in a jurisdiction, job category, and so on, thus showing evidence of bias. Under the *Ward's Cove* ruling, litigants must tie specific employer practices to underrepresentation. Then the employer can justify such practices if they are based on reasonable and usual business practices.[31] The decision shifts the burden of proof from the employer to the plaintiff and makes it easier for the employer to use standardized tests and diploma requirements even if they have an adverse impact on protected groups.

The third case, *Martin v. Wilks,* came out of Birmingham, Alabama, where a group of white firefighters sued, claiming the city's voluntary preferential hiring of blacks resulted in reverse discrimination. The Supreme Court agreed, paving the way for numerous reverse discrimination suits.[32]

REACTIONS TO COURT DECISIONS.—In response to these actions and to President Bush's veto of the 1990 Civil Rights Act, on 21 November

1991 Congress passed the 1991 Civil Rights Act. Major provisions of the legislation include[33]

- An overturning of the *Ward's Cove* decision. The burden of proof for statistical adverse impact is shifted back to the employer. A "business justification" for racial imbalance once again requires "business necessity" and "job relatedness."
- A reversal of the *Martin* v. *Wilks* decision. The reversal limits the ability for whites to claim reverse discrimination in consent decrees.

While not a reaction to a court decision, another major piece of legislation will have a significant impact on personnel practices: the Americans with Disabilities Act of 1990.[34] This legislation prohibits job discrimination in all employment areas (recruitment, benefits, testing, etc.) against people with disabilities by private and public employers. The law applies to all employers currently with twenty-five or more employees and, after 26 July 1994, with fifteen or more employees.

In an effort to mitigate the effects of the Court's decision in *Croson,* cities have undertaken "disparity studies" to justify minority set-aside programs. These studies statistically document how minorities and minority business enterprises (MBEs) have been discriminated against in government contracting.[35] Based on disparity studies, King County, Washington, and Hillsborough County, Florida, withstood court challenges to their MBE set-aside programs. With a $500,000 disparity study to draw on, officials in Atlanta are creating a program to enforce MBE set-asides. Disparity studies have been completed in Baltimore, Denver, Seattle, San Francisco, and Milwaukee.

THE COURTS AND SELECTION PROCEDURES

As noted earlier, the Civil Rights Act of 1991 overturned the U.S. Supreme Court's decision in *Ward's Cove.* In doing so, it codified the Court's earlier decision in *Griggs* v. *Duke Power Company* (1971) and subsequent *Griggs*-type decisions. The *Griggs* doctrine sets forth several key testing and selection requirements necessary for an employer to avoid racial discrimination:

- Employment practices including tests are unlawful if they differentially affect persons by virtue of their race, sex, religion, or national origin.
- To be lawful, tests must be proved valid; that is, they must be shown to be job related or predictive of performance on the job.

• Any employment practice, however fair and impartial, that tends to perpetuate the effect of prior discrimination violates the law.

The law prohibits actions that "on their face" treat "protected" classes (minorities, women) unfairly. If the requirements of a job seem to disqualify women, for example, the employer must show that the standards are a "bona fide occupational qualification" (BFOQ); otherwise they will be struck down. For instance, a city cannot require that only a woman can handle a switchboard or that only a man can drive a garbage truck. Race, by the way, is never a BFOQ.

Most municipalities have begun to recognize discriminatory treatment and eliminate it from their hiring practices. The more common issue now is disparate effect or adverse impact. Suppose the hiring or testing process for a position produces disproportionately few minority candidates. Is this discrimination? In these instances the court usually insists that the municipality show that the selection process and the test instrument are job related (validated). If the city fails to demonstrate test validity, the court then finds disparate effect and rules against the city. As a way of helping establish adverse impact, the EEOC, the Civil Service Commission, and the Departments of Justice and Labor jointly adopted an 80 percent rule: If the pass rate for minorities is not 80 percent of that for nonminority applicants, the examination procedure is considered on its face to have unequal impact. Under the 1989 *Ward's Cove* decision the mere presence of statistical adverse impact was no longer enough ammunition for protected groups to go to court. With the Civil Rights Act of 1991, the old standard may return. The expectation is that the four-fifths rule will once again be the litmus test for disparate impact.

An example of a practice with discriminatory effect is the inclusion of a minimum height and weight in the requirements for a position as police officer. On the surface these requirements, say a height of 5 feet 6 inches and weight of 140 pounds, may not seem discriminatory, but in practice they undoubtedly disqualify far more women than men; thus their impact is disparate. If the city police department could show that the criteria were essential for performance on the job (job related), the courts might accept them as legitimate. But in fact courts commonly reject height and weight requirements.[36]

How do local officials go about showing that selection procedures, most frequently tests, are job related? Validation is required.

TEST VALIDATION. — According to EEOC guidelines, tests, whether written or performance, can be validated in one of several ways. The first is to prove *criterion-related validity* (either predictive or concurrent). To establish criterion-related validity the city would have to prove that those who score highest on tests perform better on the job than those who score lower. In other words, a study would have to demonstrate that examination scores predict job success. The technique is based on statistical analysis and requires a large number of individuals in a job class or family. In essence, test scores are correlated with job performance scores. Obviously this type of validation is expensive and in many cases simply not possible, so the EEOC allows two alternative types of validity to be used: *construct validity* and *content validity*. A test is said to have construct validity when it measures a specific theoretical construct or trait, such as clerical or mechanical aptitude, that is necessary for successful job performance.[37] A content-valid test contains a representative sampling of tasks that closely resemble the duties to be performed on the job—a typing test for a job as a typist, for example. Both construct and content criteria, according to EEOC guidelines, must stem from a thorough job analysis.

AFFIRMATIVE ACTION NOW AND TOMORROW. — Much has happened in the area of affirmative action since the last edition of this book. The Rehnquist Court set new precedents in major AA cases in 1989 just to have them overturned by Congress in the Civil Rights Act of 1991. With the codification of *Griggs* by Congress, one would assume that the Court will resume a narrow interpretation of affirmative action policy guided by Nalbandian's previously discussed justification/content two-part test. The EEOC will continue to monitor and issue AA goals. Numerical quotas will continue to be anathema to the general population and avoided by the courts. Yet goals may encourage preferential hiring. If women and minorities have the post–*Ward's Cove* ability to demonstrate adverse impact more easily, employers may practice preferential hiring to avoid the hassle and cost of litigation.[38] And as Bob Cohn notes, regardless of whether one calls them goals or quotas, business must hire minorities for a host of reasons: public relations, federal mandates associated with government contracts, and the changing demographics of the American labor force.[39]

A NEW EQUAL EMPLOYMENT ISSUE
COMPARABLE WORTH

A relatively recent development that promises to complicate municipal personnel practices further is the issue of comparable worth. The Equal

Pay Act of 1963 prohibits pay differentials based on sex, thus ensuring equal pay for equal work. Comparable worth extends this concept considerably. At issue is whether the pay levels dictated by traditional market forces are fair to women. Truck drivers and equipment operators, for example, almost always command more money than do typists and secretaries. Such historical practices rarely consider whether the work requirements of the jobs really correspond with the level of pay. Comparable worth mandates that jobs be evaluated and compensated primarily on the basis of what each demands in the way of education, training, experience, and skills. If work were evaluated in this manner, employers presumably would be forced to admit that women are underpaid for much of the work they perform.

Partly because compensation plans of public entities appear less constrained by market forces than are those of the private sector, comparable worth advocates have made some headway with state and local governments. In fact, such governments have a better track record in the area of pay equity than the private sector. In 1990 women in state and local governments earned about 81 cents for every dollar earned by men. The comparable percentage in the private sector is only 71 cents.[40]

The courts have been involved hardly at all; most changes have come through legislation or bargaining agreements. What follows is what happened in one large city.

CASE STUDY

COMPARABLE WORTH IN LOS ANGELES

In May 1985 Los Angeles Mayor Tom Bradley announced that municipal pay scales would be adjusted so that salaries for jobs held mainly by women would be comparable to those for parallel positions traditionally held by men. Los Angeles thus became the largest city to adopt the controversial policy of comparable worth. The move was supported by the local president of the American Federation of State, County, and Municipal Employees, who said, "The momentum in eliminating sex bias from public-sector wage scales is now irreversible."

The problem, a difficult one, is to decide which jobs are comparable. In Los Angeles, stenographers and typists were being paid about 15 percent less than drivers and warehouse workers. Under the new system negotiated by AFSCME and city hall, all are considered to be doing comparable work. The pay agreement, estimated

to cost $12 million for 3,900 workers, was supported by male em-
ployees, who will not lose any pay in the process.

SOURCE: Adapted from "Typist = Driver: Los Angeles Adjusts Its Salaries," *Time,* 20
May 1985, 23.

Comparable worth remains controversial despite some limited gains.
Earlier in 1985 the U.S. Commission on Civil Rights had rejected comparable worth, saying it would lead to a "radical reordering of our economic system."[41] Opponents also argue that objectively determining
which jobs are comparable is an administrative nightmare, inviting discrimination, complaints, and abuse. Potentially high costs are cited as
well, because female-dominated jobs would undoubtedly be evaluated
upward with no corresponding lowering of pay for jobs held by males.
Nonetheless, several states including Minnesota and New York have
adopted versions of comparable worth, and a number of cities have
adopted comparable worth policies. N. Joseph Cayer's 1989 survey of
cities with populations of 10,000 or more residents, for example, indicates that about 10 percent of the approximately 900 survey cities have
formal comparable worth policies.[42]

SEXUAL HARASSMENT

The Anita Hill–Clarence Thomas sexual harassment controversy brought
widespread public attention to what has been called an old problem but
a new issue.[43] Both the prevalence and costs of sexual harassment in the
public workplace have been well documented. For example, surveys conducted in 1981 and 1988 by the U.S. Merit Systems Protection Board
found that at both time points about 42 percent of women and 15 percent of men had experienced some form of sexual harassment.[44] In 1980
the EEOC ruled that sexual harassment was a form of sex discrimination
and thus a violation of Title VII of the Civil Rights Act of 1964 as
amended to include governments in 1972.

Cities have begun to respond to concerns about sexual harassment.
Recent research among a group of large communities shows that most
places (84 percent) have formal sexual harassment policies.[45] About 70
percent of the cities also offer formal training programs. Almost two-
thirds reported filing one or more harassment complaints.

PERSONNEL POLICIES AND RETRENCHMENT

In addition to the disputes that arise over seniority versus affirmative action, retrenchment disrupts personnel relations in other ways. For example, organized employee groups resist cutback efforts that require layoffs, with particularly hard bargaining when employee unions feel the municipality's retrenchment compensation proposals treat them unfairly. In some places cutbacks have led to more frequent use of compulsory arbitration. This was true, for example, of the fire department in Oakland during the late 1970s. Charles Levine and his associates noted that the firefighting unions won several skirmishes with the Oakland city administration during this period of retrenchment.[46] But the unions also recognized the inevitability of some reductions and urged the city to practice reductions by attrition insofar as possible and to give the unions advance warning of necessary layoffs.

Finally, layoff and work-reduction procedures can have serious consequences for the personnel system and the efficient operation of city programs. A frequent response by city officials to budget cutbacks is reduction by attrition. This sounds reasonable, but departments with high rates of turnover suffer disproportionately. In several cities Levine and his associates observed that personnel planning and staff deployment became increasingly chaotic as hiring freezes were prolonged. And productivity can be jeopardized when key people resign or retire and are not replaced.

Labor-Management Relations

Even though public employee unions appeared as early as the nineteenth century, their real growth came only after World War II. By the early 1970s nearly two-thirds of all cities of over 25,000 population were operating under at least one collective bargaining agreement with unions or local employee associations.[47] Labor unions had become a major force to be reckoned with in most American cities of any size.

Although growth in municipal employment has slowed in recent years (the total number of employees increased by only 0.6 percent between 1986 and 1991),[48] city employee unions continue to hold their own. In 1987 almost half (48 percent) of all municipal employees were represented by a bargaining unit of some kind, compared to about 44 percent in 1977.[49] Union membership among all U.S. workers has been declining, from 34 percent in the mid-1950s to 17 percent in 1987.[50]

MUNICIPAL UNIONS

Workers join unions for a variety of reasons: economic, social, and psychological. The principal motive, especially for blue-collar workers, ap-

pears to be economic, the hope that a union will improve pay and working conditions through collective action. In short, as public administration specialist Richard Kearney notes, "Public employees join unions for
many of the same reasons as their private sector counterparts, particularly better wages and fringe benefits, improved working conditions, job
security, and a stronger voice in organizational decision making."[51] Public and private unions differ, of course. Whether these differences are sufficient to warrant special treatment of public unions continues to be debated.

PUBLIC UNIONS VERSUS PRIVATE UNIONS.—How do public and private labor-management relations differ? Probably the key distinction is
the lack of a profit motive on the part of public organizations. Some al-
lege that in the absence of profit and price competition, city councils, for
example, too easily give in to excessive employee demands. The monopo-
listic nature of most local public services means that elected officials can
pass along the increased labor costs without fear of being priced out of
business.

A second, related argument derives from the political context of municipal collective bargaining. Some feel that because local employees can
be a potent political force, a union has an undue advantage in dealing
with a local public employer. A corollary notion suggests that political
pressure may force a city council to acquiesce in a labor dispute to avoid
disrupting vital public services.[52]

A third point concerns the special nature of certain public services.
Many believe that police and fire protection cannot be jeopardized by
strikes; these services are too vital to be interrupted. Thus public labor
relations must be treated differently to ensure continuity of indispensable
functions.

Some of these public-private distinctions appear more valid than
others. Take the question of market incentives and union power. If in
fact public unions have a special advantage over their private counterparts, this should be reflected in proportionately higher wage gains for
organized public employees. Public employees who are organized apparently do realize greater economic gains than those who are not, but the
differences are slight.[53] And the percentage gains for organized public
employees apparently have not exceeded those attained by union members in private firms.[54] Thus the fear of excessive public union power remains unsubstantiated.

Political scientist Alan Saltzstein offers another angle on the question of management's inclination to cave in to union pressure.[55] His sur-

vey of council-manager cities indicates that city managers generally see themselves as "management" and thus are prone to oppose union demands. He goes on to say that managers prize their right under most charters to control personnel policy, which leads them to resist union encroachment. Finally Saltzstein notes the tendency for many city councils to overrepresent the upper-middle class in council-manager communities, which offers a supportive environment for those managers who want to take a hard line with the unions. Saltzstein's conclusion: A municipal union faces a potent force when it tangles with public management in a council-manager city.

UNIONS AND MERIT.—Some fear that the growth in public unions bodes ill for the merit principle. Unions generally do support seniority as a basis for promotion, but this is not to the exclusion of merit. As Jerry Wurf, then head of the American Federation of State, County, and Municipal Employees (AFSCME), noted, promotion should be on the basis of merit and fitness, but "seniority must be the key determination for distinguishing between qualified applicants."[56] In actual practice, of course, seniority frequently is the primary basis by which advancement comes even in the best of merit systems. When it comes to compensation, unions have fought efforts by management to create pay differentials for similar jobs except, of course, on the basis of seniority. Thus teacher organizations, for example, generally oppose any compensation plan based on performance. Although there are indications that some public employee groups are relenting a bit on the pay-for-performance issue, unions in general are still wary of such schemes, arguing that they create tensions among employees and are subject to abuse by management.

The general view today is that both collective bargaining and the merit principle are here to stay. Both management and labor, then, must get on with the task of ensuring their relative compatibility.

COLLECTIVE BARGAINING PROCEDURES

By far the most common practice among cities using collective bargaining is to grant unions exclusive recognition. This does not mean that all employees are required to join the union; *exclusive recognition* simply requires that once a bargaining agent has been properly selected, management must deal only with that employee group. Workers in these cities are not necessarily represented by just one union, however; bargaining units can be formed for a number of different components of the municipal workforce. On average, cities give exclusive recognition to five unions. In some of the very largest cities the number of bargaining units approaches the ridiculous. New York City, for example, has well over 200 separate units. In most cities there are usually separate organizations for police and firefighters, maybe separate unions for sanitation and public works employees, and then one or more unions representing the remaining line-level employees. In addition, there is a trend toward emulating the private sector and either excluding or constraining public-sector supervisors' bargaining rights.[57]

We should note several other features of collective bargaining. The chief administrative officer is most likely to be named chief negotiator for the city. In larger cities, though, the chief executive generally forms a committee to assist him or her in the actual conduct of bargaining. A recent survey found this to be the case in 86 percent of responding cities.[58] The most frequent members of the bargaining team were manager/CAO (43.7 percent), personnel director (45.6 percent), and department head (56.7 percent). Although the city council must approve all final agreements, again most authorities feel that neither this group collectively nor its individual members should actively engage in the negotiation process.

State legislation on collective bargaining tends to follow the requirements of the National Labor Relations Act in compelling good-faith bargaining. Just what this means is not always clear, although specific prohibitions sometimes are set forth in the enabling legislation. For example, an employer may be barred from interfering with the rights of employees. A city also would be forbidden to discriminate or retaliate against employees for union activities. Employees likewise may be prohibited from interfering with or coercing other employees.[59]

Collective negotiations constitute much more than a rule-bound legal process. Bargaining at the municipal level can easily become a political contest. Employees, after all, represent a sizable voting bloc. They may seek to advance their interests not only at the bargaining table but also before the council directly, in the electoral arena, and even in the state legislature. In fact, a major concern of those who fear union power is this very potential for the extensive exercise of political influence by public employee organizations. Local elections are notorious for their low turnout, as we have seen. A well-organized bloc of employees may well be able to affect the outcome of any such contest. The assumption often follows that local politicians, eager for reelection, are especially sensitive to any action that might offend employee unions. As indicated previously, however, there is no conclusive evidence that municipal unions receive larger benefits than do unions in the private sector. Still the fear remains. Undoubtedly we must recognize the political environment in which local collective bargaining takes place, but the extent to which politics produces bargaining outcomes different from those that would otherwise be negotiated remains an open question.

The political question aside, concern remains over possible union militancy. In fact, much of the literature on public-sector labor relations deals with various ways to minimize work stoppages.

IMPASSE RESOLUTION.—The purpose of collective bargaining is to arrive at a mutually acceptable agreement. When normal negotiation does not produce this outcome, labor disputes arise. Because most states prohibit strikes by public employees, some means other than striking must be found to resolve deadlocks. Over the years, three basic methods have evolved for dealing with labor-management impasses: mediation, fact finding, and arbitration. Mediation is the most common; arbitration, the least.

Mediation brings in a neutral third party, acceptable to both union and management, to help the two parties resolve the dispute themselves. If negotiations have broken down, the mediator's first task is to restore communication. A mediator ordinarily does not hold formal hearings, keep written transcripts, or release an opinion on the issues in contention. Mediation has been both popular and successful. The parties at issue are not reluctant to use the process because neither is obligated to accept the mediator's suggestions. A skilled mediator may be invaluable to parties that have had little negotiating experience.[60]

When mediation is unsuccessful, *fact finding* is often the next step. Fact finding also requires the use of a neutral third party to help resolve disputes. In this case the procedure is more formal, usually involving three stages: initiation of the process and selection of the fact finder, hearings to identify the issues, and submission of a report with recommendations.[61] Although the fact finder makes written recommendations, these are not binding on either party. Again consensus suggests that fact finding produces good results; still some contend that if the method is too readily available, it reduces incentives for genuine bargaining at any earlier stage.

Arbitration is the most drastic step in impasse resolution. Arbitration may take several forms. In *voluntary arbitration* the two parties agree without compulsion to submit specific issues to a third party for a final binding decision. Most arbitration, however, is *compulsory*. The binding-arbitration procedure is much the same as that used in fact finding: the disputants each select a representative, and the representatives in turn choose a third neutral party; hearings are held and transcripts kept; and a final recommendation is issued. Under compulsory arbitration both parties are legally bound by the arbitrator's findings. Often a decision is made that splits the difference between the union's last demand and the city's final offer.

Controversy surrounds compulsory arbitration. Historically, management has resisted having the terms of a contract dictated by an outside group; unions too have had misgivings about what might be involved. Yet binding arbitration has become widespread in the private sector, often as a tradeoff for a no-strike clause. Partly because of this growing acceptance in private business, binding arbitration has become more common in the public sector. Some feel that this resolution mechanism is also an effective deterrent to strikes. In many cities its use is limited to those public employee groups providing indispensable services—police and fire departments, for example. Whether compulsory arbitration prevents strikes remains uncertain. Despite its growing popularity, at least one authority expresses reservations about its unrestricted application to the public sector. Myron Lieberman suggests that binding arbitration for public jurisdictions be limited to questions of fact; otherwise the practice deprives management of its legitimate right to make policy. For example, an employee fired for stealing public property might submit to arbitration the question of whether the theft occurred, but could not contest the form of punishment.[62]

An interesting twist to binding arbitration—final offer arbitration (FOA)—has appeared in recent years. The approach requires the arbitrator to choose either management's or labor's last offer. There's no splitting the difference; it's winner take all. The procedure presumably forces both parties to make a final offer they can live with; otherwise the arbitrator might select the other party's offer as a more reasonable settlement. Although FOA is an ingenious device to compel reasonable final offers, it does present several problems. First, it is inflexible; the arbitrator has no choice but to accept one or the other final offer. This may not be terribly serious with respect to wages, but it can prove troublesome in nonwage disputes. Experience with FOA has been limited, but in Eugene, Oregon, the procedure seems to work reasonably well.[63] And in Eugene the FOA method does not seem to jeopardize the incentives to genuine bargaining, a fear many have concerning binding arbitration in any form.

Finally, cities sometimes create joint labor-management committees to avoid prolonged labor disputes, accelerate productivity, improve the work environment, and improve labor-management relations.[64] In Massachusetts, for example, a fourteen-member joint committee now oversees collective bargaining for the state's police and firefighters.[65] The committee includes an equal number of representatives of labor and management (six members each) plus a neutral chair and vice-chair. The group is committed to settling disputes through direct bargaining by the affected parties whenever possible, and it has the legal authority to enter a dispute even before the parties declare an official impasse. The mechanism has worked well in the Bay State; the time taken to resolve the average labor-management dispute has been cut in half—from over six months to less than three. It is also cheaper, as fewer lawyers are involved for shorter periods of time.

THE STRIKE. —Traditionally, the law prohibits strikes by public employees. This has not prevented strikes and work stoppages, however. Today the total opposition to public-sector strikes is undergoing modification. As of 1992, twelve states have legislatively granted at least some of their employees a limited right to strike,[66] usually those in nonessential work areas. Strikes remain illegal for police and fire employees and others who protect the safety and security of the public.

The strike issue is certainly the most controversial problem in public labor relations. Opponents tend to see a strike as defiance of public authority. Labor, in contrast, argues that there are no compelling differences between public and private employment, and therefore the strike should be considered a legitimate, useful weapon in all labor disputes. To some the problem appears intractable because there is merit to both sides of the question: "The public welfare must continue to be served, but at the same time the rights of employees cannot be ignored."[67] Sterling Spero and John Capozzola offer a different view. They contend the sovereignty issue is essentially phony—"a convenient technique to avoid dealing with the merits of issues in disputes." They argue further that "the public-private dichotomy fails to distinguish between necessity and convenience and takes no notice of the critical or noncritical character of the service."[68] The Canadian government seems to have arrived at a unique solution to the issue of public-sector strikes. Under Canadian law, after a union has been certified as a bargaining agent, it is required to specify one of two alternatives for impasse resolution. The first is referral to binding arbitration; the second is mediation with the right to strike. If a union opts for compulsory arbitration, legally it cannot strike. And most national public unions in Canada have chosen compulsory arbitration. Variations on the Canadian federal experience are found in several provinces. Still, even if the strike option is elected, certain employees are prohibited from striking if "necessary in the interest of the safety or security of the public."[69]

Of course, the sticky question remains: How do we designate those employees whose jobs are essential to the safety of the public? If a distinction is made, it seems appropriate to give that group access to binding arbitration. Beyond that there would seem to be no compelling reason not to give other public employees the full rights of labor, including the right to strike. The Canadian approach or some variation thereof would seem to be a way out of the intractable strike situation.

CASE STUDY

Collective Bargaining in Cincinnati

In 1948 the Cincinnati city council adopted an ordinance giving city employees the right to be represented by unions. The council directed the city manager to deal with any organized employee group. Negotiation guidelines were provided, and later that same year a system of collective bargaining was established. Over time, AFSCME became the exclusive bargaining agent for most employees, excluding police and fireworkers.

The Cincinnati city manager assigned the negotiating function to the personnel director, although the manager retained final authority over any agreements and offered broad guidelines and advice during the negotiation process. Generally the council accepted whatever the city manager recommended in the way of a contract.

Through most of the 1960s collective negotiations operated smoothly, but toward the end of the decade things began to change. The Cincinnati management had always relied on a tight fiscal condition to persuade the unions to exercise restraint at the bargaining table, and this very fiscal conservatism brought trouble in 1969, the year Cincinnati experienced its first serious municipal strike. The primary cause was the voters' rejection of a proposal to raise the local income tax from 1 to 2 percent. Nonuniformed employees apparently felt this would mean intolerable limits on wages and salaries. A strike was on.

In all, both sides acted responsibly. The city obtained but refused to enforce an injunction, and no arrests were made. According to Donald Heisel, the personnel director, "Experience elsewhere shows that strike settlements are never made in the jail house." Federal mediators were called in, and the whole affair was over in three days.

But controversy flared up again the next year. When negotiations reached a stalemate, several AFSCME unions struck, this time exhibiting none of the restraint shown the year before. The city reacted in kind. One worker commented, "This was an all-out affair with no legal holds barred." The city obtained and enforced an injunction against the striking workers. Thirty-seven arrests were made, and two strike leaders were sentenced to twenty days in jail and fined $1,000 each. The strike lasted five bitter weeks.

When the smoke cleared and the strikers went back to work, the city had agreed to substantial wage increases and other employee benefits. The jailed union officers were released, and officials promised they would drop all future legal action. But the dispute left a residue of distrust on both sides.

SOURCE: Adapted from Sterling Spero and John Capozzola, *The Urban Community and Its Unionized Bureaucracies* (New York: Dunnellen, 1973), 50–57.

MUNICIPAL UNIONS IN PERSPECTIVE

Public labor relations have moved ever closer to the industrial model. Bilateral determination of wages and working conditions is now established procedure in most large cities, and municipal workforces are the most heavily unionized of all public employee groups. What does all this mean for traditional municipal personnel practice? First, there is no clear evidence that public unions are more successful than private unions in achieving their economic goals. Second, public employee organizations are now affected in much the same way as their private-sector counterparts by the economic and social changes sweeping the nation. With overall union membership declining and cities retrenching, the possibility of a strike seems less threatening, and consequently management has become increasingly resistant to labor demands. Unions clearly are on the defensive. We have entered what John Capozzola has described as a period of "concessionary bargaining," which has stimulated considerable union interest in labor-management cooperation.[70]

Frank Swoboda makes a similar argument with respect to strikes. "The strike has become, in effect, the nuclear device in labor's arsenal of weapons, something to be used in total warfare.... "[71] Such cooperation does not signal the end of collective bargaining, of course, but it does suggest that shrewd and realistic union leaders have recognized that tactical adjustments are necessary to cope with changing times. If management is also receptive, the new era of cooperation should mean more consultation with workers and greater involvement of employees in decision making in areas that generally have not been subject to mandatory bargaining. Capozzola also sees this as an opportune time for labor to do some soul-searching:

> The aim of negotiators to get more for the existing membership at the expense of the unemployed should be reexamined. Deep-rooted work rules reduce efficiency, hamper productivity and hinder foreign competition. In a similar vein, more introspection and study is needed to reconcile valid concepts of seniority and merit.[72]

Summary

Traditional municipal personnel practices have been considerably transformed in recent years. Organization is shifting from independent employment (civil service) commissions to executive-controlled personnel staffs. Whatever their organizational structure, most cities claim to use some form of merit system in their practices. Gains have been made in staffing and employee classification, but municipalities have made only modest headway in establishing pay-for-performance compensation plans.

The quest for equal employment by minorities and women has resulted in a serious challenge to traditional concepts of merit. Minorities in particular have argued for less reliance on formal credentials and written examinations. In response to court decisions and federal pressure, cities continue to modify personnel practices in the name of affirmative action, which stress results above all. Goals and timetables seem indispensable to this effort. But the courts almost always reject numerical quotas. Other personnel procedures are undergoing change as well. The one-of-three rule is under attack; pass-fail tests are advocated; and federal courts are mandating that examinations be validated. Although almost everyone accepts validation as useful, in practice it is not easily done.

Other personnel issues have become salient in recent years. Those with disabilities have secured new rights under the Americans with Disabilities Act of 1990. The Congress demonstrated its dissatisfaction with recent Supreme Court decisions with passage of the Civil Rights Act of 1991. The old problem of sexual harassment has become a new issue.

Municipal unions—some fear they will make the local bureaucracy too powerful; others insist that there is little difference between public and private employment and that public unions should be dealt with accordingly. Certainly municipal unions are here to stay, and cities must learn to accept and understand the key features of public collective bargaining. Because most states still prohibit strikes by public employees, methods of impasse resolution—mediation, fact finding, and arbitration—are critical. Although no unanimity exists in this area, increasing attention has centered on binding arbitration and the use of limited strikes as ways to guarantee public employees the customary rights of labor while still ensuring the provision of vital public services.

Notes

1. Municipal Manpower Commission, *Governmental Manpower for Tomorrow's Cities* (New York: McGraw-Hill, 1962).

2. *A Model Public Personnel Administration Law* (Washington, D.C.: National Civil Service League, 1970).

3. N. Joseph Cayer, "Local Government Personnel Structure and Policies," in *Municipal Yearbook 1991* (Washington, D.C.: ICMA, 1991), 4–5.

4. Andrew H. Boesel, "Local Personnel Management: Organizational Problems and Operating Practices," in *Municipal Year Book 1974* (Washington, D.C.: ICMA, 1974), 94.

5. This preliminary discussion draws on Frank J. Thompson, *Personnel Policy in the City* (Berkeley: University of California Press, 1975), 4–19.

6. Elder Witt, "Are Our Governments Paying What It Takes to Keep the Best and the Brightest?" *Governing*, December 1988, 30.

7. Felix Nigro and Lloyd Nigro, *The New Public Personnel Administration* (Itasca, Ill.: F.E. Peacock, 1976), 153–54.

8. Thompson, *Personnel Policy*, 81–82.

9. Twenty-five objections to traditional testing for selection purposes are listed in Nesta M. Gallas, "The Selection Process," in *Local Government Personnel Administration*, ed. Winston Crouch (Washington, D.C.: ICMA, 1976), 134.

10. Thompson, *Personnel Policy*, 102.

11. This discussion relies on O. Glenn Stahl, *Public Personnel Administration*, 8th ed. (New York: Harper & Row, 1983), 131–32.

12. Gregory D. Streib, "Personnel Management," in *Small Cities and Counties: A Guide to Managing Services*, ed. James M. Banovetz (Washington, D.C.: ICMA, 1984), 256.

13. David H. Rosenbloom, "Equal Employment Opportunity: Another Strategy," *Personnel Administration/Public Personnel Review* 1 (July–August 1972): 38–41.

14. Jonathan Walters, "How Not to Reform Civil Service," *Governing*, November 1992, 33.

15. Nigro and Nigro, *New Public Personnel Administration*, 116.

16. Jerome S. Sanderson, "Compensation," in Crouch, *Local Government Personnel Administration,* 196–97.

17. N. Joseph Cayer, *Public Personnel Administration in the United States* (New York: St. Martin's, 1975), 70– 71.

18. Chester A. Newland, "Public Personnel: Retrenchment, Restructuring, Reorganization," in *Municipal Year Book 1982* (Washington, D.C.: ICMA, 1982), 201.

19. Steven Waldman with Betsy Roberts, "Grading 'Merit Pay,'" *Newsweek,* 14 November 1988, 45.

20. Gregory Streib and Theodore H. Poister, "Established and Emerging Management Tools A 12-Year Perspective," in *Municipal Year Book 1989* (Washington, D.C.: ICMA, 1989), 46.

21. David Osborne and Ted Gaebler, *Reinventing Government* (Reading, Mass.: Addison-Wesley, 1992).

22. David Ammons and Arnold Rodriguez, "Performance Appraisal Practices for Upper Management in City Governments," *Public Administration Review* 46 (September/October 1986): 460–67; Robert E. England and William M. Parle, "Nonmanagerial Performance Appraisal Practices in Large American Cities," *Public Administration Review* 47 (November/December 1987): 498–504.

23. Robert D. Behn, "Measuring Performance Against the 80–30 Syndrome," *Governing,* June 1993, 70.

24. Charles J. Fox, "Employee Performance Appraisal: The Keystone Made of Clay," in *Public Personnel Management: Current Concerns–Future Challenges,* ed. Carolyn Ban and Norma M. Riccucci (New York, Longman, 1991), 67–68.

25. Herbert Hill, "Preferential Hiring: Correcting the Demerit System," *Social Policy* 4 (July–August 1973): 102.

26. Catherine Lovell, "Three Key Issues in Affirmative Action," *Public Administration Review* 34 (May–June 1974): 235–37.

27. Tom Kenworthy and Thomas B. Edsall, "The Voices of Those Who Think Civil Rights Have Gone Too Far," *Washington Post National Weekly Edition,* 10–16 June 1991, 14.

28. John Nalbandian, "The U.S. Supreme Court's "Consensus" on Affirmative Action," *Public Administration Review* 49 (January/February 1989): 39.

29. Charles Fried, "Restoring Balance to Civil Rights," *Washington Post National Weekly Edition,* 3–9 June 1989.

30. For a discussion, see Ann O'M. Bowman and Michael A. Pagano, "The State of American Federalism—1989-1990," *Publius* 20 (Summer): 1–25; and Mitchell F. Rice, "Government Set-Asides, Minority Business Enterprises, and the Supreme Court," *Public Administration Review* 51 (March/April 1991): 114–22.

31. Julianne R. Ryder, "High Court Ruling Will Impact Affirmative Action," *Public Administration Times* 12 (23 June 1989): 1, 11.

32. Ibid.

33. Sue Ann Nicely, "New Civil Rights Act to Adversely Impact Employers," *Oklahoma Cities & Towns,* 14 February 1992, 1, 3. See also Paul Gewirtz, "Discrimination Endgame," *New Republic,* 12 August 1991, 18–23; and Paul Gewirtz, "The Civil Rights Bill's Loopholes?" *New Republic,* 18 November 1991, 10–13.

34. This discussion is drawn from U.S. Equal Employment Opportunity Commission, *The Americans with Disabilities Act: Your Responsibilities as an Employer* (Washington, D.C.: EEOC, 1991).

35. Ellen Perlman, "Minority Set-Aside Programs Back on Course," *City & State,* 5 November 1990, 4.

36. Nelson and Harding (attorneys), "An Introduction to Equal Employment Opportunity," *Current Municipal Problems* 9 (1982–83): 84.

37. David Robertson, "Update on Testing and Equal Employment," *Personnel Journal* 56 (March 1977): 145.

38. Gewirtz, "Discrimination Endgame," 20.

39. Bob Cohn with Tom Morganthau, "The Q-Word Charade," *Newsweek,* 3 June 1991, 17.

40. Joseph M. Winski, "Pay Equity Gap Smallest in State, Local Government," *City & State,* 18 May 1992, SG18.

41. "Typist = Driver: Los Angeles Adjusts Its Salaries," *Time,* 20 May 1985, 23.

42. Cayer, "Local Government Personnel Structure and Policies," 9.

43. Cynthia S. Ross and Robert E. England, "State Governments' Sexual Harassment Policy Initiatives," *Public Administration Review* 47 (May/June 1987): 259.

44. See U.S. Merit Systems Protection Board, Office of Merit Systems Review and Studies, *Sexual Harassment in the Federal Workplace: Is It a Problem?* (Washington, D.C.: Government Printing Office, March 1981), 2–14; and "Sexual Harassment Is Still a Problem in Government," *Wall Street Journal,* 30 June 1988, 10.

45. Connie Kirk-Westerman, David M. Billeaux, and Robert E. England, "Ending Sexual Harassment at City Hall: Policy Initiatives in Large American Cities," *State and Local Government Review* 21 (Fall 1989): 100–105.

46. The following discussion comes from Charles Levine, Irene Rubin, and George Wolohojian, *The Politics of Retrenchment* (Beverly Hills: Sage, 1981), 67–69, 193, 204.

47. Boesel, "Local Personnel Management," 87.

48. U.S. Bureau of the Census, *City Employment in 1991* (Washington, D.C.: Government Printing Office, 1992), 2.

49. U.S. Bureau of the Census, *1987 Census of Governments: Labor-Management Relations in State and Local Government* (Washington, D.C.: Government Printing Office, 1988), 1; and U.S. Bureau of the Census, *1977 Census of Governments: Labor-Management Relations in State and Local*

Government (Washington, D.C.: Government Printing Office, 1979), 7.

50. Irving O. Dawson, "Trends and Developments in Public Sector Unions," in *Public Personnel Administration: Problems & Prospects* 2d ed., ed. Steven W. Hays and Richard C. Kearney (Englewood Cliffs, N.J.: Prentice Hall, 1990), 148.

51. Richard C. Kearney, *Labor Relations in the Public Sector* (New York: Marcel Dekker, 1984), 16.

52. Jay F. Atwood, "Collective Bargaining's Challenge: Five Imperatives for Public Managers," *Public Personnel Management* 5 (January–February 1976): 24–32.

53. W. Clayton Hail and Bruce Vanderporten, "Unionization, Monopsony Power, and Police Salaries," *Industrial Relations* 16 (February 1977): 94–100.

54. James L. Freund, "Market and Union Influences on Municipal Employee Wages," *Industrial and Labor Relations Review* 27 (April 1974): 391–404.

55. Alan L. Saltzstein, "Can Urban Management Control the Organized Employee?" *Public Personnel Management* 3 (July–August 1974): 332–40.

56. Jerry Wurf, "Merit: A Union View," *Public Administration Review* 34 (September/October 1974): 433.

57. Joel M. Douglas, "Collective Bargaining and Public Sector Supervisors: A Trend Toward Exclusion?" *Public Administration Review* 47 (November/December 1987): 492.

58. Timothy David Chandler, "Labor-Management Relations in Local Government," in *Municipal Year Book 1989* (Washington, D.C.: ICMA, 1989), 90.

59. James S. Crabtree, "Development, Status, and Procedures for Labor Relations," in *Developing the Municipal Organization*, ed. Stanley Powers, F. Gerald Brown, and David Arnold (Washington, D.C.: ICMA, 1974), 255.

60. William Work, "Toward More Negotiations in the Public Sector," *Public Personnel Management* 2 (September–October 1973): 345.

61. Karl A. Van Asselt, "Impasse Resolution," *Public Administration Review* 32 (March/April 1972): 115.

62. Myron Lieberman, *Public-Sector Bargaining* (Lexington, Mass.: D.C. Heath, 1980), 99–101.

63. Peter Feuille and Gary Long, "The Public Administrator and Final Offer Arbitration," *Public Administration Review* 34 (November/December 1974): 575–83.

64. See John R. Miller and Myron Olstein, "LMCs: Helping Government Function Effectively," *City & State*, 23 October 1989, 23.

65. Jonathan Brock, "Labor-Management Conflict: Bargaining Beyond Impasse," *Washington Public Policy Notes* 12 (Spring 1984): 4–5.

66. Kearney, *Labor Relations in the Public Sector*, 283.

67. Cabot Dow, "Labor Relations," in Crouch, *Local Government Personnel Administration*, 231.

68. Sterling Spero and John Capozzola, *The Urban Community and Its Unionized Bureaucracies* (New York: Dunnellen, 1973), 313.

69. Eugene F. Berrodin, "Compulsory Arbitration in Personnel Management," *Public Management* 55 (July 1973): 13.

70. John M. Capozzolla, "Taking a Look at Unions: American Labor Confronts Major Problems," *National Civic Review* 75 (July–August 1986): 205–13.

71. Frank Swoboda, "Striking Out as a Weapon Against Management," *Washington Post National Weekly Edition*, 13–19 July 1992, 20.

72. Capozzolla, "Taking a Look at Unions," 213.

Suggested for Further Reading

Ban, Carolyn, and Norma M. Riccucci, eds. *Public Personnel Management: Current Concerns–Future Challenges.* New York: Longman, 1991.

Dresang, Dennis L. *Public Personnel Management and Public Policy.* 2d ed. New York: Longman, 1991.

Hays, Steven W., and Richard C. Kearney. *Public Personnel Administration: Problems and Prospects.* 2d ed. Englewood Cliffs, N.J.: Prentice Hall, 1990.

Kearney, Richard C. *Labor Relations in the Public Sector.* 2d ed. New York: Marcel Dekker, 1992.

Thompson, Frank J. *Classics of Public Personnel Policy.* 2d ed. Pacific Grove, Calif.: Brooks/Cole, 1991.

10

Finance and Budget

Talk to any city manager about the city's problems. The conversation won't get far before the matter of money comes up. According to local officials, few problems could not be solved or at least made much easier to handle if more money were available. The cost of programs and services imposes the greatest single constraint on local decision making.

Cities face a never-ending quest for funds. Where does the money come from? How much is really needed? What effects do certain revenue-raising schemes have on different segments of the population? What is politically feasible? What financial options are available? These are the issues with which city leaders must continually cope. And with the continuing demand for more and better services in the face of constantly increasing costs, tough decisions must be made. As we saw in chapter 7, cities of every size across the country are being forced to retrench, to practice cutback management. Now more than ever, virtually every significant policy decision must be considered in the light of available funds.

This chapter begins by examining certain features of the municipal revenue-raising system, among them sources of funds, alternative revenue-raising options, and the political issues that arise when cities search for new sources of income. Recent spending trends is the second major topic. Then we explore how funds are distributed among competing needs—the process of city budgeting. And finally we look at the overall process of financial management.

Revenue Raising

THE MUNICIPAL FINANCE SYSTEM

A fundamental feature of local government in the United States is the imbalance between the massive services cities must provide and the limitations on their existing revenue-raising structures.[1] Perhaps in no other country except Canada is local government expected to do more. Yet the higher levels of government are inherently better tax collectors; the states and especially the national government not only have access to a broader range of wealth and income than do cities but also can effect significant economies of scale in tax collection.

The congenital imbalance between service responsibility and revenue-raising capacity has brought about the large-scale system of grants flowing from higher to lower levels. This elaborate grant system is the second basic characteristic of municipal finance in this country.

Several other elements underlie the cities' revenue structure. State constitutional and statutory restrictions create severe constraints on municipal revenue-raising capacity. Federal guidelines and controls on grants-in-aid impose additional limitations on local financial policy. Also, the fragmentation inherent in local governments can divorce local resources from local needs, creating serious financial disparities within metropolitan areas. Finally, because of their limited geographic scope, cities are not adequately equipped to handle spillovers. Often they must absorb the significant costs of dealing with social problems that are not generated within their own borders.

The drawbacks associated with cities' limited geographic territory can be alleviated partly by shifting the fiscal burden of urban services to higher levels. If greater responsibility for funding were assumed by national and state governments, at least three major defects of the present system would be eliminated: inadequate handling of spillovers, disparities in service and tax levels, and fiscal imbalance among levels of government.[2] Politically, however, greater fiscal centralization does not have much appeal. States are not enthusiastic about taking on more of the financial burdens of the central cities. Suburbs and smaller communities are largely indifferent to appeals to help the big-city poor. And the prevailing commitment to a grassroots political philosophy (the fear of losing local control) remains a formidable barrier to sharing responsibility on a wider scale. Unless the states provide more help, of course, cities are not likely to have much success in shifting the financial burden upward.

REVENUE SOURCES

States traditionally have relegated the property tax to local governments as their primary means of raising revenue. This source of money remains prominent within local systems of finance, especially for schools and county governments. In recent years, however, cities have come to rely less on the property tax for financing current operations. Intergovernmental transfers (grants-in-aid) have now displaced the property tax as the principal source of municipal revenue.

Table 10.1 summarizes the changes in sources of revenue that have taken place over the past fifteen years. Not too much change occurred between 1976 and 1991 in reliance on city taxes, an increase of 1.7 percentage points. This increase is a product of the 1986–91 time period when the trend toward a declining reliance on taxes to raise revenue was reversed. Taxes provide about 44 percent of municipal revenue. In 1981, before the major effects of the Reagan domestic budget cuts, taxes furnished only 34 percent of city budgets. Property taxes are down, however, from almost 26 percent of municipal revenue in 1976 to 22.9 percent in 1991. Other taxes, consequently, are up slightly as a percentage

TABLE 10.1.
CITY GENERAL REVENUE FROM SELECTED SOURCES,
1976, 1986, AND 1991, AND
CHANGE 1976 TO 1991[a]

	1976	1986	1991	Change 1976 to 1991 (%)
General revenue (total in millions)	$55,341	$122,049	$164,319	196.9
Taxes (%)	42.2	41.7	43.9	1.7
Property	25.6	20.5	22.9	−2.7
Sales and gross receipts	9.2	12.0	11.9	2.7
Other	7.4	9.2	9.1	1.8
Intergovernmental (%)	40.2	30.4	28.1	−12.1
From state	24.9	20.2	21.2	−3.7
From federal	13.4	8.0	4.6	−8.8
From local	1.9	2.2	2.3	.5
Charges (%)	11.1	14.8	16.6	5.5
Miscellaneous (%)[b]	6.5	13.1	11.4	4.9

SOURCE: U.S. Bureau of the Census, *City Government Finances, 1975–76, 1985–1986, and 1990–1991* (Washington, D.C.: Government Printing Office, 1977, 1988, 1993).

a. General revenue excludes utility, liquor store, and insurance trust revenue.
b. Miscellaneous includes interest earnings, sale of property, and special assessments.

of the total. The big change is in intergovernmental revenue; it dropped over 12 percentage points, from 40.2 to 28.1 percent. The drop in federal aid is not surprising, but note also the relative decline in state support, of almost 4 percentage points. Charges, fees, and miscellaneous revenue are up as a proportion of the total, together accounting for over a 10-percentage-point increase. What we see here, of course, is almost an exact tradeoff; charges and miscellaneous have made up for the relative losses in intergovernmental revenue.

There is no reason to assume that the property tax trend will change significantly in the near future. Intergovernmental transfers may have finally bottomed out. Regardless of which party controls the White House, however, any revival of substantial federal aid to cities is unlikely. And states have little revenue to share. So cities will continue to fend for themselves during the 1990s.

REVENUE-RAISING ALTERNATIVES

Cities vary considerably in the degree to which they rely on certain sources of revenue, primarily because of state laws and historical tendencies. For example, many older northeastern cities continue to rely heavily on the property tax, whereas western cities use it much less extensively. What are the pros and cons of the property tax?

THE PROPERTY TAX.—Although still a mainstay of local revenue raising, the property tax is widely criticized by finance experts. First, it suffers from serious problems in administration. Large discrepancies in property evaluation inevitably result from the system of local assessment. Also property tax systems are costly and inefficient to administer compared with other tax options. Third, the property tax discourages improvements and maintenance on property. Why should an absentee landlord spend money to improve a building if the increased value simply means higher taxes? Fourth, some authorities consider the property tax, as currently levied and administered, to be mildly regressive. The argument is that because the poor spend a larger share of their income for housing than do other groups, they pay proportionately more than the well-to-do.

CASE STUDY

THE PROPERTY TAX IN TWO COOK COUNTY SUBURBS

IN an article entitled "Property-Tax Paradox: High Rate in Poor

Town," Marla Donato vividly illustrates how the property tax can vary from one community to the next and the tax's regressive nature. The real-life characters are Amy Washington and John Zeman. Amy lives in Ford Heights, one of the nation's poorest suburbs. John lives in Niles, a solidly middle-class suburb. The paradox is that Ford Heights has the highest tax rate in Cook County and Niles has the lowest.

Both Amy and John live in modest three-bedroom homes. The tax rate in Ford Heights is $18.12 per $100 of assessed valuation. In Niles the rate is $6.31. The market value of Amy's home is $19,381. Her tax bill is $854 dollars per year, about 4.4 percent of the home's value. John's home is worth $74,875. His tax bill is $1,268, or 1.7 percent of the home's value. The city of Ford Heights gets $340 of Amy's tax bill; Niles takes only $75 of John's tax bill. Why? Ford Heights is a poor community with a large number of individuals on public aid and in public housing. With a smaller tax base, fewer people must pay more. Business and industry would help ease the tax burden, but since property taxes are higher in Ford Heights for commercial as well as personal property, business has less incentive to locate in the community.

Perhaps the proportionately higher taxes results in better services for Amy? Not really. She pays for her rusty well-water bill at the Village Hall where the water fountains do not work. Not being able to pay liability insurance, the public pool has been closed for the past ten years. The library is closed for renovations, and when it was open, it was for just a few hours each week. The story is different for John, who enjoys clear Lake Michigan water. He can ride the free municipal bus to his Village Hall. His children can play on one of the manicured baseball fields, at the municipal ice rink, or at the city's new water park. At the library, which is open to 9 P.M. most nights, he can enjoy the computerized card catalog or one of eleven computer terminals for patrons.

SOURCE: Marla Donato, "Property-Tax Paradox: High Rate in Poor Town," *Chicago Tribune,* 5 September 1992, 1, 12.

Others argue that the property tax may not be any more regressive than most other sources of municipal revenue. And indeed some states and localities are reducing the tax's regressive effect by providing *circuit breakers*—tax breaks for the poor or elderly. The real issue here is a comparative one: what other revenue sources are likely to be used in lieu of the property tax, and how do they compare in regressivity with the property tax? As we see below, trading a reduction in property tax for an increase in another form of revenue may not benefit low- and moderate-income families.

Debate surrounds the property tax for other reasons as well. There is some question about the tax's elasticity—the degree to which it responds to changing economic conditions. Although property values have soared in the past quarter century, property tax collections have increased only half again as much. Presumably this adds a special burden to older central cities, which rely heavily on this source of revenue.[3]

One other problem plagues the property tax—its visibility, and thus its universal unpopularity. According to recent surveys done for the Advisory Commission on Intergovernmental Relations (ACIR), the local property tax is considered the "worst" or "least fair" tax, followed by the federal income tax.[4]

But when all is said and done, the property tax raises a great deal of revenue, can be administered by local governments, and is the only major source of tax revenue that local governments can call their own.[5] And despite its unpopularity, voters have turned down several recent efforts to discard the property tax in favor of other forms of school financing. It is doubtful, then, that we will see the wholesale abandonment of the property tax, even though several states are struggling to rectify the gross inequities in school financing that result from the heavy dependence on this form of revenue.

NONPROPERTY TAXES.—Several years ago, the ACIR's national survey on government and taxes asked, "If local governments must raise more revenue, what would be the best way?" The overwhelming choice of respondents (49 percent) was the category "charges for specific services." The next highest category, with 26 percent, was local sales tax. Only 9 percent favored a local income tax (the property tax was last with 7 percent).[6]

The *sales tax* has several potential strengths. Especially if the state collects the tax and rebates it to the city, administration is easy and efficient. The sales tax is also reasonably elastic. And people seem to favor it over other taxes in part because it seems equitable—everyone pays on the same basis. Excise taxes, however, are regressive, as the poor pay a relatively larger share of their income for items normally subject to sales tax. If certain exemptions are granted, say on food and drugs, the regressive nature of the sales tax is blunted considerably. But even these exemptions are not without problems: they are costly; they create administrative difficulties; and they open the door to tax evasion. And whether exemptions really benefit the poor may depend on how much revenue loss is absorbed by cutting services to the poor and what kinds of taxes are used as a replacement.[7]

The *local income tax* (including payroll tax) is available to cities in ten states, but widespread coverage exists only in three states: Kentucky, Ohio, and Pennsylvania. By 1991, some 3,697 local jurisdictions (including counties and school districts) had adopted the tax. Of these, only 873 were outside the state of Pennsylvania. Several of the largest U.S. cities employ a local income tax, including Detroit, New York City, Cincinnati, Cleveland, Columbus, Philadelphia, and Toledo. In Los Angeles, San Francisco, and Newark, taxes are imposed on the total payroll of employers.[8]

The income tax is normally a flat rate (often 1 percent) on wages and salaries. Typically the locality itself administers the tax, but in some places the state is authorized to do so. The administrative process raises several issues. First there is the question of taxing nonlabor income. Most cities do not levy the tax on dividends, interest, and rental income. This gives a break to the wealthy, of course, but eases administrative problems.[9] The other major issue involves taxing nonresidents. Most cities would like to levy the tax on nonresidents who work there. State law determines whether this is possible. If it is, what happens to a commuter who works in one tax-levying community and lives in another? Except in Philadelphia, double taxation is precluded by law or court decision.

Where an income tax can be imposed, it has several advantages over the property tax. It certainly is less regressive, especially if nonlabor income is included. The tax responds exceptionally well to changing economic conditions. And if it is administered centrally (perhaps by the state), the collection costs are less than those for the property tax.[10]

USER CHARGES. —In this day of tax limits and federal aid cutbacks, cities have turned to greater use of fees and charges for services. Presumably increased user charges contribute to greater economic efficiency by supplying services in response to community preferences. Also many think such charges are more equitable—people pay only for what they receive.[11]

Some communities have begun to push the outer limits of pay-as-you-go government. In the mid-1980s, St. Paul, Minnesota, faced a serious budget shortfall with little apparent chance of raising taxes.[12] For solutions to the problem, the city administration brought in the Rand

Corporation, a California-based think tank. Rand's answer was simple: Let city departments that are capable of earning money do so. A variety of options were explored. The city now plans to charge for street lighting that exceeds a prescribed standard. If residents or businesses request extra lights in front of their homes or businesses, they will have to pay for them. Merchants who want turnover in parking in front of their stores may one day have to pay for painting the curb or installing parking meters. The library, according to Rand, should provide the customary book-lending service without charge, but a special fee might be required for such special services as videotape rental and bibliographic searches. The idea, says finance director Peter Hames, is to make a profit where it can be done—logically, competitively, and without creating problems with citizens, unions, or other government bodies. David Osborne and Ted Gaebler agree. One of the "ten principles" of *Reinventing Government* is to apply market-oriented thinking to government.[13] To protect low-income residents, Rand suggests, the city might issue qualifying individuals scrip or vouchers exchangeable for certain services, an approach not unlike the food stamp program.

Concern for the poor is one of at least two issues that can arise if a city moves heavily into user charges. Such fees and charges can be regressive in their effects in somewhat the same way as sales taxes can, penalizing the less-well-to-do, who usually pay proportionately more of their income for basic services. Recent research, for example, shows that cities have replaced lost General Revenue Sharing funds by increasing user fees and charges. As a result, "much of the cost has fallen on the poor."[14] The case study that follows illustrates what can happen when a tradeoff is proposed between property taxes and user fees.

CASE STUDY

Trading the Property Tax for a User Fee

In the proposed budget submitted to the Fort Worth city council in August 1978, acting city manager Morris Matson included a provision that would lower the city's property tax rate by $.065 (per $100 valuation) and increase the residential garbage rate by $.50 a month. Mayor Hugh Palmer objected to the proposed tradeoff, claiming that the exchange was unfair to owners of modest homes. The mayor showed reporters a chart indicating that residents whose homes were valued at $15,000 would pay about $2.64 less in taxes compared to a $6 annual increase in garbage fees (the proposed increase was from $2.50 to $3 a month). He went on to say that residents with homes in higher value brackets would benefit from the proposal, for their tax cut would exceed the increase in garbage fees. Palmer indicated that 82 percent of the homes in Fort Worth were valued at $25,000 or less. "Clearly this [proposal] works to the disadvantage of nine out of ten homeowners and tax-payers," he said.

Apparently the mayor's argument was persuasive to most members of the council. In a move designed to please everyone, the council voted to lower taxes, although not as much as the city manager had proposed, but to keep the garbage rate unchanged. The revenue shortfall was made up by raising certain administrative charges against the water and sewer fund, a separate enterprise account. Still, as a result of the dispute the city later decided to create a separate enterprise fund for the garbage and trash operation, partly to show how much the cost of that service was being subsidized by other sources of revenue. Four years later the sanitation service was still not self-supporting.

SOURCE: Taken from the *Fort Worth Star-Telegram*, 19 August 1978, and from a telephone conversation with Morris Matson, assistant city manager, Fort Worth, 11 January 1983.

Equity considerations aside, others fear that an increased reliance on fees and charges might eventually undermine public support for the basic taxes on which core urban services depend. The case study that follows addresses this issue.

CASE STUDY

INCREASING USER FEES IN CONCORD

IN response to the tax-cutting measure Proposition 2½, the town of Concord, Massachusetts (population 17,000), implemented a wide-ranging search for alternative revenue sources. The fiscal situation in Concord was typical of that in smaller municipalities in Massachusetts in several ways: property taxes provided almost 80 percent of the general fund budget, most of which went for education; and exclusive of utility operations, fees and charges contributed less than 5 percent to the budget. One of the obvious ways of bringing in more money was to rely more heavily on user charges. So Concord's managers took a hard look at which programs and activities currently receiving tax subsidies might be made self-supporting. They decided that the water and sewer departments, the recreation department, and ambulance services should be financed solely by charges.

Proposition 2½ provides that no local government can impose any charge or fee in excess of the costs of furnishing a service, but it offers no guidelines for determining costs. Do costs include employee benefits, future pension liabilities, asset depreciation, and central administrative support? These were some of the issues facing Concord's management.

The decision regarding the recreation department, for example, was to pay departmental administration from the property tax but to eliminate all subsidy of actual programs. The level of program activities, then, would be determined solely by demand. Fees were revised on the basis of comparable prices charged by private recreation providers. Minimum registration levels were set for each program to ensure that fees would cover costs. The results were unexpected: the demand for certain programs fell precipitously. Although fees had been doubled in many cases, they were still below the market rates; yet a number of programs that had been oversubscribed in previous years had to be canceled. This forced the town to modify its mix of program offerings to correspond more closely with the value users placed on the department's activities.

The city's finance director, Anthony Logalbo, argues that fees and charges have an important but limited role to play in financing local government. He asserts that "injudicious use of fees and charges can undermine basic public support for the full range of local government activities. . . . It would be ironic if the move toward user charges resulted ultimately in the withering of services that remained to be financed from taxes."

SOURCE: Adapted from Anthony T. Logalbo, "Responding to Tax Limitation: Finding Alternative Revenues," *Governmental Finance* 11 (March 1982): 13–19.

THE POLITICS OF REVENUE RAISING

Cities have been forced to intensify the search for alternative revenue sources not only because of the decline in federal aid but also in response to taxpayers' resistance to higher property taxes. But user fees and charges can do only so much; cities must consider other measures as well. In many places state governments are being asked to provide more help, not just in dollar form but more fundamentally by giving municipalities the legal authority to tap new revenue sources. In 1991, for example, cities in only twenty-two states imposed a sales tax.[15] Restrictions on income taxes are even more onerous. Given that most local taxes, except the property tax, require voter approval, it seems hard to justify such state-imposed limitations.

It would be unrealistic to expect a whole lot of additional assistance from the states. Cities by and large must continue to rely on their own initiatives. This means that difficult decisions on whether or not to push for tax increases and which ones to opt for remain in the hands of local officials. Such decisions, especially when the pie is shrinking, can become quite politically controversial. How, then, might city leaders proceed?

One of the few accounts of the politics of municipal revenue raising comes from Arnold Meltsner's observations of the efforts of city officials in Oakland to obtain resources from what they believed to be a hostile environment.[16] Four operating or decision rules on the part of local officials can be distilled from Meltsner's work.

First, hide the tax. One of the great arts of the tax game is to design revenue sources so that people do not know how much tax they pay. This means resorting to a variety of indirect revenue sources. Thus cities often levy taxes on private utilities (which then pass them on to the consumer), hotel rooms, businesses or occupations, and motor vehicles (often in lieu of a property tax); they impose charges for various municipal utilities and enterprises—sewer service charges, fees for tapping into the water system for new homes and businesses, or fees for cutting street curbs. Although many of these sources do not generate huge sums, their indirect nature may reduce political opposition.

A second and related rule is to minimize taxpayer resistance by using small, low-yield taxes instead of one large levy. Not only are low taxes less visible, they also keep the taxpaying public fragmented. Most small taxes are salient only to small groups. With the exception of tax association representatives, those who care about taxes care only about specific taxes; hotel and motel owners, for example, care only about taxes that might hurt their business. A cigarette levy may be opposed only by cigarette retailers and wholesalers, and a fee for tapping into the water system or cutting curbs may draw attention only from builders and developers. Beyond these relatively small groups lies a quiescent majority that is largely unconcerned about such specialized taxes but can be mobilized if a tax issue becomes salient. The idea is to keep the attentive groups divided and the larger public quiet, if not satisfied.

A third rule concerns equity. City governments have little concern for fiscal justice; they are seldom interested in who *should* pay but rather who *will* pay. "Local officials emphasize yields and leave the problem of income distribution to the federal government," says Meltsner.

According to the fourth rule, the city manager is the fiscal innovator. Finances are almost always at or near the top of the manager's agenda. In Oakland, for example, the city manager initiated an internal study to analyze each current source of revenue and to suggest new sources to meet a projected revenue-expenditure gap. The Oakland manager also assumed an educational role with other important groups: the council, community leaders, even city department heads. The city manager normally knows the nuts and bolts of taxes, follows relevant state legislation, and tries to keep up with what other cities are doing about finance. This superior tax knowledge puts the manager in the driver's seat; the result: who pays is usually determined by the manager and the finance department staff. Council members tend not to be tax policy initiators in any case. Their main concern seems to be holding down property taxes; as elected officials, they are especially sensitive to citizen concerns over this politically unpopular and relatively visible source of municipal revenue.

To generate support for new taxes, Meltsner offers this advice. Among community leaders, stress the specific connection between a proposed revenue source and community benefit. Instead of advocating a capital program that contains a shopping list of land, buildings, and improvements, officials should emphasize potential outcomes: less crime, better health, less flooding, fewer accidents, more employment. With the larger public, Meltsner says, stress only the benefits, leaving the tax-service nexus obscure. Local officials should not be squeamish, he argues, in consciously manipulating the benefit side of a proposal. A few years ago in Oklahoma City, for example, a temporary one-cent sales tax for a new jail was sold to the voters almost solely as an anticrime measure: "Vote yes and keep the criminals off the streets." Meltsner admits that building tax coalitions is not easy, but the effort should pay off in generating the support essential for success.

Is it political folly to consider new taxes? One might think so given the recent history of tax revolts, beginning with the now-famous Proposition 13 approved by California voters in 1978. This property tax rollback measure was followed by a series of tax limitation efforts around the country. For example, Proposition 2½ in Massachusetts, which passed in 1980, prevents property taxes from exceeding 2.5 percent of the cash value of the local tax base. Yet despite these well-known examples of taxpayer rebellion, cities continue to win support for new tax levies. For example, in the early 1980s, during a time of great fiscal stress, over half of a large group of cities of 25,000 or over population reported some increase in local taxes.[17]

Still, most recent studies indicate that many cities continue to struggle to keep expenditures from outpacing revenues. As we noted earlier, efforts persist to improve productivity, to identify new operating efficiencies, and to become more entrepreneurial. There seems little doubt that the future will not bring much relief. The interminable fiscal squeeze has become a way of life for many hard-pressed city officials.

Expenditures

Cities spend most of their money on basic services. If one leaves out education, welfare, hospitals, and community development, four high-dollar services for which many cities are not responsible, in 1991 the biggest single item in the city budget, on average, is police protection—about 12 percent of direct general expenditures.[18] The next largest item is sewage and sanitation at about 11 percent, with streets third at 8 percent.

Several other general observations can be made about city expenditures. First, as suggested earlier, some cities perform more services than others. Cities that are more functionally inclusive tend to spend more per capita, of course, than do those with a more limited scope of operations. A regional bias exists here. Northeastern municipalities on average provide more services than do western cities, where special districts or counties may perform more functions. So when regional comparisons are made, northeastern cities may appear to be spendthrifts. Although labor costs may be somewhat higher for cities in the more industrialized and unionized Northeast and North Central regions, the biggest difference in spending likely is tied to the more comprehensive scope of services often provided by cities in those areas. The level of expenditure also tends to relate to city size. Big cities spend more than smaller cities on a per capita basis, again because they generally perform more functions. In addition, large urban places are likely to be called on to provide the more costly social services required for their proportionally larger dependent populations.

At the national level and especially among state governments, considerable revenue is dedicated to, or earmarked for, specific purposes, such as the gasoline tax for highway use. At the city level, considerably less earmarking occurs, except perhaps to repay revenue bonds financed from utility earnings. Most of the money for current municipal operations goes into a general fund, at which time it becomes available for spending on a variety of programs and activities. The mechanism by which these funds are allocated is the city budget, of course.

Budgeting

In simplest terms a *budget* is a plan for resource allocation. In most municipalities the chief executive prepares the budget and submits it for approval to the legislative body. Ordinarily the budget contains a schedule of sources of city revenue by category as well as an indication of the categories or service areas for which funds will be spent.

Budget making is far from a simple accounting exercise. Allocating financial resources among competing activities is an act of policymaking. The budget reflects the programs and policies the city intends to pursue. But resources are never sufficient to satisfy the demands of all interested groups, and conflict is inevitable. Because politics can be defined as conflict over public policy, budgeting obviously is a political process. But as we see later, budgeting is also a highly stable, predictable operation. It remains considerably insulated from external forces and pressures. One of the continuing debates among students of local government budgeting concerns the extent to which budgeting responds to external influences.

THE BUDGET PROCESS

Generally, budget making is a three-stage process: departmental request; executive review, modification, and consolidation; and legislative enactment. The actual budget cycle is likely to be initiated, in larger cities at least, by the budget office acting in behalf of the chief executive. Initiation of the process usually encompasses giving some guidelines to department heads concerning program emphasis or limits on requests for increases.

THE ROLE OF DEPARTMENT HEADS. —Department heads always ask for more than they were allotted last year. According to Aaron Wildavsky, an expert on public budgeting, "Padding in the expectation of cuts is part of playing the game."[19] One might assume in this age of fiscal stress that padding budgets is no longer an acceptable practice. Recent survey research suggests that this is not the case. About 65 percent of approximately 385 local officials indicate they continue to pad budgets.[20] Just as departments always ask for more, chief executives invariably cut. So department heads merely adopt a counterstrategy by submitting budget figures that can be cut. They mark up their requests by the amount they expect will be eliminated, trying to neutralize the possible adverse effects of the cuts and to end up with the amount they wanted initially.[21] Lewis Friedman characterizes department heads as advocates; their job is to push hard for their programs.

Preparing budget requests tends to be a highly incremental process dominated by well-developed practices and routines. A study of state agency heads in Illinois, for example, identified a set of routine practices that characterized budget preparation in that state. Those that might be applied to the city level include the following:[22]

- Spend all your appropriation. Failure to use up an appropriation indicates that the full amount was unnecessary in the first place, which in turn implies that your budget should be cut next year.
- Never request a sum less than your current appropriation. It is easier to find ways to spend up to current appropriation levels than to explain why you want a reduction.
- Put top-priority programs into the basic budget. Chief executives and city councils seldom challenge programs that appear to be part of existing operations.
- Make increases appear small, and describe them as though they grew out of existing operations.
- Give the chief executive and the council something to cut. This enables them to "save" money and justify their claim to promoting "economy" in government. Giving them something to cut also diverts attention from the basic budget and its vital programs.

THE EXECUTIVE ROLE. — Budgeting at the municipal level is generally an executive-centered process. A discussion of budgeting in Cleveland, Detroit, and Pittsburgh noted that the municipal budget is the mayor's budget—the mayor's policies dominate the department totals and citywide tax and wage policies.[23] Arnold Meltsner and Aaron Wildavsky attribute a similarly central role to the city manager in Oakland: "He is the key figure in making most of the decisions. . . . He guides the city council in its considerations. He feels it is his budget. And he uses it to make his influence felt throughout city government."[24]

The chief executive—mayor or manager—with the responsibility for the budget almost always compiles the separate departmental requests into a single comprehensive document. In the process cuts are inevitable. Friedman refers to the executive's role as that of economizer. The cutting process stems from two factors: the belief that most departments pad their requests and the legal requirement that municipal budgets be balanced. In larger cities the budget officer and staff play a significant part in analyzing requests for new funds. Here program analysis, productivity measurement, or program evaluation may come into play. Frequently the budget officer reaches a compromise with various departments on proposed increases before the draft budget reaches the executive. In the end the manager must judge the merits of expenditure requests. This is where the executive exerts maximum influence: "By choosing among departmental requests and by initiating his own spending proposals he has, through budgeting, the opportunity to implement his own programs and assert leadership over the direction of governmental activity."[25]

THE ROLE OF THE COUNCIL. — City councils retain the final legal authority to approve the budget. Legislative bodies are widely assumed to lack the time, expertise, and staff to do much more than make minor modifications to an executive's budget. But governing boards may not be as passive as is often thought.

First, councils may feel compelled to make overall reductions in an executive's recommended budget. Usually the percentage is small. A study of fourteen cities found that eight councils cut the budget, three increased the budget, and three accepted executive recommendations for change.[26] Second, when asked, council members indicate they are not just rubber stamps for executive proposals. They apparently examine the budget with considerable care, ask a great many questions, and require the executive to justify a number of budget choices. In fact, their role is that of overseers.[27]

THE TRADITIONAL APPROACH: LINE-ITEM BUDGETING

Traditionally, budgeting has been an incremental process. This year's budget, with a slight change in available resources, is basically the same as last year's. "This, of course, means that the budget is a slowly changing thing, consisting of a series of marginal changes from previous budgets."[28]

Budgeting by line item virtually ensures incrementalism, and most governments at all levels still employ a line-item budget. The format specifies dollar amounts by department for a host of detailed expenditures, often grouped under three basic categories: personal services, operating expenses, and capital outlay. Line-item budgeting was a natural outgrowth of the reformers' early efforts to make governments more fiscally accountable. Presumably where line items of expenditures were detailed, auditors or external critics could more easily ascertain that the city government did not overspend. Line-item budgeting, then, stems from the desire to control governmental spending, not from an interest in developing effective services and programs.

CASE STUDY

LINE-ITEM BUDGETING

AT one time in "West City," a large downstate Illinois community, line-item budgeting was the order of the day. The city manager dominated the process, although in this instance the manager did not employ the budget as an instrument to affect policy. The procedure went along these lines.

First the manager and the city clerk arrived at an estimate of revenue available to the city for the next year. Revenue estimation was somewhat haphazard, but for the most part the city relied on projections from past experience to predict its future income. In effect, this forced the manager to think of the budget as representing nothing more than "what we did last year" or "what we are now doing."

The actual budget prepared by the manager of West City was based on lump-sum amounts for object categories (e.g., personal services, supplies, contractual services). The manager apparently did not feel the need to develop a more detailed budgeting plan. In his words:

> We spend a lot of money every year here. And I don't like to waste a lot of time on items which we know we are going to have to continue to support. So if we get an item in here in a departmental budget which we know we've been spending money on for the last three or four years and it looks as though we are going to have to be spending that money for the next few years, I don't waste time trying to justify that expenditure. When I make up the budget I try to comment only on the items which represent an increase in spending or a new program of some kind that is different from what we have been doing previously.

The manager did not recommend policies to deal with specific problems, nor did he provide any detailed explanation that permitted the council to go beyond the line-item amounts found in the budget. The manager did not see himself as a policy leader. Instead he considered himself an administrator only, whose responsibilities were limited to carrying out council policy. When requested to do so by the council, the manager would suggest solutions to problems. But he refused to push his solutions on the theory that such decisions are policy matters best left to the discretion of the council.

SOURCE: Adapted from Thomas J. Anton, *Budgeting in Three Illinois Cities* (Urbana, Ill.: Institute of Government and Public Affairs, University of Illinois, 1964).

EXTERNAL INFLUENCES ON THE BUDGET.—Incremental budgeting would seem to leave little room for the influence of outside forces. This brings up one of the continuing controversies in budgeting literature: Just how much do external pressures shape municipal budgetary decisions?

Most political scientists see budgeting as a political act. The budget has even been described as the "prime expression of political decision."[29] This implies extensive negotiation, bargaining, and even conflict among contending groups. But empirical research casts doubt on the extensiveness of external group participation in the municipal budget process. John Crecine found budgeting in Pittsburgh, Cleveland, and Detroit to be so standardized and insulated that it could be successfully simulated with an elaborate computer routine. He found little evidence of external political influence in the budget-making process. He asserts that "budgets in municipal governments are reasonably abstracted documents, bearing little direct relationship to specific community pressures."[30] Crecine concludes that pressure and influence take place at different levels of decision making.

Friedman's research seems to confirm this view. He quotes one local official: "As a general rule groups do not concern themselves with budget preparation and adoption.... Agitation for programs goes on throughout the year. Interest doesn't just focus on the budget."[31] Yet outside political forces are not excluded totally from municipal budgeting. Friedman considers the attitudes of public officials toward the city's tax base and their personal views about the proper scope of government to be instances of external influence. Especially where the executive and the council hold an activist orientation to government, expenditures are likely to increase.

Finally, we might note that most city budgets are annual in nature but must be revised during the course of the year. This process, called rebudgeting, is quite common but little studied. Recent research on the topic finds that revising and updating the officially adopted budget during the fiscal year is a less visible and more technical process; it further enhances the power of administrators.[32]

BUDGETARY REFORM

For years, academics and practitioners have complained about line-item budgeting. The principal limitation is the inability of the line-item schedule to show any connection between resources (human and fiscal) and program outputs (activities). The presumptive cure is to use a budgeting format that focuses on performance or program activities. Municipal budget reform has taken several approaches. Three older, prominent, and well-known reforms include performance budgeting, planning-programming-budgeting (PPB) systems, and zero-base budgeting (ZBB). A more recent reform effort is expenditure control budgeting (ECB). Before turning to ECB, we might briefly examine the three older budget reforms.

BUDGETING REFORM: PAST EFFORTS

PERFORMANCE BUDGETING. — Performance budgeting is a product of the New Deal. Concomitant with the rise of the national government in the 1930s was the perceived need to focus more on the management of public programs. Performance budgeting differed from the previous control orientation of the line-item budget in two important ways. First, it maximized the value of effective management; the budget is a way to manage programs not simply control expenditures. Second, performance budgeting is concerned with what happens with resources after they are allocated. Objects of expenditures are not enough. Instead, the budget should be redesigned so that each agency identifies activities preformed, develops performance measures (projected cost of each activity), and prepares performance reports that compare goals and projected costs with accomplishments and actual costs. Beginning in the 1960s performance budgeting gave way to PPB and then in the 1970s to ZBB. In actuality, PPB and ZBB are nothing more than sophisticated extensions of performance budgeting; the former maximizes the value of planning in budgeting, and the latter maximizes the value of decision making in budgeting.[33]

PLANNING-PROGRAMMING-BUDGETING SYSTEMS. — The PPB approach is based on the rational-comprehensive model of decision making. Under PPB, expenditures are organized into program categories. Budget decisions are then made by analyzing alternative spending proposals, both within and among program categories. This analysis takes into account both cost and program performance.[34] PPB also incorporates long-range planning, often over a five-year period. PPB in short embraces three components: budgeting by program category, analysis, and planning.

Figure 10.1 provides an example of a program budget for the fire-suppression division of a city fire department. It includes goals, objectives, and output measures in addition to the dollar amount requested

Department	Division
Fire	Fire Suppression

Goal: To minimize harm or damage to persons and property caused by fires and explosions.

Objectives:

1. To reduce average dollar property loss for residential fires by 3 percent.
2. To reduce average dollar property loss for commercial fires by 2 percent.
3. To reduce fire deaths by 10 percent.
4. To reduce overall mean response time from 5.3 to 5.2 minutes.

Program output measures	*Actual* 1993	*Estimate* 1994	*Target* 1995
1. Average dollar property loss— residential	$21,564	$22,013	$21,353
2. Average dollar property loss— commercial	$69,724	$70,112	$68,710
3. Fire deaths per 100,000 population	5.2	5.1	4.6
4. Mean response time (min.)	5.4	5.3	5.2

Program element	*Program costs* 1993 *Actual*	1994 *Appropriated*	1994 *Expended*	1995 *Proposed*
Administration	$ 1,100,000	$ 1,144,100	$ 1,142,200	$ 1,184,400
Communications	1,283,500	1,334,800	1,332,600	1,381,800
Fire response	14,987,800	15,586,700	15,568,700	16,134,400
Training	366,700	381,400	380,700	394,800
Operation and maintenance	550,000	572,000	563,000	592,200
Contractual	47,000	50,000	49,800	52,400
Totals	$18,335,000	$19,069,000	$19,037,000	$19,740,000

FIGURE 10.1. EXAMPLE OF A PROGRAM BUDGET FOR
FIRE DEPARTMENT, SUPPRESSION DIVISION.

for each of the various program elements. It would be possible, of course, to add a line-item budget to this format rather easily by listing the costs by year for personnel, maintenance and operations, contractual items, and even capital purchases. A program budget provides quite a bit more detail than does a simple line-item budget.

By increasing the level of information and grouping activities along functional lines, PPB is supposed to contribute to more rational decision making. But implementing this new approach is not easy. A few years ago, for example, Ann Arbor, Michigan, implemented PPB. The city learned several lessons.[35] First, it is not wise to introduce a drastic new system during the normal budget period. Second, more data can easily be produced than decision makers can readily assimilate. Third, better program data are a two-edged sword, at least for departments. They can highlight weaknesses as well as justify program expansion. Fourth, the total conversion process takes a long time (perhaps three or four years). And finally, the program budget should not be converted to a line-item budget.

Because of the difficulties involved in implementing PPB, several elements appear crucial for success: strong continuing support from top management; a well-trained staff to direct and coordinate the program; a period of three to five years for full implementation; and methods for dealing with considerable resistance from some, if not most, operating departments. Irene S. Rubin and Lana Stein's case study of budget reform in St. Louis, for example, found that the city's new program and performance budget was the result of improved technology (computerization), a professional staff, and strong executive (mayoral) leadership.[36]

Implementation problems are not the only grounds on which PPB has been criticized.[37] The approach contains a strong centralizing bias that many do not like. Generally speaking, PPB is a top-down process. Critics also object to the tendency of PPB proponents to minimize or ignore the political context within which budgeting takes place. Most of the objections are virtually identical with those aimed at all forms of systems analysis (the difficulty in quantifying intangibles, too much reliance on economic cost-benefit criteria, and so on). In fact, Aaron Wildavsky's assessment seems right on target: "The simpler the problem, the fewer interdependencies, the greater the ability to measure the consequences of alternatives on a common scale, the more costs and benefits are valued in the market place, the better the chances of making effective use of [PPB]."[38]

ZERO-BASE BUDGETING. —During the 1970s zero-base budgeting enjoyed some popularity. According to Peter Pyhrr, its originator, ZBB involves two basic steps: developing and ranking decision packages.[39] Developing a decision package involves specifying a program activity, its cost, the service provided, and the level of effort required to achieve each prescribed target increase or decrease. Department heads then rank the decision packages according to priorities established at higher levels. The process of ranking the decision packages continues up the line as each management level reviews, compares, consolidates, and establishes program priorities. The chief executive prepares the final list of decision-package ranking, which is then forwarded to the city council.

According to a survey of budget directors who use ZBB, it is most helpful in reallocating resources from lower-to-higher-priority projects and in making more rational budget cuts. The main complaints: the time and paperwork required and the reluctance of department heads to offer decision packages at a funding level lower than their present appropriation. Budget directors also note the tendency of some departments to manipulate priority listings by ranking popular activities lower than activities with little chance of being funded.[40]

AN ASSESSMENT OF PAST BUDGET REFORMS. —Budgeting in American cities has changed tremendously over the past several decades. While various budgeting reforms have been institutionalized, most cities cling to the line-item budget. Program budgeting in one form or another has grown more popular, especially among larger and western communities.[41] More reformed cities also are likely to adopt budget reforms more quickly than other cities.[42] In the mid-1980s some 45 percent of a nationwide sample of cities reported using program budgeting, although usually in combination with a line-item format.[43] Only about 7 percent relied on a full-blown PPB system, even in combination with other budgeting formats. A full 78 percent of the total of 357 cities indicated that they still prepared a line-item budget, at least in part.

Zero-base budgeting has never been widely adopted at the municipal level, and interest in ZBB has waned in recent years. In the survey identified earlier, fewer than 12 percent of the cities reported employing ZBB even in combination with other budgeting approaches.

Perhaps budget expert Allen Schick best summarizes the current thinking on budgetary reform:

> There is little interest these days in big reforms of the sort that animated performance budgeting, planning-programming-budgeting (PPB), and zero-base budgeting (ZBB) in earlier decades.... It is now part of the lore of budgeting that PPB and ZBB promised more improvement than

they produced. These actual or perceived failures taught a generation of budget practitioners and scholars that comprehensive change is costly and disruptive, has uncertain prospects, and produces unintended side effects.[44]

This is not to suggest that efforts to reform the municipal budgeting have been unsuccessful or are over. Stanley Botner notes that today "a professional budgetary system might well include features of performance budgeting in addition to the object and program approaches."[45] In short, the contemporary municipal budget is a hybrid, line item in format but possessing performance and program budgeting characteristics. And there is a new budgeting reform in town, most frequently called expenditure control budgeting (ECB).

BUDGETING REFORM: THE NEW WAVE

ECB is part of a new thrust of budgetary reform called "entrepreneurial budgeting."[46] Included in this wave of reform are mission-driven budgeting and budgeting for results. Perhaps the principal advocates of entrepreneurial budgeting are David Osborne and Ted Gaebler.[47] In their opinion the process of "reinventing government" must include freeing managers from the line-item budget. They insist that traditional line-item budgeting encourages waste because agency officials must spend money or lose it, and stifles initiative because managers have little discretion in spending. Instead, they propose that budgeting should be mission-driven and aimed at results. Mission-driven budgeting and budgeting for results are nothing more than recycled versions of performance/program budgeting. They focus on program goals, outputs, outcomes, and employee performance. Expenditure control budgeting, in contrast, offers a new approach to municipal budgeting. It encompasses a *process* one can use to budget for results and implement mission-driven budgeting.

ECB is the product of Oscar Reyes, an assistant finance director in Fairfield, California. Nationally honored and recognized city manager Gale Wilson (see case study in chapter 12 for a profile) installed the innovation in 1979 after Proposition 13. Six months later, then city manager Ted Gaebler brought the budgeting reform to Visalia. "To date, the application of ECB is limited,"[48] but it can be found in a dozen or so jurisdictions.

Political scientist Eric Herzik has defined ECB as "a comprehensive budgetary system that uses retained savings to promote managerial innovation."[49] In Fairfield, California, where the innovation was originated, ECB basically produced three results: eliminated line items, allowed departments to keep what they did not spend, and turned the city council budget into a two-page document that set expenditure limits.[50] In essence, department heads are given block grants and plenty of discretion. Retained savings accrue and carry over from one year to the next and must be used to fund new programs, projects, or maintain existing services in a period of retrenchment.

An expenditure control budget includes several general operating features:

- Each department receives a base budget that is annually adjusted for population growth and the cost of living (inflation).
- The base budget assumes existing service levels. The chief executive and council must approve service level changes, and the chief executive can adjust base budgets to correct minor imbalances.
- Department heads are responsible for future costs of programs and must pay for service expansions from retained savings.
- A proportion or all savings generated from productivity are carried over to the next year.

In operation ECB is very different from previous budgetary reforms. It starts out as a top-down process, but ends up giving more autonomy to operating departments. The council monitors performance and demands accountability for results.

One problem associated with ECB is overcoming bureaucratic inertia. Departments that enjoy favored status may lose their positions of privilege, and departments that are not favored may feel they deserve a higher base budget to compensate for past actions. Another problem is the unwillingness of elected officials to decentralize power to agency personnel. The legacy of political control through the line-item budget is hard to overcome.[51]

The benefits of ECB are improved efficiency and innovation. Fairfield officials contend they saved about $5 million in an eight-year period. In fiscal year 1986–87 Chandler, Arizona, saved over $2 million.[52] Perhaps just as important, ECB fosters trust between those who rule and those who are responsible for the delivery of public services.

Regardless of format, the budgetary process involves considerable interaction and consultation, if not negotiation, among a relatively limited set of internal actors. Certainly values and beliefs come into play when the budget pie is cut, as various individuals and departments pursue their objectives and protect their turf. One must not forget that the budget is a political document.

CAPITAL IMPROVEMENT PLANNING AND BUDGETING

In addition to an annual operating budget, most cities of any size prepare a capital improvement budget. Cities need to anticipate and plan for the construction and financing of large-scale public improvements. A capital facilities plan is supposed to ensure that these projects are carried out according to a well-prepared program that reflects the city's needs and ability to pay. Because major capital improvements substantially affect city taxes, capital planning can reduce tax-rate fluctuation by systematically staggering projects.[53]

Planning and budgeting for capital needs is usually a sequential process.[54] It begins with the preparation of a comprehensive city plan, or master plan. This planning document may project in broad outline form the capital requirements over a period of, say, twenty-five years. The next step is preparation of the capital improvement program or schedule; it has a much shorter time horizon, perhaps five to eight years. This document sets forth a year-by-year list of projects and facilities to be constructed or renovated. Finally, a capital budget makes specific provisions for the first year of the improvement program. The capital budget is then revised annually to reflect completion of projects and necessary modifications.

Figuring out how to pay for capital needs is a major concern of capital planning and budgeting. In most cities nowadays, making large-scale capital improvements means going into debt. Where debt financing is required, cities usually have two options: general obligation (GO) bonds or revenue bonds. GO bonds require a vote of the people because their repayment is guaranteed by the full taxing power of the issuing government; ordinarily the debt is serviced by increasing the property tax. Revenue bonds, however, often can be issued without a popular vote; ordinarily the city simply pledges to use a certain portion of the revenue from some municipal revenue-producing facility for debt retirement. Improvements to the water and sewer systems frequently are accomplished using revenue bonds. The city council (or utility authority) may raise the utility rates to pay off the bonds. Because revenue bonds are not backed by the "full faith and credit" of the city, they generally bear an interest rate 1 percent or so above that of GO bonds. So the city pays more in debt service to issue revenue bonds.

Because most cities use debt financing for capital improvement, the capital budget may have little or no connection with the operating budget. Partly for this reason and partly because of the uncertainties in funding, capital programming and budgeting undergo frequent change.

Projects are modified, postponed, or in some cases accelerated depending on circumstances. Certainly the availability of federal or state grant money affects the process. Capital planning and budgeting, then, are not as orderly as many would like. There are no automatic neat linkages flowing from the comprehensive plan to the capital improvement program, to the capital budget, and on to the operating budget.[55]

WHITHER CITY BUDGETING?

Cities have been urged for years to reform their budget making. PPB, ZBB, and ECB have captured the support of reformers, but most cities have resisted giving up line-item budgeting completely. To wrap up our consideration of municipal budgeting we should examine the provocative advice of Meltsner and Wildavsky, which is reflected in the title of their paper "Leave City Budgeting Alone!"[56]

Meltsner and Wildavsky contend that municipal budgeting is not just a way of allocating resources. Its real purpose is control—to permit officials to hold down costs so that expenditures do not exceed income and necessitate new taxes. The city's budget cutters lack the information, time, and staff to explore programmatic changes in any detail during budget time. The authors argue that no proposal to change city budgeting is acceptable if it makes the budget appreciably less useful for control and cutting purposes, calls for a large increase in personnel, requires a high level of analytic talent, or depends on the existence of, or the likelihood of obtaining, good data relevant to actual decisions. In short, they believe that strong political leadership and the intelligent but modest use of program analysis can help cities more than drastic budgetary reform. Apparently a lot of city officials agree.

Managing Municipal Finances

Although budgeting is certainly at the heart of municipal financial management, that process incorporates a series of interrelated basic functions of which budgeting is only one part. Figure 10.2 shows five of these functions and identifies the linkages among them.

FORMING GOALS AND OBJECTIVES

The degree to which municipalities formally define their goals varies considerably. To the extent that they are written out, larger objectives are most likely to appear in the city budget, perhaps separately for each department. Whatever the degree of formality, top management and department heads presumably engage in an ongoing process of identifying

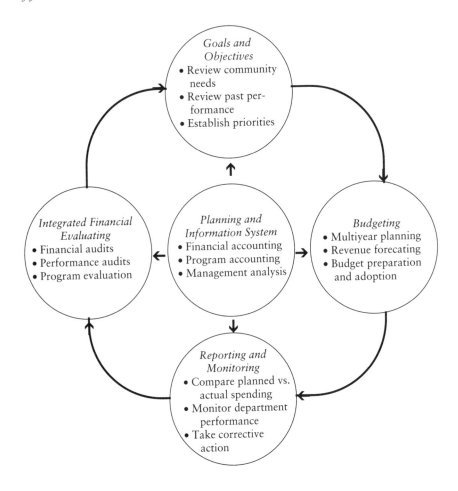

FIGURE 10.2. INTEGRATED MUNICIPAL FINANCIAL
INFORMATION SYSTEM.

SOURCE: Adapted from *Program Measurement Handbook,* Office of the Mayor, City and
County of San Francisco, February 1980, as reproduced in *Linkages: Improving Financial
Management in Local Government,* by F.O'R. Hayes et al. (Washington, D.C.: Urban Insti-
tute, 1982), 6.

the community problems and needs toward which city programs should
be directed. Likewise, municipal managers—if not continuously, at least
at budget time—enter into a process of reviewing past performance in
addressing those issues and concerns. Perhaps through the use of per-

formance evaluation or MBO, program managers may decide to shift priorities to the areas showing the greatest need. Or possibly the city council or city manager, responding to community pressures, may force a reordering of the agency agenda. This sort of needs assessment and analysis, even if it is largely a muddling-through process, occurs in cities of all sizes.

Planning and Budgeting

The next step is to incorporate community needs and objectives in the formal document that allocates financial resources—the city budget. Whatever the budget format, it should incorporate multiyear financial planning, which is not an easy matter. In noting the rarity of long-term financial planning in the public sector, Jacob Ukeles observes that "politicians in general, out of long and bitter experience, are notoriously uninterested in being pinned down with regard to decisions they may take affecting the next several months, let alone two, three, or four years in the future."[57] But he goes on to compare cities and states with large corporations, insisting that public entities, like those corporations, must look ahead to manage effectively. What does advance planning do? It facilitates cash-flow management, focuses attention on infrastructure maintenance needs, and removes the element of surprise should revenue receipts diverge from past trends.

How can cities plan over a multiyear period? Daron Butler, budget director of Austin, Texas, suggests several steps cities can take to establish a base for projecting revenues.[58] First the city should prepare a written revenue projection plan to accompany the municipal budget. The plan should list specific revenue sources, assumptions used, and comparisons of budget-year projections to current-year estimates and prior-year receipts. A projection is only as good as the assumptions on which it is based, so full disclosure of all assumptions is critical. This three-year prospective provides city management and the city council with a means for judging how well the city has estimated revenue in the past.

Reporting and Monitoring

Several issues arise in reporting and monitoring the financial developments in city government. First, an Urban Institute volume on financial management by Frederick Hayes and his associates emphasizes the need to include measurable objectives and targets as part of the budget, to facilitate both the monitoring process and accountability.[59] This might involve tying an MBO system into the budgeting process. Or in the terminology of *Reinventing Government*, managing for results. In addition to the use of program performance measures, financial monitoring demands regular reporting.

Small- and even medium-sized cities may experience considerable difficulty in developing the capacity to monitor financial trends. To assist these cities the ICMA issued a series of handbooks for evaluating a city's financial condition. The second handbook, *Financial Trend Monitoring System*, contains information on collecting data, charting trends, and interpreting the results of thirty-six financial indicators.[60] These indicators include uncollected property taxes, user charge coverage, revenue shortfalls, operating deficits, enterprise losses, long-term and short-term debts, pension liability, and level of capital outlay. The approach asks the city to construct these indicators from existing data over a five-year period and to observe how they change. The indicators are then updated each year to enable the city to identify financial problems and plan corrective action.

EVALUATING

Evaluating the financial system demands auditing in one form or another. In the past this usually involved a once-a-year financial audit, perhaps by an outside auditing firm, to determine whether the city's financial practices conformed to accepted standards and legal requirements. This is still common practice, but some cities are taking a closer look at program results. As Hayes and his coauthors point out, the program results audit is really a form of program evaluation.[61] As with any such evaluation, an effort is made to determine how well the program is working, whether it is meeting its objectives, and how much the program itself has contributed to observable changes. The Urban Institute volume notes that program audit findings are a basis for terminating marginal programs and for changing others.

THE INTEGRATED FINANCIAL INFORMATION SYSTEM

Linking the basic components of the financial management system is the primary emphasis of Hayes and his colleagues. A fully integrated system is built on a unified database that includes both financial and program information. The authors admit there are no prescribed steps that can be followed by every city to create essential linkages. They mention, though, that often the first step toward integration is to tie together the basic accounting and budgeting functions. They also discuss the potential usefulness of a financial management improvement committee.[62] This group would consist of the mayor or city manager, the chairperson of the council's finance committee (if one exists), the finance director, the budget director, and the chief internal auditor. Heads of some operating agencies might be included as well. The committee would develop basic policies and strategies, identify priorities, review projects, and assess progress periodically. The committee, as such, would not have managerial responsibility because most specific financial functions would be carried out by the separate agencies represented on the committee. Hayes and his colleagues acknowledge that few local governments can develop a fully integrated, comprehensive financial management system without help from outside consultants and contractors.

Although a fully developed, interrelated financial management system may be a long way off for most cities, today's fiscal realities demand more and better financial information and the capacity to use that information more effectively. Revenue slowdowns and retrenchment make staying on top of the city's financial affairs doubly critical. Otherwise financial duress may lead to a real debacle.

Summary

In this country cities must raise most of their revenue within their own borders. Yet the most efficient revenue-raising machinery and the most productive tax sources belong to the federal and state governments. This intrinsic fiscal imbalance creates considerable pressure for cities to seek federal and state aid. Yet in recent years that source of funding has dwindled considerably. Cities have been forced to turn inward, to cut spending or to rely on their own resources for new revenue.

Some also contend that cities should accelerate the move away from heavy reliance on the property tax. Sales and income taxes are becoming more popular in many places. A case also can be made for greater reliance on user charges—charges that place a larger burden on those who are especially heavy users of certain services and facilities.

As cities try to pull themselves up by their bootstraps, figuring out how to pry more dollars out of the local citizenry becomes a high priority. Several suggestions can be gleaned from the case-study literature: hide the tax and use small and indirect taxes, all to avoid or minimize citizen resistance. Although a number of cities have been successful in raising taxes in the past few years, the prognostication is still for lean times ahead.

How do cities allocate the funds they have? The budgetary process represents a significant political act by which scarce resources are apportioned among competing needs. But research also shows municipal budgeting is a highly incremental process that to a considerable extent remains isolated from external influences. Incrementalism apparently results in part from the widespread practice of line-item budgeting. Because of the many alleged shortcomings of this budget format, reformers have urged its replacement. PPB, ZBB, and more recently ECB are being lauded as substitutes. But do these approaches to municipal budgeting meet the needs of city officials? Do they allow the budget to serve its vital control and cost-cutting functions? Their limited acceptance suggests that many city officials do not think so.

Most authorities now recognize that budgeting is only one step in the process of managing the city's finances. An integrated financial management system includes several related elements—goal setting, long-range planning and budgeting, reporting and monitoring, and evaluating—and the integrated information system that links them together. Whatever approach the city takes in its revenue-raising, spending, and budgeting activities, the continuing shortage of resources demands that today's urban managers monitor financial practices more closely than ever before.

Notes

1. Dick Netzer, *Economics and Urban Problems,* 2d ed. (New York: Basic Books, 1974), 65.

2. Ibid., 231.

3. Ibid., 64.

4. ACIR, *Changing Public Attitudes on Governments and Taxes, 1991* (Washington, D.C.: Government Printing Office, 1991), 1.

5. Arthur D. Lynn, Jr., "The Property Tax," in *Management Policies in Local Government Finance,* ed. J. Richard Aronson and Eli Schwartz (Washington, D.C.: ICMA, 1975), 104.

6. ACIR, *Changing Public Attitudes on Governments and Taxes, 1986* (Washington, D.C.: Government Printing Office, 1986), 5.

7. L. Laszlo Ecker-Racz, *It's Your Business: Local and State Finance* (New York: National Municipal League, 1976), 80.

8. ACIR, *Significant Features of Fiscal Federalism: Budget Processes and Tax Systems—1992,* Vol. 1 (Washington, D.C.: Government Printing Office, 1992), 73–75.

9. John Due and John Mikesell, "Local Sales and Income Taxes," in Aronson and Schwartz, *Management Policies,* 142–43.

10. Christopher Gadsden and Roger Schmenner, "Municipal Income Taxation," in *Local Public Finance and the Fiscal Squeeze,* ed. John Meyer and John Quigley (Cambridge, Mass.: Ballinger, 1977), 81.

11. Seymour Sacks and Ralph Andrews, "User Charges and Special Districts," in Aronson and Schwartz, *Management Policies,* 177.

12. Gale Tollin, "City Paying Its Own Way," *Norman Transcript,* 17 March 1983.

13. See chapter 10 of David Osborne and Ted Gaebler, *Reinventing Government* (Reading, Mass.: Addison-Wesley, 1992).

14. John Forrester and Charles J. Spindler, "Assessing the Impact on Municipal Revenues of the Elimination of General Revenue Sharing," *State and Local Government Review* 22 (Spring 1990): 82.

15. ACIR, *Significant Features of Fiscal Federalism, 1992,* Vol. 1, 96.

16. This section draws on Arnold J. Meltsner, *The Politics of City Revenue* (Berkeley: University of California Press, 1971).

17. David R. Morgan and William J. Pammer, Jr., "Municipal Fiscal Austerity: Examining the Use of Retrenchment Strategies," *Management Science and Policy Analysis* 3 (Fall 1985): 1–9.

18. U.S. Bureau of the Census, *City Government Finances, 1990–91* (Washington, D.C.: Government Printing Office, 1993), 1.

19. Aaron Wildavsky, *The New Politics of the Budgetary Process* (Glenview, Ill.: Scott, Foresman/Little, Brown, 1988), 235.

20. Len Wood, "Budget Tactics: Insights from the Trenches," *Public Management,* October 1993, 16.

21. Lewis Friedman, *Budgeting Municipal Expenditures* (New York: Praeger, 1975), 62.

22. Thomas J. Anton, *The Politics of State Expenditures in Illinois* (Urbana: University of Illinois Press, 1966), 49–52, as adapted in Thomas R. Dye, *Understanding Public Policy,* 2d ed. (Englewood Cliffs, N.J.: Prentice Hall, 1975), 226.

23. John Crecine, *Governmental Problem-Solving: A Computer Simulation of Municipal Budgeting* (Chicago: Rand McNally, 1969), 38.

24. Arnold Meltsner and Aaron Wildavsky, "Leave City Budgeting Alone! A Survey, Case Study, and Recommendations for Reform," in *Financing the Metropolis,* ed. John Crecine (Beverly Hills: Sage, 1970), 344.

25. Friedman, *Budgeting Municipal Expenditures,* 76.

26. Bryan Downes and Lewis Friedman, "Local Level Decision-Making and Public Policy Outcomes: A Theoretical Perspective," in *People and Politics in Urban Society,* ed. Harlan Hahn (Beverly Hills: Sage, 1972), 329–30.

27. Friedman, *Budgeting Municipal Expenditures,* 79.

28. Crecine, *Governmental Problem-Solving,* 41.

29. Kenneth Boulding, *The Parameters of Politics* (Urbana: University of Illinois Press, 1966), 10.

30. Crecine, *Governmental Problem-Solving,* 192.

31. Friedman, *Budgeting Municipal Expenditures,* 206.

32. John Forrester and Daniel R. Mullins, "Rebudgeting: The Serial Nature of Municipal Budgetary Processes," *Public Administration Review* 52 (September/October 1992): 467.

33. George J. Gordon, *Public Administration in America,* 4th ed. (New York: St. Martin's, 1992), 357.

34. Downes and Friedman, "Local Level Decision-Making," 323.

35. This discussion is drawn from Donald J. Borut, "Implementing PPBs: A Practitioner's Viewpoint," in Crecine, *Financing the Metropolis,* 304.

36. Irene S. Rubin and Lana Stein, "Budget Reform in St. Louis: Why Does Budgeting Change?" *Public Administration Review* 50 (July/August 1990): 426.

37. See Michael Babunakis, *Budgets: An Analytical and Procedural Handbook for Government and Nonprofit Organizations* (Westport, Conn.: Greenwood, 1976), chap. 5.

38. Aaron Wildavsky, "The Political Economy of Efficiency: Cost-Benefit Analysis, Systems Analysis, and Program Budgeting," *Public Administration Review* 26 (December 1966): 303.

39. Peter A. Pyhrr, *Zero-Base Budgeting* (New York: Wiley, 1973), xii, 5–18.

40. Perry Moore, "Zero-Base Budgeting in American Cities," *Public Administration Review* 40 (May/June 1980): 253–58.

41. Glen H. Cope, "Municipal Budgetary Practices," *Baseline Data Report* 18 (May-June, 1986): 5–7.

42. Irene S. Rubin, "Budget Reform and Political Reform: Conclusions from Six Cities," *Public Administration Review* 52 (September/October 1992): 454.

43. These figures come from Cope, "Municipal Budgetary Practices," 5–7.

44. Allen Schick, "Micro-Budgetary Adaptations to Fiscal Stress in Industrialized Democracies," *Public Administration Review* 48 (January/February 1988): 532.

45. Stanley B. Botner, "Trends and Developments in Budgeting and Financial Management in Large Cities in the United States," *Public Budgeting and Finance* 9 (Autumn 1989): 39.

46. Dan A Cothran, "Entrepreneurial Budgeting: An Emerging Reform?" *Public Administration Review* 53 (September/October 1993): 445.

47. See Osborne and Gaebler, *Reinventing Government.*

48. Ibid., 4.

49. Eric B. Herzik, "Improving Budgetary Management and Fostering Innovation: Expenditure Control Budgeting," *Public Productivity and Management Review* 14 (Spring 1991): 239.

50. Cothran, "Entrepreneurial Budgeting," 446.

51. Herzik, "Improving Budgetary Management and Fostering Innovation," 243.

52. Cothran, "Entrepreneurial Budgeting," 446–47.

53. Bruce E. Benway, *Introduction to Modern Municipal Budgeting* (Orono, Me.: Bureau of Public Administration, University of Maine, 1973), 5.

54. James E. Jernberg, "Financial Administration," in *Managing the*

Modern City, ed. James Banovetz (Washington, D.C.: ICMA, 1971), 355.
55. Ibid., 358.
56. Meltsner and Wildavsky, "Leave City Budgeting Alone!" 348.
57. Jacob B. Ukeles, *Doing More with Less* (New York: AMACOM, 1982), 87.
58. Daron K. Butler, "Revenue Forecasting and Management," *Public Management,* June 1979, 10–11.
59. Frederick O'R. Hayes, David Grossman, Jerry Mechling, John Thomas, and Steven Rosenbloom, *Linkages: Improving Financial Management in Local Government* (Washington, D.C.: Urban Institute, 1982), chap. 7.
60. Sanford M. Groves, *Financial Trend Monitoring System: A Practitioner's Workbook,* vol. 2 (Washington, D.C.: ICMA, 1980).
61. Hayes et al., *Linkages,* 154–55.
62. Ibid., 161–62.

Suggested for Further Reading

Aronson, J. Richard, and Eli Schwartz, eds. *Management Policies in Local Government Finance.* 3d ed. Washington, D.C.: ICMA, 1987.
Clark, Terry N., G. Edward DeSeve, and J. Chester Johnson. *Financial Handbook for Mayors and City Managers.* 2d ed. New York: Van Nostrand Reinhold, 1985.
Hayes, Frederick O'R., David Grossman, Jerry Mechling, John Thomas, and Steven Rosenbloom. *Linkages: Improving Financial Management in Local Government.* Washington, D.C.: Urban Institute, 1982.
Martin, Joan K. *Urban Financial Stress: Why Cities Go Broke.* Boston: Auburn House, 1982.
Meltsner, Arnold. *The Politics of City Revenue.* Berkeley: University of California Press, 1971.
Rubin, Irene S. *The Politics of Public Budgeting.* Chatham, N.J.: Chatham House, 1990.

PART FOUR

The Urban Future

Urban Economic Development

The news comes hard. Metrovale's widget manufacturing plant has decided to close; competition from Japanese widgets has finally forced this
drastic step. What now, ask community leaders. The plant employed
more than 500 workers and furnished a sizable chunk of the local tax
base. Everyone quickly agrees—we must find something to replace the
plant; we need to diversify the local economy; we need, in other words,
local economic development.

This scenario may take place in only a few communities, but almost
every area, regardless of its current economic condition, has become extremely interested in economic development. In fact, the question of who
wins, who loses, and why in the battle among communities, states, and
regions for economic development clearly represents one of the most
compelling urban issues to emerge in this decade. New York accuses
New Jersey of deliberately attempting to steal jobs and economic activity
from Manhattan. In the sunbelt Phoenix, San Diego, Dallas, and Austin,
among others, find themselves blamed for the economic troubles beset-
ting older cities in the Northeast.[1] Lest we think only large northeastern
cities are worried about economic changes, a nationwide survey of local
officials by the National League of Cities revealed that the ability to attract new industry and jobs is the number-one problem facing America's
small cities and towns.[2] This trend, of course, reflects in part the continued transition of the nation's economy, what futurist John Naisbitt refers to as the shift from an industrial to an information society.[3] Whether
we call it an information or a service economy, the fact is that almost all
the new jobs in this country are in the information, knowledge, and ser-

vice sectors. And virtually every community wants its share. So we find local public officials and business leaders alike pursuing a variety of plans and projects designed to make their areas more attractive for development. The object: to create more and better jobs, revitalize downtowns, redevelop older neighborhoods, and establish a stronger tax base.

In this chapter we first consider the process of economic development and the steps necessary to implement a development plan. Next, the more common strategies and tools now employed in the name of local economic development are examined. Then we consider the municipal government's role in development. Finally, we step back to examine some of the problems and broader issues that arise as cities pursue various efforts to maintain and perhaps enlarge their economic base.

Economic Development as a Process

What is economic development and why do we need it? Basically, *local economic development* is a process for achieving and maintaining the economic health of a community through the retention, expansion, and attraction of commerce and industry. The more specific purposes of economic development (ED) may vary by community. Development specialist Robert Weaver makes a useful distinction between two basic types of communities—"haves" and "have nots."[4] The "haves" see ED as a tool for *managing* growth; the "have nots" initiate programs to *encourage* growth. The "haves" tend to be cities where considerable economic or residential expansion is under way, such as the larger suburbs of a major metropolitan area or a city such as Austin, Texas, which has benefited greatly from high-tech industry. The main objective of these places may be to establish policies that will channel growth into the kinds of development and areas of the city where it will cause the least harm to the quality of life and will produce the greatest net gain in local revenue.

"Have-not" communities may be suffering from a declining or stagnant population and tax base. With little new growth and development to manage, these localities are much more interested in policies designed to reduce unemployment and expand and diversify the local economy. Frequently such places are burdened with special problems. They may be overly dependent on a single industry or economic sector such as agriculture; they may lack transportation facilities or skilled labor pools; or they may be experiencing local problems resulting from changing national or international trade practices. In many instances these economic difficulties are rooted in conditions over which the community has little control—the movement of industry overseas, a decline in manufacturing jobs, a drop in world oil prices, or a negative export/import ratio.

Economic development and entrepreneurship have moved near the top of the municipal agenda for at least two other reasons. The first is recent changes in federal policy. Although cities were becoming more self-sufficient before 1980, the Reagan administration pushed communities further in that direction, instructing them to wean themselves from dependence on federal aid and to prepare themselves for free-market competition.[5] Under this philosophy, cities were urged to gain control over their own destinies, become attractive to business, compete with one another, and adapt to changing national and international economic trends. City officials were asked to become more than experts at grantsmanship; they were asked to become entrepreneurs. This trend toward self-sufficiency or "fend-for-yourself" continues today. The second reason for the enormous interest in ED is that development is one means of raising local government revenue without increasing taxes. As public officials are forced to retrench and hold the line on services, anything that promises a little fiscal relief is most welcome.[6]

THE ECONOMIC DEVELOPMENT PLAN

As desirable as it may be, economic development does not just happen; communities must make a conscious decision to create a stronger local economy. Planning thus becomes essential. A series of steps such as the following will likely be necessary to establish a development plan:[7]

- Analyzing the local economic structure and community attributes
- Setting local goals and priorities
- Adopting strategies for goal achievement
- Identifying obstacles to the development plans and taking action to overcome them

Each of these steps requires some elaboration.

Step 1: Analyzing Local Attributes. Three activities might be undertaken to develop the knowledge necessary to decide which ED strategies fit a given community best: an economic base analysis, a business survey, and a community survey.

A big city may elect to hire a consulting firm to perform its economic base analysis, given the complexity of such a task in a large community. The essential purpose, however, is straightforward: to determine which businesses and industries make up the economic base of the community and whether these are *export* or *nonexport firms*. Export industries sell goods and services to customers outside the community, whereas nonexport firms concentrate on sales inside the community. Export industries are the most valuable because they bring dollars into the community, which in turn helps generate new jobs and economic growth. Export activity thus has a multiplier effect.

Economic base analysis requires tracking the performance of local industries over time, using census data in addition to local sources of information. The undertaking may include comparing the percentage of workers employed locally in a particular industry to the percentage employed nationally in that industry. Such questions as growth rates and the mix or diversity of industrial types may be addressed. "The economic base study serves as the starting point for formulating an effective local economic development strategy."[8]

Conducting a business survey is an effective way of gathering information about the plans and priorities of existing businesses. Such information might be collected through door-to-door, telephone, or mail surveys of all businesses over a certain size. Topics covered in a survey might include the type of business, number of employees, growth and location plans, needs for land and buildings, and satisfaction with city services.

The purpose of a community analysis is to collect information on the community. What attributes does the community possess that might be considered attractions for business and industry? What are its negative features? Considerable research emphasizes the critical nature of the labor force, transportation facilities, and access to materials and markets. Additionally, the quality of life, educational facilities, possible financial incentives, and even the physical appearance of the community may affect industrial location or expansion decisions.

Step 2: Setting Goals. Goals and priorities might be established by an "action team" made up of key leaders from local government, business and finance, and community organizations, as well as local university personnel. An ICMA report stresses the importance of involving representatives of the banking community because they have the most knowledge of business activity in the community. They continually monitor the local economy through review of loan requests and deposit trends, they regularly talk with other business leaders, and they can provide "the skills in packaging loans, examining business plans, and assessing the management capabilities of entrepreneurs."[9]

The action team examines and analyzes the information collected in the light of current local and national economic trends. Broad economic goals may be formulated at this point, to be followed by a set of strategies and objectives that should move the community in the proper direction. Although the goal-setting process may seem relatively straightforward, in actuality disagreements over priorities and specific interests will undoubtedly arise, requiring negotiation and compromise.

Step 3: Formulating Development Strategies. Essentially three principal strategies are available to enhance the economic vitality of the community: retain and expand existing industries, attract outside businesses, and provide development programs for new businesses. In the past, at least, many cities concentrated on attracting enterprises from outside the community. Considerable research shows, however, that most new jobs are created by the expansion of existing industry and the start-up of new businesses. Retaining and expanding existing businesses may require reducing barriers to expansion and stimulating demand for their products. Several barriers to expansion are often identified: an inadequate labor force, lack of sites for expansion, and, most often, a shortage of capital.

Encouraging the start-up of new businesses may take several forms. Leveraging funds from federal grants, such as a CDBG, can play a vital role. Access to capital funds is probably more critical to emerging entrepreneurs than to existing businesses. The use of community development corporations—usually private, nonprofit entities—may also prove beneficial in getting new enterprises off the ground. The next section of this chapter examines specific tools and strategies at greater length.

Although most authorities agree that attracting new industry should not be the cornerstone of an economic development plan, most communities include such an effort as part of their overall scheme, if only because every other place does and they want to be competitive. It may also be a good way to diversify the community's economic base. The ICMA emphasizes the importance of building on the community's existing assets in efforts to attract outside firms.[10] Recently some cities have initiated vigorous marketing strategies to enhance economic development. In Wichita, Kansas, for example, some $2.5 million has been spent to create and advertise a new image for the city. Now, in addition to the traditional economic elites of oil, agriculture, and aviation, Wichita has expanded to become the corporate home to telemarketing and franchising industries. More than 2,000 jobs have been created.[11]

Step 4: Identifying and Overcoming Obstacles. The last step in the overall effort at economic development requires monitoring, feedback, and modification of the program. Implementation does not take place automatically or without hitches. Some activities may pay off quickly, whereas others may lag or encounter unexpected obstacles. A process of continually assessing and reassessing how the overall effort is working ultimately may be the best assurance of success. The ICMA report on enterprise development suggests that one of the biggest and most difficult obstacles to overcome is community resistance to change. The ICMA urges a "can do" attitude on the part of the development team, partly as a means of promoting a positive attitude toward development within the community.[12]

The case study that follows illustrates how one jurisdiction prepared itself for community development.

CASE STUDY

GENERATING NEW JOBS IN CHESTER COUNTY

CHESTER COUNTY, Pennsylvania, is a mid-sized county west of Philadelphia. Much of its economy depends on agriculture, with some recent high-tech additions. The northern section, however, has long been a steel-producing center. So although the overall economy of the county was healthy, the areas dependent on the steel industry—particularly the communities of Coatesville and Phoenixville—had suffered serious economic decline and high unemployment.

Through participation in a national Employment/Economic Development Connection project, a county ED task force was established, which was headed by the chairman of the County Board of Supervisors. The task force formed subcommittees for the two steel towns, bringing together key public and private leaders. Both communities acknowledged the need to diversify their economies and reduce their dependence on steel. In addition, leaders from the two towns recognized that new and small business development offered the best prospects for economic revival.

The county's Office of Economic Development took the lead in identifying strategies for promoting small business in the county generally and in these two steel towns in particular. Elements of the strategy included

- Financing for small business, provided through a CDBG-funded $500,000 loan
- Entrepreneurial training for new and potential business operators through a program called "Be Your Own Boss" (BYOB), run in cooperation with the federal Small Business Administration (SBA)

- Special training for employees of new and small businesses through a set-aside of fifty Job Training Partnership Act slots for each steel community
- A small business incubator for each community, to be developed in collaboration with the University of Pennsylvania, the state's ED program, and the SBA
- Potential establishment of a purchasing program under which certain high-tech firms would buy locally produced goods, following a feasibility analysis by a local university and consultation with the purchasing agents of the firms

SOURCE: Adapted from National Alliance of Business, *The Employment/Economic Development Connection: New Tools, New Roles, New Directions, a Guidebook* (Washington, D.C.: Council of State Planning Agencies, 1981), 87.

Strategies and Tools for Economic Development

The list of strategies, tools, and activities available for ED is almost boundless. They range from the creation of community development corporations to tax incentives, job-training programs, and the leveraging of state and federal funds. In general, though, we can identify three basic categories of strategies that communities can and do pursue: financial incentives, public improvements, and public-private partnerships.

FINANCING ECONOMIC DEVELOPMENT

If a community is to pursue economic development seriously, it must consider mechanisms to finance various projects and activities early in the game. We are speaking here mainly of tax incentives or other government-provided financial subsidies that may be necessary to get a project off the ground or otherwise make the community attractive for private investment. Financial incentives are often controversial, especially tax abatements. And considerable research indicates that financial inducements are quite low on the list of state and community characteristics considered important in business location or expansion decisions.[13] Nonetheless, local governments continue to offer financial inducements regularly. Seventy-eight percent of cities responding to a 1989 nationwide ICMA survey stated that they use municipal revenue to support their economic development programs. The comparable percentage in 1984 was only 61 percent.[14]

The reason businesses do not consider financial incentives decisive is really fairly simple: other locational characteristics invariably outweigh tax advantages or financial incentives. Most authorities consider requirements as paramount in determining the location of an industrial enterprise. Other influences generally thought to be more critical than taxes or monetary incentives include availability of labor, transportation, and land; energy costs; and the quality of life of an area. Probably the biggest reason cities continue to offer financial incentives is fear of the competition. The stakes are high. In 1991, for example, some ten cities competed in a version of "let's make a deal" for a $1 billion United Airlines maintenance facility. Near the end of the competition, Louisville, Oklahoma City, and Indianapolis were still in the hunt for the expected 5,000 new jobs associated with the facility.[15] In June of 1991 Transportation Secretary Samuel Skinner was in Oklahoma City and had this to say about United's tactics:

> United's operating mode in big contracts is to "put everybody in a room, say 'Here's the deal, can you beat it?'" Skinner said. "I'm surprised United hasn't called them all in ... and said, 'What's your best deal? We're going to make a decision today.'"[16]

Eventually Indianapolis secured the facility with an estimated $300 million incentive package.

Because everyone else does it, communities must compete so as not to put themselves at a comparative disadvantage. Moreover, evidence does show that if a business is considering various locations within a specific geographic region, the importance of taxes and fiscal incentives increases. Transportation, labor cost, and market differentials tend to decrease as the area under consideration diminishes, making monetary incentives more significant.[17]

The two most common ways of providing financial incentives are offering fiscal incentives and using public funds to leverage sizable private investments.

FISCAL INCENTIVES. — Of the several possibilities for offering financial incentives, a common technique has been the issuance of local industrial revenue bonds (IRBs), also known as industrial development bonds. These bonds are often issued by a local government or some other local public authority created by the city or county government, without a vote of the people. The ICMA survey found that about 18 percent of responding cities used revenue bonds and about another 17 percent used special assessment district revenue to finance economic development projects.[18] The purpose is to provide a pool of money to buy land, construct buildings, and purchase capital equipment. IRBs are tax exempt, and the lower costs are passed on to the borrower.[19] The principal advantages of IRBs are access to long-term financing, low interest, and the absence of federal income tax on the interest earned by the bond or holder.

Because the federal Treasury is affected by the issuance of IRBs, the national government has imposed a number of restrictions on the way these bonds may be used. The Tax Reform Act of 1986, for example, eliminates a number of uses of IRBs and establishes a state-by-state limit on the amount of private-purpose bonds that may be issued; no longer may tax-exempt bonds be used to finance sports, conventions, or parking facilities or industrial parks.

A second device employed as a fiscal inducement for ED is tax increment financing (TIF). The idea of TIF originated in California in the 1950s, although most TIF districts were created in the 1980s.[20] The 1989 ICMA survey found that 26 percent of responding cities used TIFs in their development effort.[21] Tax increment financing requires the creation of a special district or area to which the increased taxes received by the local government, as a result of economic expansion, are returned to finance public improvements in that specific area. The additional tax receipts (the increment) may be used to fund improvements on a pay-as-you-go basis or may be pledged to repay revenue bonds issued for long-term improvements.[22]

Currently forty-four states allow their cities to use tax increment financing. But according to Penelope Lemov, "tough times" are ahead for TIF.[23] Problems include, for example, those in St. Petersburg, where a $5.2 million bond payment is due but only $1.8 million in taxes has been collected. Others argue that TIF is not attracting enterprises from another state but simply moving shopping centers from one suburb to another or jobs from the central city to the suburb. Finally, TIF districts may result in the loss of revenue for counties and school districts since they do not get a share of new revenue. In contrast to these arguments, empirical research has shown that tax increment financing is "generally equitable, effective, and efficient.... Failures associated with TIF districts result from poor planning ... and a lack of effective communication with the individuals who claim financial disparity."[24]

Cities may also offer tax abatements (or exemptions) to private firms in accordance with state law. In many instances such tax breaks are granted as part of an urban enterprise zone program. Other arrangements are possible as well. In Texas, for example, the law permits cities to abate taxes in specially designated areas called "reinvestment zones."[25] The municipality may then enter into agreements with property owners to exempt some or all of their property from city taxes for a specified period, not to exceed fifteen years. In return, the owners must agree to make certain improvements or repairs to their property.

LEVERAGING PRIVATE INVESTMENT. — One of the most common and obvious examples of the use of public funds to attract additional private investment involved the old Urban Development Action Grant (UDAG) program. Many UDAG projects were aimed at downtown development. They often included the construction of hotels, parking facilities, and shopping malls plus the provision of public infrastructure—street widening, sidewalk construction, and extension of water and sewer lines. It might be noted that UDAG projects often revolved around the issuance of IRBs and took advantage of other public money—for example, funds from Community Development Block Grants and from the city treasury itself—in order to create the most comprehensive financing package possible. The case study that follows shows how the process worked in San Antonio, Texas.

CASE STUDY

UDAG IN SAN ANTONIO

IN September of 1978, HUD awarded $6.5 million in UDAG funds to the city of San Antonio for the Alamo Plaza–Paseo del Rio Linkage Project, also known as the Hyatt UDAG project. A number of activities were planned, but the keystone of the project was the construction of a 633-room Hyatt Regency Hotel and parking garage. The federal funds were committed for the purpose of land acquisition and the construction of a pedestrian linkage to San Antonio's famous river walk, plus some utility relocation, site preparation, landscaping, and related construction costs. The entire project cost almost $62 million, with 83 percent of this amount coming from private sources. A total of $10.2 million came from public funds, as follows:

$6.5 million	UDAG grant
$2.3 million	CDBG funds
$597,000	Department of Transportation (mass transit) funds
$313,000	City funds

$300,000	Economic Development Administration funds
$97,000	State of Texas
$52,000	VIA Metropolitan Transit (authority)

A six-block area in the heart of San Antonio's historic downtown commercial area was affected. In addition to the construction of the hotel, parking structure, and river-walk linkage, long-term plans called for the building of a partially enclosed commercial mall, the restoration of the facades of certain historic buildings, and the construction of special bus lanes in front of the historic Alamo chapel.

According to an evaluation by the U.S. General Accounting Office (GAO), 690 permanent new jobs were created as a result of the overall project. Over half of these were filled by racial minorities. In 1982 nearly $1.2 million in state and local taxes had been generated, almost double the amount originally estimated. By 1984 the figure had reached $2.1 million. The 1985 GAO survey also found that most Hyatt employees felt their new jobs offered better pay and working conditions than had their previous employment. The GAO offered the following summary: "The Hyatt UDAG project has, for the most part, successfully accomplished what was specified in the grant agreement. This project was completed ahead of schedule. The number of jobs created, the amount of private investment generated, and the taxes collected all exceeded the expectations for the project."

Question: Would Hyatt have built the hotel anyway?

SOURCE: Adapted from U.S. General Accounting Office, *Urban Action Grants: A Review of Two San Antonio, Texas, Development Projects* (Washington, D.C., January 1986).

As the San Antonio case points out, it is not uncommon for cities to use federal or state grants to leverage private investment. In fact, the 1989 survey by the ICMA showed that some 53 percent of cities use federal grants and 32 percent use state grants-in-aid to finance local economic development.[26]

PUBLIC IMPROVEMENTS

Financing a host of public improvements—from streets to sewers to parking garages or recreation facilities—is a major strategy employed by local governments in behalf of economic development. Some of these actions, perhaps most, are directly tied to the investment of private capital, the primary purpose often being to reduce overall private development costs. Public spending for development-related infrastructure must compete, of course, with other potential uses for those dollars.

On what basis might a city government decide to spend public funds for projects designed primarily to facilitate or aid private development? George Whelan, capital program director for the city of Philadelphia, contends that the prospect of new taxes is usually the compelling factor.[27] New tax revenue may be generated in several ways, not only from the construction of new buildings but also from the creation of new jobs and the inducement of surrounding businesses to upgrade and improve their structures. Job creation in itself certainly represents another common argument in favor of public support for ED.

Just how far should a public entity go in providing physical improvements for development? Must the public's involvement be limited to very specific, concrete projects? How much financial speculation is tolerable? These are not easy questions to answer, of course. Whelan thinks that a certain amount of cautious speculation may be acceptable and that it is probably essential at all times. He mentions Philadelphia's Penn's Landing project as a case in point. By mid-1985 the city and state had spent $52 million on a twenty-five-acre waterfront property along the Delaware River. An old ferry site was dismantled and replaced by an embarcadero and boat harbor. An adjacent pier was closed and restored as an indoor tennis complex. The larger plans call for an estimated $200 million for private office space, condominiums, garages, hotel, and retail space. In Whelan's words, "The dredging, bulkheading and filling at the public's expense literally provide the foundation for the larger complex."[28]

Penn's Landing was not one large project; it evolved incrementally. Some of the bulkheading was begun, for example, in the late 1960s. Much of the final private development has not yet been nailed down. One of the advantages of this drawn-out process is the spreading of the public costs over a period of years. The key criterion, according to Whelan, is the estimated marketability of the site once the improvements are complete. He observes that many localities possess seemingly useless parcels of land in otherwise attractive locations where some public investment might produce long-term benefits. After all, Penn's Landing was once no more than a muddy riverbank.

Making public improvements may take forms other than providing infrastructure or assembling land parcels. As Howard Gudell and Russell Smith point out, the way a community handles enabling powers such as zoning, eminent domain, code enforcement, and enforcement of development regulations can greatly encourage or discourage private development.[29] Lest these matters be considered trivial, we should take note of a study done in the 1970s in which a group of business leaders were asked what cities could do to improve their business climate. Reducing rules and regulations, cutting red tape, shortening inspection time, improving the city's attitude, and ending "harassment by city inspectors" accounted for 48 percent of the responses.[30] Some cities now have one-stop permit centers, and many places have begun to reexamine the whole set of regulations in the hope of removing impediments and streamlining the city's role in the development process.

PUBLIC-PRIVATE PARTNERSHIPS

Some might contend that almost by definition urban economic development requires a partnership between the public and private sectors. Certainly the foregoing discussion reveals the extensive nature of the public-private collaboration frequently essential for successful development. Here we examine public-private partnerships that take a somewhat different, and in some instances more enduring, form.

ECONOMIC DEVELOPMENT CORPORATIONS. — Quasi-public economic development corporations have sprouted up all over the country, primarily to provide a permanent planning and financing structure to facilitate ED. They also are useful because laws in some states prohibit cities from providing direct funding for business development. These corporate entities normally include both business leaders and public officials on their boards of directors. Arranging the financial package necessary for development may well be a prime responsibility of such an organization, as it was in the case of the Stouffer Hotel complex in downtown Dayton, Ohio.[31] Assembled by the Dayton City-wide Development Corporation (DCWDC), the financial package included secured debt from lending institutions, county revenue bonds, federal Model Cities and CDBG funds, twenty-year property tax exemptions, seed equity from DCWDC, equity financing raised through sale of partnership units in a quasi-public general partnership, and direct investment by the Stouffer Company. Complex indeed—no wonder a separate corporate entity was required to put that one together. The case study that follows illustrates a simpler arrangement.

PUBLIC-PRIVATE COOPERATION IN ROCK HILL

THE community of Rock Hill, South Carolina (population about 38,000), has long been heavily dependent on the textile industry. In recent years, with industrial modernization and foreign competition, employment in textiles has declined. In the mid-1980s, for example, Rock Hill lost about 4,000 jobs. In response to job loss and the clear need to diversify economically, Rock Hill business and political leaders got together to form the Rock Hill Economic Development Corporation (RHEDC). Its membership is drawn from business and community organizations and local government.

In order to make the area more appealing to new industry and to facilitate expansion of existing businesses, RHEDC, with federal and state funds, developed a 100-acre industrial park next to the local airport and acquired an additional 150 acres of land for a business, research, and technology park. Three new industries, employing over 300 people, quickly located in the Airport Industrial Park.

Loan packaging and financial assistance are provided to businesses. Using CDBG funds, the corporation has capitalized a revolving loan fund of more than $500,000. Its purposes are to assist businesses that will create jobs and to leverage additional private investment. Within the first couple of years, five loans for a total of $230,000 were made from the fund. The result: new investment of $2.3 million and the potential for 150 new jobs.

As an aid in business formation, RHEDC cooperated with the state of South Carolina and Control Data Worldtech to create a 120,000-square-foot business incubator. This facility, which offers technical assistance to new business, is tied to Control Data's Business and Technology Center program. In association with the incubator, the development corporation has initiated two more programs to help create new business—the Business Formation and Assistance Office and a seed capital fund. The city of Rock Hill has committed $180,000 in federal community development funds for seed capital and is working with the local chamber of commerce to secure additional private funds.

The director of planning and economic development for Rock Hill, Jim Reese, has high praise for the public-private partnership approach. Not only has this effort received strong support from the business community, but the city government has contributed significantly to its success. Reese credits in particular the guidance and leadership of the city manager, who has been an active supporter of economic development. Reese provided the following overall assessment: in only two years, RHEDC has proven itself an effective vehicle in the creation of jobs and in the diversification of the economic base of the city of Rock Hill.

SOURCE: Adapted from Jim Reese, "Public/Private Cooperation in Rock Hill, South Carolina," *Public Management* 67 (December 1985): 14–15.

Many participants praise these quasi-public economic development corporations for their capacity to raise money and expedite the development process. Other observers criticize them because they are not under direct public control. Political scientist Robert Stoker calls them "shadow governments," partly because they are designed to operate out of the public eye and limit popular participation.[32] More will be devoted to this issue in the section on the politics of development.

EMPLOYMENT AND JOB TRAINING. — Another arena in which collaboration between the public and private sectors can be effective is employment and job training. As a recent publication of the National Alliance of Business (NAB) notes, "employment and training and economic development activities need to be closely linked—economic development is more dependent than ever on a skilled labor force, and employment and training opportunities simply cannot happen without economic development."[33] A key federal program can help here—the Job Training Partnership Act (JTPA). JTPA provides states with block grant funding, which then is distributed by formula to communities to be used according to plans developed by private industry councils and local governments. These plans may specify the design of training programs, indicate those occupations to be included in such programs, establish criteria for training, and provide for the monitoring of training efforts.

Cities are pursuing a range of strategies in the effort to link the public and private sectors for employment and training purposes. Attempting to meet the needs of hard-to-employ groups, dealing with plant closings, developing retraining programs, and working with new and small businesses to create or retain jobs are among a sampling of the activities being undertaken in various communities. According to NAB, an important underlying objective should be the creation of institutional arrange-

ments that will form the basis for ongoing efforts to address employment
and development needs.

PUBLIC-PRIVATE COOPERATION IN INFRASTRUCTURE DEVELOP-
MENT. — We usually think of infrastructure improvements as being solely
the responsibility of the public sector. Not necessarily. A growing number of cities now recognize that the quality of life can help or hinder their
economic development efforts, particularly if they are trying to woo
high-tech industries that can pick and choose from the most desirable locations.[34] Thus cities are beginning to include amenity infrastructure as
part of their ED strategy—an ambitious undertaking that requires substantial public-private cooperation. The amenity infrastructure can include a wide range of facilities: civic and convention centers, sports are-
nas, facilities for the performing and visual arts, and museums.

The experience of the city of Indianapolis illustrates the potential
value of this approach. Between 1974 and 1984 some $136 million was
invested there in sports facilities, with another $850 million in related
downtown development. This mammoth commitment produced the
Hoosier dome, home of the Indianapolis Colts professional football
team, along with a tennis sports center, the Indiana University/Purdue
University Natatorium (swimming and diving), a track and field stadium,
and the Major Taylor Velodrome (cycling). This enormously successful
program has helped turn around a slumping economy and has put Indianapolis on the map as the amateur sports capital of the nation. This
was not the work of the city government alone, although two powerful
mayors—now-Senator Richard Luger and William Hudnut—deserve
considerable credit. Generous private-sector contributions, led by the
city's Eli Lilly Endowment, greatly facilitated the transformation. Mayor
Hudnut has called this combination of public action with private
entrepreneurship the "new civics," a phrase that shows, in his words,
that "community involvement is as much a matter of enlightened self-interest as a matter of obligation."[35]

Organizing for and Managing
Economic Development
ORGANIZATION MODELS

Two principal models exist for organizing for economic development.[36]
One involves the creation of a quasi-official corporation to handle the
operation, perhaps working closely with certain agencies of city government. The use of economic development corporations was outlined ear-

lier. The second approach places the responsibility for development directly with city government. St. Louis recently reorganized its planning department to include ED, and Oakland merged its community development and its employment and training offices into a superagency—the Office of Economic Development and Employment.[37] The model chosen by a given community will depend on a variety of local conditions and past history.

Alan Gregerman, research director of the National Council of Urban Economic Development, suggests that the public approach may work well in cities where the local government has given a high priority to ED and the private sector is already actively involved.[38] In contrast, he says that a quasi-public corporation may be more effective where development is not a top municipal priority or where the private sector is uneasy about working directly with local government. Increasingly, Gregerman notes, communities are pursuing the quasi-public route. Not without opposition from some quarters, however. In Chicago, for example, Robert Mier, who was appointed economic development commissioner by Mayor Harold Washington, expressed concern over the idea of putting too much power in the hands of a private body. "The major question," says Mier, "is the degree to which economic development gets privatized. The city must retain responsibility for policy making, and it must remain accountable for its use of public resources."[39] Cities do devote considerable fiscal and human resources to economic development efforts. The 1989 ICMA survey found that almost half of the responding cities (46.4 percent) spent $100,000 or more for economic development; 45 percent of cities with 250,000 or more residents spend over $500,000 per year. Fifty-eight percent of cities over 250,000 report having a staff of more than ten people in addition to the economic development director.[40]

LEADING AND MANAGING

Regardless of the organizational structure used, aggressive foresight, planning, and leadership may spell the difference between success and failure. If so, whose job is it to provide that leadership? Many, such as Mier, would argue that the city government must do it, especially the mayor and perhaps the city manager. But apparently that does not always happen. The 1989 ICMA survey alluded to frequently in this chapter asked cities where the key responsibility for facilitating ED lay. The answers were a bit surprising—only 41 percent (down from 55 percent in 1984) of the cities indicated the municipal government was the key facilitator, 29 percent named a local development corporation (up from

15 percent in 1984), and a full 26 percent said private business in general was the most active (down slightly from 30 percent in 1984).[41]

Because of the diversity of activities that may take place under the heading of ED, Robert Weaver stresses the need for unified management.[42] Coordination will likely be severely impaired if no single person or group is in charge. Thus he says that overall management authority and responsibility must be clearly assigned and acknowledged by all actors involved. It would seem difficult to achieve such a condition if the key responsibility for development lies within the business community generally. Yet private organizations and corporations—even the local chamber of commerce—can lead and are leading the development effort in many communities, and city hall may acquiesce willingly. In fact, a private organization can be the focal point of various public-private cooperative ventures. For example, in Denver, Mayor Federico Peña announced in July 1984 that the city and the Denver Partnership, the downtown development corporation, would collaborate on a downtown master plan to promote and direct development in and around the central business district. Denver's downtown planner explained that the Denver Partnership would take the lead in the downtown plan because "we just didn't have the core staff or the money to do it ourselves."[43]

In some instances the city manager may be a key figure in facilitating economic development. Most of the literature suggests that such an essentially political position is best reserved for elected officials. But with local government having such a vital stake in ED, communities with city managers may find this individual in the thick of the fight. What follows is a case study in which the city manager of a large city played a critical role in downtown redevelopment.

CASE STUDY

THE CITY MANAGER IN CINCINNATI'S DOWNTOWN REDEVELOPMENT

ALTHOUGH many large, older central cities have seen their inner core decline, Cincinnati's downtown has remained a vital hub of commercial and financial activity. Nonetheless, in the early 1970s development had slowed, partly because of a tight money market and lack of strong leadership. Soon after city manager William Donaldson arrived in 1975, he was approached by representatives of the chamber of commerce and the Cincinnati Business Committee who sought his leadership in redeveloping the premier city block in the downtown core.

Donaldson's first step was the creation of a project task force made up of a hand-picked group of middle-management city employees. A plan was then developed for an 80,000-square-foot block to be called Fountain Square South. Financing of a proposed office building and hotel was facilitated by a state law providing property tax relief for the developer. It permitted the developer to make annual "service payments" directly and exclusively to the city, in lieu of paying property taxes. Donaldson elected to plow that money back into other development as "seed money," as a form of tax increment financing. The project developers apparently felt such an arrangement was essential to help create the proper business climate for additional downtown development. In the meantime, the city council authorized the sale of $4.4 million in municipal bonds to support the overall project. The final package of financing, condemnation, demolition, and tract preparation was pushed through by the city manager in less than two years.

Donaldson hoped the Fountain Square South project would become the cornerstone of an overall program of downtown development. He wanted a master plan with a built-in multiplier effect. Donaldson was convinced that tax incentives such as those arranged for Fountain Square South were needed to place the central city on a competitive basis with the suburbs. He underscored this concept with these words to the city council: "Because of the policy of the national government subsidizing transportation facilities and utilities in the suburbs ... it is cheaper to develop raw land than to develop sites in the existing city." Donaldson recognized that tax breaks were controversial, but he argued that downtown redevelopment was critical and that in the long run it would lead to more jobs and a healthier tax base.

"It's a tradeoff," the city manager admitted. "I'd like to think that the strongest incentive a city can offer is to be pleasant and helpful to potential developers. Unfortunately, we are at a competitive disadvantage of the suburbs and need this [tax] incentive to overcome those negative factors. I believe in the revitalization of this city, and short-term loss of property tax is not too great a price to pay." The city council bought the argument. After six years of tax incentive financing, some twenty projects are under way, which their developers say would have been impossible without financial assistance from the city.

Many observers believe Donaldson's forceful leadership was the catalyst necessary to put the project in motion. Admittedly, some observers might consider such leadership as beyond the bounds of the manager's job description; but others would insist that Donaldson assumed command largely in the absence of council or mayoral leadership.

SOURCE: Adapted from David Sink, "The Political Role of City Managers in Economic Redevelopment Programs: Theoretical and Practical Implications," *State and Local Government Review* 15 (Winter 1983): 10–15.

The Politics of Urban Development

Despite its widespread appeal, economic development is not beyond controversy, especially when questions of tax relief or control of the process arise. Indeed, political disputes may be unavoidable. At least three issues bear on the political dimension of ED. One is how to build the political consensus necessary for success. The other two are more fundamental questions of values and ideology—who participates in the process and who benefits.

CONSENSUS BUILDING

As we noted earlier, development requires teamwork and cooperation to be successful. Creating an action team may be a way of involving certain groups in the community who have a stake in the process. Identifying key team members from the city government may not be too difficult—perhaps the city manager or mayor accompanied by certain staff or technical specialists such as the planning director or the person in charge of an ED department or division. But what about those outside municipal government? Part of the answer here depends on where the idea originated. If the business community has taken the lead, its representative in effect may invite or urge city officials to join the effort. In such instances the city's participation may be secondary to the main enterprise being directed by business interests. The city likely will be needed, of course—perhaps to issue bonds or provide public works improvements and technical assistance—but municipal officials may be limited to a distinctly supporting role.

No matter who takes the lead, even when agreement has been reached in general over the course of development, it is often difficult to achieve the necessary consensus on specific activities. One of the basic problems, according to Weaver, is that "various local interests can look at the economy of the city and arrive at very different conclusions about its economic development needs and goals."[44] Thus consensus building may be a difficult process in which some person or group may be called on to broker the various interests. The city manager might play this role, as in the Cincinnati case, or the mayor may be a more appropriate broker in some communities. As we see later, whether the business community or the city government takes the lead, the larger public or affected neighborhood groups may not follow, at least willingly.

WHO PARTICIPATES AND WHO BENEFITS

The push for economic development is based on a fairly simple model: business investment leads to more jobs and an expanded tax base, from which everyone in the community benefits. As political scientists Dennis Judd and Margaret Collins have observed, "It is easy to understand how downtown business interests equate their own investment decisions with the general public good and why they become infuriated when 'minority factions' get in the way of progress."[45] Yet as John Schwarz and Thomas Volgy argue in their book, *The Forgotten Americans: Thirty Million Working Poor in the Land of Opportunity*, there "is little evidence that the billions of dollars spent annually on economic development by states and localities have resulted either in higher wages or fewer working poor."[46] Similarly, in an empirical study of 212 U.S. cities, Richard Feiock found that "local economic development policies have a significant effect on capital investment but little effect on employment growth."[47]

What some see, in effect, is an unbalanced public-private partnership, which in a number of cities permits development decisions with far-reaching consequences to be made by a business-dominated elite with very little input from the larger community. Based on an extensive case study of neighborhoods and public-private partnerships in Pittsburgh, for example, sociologist and urban affairs expert Louise Jezierski offers this assessment of the process: "Partnerships alter the governing structure of a community by limiting participation to enhance efficiency."[48] Jane Grant's analysis of locating a General Motors truck plant in Fort Wayne, Indiana, reaches a similar conclusion: public input was limited.[49] Perhaps Max Stephenson best captures the essence of the controversy in his critical overview of public-private partnerships:

> Partnerships are unlikely to vanish from the nation's political scene soon. Their apparent promise is simply too great and city needs too vast for officials to ignore the very real economic and political benefits that

such efforts may bring. But great uncertainty exists about the issue of whether such arrangements can address the long-term needs of the community and not simply fulfill the agendas of the best organized groups within them.[50]

Some would argue that there are good reasons why development decisions are not widely shared. Political scientist Paul Peterson, for example, identifies two related reasons for limiting public participation in ED policymaking. First, by keeping mass involvement at a minimum, the city can avoid conflict over "economically productive policies." He argues that development is so fundamental to a city's well-being that it should not be derailed by disagreement and dissension. Moreover, Peterson thinks the development process can be accomplished more effectively when conducted out of the public eye, relying on "highly centralized decision-making processes involving economic elites."[51] When consensus has been obtained, broader support may be sought.

Peterson's description of developmental politics contrasts sharply with the nature of allocational politics. These stark differences have prompted urban affairs expert Elaine Sharp to offer a "bifurcated model" of politics as a way of understanding who rules in urban America.[52] It may vary from community to community, of course, but frequently the politics of development is relatively closed, nonconflictual, and elite dominated. The players are prominent economic interests: bankers, land developers, corporate leaders, and downtown business representatives. In contrast, the politics of allocation is more open, conflictual, and pluralistic. Here various interests compete over the most routine issues and problems surrounding service delivery. In its extreme version, you have Yates's street-fighting pluralism. Neighborhood groups, city unions, business interests, and politicians all mix it up.

No doubt in some places the process closely parallels Peterson's description. Consider Baltimore. Widely acknowledged as an innovator and leader in development, Baltimore has an ED process dominated by a complex of business-controlled development corporations. The reason is one Peterson recognizes—to "infuse Baltimore's development process with speed, flexibility, and technical expertise so as to manage development initiatives more effectively."[53] But according to Robert Stoker, another outcome is that popular control is circumvented and the real costs of development projects are masked. The fundamental issue here is, in his words, "striking a balance between accomplishment and accountability."[54]

In addition, projects may well produce unintended consequences.

For example, a recent analysis of casino development in Atlantic City indicates that substantial social costs have accompanied the immediate gain in jobs and taxes.[55] Increased land values may bring higher taxes or rents for those on fixed incomes. New job opportunities may not go to inner-city dwellers but to suburbanites. High-rise development may discourage the street trade many small retailers rely on. As political scientist Clarence Stone asks, "Why should a city government embrace policies that help some people while neglecting or harming others?"[56] Or, at the least, are these not matters that should be considered openly in a forum accessible to all who might be affected?

Not all development efforts exclude the larger public or affected neighborhood groups, of course, as the Neighborhood Redevelopment Renaissance Project in Columbus, Ohio, illustrates. In the mid-1970s the Battelle Memorial Institute, an internationally known scientific research foundation, initiated a revival project in its Columbus neighborhood. The for-profit subsidiary created for this task organized community meetings and invited suggestions for projects from residents, organizations, and city staff. A multiyear plan was created involving housing renovation, shopping center development, and infrastructure improvements. The housing needs of low- and moderate-income families were explicitly included as well. After six years the results are impressive. The neighborhood has been significantly upgraded: more than 200 homes were improved, 30 new homes were built, and 130 homes were rehabilitated for low- and moderate-income tenants.[57]

The position one takes on how much politics should affect the development process may depend ultimately on one's ideology. No one expects all decisions involving the obligation of public funds to be put to a vote. That is why we have a representative democracy. And almost everyone recognizes that a substantial private commitment is a must for development to work. The local government, however, clearly has a role to play. Should it initiate and direct the process, or should it merely be a handmaiden to decisions made behind closed corporate doors? Can a true balance be achieved? These questions are not easily answered, but the proper relationship between the public and private sectors is a legitimate concern for all who are committed to economic development.

Summary

Entrepreneurship and competitiveness—these are the slogans now being embraced by a growing number of city officials. Federal aid to municipalities is down, and with this decline has come an increasing awareness that greater independence for cities is not only inevitable but also desirable. Yet some communities have a tougher time than others in standing on their own feet; they have lost population and jobs over the past few decades, their inner core has collapsed, their tax base has seriously eroded. Such places have begun to fight back, trying to improve their economic base and make the community more attractive to new private investment. In short, economic development in many communities now occupies a niche at or near the top of municipal priorities. Mayors such as Jan Coggeshall of Galveston, Texas, say they now spend half their time trying to lure economic development projects, often without the tools offered by the federal government in earlier years. "Traditionally, the job was to pick up the garbage and deliver the water. Today that's changed," Coggeshall said, recalling that one businessman told her, "I want a salesman, not an accountant" for mayor.[58]

Even though less federal help is available now, cities continue to use federal dollars as a way of leveraging private investment for development. A variety of other strategies and techniques are widely used as well. Many involve financial incentives from the local treasury or require the obligation of local funds for public works improvements. Much of this activity takes place under the currently popular rubric "public-private partnership." Although most observers recognize that both sectors must participate for many projects to succeed, some have raised questions about the proper relationship between the public and private sectors. One group contends that privatizing development reduces delays and red tape, allowing the whole process to occur more efficiently. Others fear that business dominance, perhaps operating largely out of the public eye, keeps the process from being accountable to the larger community. As Judd and Ready assert, growth politics has been partially depoliticized. "Nevertheless, it will continue as the subject of political controversy."[59] With so much at stake—business expansion, jobs, taxes —would we want it any other way?

Notes

1. Rita J. Bamberger and David Parham, "Leveraging Amenity Infrastructure: Indianapolis's Economic Development Strategy," *Urban Land* 43 (November 1984): 12.

2. *Public Administration Times,* 11 September 1987, 1.

3. John Naisbitt, *Megatrends* (New York: Warner, 1984), chap. 1.

4. Robert R. Weaver, *Local Economic Development in Texas* (Arlington: Institute of Urban Studies, University of Texas at Arlington, 1986), 4–6.

5. Dennis Judd and Randy Ready, "Entrepreneurial Cities and the New Politics of Economic Development," in *Reagan and the Cities,* ed. George Peterson and Carol Lewis (Washington, D.C.: Urban Institute, 1986), 210.

6. Roger L. Kemp, "Economic Development: Raising Revenue without Increasing Taxes," *Public Administration Survey* 34 (Autumn 1986–Winter 1987): 1–2.

7. This discussion of development planning is drawn from ICMA, "Strategies for Local Enterprise Development," *MIS Report* 18 (February 1986): 1–7; and *Making Sense Out of Dollars: Economic Analysis for Local Government* (Washington, D.C.: National League of Cities, 1978), 5–6.

8. *Making Sense Out of Dollars,* 6.

9. ICMA, "Strategies for Local Enterprise Development," 2.

10. Ibid., 7.

11. Todd Sloane, "New Image Paves Way for Wichita," *City & State,* 13 August 1990, 12–13.

12. ICMA, "Strategies for Local Enterprise Development," 7.

13. For example, see Michael Kieschnick, *Taxes and Growth: Business Incentives and Economic Development* (Washington, D.C.: Council of State Planning Agencies, 1981), 87.

14. Cheryl Farr, "Encouraging Local Economic Development: The State of the Practice," *Municipal Year Book 1990* (Washington, D.C.: ICMA, 1990), 26.

15. Mary Jo Nelson, "Kentucky Ups United Offer," *Daily Oklahoman,* 6 September 1991, 15.

16. "United Searches for Best Deals," *Daily Oklahoman,* 27 June 1991, 15.

17. Barry Rubin and C. Kurt Zorn, "Sensible State and Local Economic Development," *Public Administration Review* 45 (March/April 1985): 335.

18. Farr, "Encouraging Local Economic Development," 26.

19. The discussion of IRBs comes from Wardaleen Belvin, "Industrial Revenue Bonds," in *Local Economic Development,* ed. Sherman Wyman and Robert Weaver (Arlington: Institute of Urban Studies, University of Texas at Arlington, 1987), 52.

20. This discussion comes from Fred Allen Forgey, "Tax Increment Financing: Equity, Effectiveness, and Efficiency," *Municipal Year Book 1993* (Washington, D.C.: ICMA, 1993), 25–33.

21. Farr, "Encouraging Local Economic Development," 26.

22. For a general discussion of TIF issues and methods, see Forgey, "Tax Increment Financing," 25–33; and Don Davis, "Tax Increment Financing," *Public Budgeting and Finance* 9 (Spring 1989): 63–73.

23. This discussion comes from Penelope Lemov, "Tough Times for TIF," *Governing,* February 1994, 18–19.

24. Forgey, "Tax Increment Financing," 32.

25. Weaver, *Local Economic Development in Texas,* 28.

26. Farr, "Encouraging Local Economic Development," 26.

27. George Whelan, "Public Budgeting Criteria for Assisting Economic Development," in *Long-Term Financial Planning,* ed. Jeffrey Chapman (Washington, D.C.: ICMA, 1987), 70.

28. Ibid., 71.

29. Howard Gudell and Russell Smith, "Economic Development," in *Small Cities and Counties: A Guide to Managing Services,* ed. James M. Banovetz (Washington, D.C.: ICMA, 1984), 78.

30. Cited in Roger J. Vaughn, *State Taxation and Economic Development* (Washington, D.C.: Council of State Planning Agencies, 1979), 27.

31. This example comes from Committee for Economic Development, *Public-Private Partnership* (New York: CED, February 1982), 40.

32. Robert Stoker, "Baltimore: The Self-Evaluating City?" in *The Politics of Urban Development,* ed. Clarence Stone and Heywood Sanders (Lawrence: University Press of Kansas, 1987), 258.

33. National Alliance for Business, *The Employment/Economic Development Connection,* 5.

34. This section draws on Bamberger and Parham, "Leveraging Amenity Infrastructure."

35. Ibid., 16.

36. Weaver, *Local Economic Development in Texas,* 41–42.

37. This discussion is based on Ruth Knack, James Bellus, and Patricia Adell, "Setting Up Shop for Economic Development," in *Shaping the Local Economy,* ed. Cheryl A. Farr (Washington, D.C.: ICMA, 1984), 42–43.

38. Ibid., 43.

39. Quoted in ibid., 43.

40. Farr, "Encouraging Local Economic Development," 26–27.

41. Ibid., 19.

42. Weaver, *Local Economic Development in Texas,* 43.

43. Quoted in Judd and Ready, "Entrepreneurial Cities," 226.

44. Weaver, *Local Economic Development in Texas,* 45.

45. Dennis Judd and Margaret Collins, "The Case of Tourism: Political Coalitions and Redevelopment in the Central Cities," in *The Changing Structure of the City,* ed. Gary Tobin (Beverly Hills: Sage, 1979), 183.

46. John E. Schwarz and Thomas J. Volgy, "Commentary: How Economic Development Succeeds and Fails at the Same Time," *Governing,* November 1992, 10–11.

47. Richard C. Feiock, "The Effects of Economic Development Policy on Local Economic Growth," *American Journal of Political Science* 35 (August 1991): 653.

48. Louise Jezierski, "Neighborhoods and Public-Private Partnerships in Pittsburgh," *Urban Affairs Quarterly* 26 (December 1990): 242.

49. Jane A. Grant, "Making Policy Choices: Local Government and Economic Development," *Urban Affairs Quarterly* 26 (December 1990): 148–69.

50. Max O. Stephenson, "Wither the Public-Private Partnership: A Critical Overview," *Urban Affairs Quarterly* 27 (September 1991): 123.

51. Paul E. Peterson, *City Limits* (Chicago: University of Chicago Press, 1981), 129–32.

52. Elaine B. Sharp, *Urban Politics and Administration* (New York: Longman, 1990), 261.

53. Stoker, "Baltimore," 261.

54. Ibid.

55. Cited in Clarence N. Stone, "The Study of the Politics of Urban Development," in Stone and Sanders, *Politics of Urban Development,* 7.

56. Ibid., 8.

57. Dale F. Bertsch, "Non-Profit Institutions and Urban Revitalization," in Porter and Sweet, *Rebuilding America's Cities,* 54–56.

58. Quoted in *Washington Post,* 24 June 1985, A10.

59. Judd and Ready, "Entrepreneurial Cities," 244.

Suggested for Further Reading

Gordon, Gerald. *Strategic Planning for Local Government.* Washington, D.C.: ICMA, 1993.

Hatry, Harry P., Mark Fall, Thomas O. Singer, and E. Blaine Liner. *Monitoring the Outcomes of Economic Development Programs.* Washington, D.C.: Urban Institute, 1990.

Luke, Jeffrey S., Curtis Ventriss, B.J. Reed, and Christine M. Reed. *Managing Local Economic Development: A Guide to State and Local Leadership Strategies.* San Francisco, Calif.: Jossey-Bass, 1988.

McGowan, Robert, and Edward J. Ottensmeyer. *Economic Development Strategies for State and Local Governments.* Chicago, Ill.: Nelson-Hall, 1993.

Mollenkopf, John H. *The Contested City.* Princeton, N.J.: Princeton University Press, 1983.

Sharp, Elaine. *Urban Politics and Administration: From Service Delivery to Economic Development.* New York: Longman, 1990.

Stone, Clarence N., and Heywood T. Sanders, eds. *The Politics of Urban Development.* Lawrence: University Press of Kansas, 1987.

Managing the
Urban Future

Although city political and administrative officials have never had an easy job, today their job seems almost impossible. A host of competing interest groups clamor for their "fair share" of government goods and services. The local tax base in many places is obsolete, and federal and state aid continues to decline. Local taxpayers want more and better services, but are unwilling to pay for them. In all, the pressures on urban managers have never been greater to provide local services efficiently and effectively while still meeting the more political criteria of equity and responsiveness in service delivery.

What does the future hold for our cities and their leaders? Obviously we cannot know for sure, but we can recognize certain trends. Several recent assessments of the urban future arrive at similar conclusions, at least in a general sense. A book by three practitioners refers to what lies ahead as an "era of revenue reduction."[1] Another attempt to look forward uses the broader phrase *postaffluent America* to signify changes even more drastic than those associated with the term *postindustrial*.[2] Almost everyone agrees, then, that for the foreseeable future city governments will have fewer resources than they have had in the past. The "politics of scarcity" seem to be here to stay. What developments are we likely to see in an era of fiscal limitations? And how will these trends affect the jobs of those responsible for leading and managing our cities?

The Politics of Scarcity

Most observers think the municipal fiscal crisis will continue indefinitely. There seems little doubt, then, that cities across the country will be forced to continue or even step up their quest for ways of cutting costs, improving productivity, and reducing the demand for services. An ICMA study refers to the process as "getting by modestly," which translates into a host of prescriptions for local governments, including the following:[3]

- *Greater public-private cooperation*—including more private-sector support for local government decision making and greater private-firm participation in service delivery, especially through contracting out
- *Greater use of volunteers*—training volunteers to perform medical, patrol, and maintenance functions as well as the more traditional activities at libraries, recreation centers, and social service agencies
- *Increased reliance on self-help*—not voluntarism, but asking people to do more for themselves

The ICMA report also stresses the importance of decentralization and effective citizen participation, especially at the neighborhood and block levels. Indeed this authoritative group argues that the neighborhood is the "essential community." This emphasis on citizen involvement in an era of fiscal contraction has led some to press for a greater degree of formal cooperation between service providers and recipients. This process, called *coproduction*, envisions direct citizen involvement in the design and delivery of municipal services.[4] Presumably by supplementing, or perhaps supplanting, the work of paid employees with the efforts of private citizens, this approach would result in cost savings and enhance citizen ownership of public services. Coproduction might take several forms, among them making greater use of volunteers in the protective services and reducing service levels in areas where citizens can share responsibility with the municipal workforce (neighborhood watch programs, separating garbage and trash, serving as volunteer police or fire personnel, or adopting a city park, for example). Some of these activities have been going on for some time now; others are more novel. Regardless, as a recent ICMA survey shows, coproduction activities among cities and counties have increased, especially in the areas of crime prevention control, programs for the elderly, and operation of recreational and cultural programs.[5]

CASE STUDY

Municipal Self-Service in Detroit

In April 1980, as part of his annual budget message, Detroit Mayor

Coleman Young unveiled his self-serve city program. In response to the terrible state of the local economy and a huge budget deficit, Young announced: "It may very well be that for the near future we will have to get used to doing things for our city that we have come to expect our city to do for us." The mayor's plan included the following proposals:

- An expansion of the ranks of Detroit's police reserve, made up of citizens ages eighteen to fifty, who receive eighty hours of training, a gun, and a uniform and then either accompany regular officers in scout cars or help handle traffic and crowds at special events
- Revival of the fire department auxiliary, a volunteer unit disbanded after a brief existence during the 1950s (The fire chief explains: "The idea is to train the people in the neighborhoods to protect themselves.")
- Adopt-a-Park, a program that asks neighborhood groups to cut the grass and pick up litter in the nearest city park
- An admonition to those who complain of weeds in vacant lots to get out their lawnmowers (the city has twenty-three workers to cut weeds on some 25,000 vacant lots)
- The Detroit Christmas Catalogue, a booklet of "gifts" for the city (a honeysuckle shrub for $15, a picnic table for $120, a swing set for $800, or the ultimate gift—a combination senior citizens' center and regional arts complex for $3.5 million)

Just how well has Detroit's self-service program worked? There are several encouraging signs. For example, public parks adopted by local block clubs suffer less vandalism and litter than those maintained by the city. Yet as the director of the department of public works comments, "Some things people can do. But they can't turn the whole operation around with volunteer work."

SOURCE: Adapted from Kirk Cheyfitz, "Self-Service," *New Republic,* 15 November 1980, 14–15.

Turbulent times demand creative and innovative solutions. How does one get by modestly when the problems are more pressing and complex than ever? According to San Francisco's former mayor and current California U.S. Senator Dianne Feinstein, today's urban leaders face problems their predecessors never dreamed of. America's busiest executives are no longer in the private sector; they are modern mayors, city managers, and other top-level urban officials beleaguered by a seemingly infinite variety of issues, problems, and complaints. In Feinstein's words, "Mayors who once worried about clean streets now have to worry about clean air, toxic wastes, controlling development, job training, teenage pregnancy, narcotics, labor relations and, of course, the economic viability of their cities."[6]

What's a city to do? As we noted earlier, cities cannot hope for much help from Uncle Sam anymore, and obtaining additional assistance from the states in the "decade of red ink" (see chapter 1) will certainly be problematic. Simply put, *cities are on their own,* and local chief executives are under the gun. As Feinstein says, "If the bus doesn't come on time, the motto is 'Blame the mayor.' " No one has any simple answers, of course, but certainly Feinstein is correct that the burden will fall most heavily on the urban executive. Just what qualities are demanded here? What knowledge, skills, and abilities must the top executive possess in order to provide the organization with the capacity to move forward in these changing times? It seems important to take a closer look at what the job of the urban manager demands in these days of limited resources, rapid change, and increasing complexity.

The Job of the Urban Manager

Before examining some of the more specific requirements of the municipal manager's job, we should consider briefly the more general issue of what makes a good executive. In a seminal article in the *Harvard Business Review,* Robert Katz argues that effective administrative performance depends on fundamental skills rather than personality traits.[7] In particular, he states that effective administration rests on three kinds of developable skills—technical, human, and conceptual. *Technical skill* refers to an understanding of and proficiency in a specific activity involving methods, processes, procedures, or techniques. Technical skill involves specialized knowledge, in other words. *Human skill* is the "executive's ability to work effectively as a group member and to build a cooperative effort within the team he leads." This skill involves not only communicating with others but also setting an example through one's own behavior. Katz also mentions the necessity of creating an atmosphere of approval and security in which subordinates feel free to express themselves, to participate, and to carry out activities without constant supervision. Finally, *conceptual skill* is the ability to see the enterprise as a whole and how it relates to other organizations and the larger community. In a way, conceptual skill encompasses both technical and human skills. It becomes increasingly critical at the top level of administration. Even if a leader has good technical and human skills, weak conceptual skills may jeopardize the success of the whole organization.

More recently, other ways of perceiving the nature of executive leadership have appeared. One of the best efforts to synthesize several of the newer empirical studies on leadership comes from George Barbour, Jr., and George A. Sipel, at the Center for Excellence in Local Government in Palo Alto, California. They see effective leadership as growing out of four behaviors: visioning, communicating the vision, acting on the vision, and caring about people and the organization.

"Vision is based on the beliefs and values that constitute the leader's motivating force for action."[8] This statement is related to a key theme of Osborne and Gaebler's book *Reinventing Government*—catalytic government. Catalytic government requires that leaders separate policy decisions, what Osborne and Gaebler call "steering," from service delivery, or "rowing." They argue that "visionary public leaders now concentrate more on catalyzing and facilitating change than on delivering services—why they provide less government, but more governance."[9] These visionary leaders are able "to see the entire universe of issues and possibilities and can balance competing demands for resources."[10] Competition among service providers, flexibility in procedures and to changing environmental circumstances, and accountability for quality performance through the use of performance contracts/standards are some of the tools visionary leaders can use to effectuate catalytic government.

Having a vision is one thing, getting employees to share your vision is another. How do executives get employees to internalize shared beliefs? They communicate the beliefs constantly, not only by word but by example. According to Michael Walsh, CEO of Tenneco Inc. (one of the nation's top-30 diversified industrial companies) and a former U.S. attorney for the Southern District of California, visionary leadership requires "communicating [organizational goals] and the need to change to people at all levels of an organization."[11] For example, when Walsh was CEO of Southern Pacific Railroad, he conducted a series of "town meetings" over two months that included virtually every one of the company's approximately 30,000 employees. His talks focused on the company's need to change.

The third behavior, acting on the vision, requires creating conditions under which subordinates are encouraged to work to their full potential. As Roy Pederson, former city manager of Scottsdale, Arizona, comments, "Insist on some values—absolutely and unswervingly. And then get out of the way. Give people a challenge and leeway to move. Let them breathe. Don't get in their way vicariously either by loading the organization down with lots of formal rules and regulations."[12] In the words of *Reinventing Government,* public officials must "decentralize government" and "empower" employees.[13]

The fourth and final behavior of effective leadership, according to Barbour and Sipel, is caring about people and the organization. Caring about people means treating both employees *and* citizens with respect. Employees should be treated in a humane way and not simply as cogs in the organizational machinery. They should be provided a safe work environment and paid a decent wage. They should be empowered and included in the decision-making process. With respect to citizens, Osborne and Gaebler emphasize customer-driven government—meeting the needs of the customer (citizen) and not the bureaucracy (government worker). As David Couper, chief of police in Madison, Wisconsin, notes: "Quality is determined only by customers."[14] Excellent leaders believe in and take pride in the organization; "they believe that what they and the people who work with them accomplish makes a difference."[15]

LEADERSHIP WITHIN THE MUNICIPAL ORGANIZATION

Is formulating a set of core values (e.g., vision) more difficult for a public organization than for a private firm? Kenneth Gold studied ten highly successful organizations, five public and five private.[16] Two noteworthy general characteristics were found to be common to all ten organizations. First, organizational objectives were extremely well articulated and clearly communicated to all levels. Second, employees believed that their organization was special in some way and were generally proud to be a part of it. Not surprisingly, Gold observed that public agencies had more trouble than private firms in stating a clear and consistent mission. He noted that several federal agencies possessed a higher degree of mission awareness than is found in the typical public organization primarily because their scope of service was relatively narrow (e.g., the U.S. Forest Service and the Customs Service). The more diverse the mission, the harder it is to develop and promulgate a sense of shared commitment. What common denominator exists, for example, between a city's firefighters and garbage truck drivers, except that both work for the city?

Gold points out an example of a municipal organizational culture that gave rise to a clear and consistent organizational mission. Administrators in Charlotte, North Carolina, identified "professionalism" as their guiding principle. These officials felt that the key to the success of their organization was an uncommonly bright, talented staff dedicated to doing everything they undertook in the best manner possible. This professionalism, moreover, was subject to a minimal degree of political interference. Charlotte's success notwithstanding, the local government manager may find a special challenge in identifying and effectively communicating an organizational vision or special sense of mission.

Are there other unusual or special conditions that may influence the role of today's urban manager? As municipalities are forced to become more independent (both programmatically and fiscally) and entrepreneurial, local administrators must become more effective in mobilizing community resources—public, private, and community groups—to solve communitywide problems.[17] Again, more "steering," less "rowing." The separation of public and private at the local level is breaking down; interdependence is the operative phrase now. This interdependence emphasizes the necessity of a collaborative approach to problem solving. City managers must identify strategic partners and learn to form alliances and joint ventures that extend beyond conventional public-private partnerships. This process of negotiating and collaborating with policy actors and concerned citizens outside city hall can take several forms. An increasingly frequent development is some form of service sharing or interlocal agreement. Examples include the following:[18]

- In Wilmington, North Carolina, a public housing authority provides the facilities, the city provides the staff; together they share the cost of providing a recreation program.
- The construction and operation of a fiber-optic communications network was financed through a nonprofit organization created by the city of Austin, the Austin Independent School District, the State of Texas, the University of Texas, and Austin Community College.
- Winnetka, Illinois, shares an attorney with a neighboring city.
- Thornton, Colorado, and Adams County share the cost of an emergency dispatch center.

Shared alliances and joint ventures demand unusual public leadership and entrepreneurial skills. The case study that follows illustrates some of the things a city manager can do to provide this critical community leadership.

PORTRAIT OF A "REINVENTING GOVERNMENT" CITY MANAGER

B. GALE WILSON served as city manager of Fairfield, California (population about 68,000), from 1956 until his retirement in 1988. For over thirty years he reinvented government, long before it was popular to do so. During his tenure he earned a national reputation as a shrewd negotiator and businesslike manager. He can best be characterized as someone who did not mind taking risks in the face of adversity. His entrepreneurial skills contributed to the following developments:

- A real-estate developer, who was seeking permission to build a small retail shopping center, was persuaded to build a regional center (the only one in the county), with the city buying the land, working out the zoning arrangements, and providing building permits. Under an innovative financial arrangement, 15 percent of the stores' net cash flows back into city coffers.
- The city built a $1.2 million cogeneration plant to heat and power civic-center buildings, saving about $120,000 a year in utility bills.
- Through quick action, the city was able to persuade the Southern Pacific Railroad to purchase 600 acres of prime industrial land before it fell into the hands of residential subdividers. As a result, more than ten major industries were attracted to the area.

Wilson credits much of the city's success to his staff and to "trust, delegation, and teamwork." Effectiveness can best be attained, he believes, by leaving subordinate managers alone to control their own funds, employees, and programs. This style, which is held together by the core values of trust and teamwork, frees him to consider more long-range policy matters. He also credits the council with making his job easier. "I have had great support from a city council that, on the whole, has had the best interests of the city at heart," he said. "They've never had their own axe to grind."

This activist manager has not been immune from criticism. The city has faced several lawsuits surrounding efforts to annex land to control development. Also, the city's policies on annexation and the amount it collects from its redevelopment agency have created dif-

ferences between the city and the county. Wilson responds by saying that his policies will endure the test of time.

SOURCE: This case is drawn from three sources: Ben Merritt, "A Man and His City:
B. Gale Wilson, Fairfield's City Manager," *Public Management*, August 1986,
18–19; Robert Duckworth, John Simmons, and Robert McNulty, *The Entrepreneurial American City* (Washington, D.C.: Partners for Livable Places, 1985), 13; and telephone interview with a staff person in the office of the city manager of Fairfield on
8 November 1993.

Who should provide the real leadership that everyone thinks is so
crucial in the modern city—the professional manager or the elected official? As we noted in earlier chapters, in the idealized council-manager
plan political and policy leadership resides in the hands of the elected
city council members. The manager provides policy advice, of course,
but he or she operates behind the scenes so as not to steal the political
spotlight from elected officials. Is this concept completely outmoded today? One current model of the relationship between manager and council (see chapter 3) still shows elected officeholders as primarily responsible for determining the mission of the organization—establishing the
fundamental values and direction for the municipal corporation. Perhaps
that is how it should be. But public administration professor John Nalbandian sees a different scenario, one in which the city manager plays a
much more prominent community leadership role.

Nalbandian contends that managers are forced to play a growing
political role in response to the abdication or ineptness of political leadership by elected officials.[19] This is not a new observation, of course; others have recognized this as a problem of council-manager government for
sometime. Yet Nalbandian sees certain developments that he believes are
"democratizing" and legitimizing this political role of the manager. First,
he insists that in a diverse community some mechanism, structure, or
forum must exist for debating values. If the council cannot or will not
fulfill that obligation, we should not be surprised to see the chief administrator fill the void. Even if the council tacitly endorses or at least acqui-
esces in this arrangement, Nalbandian thinks a question of oversight and
political legitimacy remains. In many instances, he contends, councils are
not effectively fulfilling their role even as overseers. Are there other ways
of holding activist managers accountable? Nalbandian places his hope in
the development of the new partnerships mentioned earlier. In particular,
he endorses the heightened activity of community groups—boards, com-

missions, hearings, advisory councils, neighborhood associations, and the like. One might add private organizations to the list as well—chambers of commerce, banks, economic development corporations, and so on.

These new or expanded relationships can provide a source of community influence and legitimacy that supplements and enlarges the oversight and control exercised by the city council. In responding to the city manager's initiatives, Nalbandian sees two roles for the council. It passes judgment on the technical complexity and political feasibility of the proposal. But it also reacts to the manager's interpretation and response to community values and goals as manifested by these extragovernmental groups. Thus as participation increases, new partnerships and interorganizational networks are formed, ensuring political control over the city manager's enlarged leadership role.

In sum, a consensus has been reached on the future role of the urban executive: she or he will have to be a leader as well as a manager. Managers manage people and work; they make sure that the right things get done by the right people using the right procedures at the right time. Leaders lead; they have a vision of what can be and communicate this vision to organizational *colleagues* in such a way as to engender support and enthusiasm. Leaders are entrepreneurs, they take chances (and subsequently they fail at times), they reinvent government. We have an ample stock of excellent managers in American cities, but as never before we need managers who are also leaders. How do we prepare for these arduous roles? Can we educate people to perform these tasks? If so, how?

EDUCATING URBAN EXECUTIVES

Although research identifies as many as four or five basic functions performed by public executives,[20] let us return to Katz's typology, which lists three basic developable skills as essential to effective administration—technical, human, and conceptual. To these three we might add policy leadership as a fourth fundamental skill required of the modern urban chief executive. How can public administrators gain these skills?

The argument over the extent to which management skills can be taught as part of a formal educational curriculum may never be settled. Historically, both in the private and in the public sector, it has been assumed that many skills can be acquired through undergraduate and especially graduate education, leading perhaps to a masters of business administration (MBA) or a masters of public administration (MPA). Of the preceding four skills, the technical skills are the ones most widely believed to be effectively imparted through schooling; after all, engineering schools, business schools, and even law schools have been teaching high-level technical knowledge and skills for years. Among urban administrators we find considerable agreement that the technical skills of finance and budgeting are probably the most critical.[21] In addition, many would argue that human relations skills can be taught at the university level or through intensive workshops and job-related seminars. Such topics as personnel administration, human relations, and organizational behavior are likely to be found in curricula for both public and private managers-to-be. In fact, following the lead of business schools, the National Association of Schools of Public Affairs and Administration (NASPAA) has now stipulated a set of basic curriculum requirements for universities wishing to offer accredited MPA degrees. The five subject areas in which public managers should have competence are the political, social, and economic context; analytic tools; individual, group, and organizational dynamics; policy analysis; and administrative management processes. NASPAA and the ICMA, in a joint statement, also urged that greater use be made of internships and practitioners in the classroom.[22]

Has a common curriculum core emerged among schools of public administration? Based on a recent survey conducted by Robert E. Cleary of the 215 public affairs/public administration masters' programs affiliated with NASPAA, the answer to this question is no: the "survey produced no evidence of a standardized core curriculum in public administration programs."[23] While neither a common core nor a consistent core pattern was found, there was some tendency toward an "inner core" consisting of six areas: public administration theory, research methods, public finance, policy analysis, personnel, and political institutions and processes. When queried about perceived gaps in curriculum offerings, those areas most frequently cited were management information systems/computers, nonprofit sector, politics, and ethics. Of these perceived skill gaps, the first two can be relatively easily "taught." The same is not true for the last two. Let us examine each of these issues—politics and ethics—in turn.

The Politics of Urban Management

Some observers have concluded that public administration may be an "occupation, an activity, an applied art—but it is most certainly not a true profession."[24] A former city manager, William Donaldson, prefers to think of the job as a craft heavily steeped in politics.[25] He contends the first problem in improving municipal management is to make managers better politicians. John Isaacson, who has spent decades head-hunting top executives for state and local governments, agrees: "Too much of an emphasis on public policy study and not enough on political survival means that schools have been pumping out a generation of administrators unprepared for life in the big city."[26] He argues that a degree in public administration should include "some combat training" in the meaning and nature of politics.

How do we impart the more intangible political skills to future urban administrators? Is it possible to provide postentry, much less preentry, training that can help urban managers become more successful executive leaders? Astrid Merget, director of Ohio State University's School of Public Policy and Management, argues for more practitioner-teachers. Many observers urge greater use of internships and practicums, where students work on real problems with real public administrators. Sabbaticals for city executives, similar to those available to federal-level members of the Senior Executive Service, might prove useful. Some "flagship" schools such as Harvard, Berkeley, Michigan, and Princeton are moving back to a more practical orientation in their public affairs/administration programs.[27] Harvard's use of the case-analysis method for teaching administrative and political skills is well known.

Traditionally, political skills have been learned through experience—in the school of hard knocks. According to former manager Donaldson, political skills can be improved or even developed by taking part in political campaigns.[28] For city managers, this would mean being involved in school board elections, state legislative battles, or special district elections. Or running for some allegedly nonpolitical office in a church or other organization might help. Donaldson's whole idea is to experience firsthand the give and take of elected office. In some communities too much active politicking on the part of a city manager would raise eyebrows. The manager would certainly have to operate with considerable caution and would be well advised to secure the approval of the city council before plunging into a school board or legislative election.

Although the value of direct political participation is hard to dispute, it may be possible nonetheless to sketch out some guidelines and suggestions from which even novice administrators might profit. We do know something about political behavior and political institutions, after all. We know, for example, that power is vital to effective political leadership; that in modern society bureaucracies are the depositories of expertise; and that the urban manager who does not understand the importance of external influences on city affairs is doomed to failure.

Richard Neustadt's book *Presidential Power* is instructive about the power of a chief executive in any governmental arena. According to Neustadt, "presidential *power* is the power to persuade."[29]

Administrators must exercise power to implement, defend, and improve controversial programs. Even for programs that are less visible and less controversial, the use of power may be required to ensure success.[30] The skillful use of power greatly enhances an executive's capacity to get things done. Political scientist Norton Long puts it in more dramatic terms: "the lifeblood of administration is power."[31]

The politics of urban management may involve power relationships between the local chief executive and three principal constituencies—the city council, the bureaucracy, and a myriad of external groups. In chapter 3 we considered the relationship between the city manager and city council. Now we examine how the manager can influence the other two constituencies—the bureaucracy and external groups.

We can identify two basic ways to produce bureaucratic change. First there is organization development, a method discussed in chapter 8. Outside consultants are brought in and training programs initiated, all to make the workforce more forthright, trusting, and cooperative. The assumption of course is that this effort will enable the organization and its individual members to grow, to become more effective in and more adaptable to a rapidly changing environment. In a less formal way creative leaders can undertake a variety of additional steps, as we saw in chapter 8. They can encourage employee involvement in hopes of producing a more committed and productive workforce.

Another approach to organizational change takes a different tack. It is based on the theory of economic man—people do not change their behavior unless it pays them to do so. Anthony Downs articulates the approach in his book *Inside Bureaucracy*. Downs assumes all participants—officials, politicians, citizens, bureau clients—are *utility maximizers*. That is, each person implicitly assigns certain values, preferences, or utilities to various options or courses of action. The individual then compares utilities and chooses the act or combination of acts that produces the most total utility.[32] Thus, organizations (and their individual members) are unlikely to change unless the perceived benefits of some new behavior outweigh the costs of the change:[33] Considerable inertia is built into any large organization. Existing practices represent a considerable sunk cost—years of effort, thousands of previous decisions, and a wide variety of experiences. Change is harder to effectuate (1) when there is a reduction in things of value to bureaucrats (e.g., personal or organizational power, prestige, income, and security), (2) the larger the degree of change required, (3) the more officials affected by the change, and (4) the larger the organization.

Forces that favor bureaucratic change include

- *The desire to do a good job.* Bureaucrats who are ambitious or strong advocates of the agency's goals can become dissatisfied with the status quo and propose new ideas and methods.
- *The desire for aggrandizement.* The desire to aggrandize breeds innovation. Bureaucratic expansion may produce gains in power, income, and prestige for individual officials.
- *Self-defense.* Change in the organization is often defensive, a reaction to external pressure.

Despite these forces for change, Downs argues that inertia usually wins out. His major point is that producing change within the organization can be difficult and time-consuming. The key to modifying existing behavior, then, is to be sure that individual employees perceive a personal payoff from any proposed change. If people can be *persuaded* that the benefits of a proposed action outweigh its costs, the opportunities for change improve greatly. Indeed, here the exercise of influence would seem to depend on the power of persuasion.

Finally, as systems analysts remind us, the external environment has a significant impact on organizational activities. Debate continues over the extent to which an appointed administrator can openly solicit political support. Yet a study of managers in the Bay Area revealed that a slight majority of the officials endorse the idea of advocating policies even when important parts of the community are hostile.[34] Assuming that external support is essential for the success of such policies, how does one go about creating it?

The answer is interpersonal techniques, a battery of methods often used by politically successful strong mayors. The heads of executive-centered coalitions rarely command; they negotiate, bargain, and persuade. And today's urban administrators must have the resources to do the same.

First, tremendous political support can be garnered from running a city government effectively. Even the best politicians recognize this fact. The late mayor of Chicago Richard J. Daley always insisted that good government was good politics. A second source of support, especially with the city council, is a reputation as a reliable source of information. Credibility is an administrator's stock in trade. Policy leadership would be impossible if elected officials and other interested parties could not rely on managers as a prime source of timely, dependable information.

So urban administrators must know their business and their city. Knowledge is indeed power.

Practitioners Rapp and Patitucci provide some guidelines and suggestions for executives who want to enhance their political influence. The authors acknowledge that in the last analysis skill in doing is best learned by doing. Yet they contend that useful information can be derived from the experience of others. Here is some of their advice for getting results when working with various groups:[35]

1. *Understand the status quo.* It is important—indeed, imperative —to understand the reasons for and the beneficiaries of the existing conditions you are trying to change. Although the benefits are not always obvious on the surface, some person or group profits from the policies, programs, and procedures that now exist and may well resist changing them. Figure out who benefits and why, in order to anticipate opposition.

2. *Recognize power where it exists.* If the change is large, invariably more than one person, group, or institution will be affected. Thus, achieving a desired change will likely depend on putting together the proper coalition. Who has the power to bring others in? Who might have the power to veto a proposed course of action? Following this guideline requires open-mindedness.

3. Create *a sense of due process.* No matter how good an idea is, implementation may be severely undermined if those affected do not perceive the process by which the decision was made as fair. At the least, affected parties must be given a genuine opportunity to be heard; such groups must also believe that their ideas are being received with an open mind.

4. *Understand the importance of timing.* "Knowing when to push for a decision and when to pull back is a skill that characterizes managers who are consistently able to achieve good performance."[36] Often, of course, it is difficult to persuade people (e.g., elected officials) to act when no crisis is at hand. This predisposition is reflected in the common saying "If it ain't broke, don't fix it." Yet there may be times when the manager must try to persuade others that the appropriate time to move on a project is before a crisis hits. How does one know when to push? Experience and judgment are about all that will help here.

5. *Know when to compromise.* Rapp and Patitucci insist that "one of the most oversold and least understood concepts in politics and public management is the notion that getting things done is the

art of compromise."[37] They argue that some decisions involve compromise; others do not. Even more problematic, sometimes it may not be clear when or how much compromise is necessary. The authors are surely correct in insisting, however, that compromise should not be the strategy of first resort.

Finally, Rapp and Patitucci maintain that creating external support requires spreading the credit for success, recognizing that change takes time, and understanding the necessity for follow-up (public decisions are rarely final).

Obviously, initiating and guiding urban change is no easy task. Enacting a policy proposal and seeing it through to a successful conclusion require an enormous talent to make diverse interests work together—a skill essential to produce both internal and external change.

One final cautionary note: There are still those who think city managers are not ideally situated to function as community change agents. After all, they are only "hired hands." The community is not really theirs; it belongs to the people, who elect their representatives to provide the basic tone and direction of city government. Remember, too, that many if not most council members still cling to the politics-administration dichotomy. Wise managers move cautiously, avoid the public eye, and give all the credit to the elected political leadership.

Ethics in the Public Service

Before moving to a final word, it is imperative that we discuss, albeit briefly, the issue of ethics in the public sector. On taking office, every public servant, elected or appointed, enters into a covenant with the people. This covenant requires that the officeholder not use her or his position for personal gain. Additionally, public officials must ensure that policymaking and service delivery occur without favoritism or discrimination.

Ethics is hard to define and according to some, like politics, impossible to teach. Nevertheless, Cleary's survey of public affairs/administration programs revealed a "perceived gap" in the study of ethics.[38] What, then, are we to do? Public administration expert Grover Starling provides some answers.

Ethical behavior normally involves a commitment to high moral principles or high standards of professional conduct. Even though there are no absolute standards of right or wrong, Starling insists that ethical behavior can be taught. In fact, he says that learning more about value systems and ethical conduct can have practical payoffs for the public administrator.[39]

- The study of ethics can facilitate decision making. Having wrestled with the value conflicts underlying previous decisions, officials can more readily identify and resolve pending ethical questions.
- A knowledge of ethics can help promote greater consistency in decision making. Reliance on a coherent set of principles engenders respect from employees who see the administrator as fair.
- The study of ethics can help public servants make more reflective decisions.

Finally, an ethical code might operate as another means of ensuring bureaucratic accountability. We can identify various external forces that govern the actions of administrative officials: public opinion, group pressures, professional standards, and, of course, legislative oversight. But an individual's internal norms may play a powerful role as well. A basic grasp of right and wrong coupled with a firm commitment to the public interest can help keep public officials on the right track.

Despite a growing interest in ethical behavior, a recent ICMA survey reveals that less than half (41 percent) of the nation's cities have formal codes of ethics.[40] Responding cities have not ignored the issue, however. Cities are pursuing several legal and institutional strategies to elevate core values and improve their ethical climate. The most common are protection for whistle blowers (59 percent); a requirement for approval of outside employment (56 percent); and an insistence on financial disclosure (53 percent).

A Final Word

Most urban administrators carry a heavy load. If they attempt to handle everything alone, they themselves may become the choke point in the system—"the point where all of the bucks stop, where all decisions must be made, where all communication is routed, where all urban change is implemented, where all solutions are created, where all evaluations are made, and where all plans are laid."[41] Obviously a role this expansive could throttle orderly progress within the organization.

Administrator Thomas Downs suggests that managers of big cities can no longer do everything themselves. But more specialists, advisers, and staff are not what is needed. Downs proposes co-managers. He believes that urban administrators should create management teams—groups that contain "the mix of talent, perspective, temperament, interest, skills, and background which can fill the man-killing job description."[42] We should not take Downs's suggestion lightly. Decision by group or committee is a hallmark of the Japanese approach to management.

Whether or not we see a growing use of management teams, we still must be concerned about the best way to prepare people for top administrative positions. Obviously much of the knowledge and skill required to perform effectively cannot be learned from textbooks or in classrooms. This does not mean that advanced degrees or continuing education programs are irrelevant for administrators. But we must be realistic about what to expect from that learning.

What advantages can formal education offer urban managers? Increasingly public administration curricula offer exposure to valuable tools and applied techniques. Today's masters of public administration have received a good deal of training in applied skills that are relevant to real-world job experience. But perhaps this is not the most significant benefit of graduate education. Plenty of studies show that formal education is associated with a number of desirable traits and attitudes. People with more education generally are more open-minded, more progressive, less tied to the ways of the past, less dogmatic, and less authoritarian.[43] Surely these characteristics will benefit anyone who must continually deal with a diversity of people, who must adapt to change, and who must perpetually offer new ideas for solving complex problems. Research also shows that better-educated city managers are more worldly than those with less education. And formal learning is positively related to managers' interest in playing a more active policy role.[44]

How can we improve the educational experience of urban administrators? No one has the definite answer, of course. But there does appear to be a growing consensus on two areas of need: more involvement by practitioners in teaching and curriculum development, and greater use of internships. And one former city manager, who recognizes the pervasive political nature of the job, advocates more actual practice in the political process.

And, finally, must we "reinvent" local government? We have made reference to David Osborne and Ted Gaebler's influential book in practically every chapter. Is *Reinventing Government* really worth reading? Yes, but with two caveats in mind.

First, local executives have been reinventing government for a long time. They just called it productivity enhancement, performance budgeting, participative management, and so on. As we stated earlier, and as the authors concede in the preface, the book offers little that is new or novel. Moreover, the book is long on prescription and short on implementation specifics. We agree with Jonathan Walters's assessment. In an article summarizing the views of some of the nation's top state and local government leaders who met to discuss "Reinventing Government," he notes:

> [Reinventing Government] ... offers an optimistic view of how governments can break old habits. Realistically, how to go about pursuing such change may not be something that can come out of a book. It may ultimately, and simply, be a very personal decision. If all Reinventing Government does is inspire such decisions, then it already has proven valuable.[45]

Second, scholar Charles Goodsell identifies two other weaknesses in the book. He contends that Osborne and Gaebler overgeneralize from a limited number of success stories. And they rely too much on "quoted wisdom" as if it were established fact.[46] Thomas Vocino, another public administrationist, criticizes Reinventing Government for downplaying the importance of politics and coalition building.[47] Rather clearly, the ideas of the book owe more to management gurus such as Peter Drucker, Thomas Peters, and W. Edwards Deming than to students of the political process. But unless administrators can mobilize the essential political support for program change, the most creative and visionary proposals may come to naught. Solutions must be not only technically correct but politically feasible.

In the final analysis the real impediment to superior leadership required at the local level may be that the very best may eschew public service. Alan Altshuler argues that the real crisis in governance is the ability of governments to lure top people to public-sector jobs given low salaries and the loss of privacy in today's high-profile political arena. "The question is, how do you get first-rate people to put up with this? The amazing thing, really, is that you still see so many terrific people for whom the call of public service is so strong."[48]

No more challenging job exists in today's complex society than that of the urban manager. Only those with a genuine commitment to making the urban world a better place to live need apply.

Notes

1. James Mercer, Susan Woolston, and William Donaldson, *Managing Urban Government Services* (New York: AMACOM, 1981), 1.

2. Gary Gappert, "The Political Future of the City in the Year 2000," in *Municipal Year Book 1979* (Washington, D.C.: ICMA, 1979), 11.

3. Laurence Rutter, *The Essential Community: Local Government in the Year 2000* (Washington, D.C.: ICMA, 1980), 95–97.

4. See Jeffrey L. Brudney and Robert E. England, "Toward a Definition of the Coproduction Concept," *Public Administration Review* 43 (January/February 1983): 59–65.

5. Elaine Morley, "Patterns in the Use of Alternative Service Delivery Approaches," in *Municipal Year Book 1989* (Washington, D.C.: ICMA, 1989), 40.

6. Dianne Feinstein, "Who Are the Nation's Busiest Execs? Mayors," *City and State*, November 1987, 12.

7. Robert L. Katz, "Skills of an Effective Administrator," *Harvard Business Review* 33 (January/February 1955): 33–42.

8. George Barbour, Jr., and George A. Sipel, "Excellence in Leadership: Public Sector Model," *Public Management*, August 1986, 3–5.

9. David Osborne and Ted Gaebler, *Reinventing Government* (Reading, Mass.: Addison-Wesley, 1992), 34–35.

10. Ibid., 35.

11. Jonathan Walters, "Reinventing Government: Managing the Politics of Change," *Governing*, December 1992, 32.

12. Roy R. Pederson, "Solving the Management Equation," *Public Management*, August 1986, 9.

13. Osborne and Gaebler, *Reinventing Government,* see chap. 9.

14. As quoted in ibid., 166; for a discussion of customer-driven government, see chap. 6 of *Reinventing Government.*

15. Barbour and Sipel, "Excellence in Leadership," 5.

16. Kenneth A. Gold, "Managing for Success: A Comparison of the Private and Public Sectors," *Public Administration Review* 42 (November/December 1982): 568–75.

17. Jeff S. Luke, "Finishing the Decade: Local Government to 1990," *State and Local Government Review* 18 (Fall 1986): 132–37.

18. Penelope Lemov, "In Hard Times, Even Governments Must Share," *Governing*, September 1993, 26.

19. John Nalbandian, "The Evolution of Local Governance: A New Democracy," *Public Management*, June 1987, 2–5; see also John Nalbandian, "Professionalism in City Management," in *Ideal and Practice in Council-Manager Government,* ed. H. George Frederickson (Washington, D.C.: ICMA, 1989), 182–94.

20. For example, Alan Lau, Arthur Newman, and Laurie Broedling, in "The Nature of Managerial Work in the Public Sector," *Public Administration Review* 40 (September/October 1980): 513–20, identify four basic components of the work performed by high-level civilians working for the U.S. Navy—(1) leadership and supervision; (2) executive decision making, planning, and resource allocation; (3) technical problem solving; and (4) infor-

mation gathering and dissemination (listed in order of importance).

21. Richard J. Stillman II, "Local Public Management in Transition: A Report on the Current State of the Profession," *Municipal Year Book 1982* (Washington, D.C.: ICMA, 1982), 172.

22. See the symposium edited by Lynn Miller and Laurence Rutter, "Strengthening the Quality of Urban Management Education," *Public Administration Review* 37 (September/October 1977): 567–630.

23. Robert E. Cleary, "What Do Public Administration Master's Programs Look Like? Do They Do What Is Needed?" *Public Administration Review* 50 (November/December 1990): 671.

24. Richard L. Schott, "Public Administration as a Profession: Problems and Prospects," *Public Administration Review* 36 (May/June 1976): 256.

25. William V. Donaldson, "Continuing Education for City Managers," *Public Administration Review* 33 (November/December 1973): 504–8.

26. Quoted in Jonathan Walters, "Combat Training for the Impossible Job?" *Governing*, July 1993, 56.

27. Jonathan Walters, "Can Innovation Be Taught?" *Governing*, November 1993, 56.

28. Donaldson, "Continuing Education for City Managers," 507.

29. Richard Neustadt, *Presidential Power* (New York: Signet, 1960), 23.

30. Robert C. Fried, *Performance in American Bureaucracy* (Boston: Little, Brown, 1976), 193.

31. Norton Long, "Power and Administration," *Public Administration Review* 9 (Winter 1949): 257.

32. Anthony Downs, *Inside Bureaucracy* (Boston: Little, Brown, 1967), 81.

33. This discussion comes from ibid., chap. 16.

34. Ronald O. Loveridge, *City Managers in Legislative Politics* (Indianapolis: Bobbs-Merrill, 1971), 49.

35. Brian Rapp and Frank Patitucci, *Managing Local Government for Improved Performance* (Boulder, Colo.: Westview Press, 1977), 336–44.

36. Ibid., 340.

37. Ibid., 341.

38. Cleary, "What Do Public Administration Master's Programs Look Like? 670.

39. Grover Starling, *Managing the Public Sector*, 5th ed. (Belmont, Calif.: Wadsworth, 1993), 170–71.

40. Jonathan West, Evan Berman, and Anita Cava, "Ethics in the Municipal Workplace," *Municipal Year Book 1993* (Washington, D.C.: ICMA, 1993), 3–16.

41. Thomas M. Downs, "Commentary on the Watt-Parker-Cantine Paper," in *Education for Urban Administration*, ed. Frederic Cleaveland and Thomas Davy (Philadelphia: American Academy of Political and Social Sci-

ence, 1973), 82.

42. Ibid., 85.

43. For example, see Samuel A. Stouffer, *Communism, Conformity, and Civil Liberties* (New York: Doubleday, 1955); and Herbert McClosky, "Conservatism and Personality," *American Political Science Review* 52 (March 1958): 27–45.

44. Timothy A. Almy, "Local-Cosmopolitanism and U.S. City Managers," *Urban Affairs Quarterly* 10 (March 1975): 243–72.

45. Walters, "Reinventing Government," 40.

46. Charles T. Goodsell, "Reinvent Government or Rediscover It?" *Public Administration Review* 53 (January/February 1993): 85–87.

47. Thomas Vocino, "Is 'Reinventing Government' the Answer?" *PA Times*, 1 May 1993, 9.

48. As quoted in Walters, "Combat Training for the Impossible Job?" 56.

Suggested for Further Reading

Doctors, Samuel I., W. Henry Lambright, and Donald C. Stone. *Educating the Innovative Public Manager.* Cambridge, Mass.: Oelgeschlager, Gunn, and Hain, 1983.

Frederickson, H. George, ed. *Ideal and Practice in Council-Manager Government.* Washington, D.C.: ICMA, 1989.

Harlow, LeRoy. *Without Fear or Favor: Odyssey of a City Manager.* Provo, Utah: Brigham Young University Press, 1977.

Peters, Thomas J., and Nancy Austin. *A Passion for Excellence.* New York: Random House, 1985.

Redford, Emmette S. *Democracy in the Administrative State.* New York: Oxford University Press, 1969.

Rutter, Laurence. *The Essential Community: Local Government in the Year 2000.* Washington, D.C.: ICMA, 1980.

Stillman, Richard J. *The Rise of the City Manager.* Albuquerque: University of New Mexico Press, 1974.

Name Index

Place Index

Subject Index

About the Authors

David R. Morgan is professor of political science at the University of Oklahoma, Norman, where he also received his Ph.D. He is the author or coeditor of *Intergovernmental Relations and Public Policy, The Oklahoma Voter*, and *Urban Political Analysis*. His articles have appeared in such journals as the *American Political Science Review, Social Science Quarterly*, and *Urban Affairs Quarterly*. He has five years' experience in city government, and he served as the first city manager of Yukon, Oklahoma.

Robert K. England, professor of political science at Oklahoma State University, is coauthor of *Race, Class, and Education: The Politics of Second Generation Discrimination*. His articles have been published in *American Political Science Review, American Journal of Political Science, Journal of Politics, Social Science Quarterly, Western Political Quarterly*, and *Public Administration Review*.

Morgan and England have coauthored two other books: *Desegregating Big City Schools*, which grew out of England's dissertation, written under Morgan's direction, and *Oklahoma Politics and Policies* (with George Humphreys), which won the Oklahoma Center for the Book nonfiction award for 1992.